Lecture Notes in Computer Science   7149

Commenced Publication in 1973
Founding and Former Series Editors:
Gerhard Goos, Juris Hartmanis, and Jan van Leeuwen

Claudio Russo   Neng-Fa Zhou (Eds.)

Practical Aspects of Declarative Languages

14th International Symposium, PADL 2012
Philadelphia, PA, USA, January 23-24, 2012
Proceedings

 Springer

Volume Editors

Claudio Russo
Microsoft Research Ltd
7 JJ Thomson Ave, Cambridge, CB3 0FB, UK
E-mail: crusso@microsoft.com

Neng-Fa Zhou
Brooklyn College
Dept. of Computer and Information Science
2900 Bedford Ave, Brooklyn, NY 11210-2889, USA
E-mail: zhou@sci.brooklyn.cuny.edu

ISSN 0302-9743   e-ISSN 1611-3349
ISBN 978-3-642-27693-4   e-ISBN 978-3-642-27694-1
DOI 10.1007/978-3-642-27694-1
Springer Heidelberg Dordrecht London New York

Library of Congress Control Number: 2011944653

CR Subject Classification (1998): D.3, D.1, F.3, D.2, I.2

LNCS Sublibrary: SL 2 – Programming and Software Engineering

Typesetting: Camera-ready by author, data conversion by Scientific Publishing Services, Chennai, India

Printed on acid-free paper

Springer is part of Springer Science+Business Media (www.springer.com)

Preface

This volume contains the proceedings of the 14th International Symposium on Practical Aspects of Declarative Languages (PADL 2012), held in Philadelphia, Pennsylvania, during January 23–24, 2012. PADL is an annual forum where researchers and practitioners present original work emphasizing new ideas and approaches pertaining to applications and implementation techniques of declarative languages. This year's topics of interest included:

- Innovative applications of declarative languages
- Declarative domain-specific languages and applications
- Practical applications of theoretical results
- New language developments and their impact on applications
- Evaluation of implementation techniques on practical applications
- Novel implementation techniques relevant to applications
- Novel uses of declarative languages in the classroom
- Practical experiences

PADL solicited both full technical papers and shorter application papers. In both categories we initially received 52 abstracts, which materialized into 41 papers (38 technical papers and three application papers). Each submission was reviewed by at least three Program Committee members and each member was asked to referee at least one paper outside their usual area. In the end, the Program Committee decided to accept 19 technical papers.

The set of accepted papers present a variety of contributions ranging from implementation techniques, applied dependent types, (embedded) domain-specific languages, declarative modelling and hardware design, concurrent and parallel programming, constraint programming, attribute grammars, distributed policy languages and work on new language features and type systems. The conference program also included an invited paper, "Recent Advances in Declarative Networking," presented by Boon Thau Loo (University of Pennsylvania), and an invited talk "Make Things Now! Pragmatic Functional Programming in Haskell" by Don Stewart (Standard Chartered Bank).

The PADL symposium was co-located with the ACM Symposium on Principles of Programming Languages (POPL 2012). We would like to thank the ACM, the POPL organizers, the Association for Logic Programming and Microsoft Research for their support, the developers of the EasyChair conference management system for easing the lives of the Program Committee chairs and the Springer staff responsible for producing the LNCS series. We would also like to express our gratitude to all the authors who submitted papers, the participants for making the event a success, and the Program Committee members and external reviewers – the symposium would not have been possible without their dedicated and outstanding work. We are also indebted to Gopal Gupta for his guidance and practical help and Ricardo Rocha for access to past materials.

November 2011

Claudio Russo
Neng-Fa Zhou

Organization

Program Committee

Marcello Balduccini	Kodak Research Laboratories, USA
Edwin Brady	University of St. Andrews, UK
Henning Christiansen	Roskilde University, Denmark
Agostino Dovier	University of Udine, Italy
Matthew Flatt	University of Utah, USA
Gopal Gupta	University of Texas at Dallas, USA
John Hughes	Chalmers University of Technology, Sweden
Gabriele Keller	University of New South Wales, Australia
Lunjin Lu	Oakland University, USA
Marc Pouzet	École Normale Supérieure, France
Ricardo Rocha	University of Porto, Portugal
Andreas Rossberg	Google Germany GmbH, Germany
Claudio Russo	Microsoft Research, UK
Kostis Sagonas	Uppsala University, Sweden; NTUA, Greece
Satnam Singh	Microsoft Research, UK
Zoltan Somogyi	The Univerity of Melbourne, Australia
Eijiro Sumii	Tohoku University, Japan
Terrance Swift	Universidade Nova de Lisboa, Portugal; Johns Hopkins University, USA
Andrew Tolmach	Portland State University, USA
Jan Wielemaker	University of Amsterdam, The Netherlands
Roland Yap	National University of Singapore, Republic of Singapore
Kwangkeun Yi	Seoul National University, Korea
Neng-Fa Zhou	City University of New York, USA

Additional Reviewers

Antoy, Sergio	Cruz, Flávio
Axelsson, Emil	Devries, Brian
Bordeaux, Lucas	Dutra, Ins
Brand, Sebastian	Fiore, Marcelo
Caillaud, Benoît	Formisano, Andrea
Carlsson, Mats	Gelfond, Gregory
Chakravarty, Manuel	Hamlen, Kevin
Chintabathina, Sandeep	Hobor, Aquinas
Cohen, Albert	Hur, Chung-Kil

Kim, Sangsig
Komendantskaya, Ekaterina
Lee, Wonchan
Lee, Wooseok
Mainland, Geoffrey
Marple, Kyle
Montanari, Angelo
Oh, Hakjoo
Omodeo, Eugenio
Pace, Gordon

Park, Sungwoo
Piazza, Carla
Rosendahl, Mads
Santos Costa, Vitor
Sasano, Isao
Schulte, Christian
Tamura, Naoyuki
Theil Have, Christian
Van Wyk, Eric

Table of Contents

Recent Advances in Declarative Networking 1
  Boon Thau Loo, Harjot Gill, Changbin Liu, Yun Mao,
  William R. Marczak, Micah Sherr, Anduo Wang, and Wenchao Zhou

Make Things Now! Pragmatic Functional Programming in Haskell 17
  Don Stewart

A Declarative Approach for Software Modeling 18
  Mayer Goldberg and Guy Wiener

Contracts and Specifications for Functional Logic Programming........ 33
  Sergio Antoy and Michael Hanus

The Environment as an Argument: Context-Aware Functional
Programming.. 48
  Pedro M. Martins, Julie A. McCann, and Susan Eisenbach

Weighted-Sequence Problem: ASP vs CASP and Declarative vs
Problem-Oriented Solving 63
  Yuliya Lierler, Shaden Smith, Miroslaw Truszczynski, and
  Alex Westlund

Practical and Methodological Aspects of the Use of Cutting-Edge ASP
Tools 78
  Marcello Balduccini and Yuliya Lierler

Efficient Tabling of Structured Data Using Indexing and Program
Transformation 93
  Christian Theil Have and Henning Christiansen

Optimizing Inequality Joins in Datalog with Approximated Constraint
Propagation 108
  Dario Campagna, Beata Sarna-Starosta, and Tom Schrijvers

Symbolic Execution of Concurrent Objects in CLP 123
  Elvira Albert, Puri Arenas, and Miguel Gómez-Zamalloa

A Segment-Swapping Approach for Executing Trapped
Computations 138
  Pablo Chico de Guzmán, Amadeo Casas, Manuel Carro, and
  Manuel V. Hermenegildo

Palovca: Describing and Executing Graph Algorithms in Haskell   153
    Michael Lesniak

LEARNPADS++: Incremental Inference of Ad Hoc Data Formats   168
    Kenny Q. Zhu, Kathleen Fisher, and David Walker

The Kennedy-Warren Algorithm Revisited: Ordering Attribute
Grammars   183
    *Jeroen Bransen, Arie Middelkoop, Atze Dijkstra, and
    S. Doaitse Swierstra*

Distributed Policy Specification and Interpretation with Classified
Advertisements   198
    Nicholas Coleman

Handshaking in Kansas Lava Using Patch Logic   212
    Andy Gill and Bowe Neuenschwander

Virtualizing Real-World Objects in FRP   227
    Daniel Winograd-Cort, Hai Liu, and Paul Hudak

Resource-Safe Systems Programming with Embedded Domain Specific
Languages   242
    Edwin Brady and Kevin Hammond

Node-Based Connection Semantics for Equation-Based Object-Oriented
Modeling Languages   258
    David Broman and Henrik Nilsson

A Declarative Specification of Tree-Based Symbolic Arithmetic
Computations   273
    Paul Tarau

Typing the Numeric Tower   289
    *Vincent St-Amour, Sam Tobin-Hochstadt, Matthew Flatt, and
    Matthias Felleisen*

Author Index   305

Recent Advances in Declarative Networking

Boon Thau Loo[1], Harjot Gill[1], Changbin Liu[1], Yun Mao[2],
William R. Marczak[3], Micah Sherr[4], Anduo Wang[1], and Wenchao Zhou[1]

[1] University of Pennsylvania
{boonloo,gillh,cliu,anduo,wenchaoz}@cis.upenn.edu
[2] AT & T Labs Research
maoy@research.att.com
[3] University of California Berkeley
wrm@berkeley.edu
[4] Georgetown University
msherr@cs.georgetown.edu

Abstract. Declarative networking is a programming methodology that enables developers to concisely specify network protocols and services, and directly compile these specifications into a dataflow framework for execution. This paper describes recent advances in declarative networking, tracing its evolution from a rapid prototyping framework towards a platform that serves as an important bridge connecting formal theories for reasoning about protocol correctness and actual implementations. In particular, the paper focuses on the use of declarative networking for addressing four main challenges in the distributed systems development cycle: the generation of safe routing implementations, debugging, security and privacy, and optimizing distributed systems.

1 Introduction

Declarative networking [27,28,29,31] is a programming methodology that enables developers to concisely specify network protocols and services using a distributed recursive query language, and directly compile these specifications into a dataflow framework for execution. This approach provides ease and compactness of specification, and offers additional benefits such as optimizability and the potential for safety checks. The development of declarative networking began in 2004 with an initial goal of enabling safe and extensible routers [30].

As evidence of its widespread applicability, declarative techniques have been used in several domains including fault tolerance protocols [52], cloud computing [4], sensor networks [11], overlay network compositions [33], anonymity systems [51], mobile ad-hoc networks [37,24], wireless channel selection [23], network configuration management [10], and as a basis for course projects in a distributed systems class [14] at the University of Pennsylvania. An open-source declarative networking system called *RapidNet* [3] has also been integrated with the emerging ns-3 [40] simulator, demonstrated at SIGCOMM'09 [38], and successfully deployed on testbeds such as PlanetLab [44] and ORBIT [42].

This paper will first present a background introduction to declarative networking (Section 2). We trace its evolution from a rapid prototyping framework

C. Russo and N.-F. Zhou (Eds.): PADL 2012, LNCS 7149, pp. 1–16, 2012.
© Springer-Verlag Berlin Heidelberg 2012

to a platform that serves as an important bridge connecting formal theories for reasoning about protocol correctness and actual implementations. The ability to bridge this gap is a major step forward compared to traditional approaches in which formal specifications, proof of protocol correctness and implementations are decoupled from one another; this decoupling leads to increased development time, error prone implementations, and tedious debugging.

Specifically, this paper describes recent work carried out within the NetDB@Penn [39] research group to address four significant challenges in distributed systems: generating safe routing implementations (Section 3), securing distributed systems (Section 4), debugging distributed systems (Section 5), and optimizing distributed systems (Section 6).

2   Background

The high level goal of *declarative networks* is to build extensible architectures that achieve a good balance of flexibility, performance and safety. Declarative networks are specified using *Network Datalog (NDlog)*, a distributed recursive query language for querying networks.

NDlog enables a variety of routing protocols and overlay networks to be specified in a natural and concise manner. For example, traditional routing protocols such as the path vector and distance-vector protocols can be expressed in a few lines of code [31], and the Chord distributed hash table in 47 lines of code [29]. When compiled and executed, these declarative protocols perform efficiently relative to imperative implementations.

In addition to ease of implementation, another advantage of the declarative networking approach is its amenability to formal and structured forms of correctness checks. These include the use of theorem proving [53], algebraic techniques for constructing safe routing protocols [54], and runtime verification [61]. These formal analysis techniques are strengthened by recent work on formally proving correct operational semantics of *NDlog* [41]. Finally, the dataflow framework used in declarative networking naturally captures information flow as distributed queries, hence providing a natural way to use the concept of *network provenance* [60] to analyze and explain the existence of any network state.

NDlog is based on Datalog [46]: a Datalog program consists of a set of declarative *rules*. Each rule has the form p :- q1, q2, ..., qn., which can be read informally as "q1 and q2 and ... and qn implies p". Here, p is the *head* of the rule, and q1, q2,...,qn is a list of *literals* that constitutes the *body* of the rule. Literals are either *predicates* with *attributes* (which are bound to variables or constants by the query), or boolean expressions that involve function symbols (including arithmetic) applied to attributes.

Datalog rules can refer to one another in a mutually recursive fashion. The order in which the rules are presented in a program is semantically immaterial; likewise, the order predicates appear in a rule is not semantically meaningful. Commas are interpreted as logical conjunctions (*AND*). Conventionally, the names of predicates, function symbols, and constants begin with a lowercase letter, while variable names begin with an uppercase letter. Function calls are additionally prepended by f_. Aggregate constructs are represented as functions with attribute variables within angle brackets (<>). We illustrate *NDlog* using a simple two rule program that computes all pairs of reachable nodes in a network:

```
r1 reachable(@S,N) :- link(@S,N).
r2 reachable(@S,D) :- link(@S,N), reachable(@N,D).
```

Rules r1 and r2 specify a distributed transitive closure computation, where rule r1 computes all pairs of nodes reachable within a single hop from all input links (denoted by the link predicate), and rule r2 expresses that "if there is a link from S to N, and N can reach D, then S can reach D." The output of interest is the set of all reachable(@S,D) tuples, representing reachable pairs of nodes from S to D. By modifying this simple example, we can construct more complex routing protocols, such as the distance vector and path vector routing protocols.

NDlog supports a *location specifier* in each predicate, expressed with the @ symbol followed by an attribute. This attribute is used to denote the source location of each corresponding tuple. For example, all reachable and link tuples are stored based on the @S address field.

2.1 Query Evaluation

In declarative networking, each node runs its own set of *NDlog* rules. Typically, these rules are common across all nodes (that is, all nodes run the same protocol), but may further include per-node policy customizations. *NDlog* rules are compiled and executed as *distributed dataflows* by the query processor to implement various network protocols. These dataflows share a similar execution model with the Click modular router [21], which consists of elements that are connected together to implement a variety of network and flow control components. In addition, elements include database operators (such as joins, aggregation, and selections) that are directly generated from the *NDlog* rules. Messages flow among dataflows executed at different nodes, resulting in updates to local tables, or query results that are returned to the hosts that issued the queries. The local tables store the network state of various network protocols.

To execute *NDlog* programs, we use the *pipelined semi-naïve* (PSN) model [27]. PSN extends the traditional *semi-naïve* Datalog evaluation strategy [9] to work in an asynchronous distributed setting. PSN relaxes semi-naïve evaluation to the extreme of processing each tuple as it is received. This provides opportunities for additional optimizations on a per-tuple basis. New tuples that are generated from the semi-naïve rules, as well as tuples received from other nodes, are used immediately to compute new tuples without waiting for the current (local) iteration to complete.

In practice, most network protocols execute over a long period of time and incrementally update and repair routing tables as the underlying network changes (for example, due to link failures, and node departures). To better map into practical networking scenarios, one key distinction that differentiates the execution of *NDlog* from earlier work in Datalog is our support for continuous rule execution and result materialization, where all tuples derived from *NDlog* rules are materialized and incrementally updated as the underlying network changes. As in network protocols, such incremental maintenance is required both for timely updates and for avoiding the overhead of recomputing all routing tables "from scratch" whenever there are changes to the underlying network. In the presence of insertions and deletions to base tuples, our original incremental view maintenance implementation utilizes the count algorithm [17] that ensures only tuples that are no longer derivable are deleted. This has subsequently been improved [36] via the use of a compact form of data provenance encoded using binary decision diagrams shipped with each derived tuple.

2.2   Language Extensions

In our original work [29], predicates are allowed to be declared as *soft-state* with lifetimes. In the extreme case, *event predicates* form transient tables which are used as input to rules but are not stored. To support wireless broadcast [24,37], we have introduced a *broadcast location specifier* denoted by @* which causes a tuple to be broadcast to all nodes within wireless range of the node on which the rule is executed. In order to support network functionality composition and code reuse, we introduced *Composable Virtual Views* [33], which define rule groups that perform a specific functionality when executed together. These extensions offer different levels of declarativity [32] to meet various application demands.

The meaning of a *NDlog* program is defined to be the behavior and output obtained by running the program through PSN evaluation [27,41]. The *Dedalus* [19,5] language is similar to *NDlog*, except its behavior and output is defined in terms of a model-theoretic semantics. Dedalus also allows users to write rules that mutate state.

Dedalus takes base Datalog, and adds an integer *timestamp* field to every tuple. State update is expressed as locally-stratified recursion through negation. Message delay and re-ordering is captured by requiring all rules to derive non-local tuples at some non-deterministic future timestamp. Dedalus uses Saccà and Zaniolo's `choice` construct [49] to model this non-determinism, which manifests itself in multiple *stable models* [13] – one model for each possible choice of timestamp.

An interesting question is to what extent the behavior and output of the program is "well-behaved." The *CALM Conjecture*, posed by Hellerstein [19] states that monotonic *coordination-free* Dedalus programs are *eventually consistent*, and non-monotonic programs are eventually consistent when instrumented with appropriate coordination. Recently, Ameloot et al. explored Hellerstein's CALM conjecture using relational transducers [6]. They proved that monotonic first order queries are exactly the set of queries that can be computed in a coordination-free fashion in their transducer formalism. Their work uses some different assumptions than traditional declarative networking—for example, they assume that all messages sent by a node are multicast to a fixed set of neighbors, whereas *NDlog* permits arbitrary unicast.

3   Generating Safe Routing Implementations

Our *Formally Verifiable Routing (FVR)* project addresses a long-standing challenge in networking research: bridging the gap between formal routing theories and actual implementations. The application of declarative networking is especially useful here, serving as an intermediary layer between high-level formal specifications of the network design and low-level implementations.

3.1 Formally Safe Routing Toolkit

The *Formally Safe Routing (FSR)* toolkit [54] attempts to bridge this gap in the context of interdomain routing by unifying research in routing algebras [16] with declarative networking to produce provably correct distributed implementations. Specifically, FSR automates the process of analyzing routing configurations expressed in algebra for safety (i.e. convergence) using the Yices SMT solver [55], and automatically compiles routing algebra into declarative routing implementations.

To enable an evaluation of protocol dynamics and convergence time, FSR uses our extended routing algebra [54] to automatically generate a distributed routing-protocol implementation that matches the policy configuration — avoiding the time-consuming and error-prone task of manually creating an implementation. FSR generates a provably correct translation to a *NDlog* specification, which is then executed using the RapidNet declarative networking engine.

Our choice of *NDlog* as the basis for FSR is motivated by the following. First, the declarative features of *NDlog* allow for straightforward translation from the routing algebra to *NDlog* programs. Second, *NDlog* enables a variety of routing protocols and overlay networks to be specified in a natural and concise manner. Given that *NDlog* specifications are orders of magnitude less code than imperative implementations, this makes possible a clean and concise proof (via logical inductions) of the correctness of the generated *NDlog* programs with regard to safety. The compact specifications also make it easy to incorporate alternative routing mechanisms to the basic path-vector protocol, as we have previously demonstrated [54]. Finally, when compiled and executed, these declarative protocols perform efficiently relative to imperative routing implementations.

Our recent prototype demonstration at SIGCOMM'11 [48] shows how FSR can detect problems in an AS's iBGP configuration (using realistic topologies and policies). We have also used our system to prove sufficient conditions for BGP safety and empirically evaluate protocol dynamics and convergence time.

FSR serves two important communities. For researchers, FSR automates important parts of the design process and provides a common framework for describing, evaluating, and comparing new safety guidelines. For network operators, FSR automates the analysis of internal router (iBGP) and border gateway (eBGP) configurations for safety violations. For both communities, FSR automatically generates realistic protocol implementations to evaluate real network configurations (e.g., to study convergence time) prior to actual deployment.

3.2 Declarative Network Verification

In addition to the FSR toolkit, we have also explored the use of theorem proving for verifying declarative networking programs. We have developed the *DNV (Declarative Network Verification)* [53] toolkit that demonstrate the feasibility of automatically compiling declarative networking programs written in *NDlog* into formal specifications recognizable by a theorem prover (e.g., PVS [2]) for verification. Unlike model checkers, DNV can express properties beyond the temporal properties to which most model-checking techniques are restricted. They also avoid the state exploration problem inherent in model checking. Theorem proving techniques are also sound and complete: once a property is verified, it holds for all instances of the protocol. Moreover, modern theorem provers come with powerful proof engines that support a large portion of automated proof exploration, enabling the proof of non-trivial theorems with relatively modest human effort.

4   Securing Distributed Systems

The *Declarative Secure Distributed Systems* (DS2) platform provides high-level programming abstractions for implementing secure distributed systems, achieved by   unifying   declarative   networking   and   logic-based   access   control specifications [12]. DS2 has a wide range of applications, including reconfigurable trust management [35], secure distributed data processing [34], and tunable anonymity [51].

DS2 is motivated in part by the observation that distributed trust management languages share similarities with both data integration languages and the distributed Datalog languages proposed for declarative networking. These languages support the notion of *context* (location) to identify *components* (nodes) in distributed systems. The commonalities between these languages indicate that ideas and methods from the database community are also applicable to processing security policies, suggesting the unification of these declarative languages to create an integrated system.

The DS2 system is currently available for download [47].

4.1   Secure Network Datalog

We developed the *Secure Network Datalog (SeNDlog)* language [59] that unifies *NDlog* and logic-based languages for access control in distributed systems. *SeNDlog* enables network routing, information systems, and security policies to be specified and implemented within a common declarative framework. We have additionally extended existing distributed recursive query processing techniques to execute *SeNDlog* programs to incorporate secure communication among untrusted nodes.

In *SeNDlog*, we bind a set of rules and the associated tuples to reside at a particular node. We do this at the top level for each rule (or set of rules), for example by specifying:

```
At N,
   r1 p :- p1,p2,...,pn.
   r2 p1 :- p2,p3,...,pn.
```

The above rules r1 and r2 are in the context of N, where N is either a variable or a constant representing the principal where the rules reside. If N is a variable, it will be instantiated with local information upon rule installation. In a trusted distributed environment, N simply represents the network address of a node: either a physical address (e.g., an IP address) or a logical address (e.g., an overlay identifier). In a multi-user multi-layered network environment where multiple users and overlay networks may reside on the same physical node, N can include the user name and an overlay network identifier. This is unlike declarative networking in which location specifiers denote physical IP address.

SeNDlog allows different principals or contexts to communicate via import and export of tuples. The communication serves two purposes: (1) maintenance messages as part of a network protocol's updates on routing tables, and (2) distributed derivation of security decisions. Imported tuples from a principal N are automatically quoted using "N says" to differentiate them from local tuples. During the evaluation of *SeNDlog* rules, we allow derived tuples to be communicated among contexts via the use of *import predicates* and *export predicates*:

- An *import predicate* is of the form "N says p" in a rule body, where principal N asserts the predicate p.
- An *export predicate* is of the form "N says p@X" in a rule head, where principal N exports the predicate p to the context of principal X. Here, X can be a constant or a variable. If X is a variable, in order to make bottom-up evaluation efficient, we further require that the variable X occur in the rule body. As a shorthand, we can omit "N says" if N is the principal where the rule resides.

By exporting tuples only to specified principals, the use of export predicates ensures confidentiality and prevents information leakage. With the above definitions, a *SeNDlog* rule is a Datalog rule where the rule body can include import predicates and the rule head can be an export predicate.

We provide a concrete example based on the declarative path vector protocol as presented in the original declarative routing [31] paper: At every node Z, this program takes as input neighbor(Z,X) tuples that contain all neighbors X for Z. The program generates route(Z,X,P) tuples, each of which stores the path P from source Z to destination X. The basic protocol specification is similar to the all-pairs reachable example presented in Section 2, with additional predicates for computing the actual path using the f_concat function which prepends neighbor X to the input path P.

The input carryTraffic and acceptRoute tables respectively represent the export and import policies of node Z. Each carryTraffic(Z,X,Y) tuple represents the fact that node Z is willing to serve all network traffic on behalf of node X to node Y, and each acceptRoute(Z,Y,X) tuple represents the fact that node Z will accept a route from node X to node Y. A more complex version of this protocol will have additional rules that derive carryTraffic and acceptRoute, avoid path cycles and also derive shortest paths with the least hop count.

The path-vector protocol is used for inter-domain routing over the Internet and is known to be vulnerable to a variety of attacks due to the lack of mechanisms for verifying the authenticity and authorization of routing control traffic. One potential solution is to authenticate every routing control message, as proposed for Secure BGP [50].

```
At Z,
  z1 route(Z,X,P) :- neighbor(Z,X), P=f_initPath(Z,X).
  z2 route(Z,Y,P) :- X says advertise(Y,P), acceptRoute(Z,X,Y).
  z3 advertise(Y,P1)@X :- neighbor(Z,X), route(Z,Y,P),
      carryTraffic(Z,X,Y), P1=f_concat(X,P).
```

In our example program, we can specify such authentication naturally via the use of "says" to ensure that all advertise tuples are verified by the recipients for authenticity. Rule z1 takes as input neighbor(Z,X) tuples, and computes all the single hop route(Z,X,P) containing the path [Z,X] from node Z to X. Rules z2 and z3 compute routes of increasing hop counts. Upon receiving an advertise(Y,P) tuple from X, Z uses rule z2 to decide whether to accept the route advertisement based on its local acceptRoute table. If the route is accepted, a route tuple is derived locally, and this results in the generation of an advertise tuple which is further exported by node Z via rule z3 to some of its neighbors X as determined by the policies stored in the local carryTraffic table.

SeNDlog is able to compactly specify a variety of secure distributed protocols. Our earlier work [59] has demonstrated, for example, the use of *SeNDlog* for performing secure distributed joins and securing distributed hash tables [8].

4.2   Reconfigurable Security

Although one can achieve a high level of security using a "one-size-fits-all" solution with fixed constructs like says, an *extensible trust management* framework where users can write and reconfigure their own constructs like says is applicable to a much broader range of settings. For example, programmers could customize the security protocols used by their application based on the execution environment without modifying the application logic. In the *LBTrust* [35] work, we extended SeNDlog to support user-defined security constructs that can be customized and composed in a declarative fashion. To validate our ideas in a production system, we implemented our extension in the LogicBlox [26] system, an emerging commercial Datalog-based platform for enterprise software systems.

We enhanced LogicBlox to support *meta-rules* — Datalog rules that operate on the rules of the program as input, and produce new rules as output — and *meta-constraints* — Datalog constraints that restrict the allowable rules in the program. Security constructs are written using these two ingredients. For example, the says construct would consist of meta-rules that rewrite the program to perform signing of all exported messages, and constraints that ensure that all imported messages have valid signatures. We demonstrate that a variety of security primitives for authentication, confidentiality, integrity, speaks-for, and restricted delegation can be supported. Based on these primitives, several existing distributed trust management systems (e.g., Binder [12], SD3 [20], Delegation Logic [22], and SeNDlog) can be implemented in LBTrust.

A follow-up to LBTrust is the *SecureBlox* [34] system, which restricts the use of meta-programming to make it a fully static, compile-time operation. We added support for physical distribution to LBTrust, and looked at performance-security tradeoffs between different constructs in distributed systems. Similar to LBTrust, SecureBlox allows meta-programmability for compile-time code generation based on the security requirements and trust policies of the deployed environment.

While we specifically study security in the LBTrust and SecureBlox work, the general pattern of using meta-programming to decompose a logic program into different aspects representing cross-cutting concerns is more broadly applicable.

4.3 Application-Aware Anonymity

To further illustrate the feasibility of our methods and technologies for the development of secure distributed systems, we have conceptualized and implemented the *Application-Aware Anonymity (A^3)* system [7,51], a distributed peer-to-peer service that provides high-performance anonymity "for the masses". A^3 uses *SeNDlog* for implementing an extensible policy engine for customizing its relay selection and instantiation strategies. A^3 allows applications to construct anonymous Onion [15] paths that adhere to application specific constraints (e.g., end-to-end latency). Unlike existing anonymity systems that construct paths according to predefined criteria, A^3 enables applications to specify the requirements of their anonymous paths. For example, anonymized Voice-over-IP services can request paths with low latency and modest bandwidth requirements, while streaming video broadcasts can request high bandwidth anonymous paths without regard for latency. A^3 is open-source and available for download [7].

5 Debugging Distributed Systems

In the context of distributed systems, it is very common for system administrators to perform analysis tasks that essentially amount to *network provenance* [60] queries. For example, they might ask diagnostic queries to determine the root cause of a malfunction, forensic queries to identify the source of an intrusion, or profiling queries to find the reason for suboptimal performance.

The *NetTrails* [58,60] system is a declarative platform for incrementally maintaining, interactively navigating, and querying network provenance in a distributed system. During the system execution, *NetTrails* incrementally maintains provenance information using RapidNet as its distributed query engine. Our architecture offers a unifying framework, as both maintenance and querying functionalities are specified as *NDlog* programs.

NetTrails consists of two subcomponents: First, a *maintenance engine* takes as input either *NDlog* programs or input/output dependencies captured from legacy applications, and then incrementally computes and maintains network provenance information as distributed relational tables. Second, a *distributed query engine* executes user-customizable provenance queries that are evaluated across multiple nodes. Legacy systems are supported either by modifying the application's source code to explicitly report provenance, or by using an external specification of the application's protocol to derive provenance information by observing a node's inputs and outputs [57].

5.1 Network Provenance Model

In *NetTrails*, the provenance graph is internally maintained as relational tables which are distributed and partitioned across all nodes in the network. Network

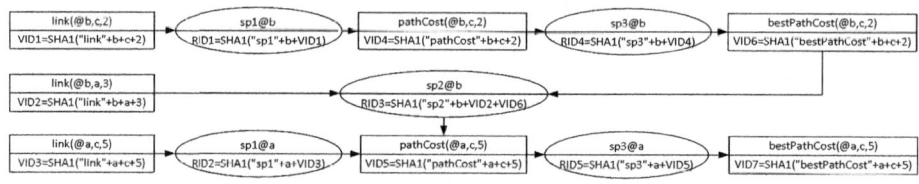

Fig. 1. The provenance graph of the tuple `bestPathCost(@a,c,5)` derived from the execution of the MINCOST program

provenance is modeled as an acyclic graph $G(V, E)$. The vertex set V consists of *tuple vertices* and *rule execution vertices*. Each tuple vertex in the graph is either a base tuple or a computation result, and each rule execution vertex represents an instance of a rule execution given a set of input tuples. The edge set E represents dataflows between tuples and rule execution vertices.

To illustrate, we consider an example network consisting of three nodes a, b and c connected by three bi-directional links (a,b), (a,c) and (b,c) with costs 3, 5 and 2 respectively. We further consider the following three-rule MINCOST program that computes the minimal path cost between each pair of nodes:

```
sp1 pathCost(@S,D,C)     :- link(@S,D,C).
sp2 pathCost(@S,D,C1+C2) :- link(@Z,S,C1), bestPathCost(@Z,D,C2).
sp3 bestPathCost(@S,D,min<C>) :- pathCost(@S,D,C).
```

Figure 1 shows the provenance for a specific derived tuple `bestPathCost(@a,c,5)`, based on the dependency logic captured by the MINCOST program. For instance, the figure shows that `bestPathCost(@a,c,5)` is generated from rule sp3 at node a taking `pathCost(@a,c,5)` as the input. To trace further, `pathCost(@a,c,5)` has two derivations: the locally derivable one-hop path $a \rightarrow c$ and the two-hop path $a \rightarrow b \rightarrow c$ that requires a distributed join at b.

5.2   Distributed Maintenance and Querying

Given the adoption of a declarative networking engine, data dependencies are explicitly captured in derivation rules.[1] The provenance maintenance in a dynamic system execution can be performed in a straightforward manner: an automatic rule rewrite algorithm takes as input a set of derivation rules, and outputs a modified program that contains additional rules for capturing the provenance information. These additional rules define network provenance in terms of views over base and derived tuples. As the network protocol executes and updates network state, views are incrementally recomputed.

Once generated, network provenance can be queried by issuing distributed queries. Since provenance information is distributed across nodes, query execution performs a traversal of the provenance graphs in a distributed fashion.

NetTrails allows users to customize the provenance queries. For instance, users can query for a tuple's lineage, the set of nodes that have been involved in

---

[1] For legacy applications, the data dependencies (reported by the modified source code or inferred from the observed I/Os) can be formulated as derivation rules as well [57].

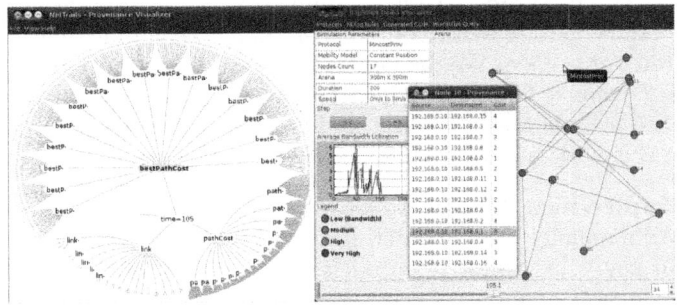

Fig. 2. A screenshot of the *NetTrails* demonstration at SIGMOD'11

the derivation of a given tuples, and/or the total number of alternative derivations. To reduce querying overhead, *NetTrails* adopts a set of optimization techniques [60], including caching previously queried results, leveraging alternative tree traversal orders, and performing threshold-based pruning.

An early prototype of *NetTrails* was presented at SIGMOD'11 [58]. Figure 2 shows an example execution of the current version of the demonstration that highlights the provenance of the system state (captured as tuples) for a running MINCOST program. One may further issue customized provenance queries and visually inspect the progressive steps of the distributed querying.

5.3 Security and Temporal Extensions

NetTrails provides functionality required for richer provenance queries by adding (i) new provenance models and maintenance strategies for capturing the time, distribution, and causality of updates in distributed systems [56], and (ii) novel query processing and optimization techniques for efficiently and securely answering queries at scale [57].

NetTrails explicitly captures *causality*: if some network state α depends on some other state β, and β is changed, the provenance of the *change* in α is attributable to the change in β. Additionally, since one of our potential use cases is forensics, *NetTrails* achieves strong *security guarantees* even in the presence of misbehaving and potentially malicious nodes. *NetTrails* utilizes *secure network provenance* [57] to provide the strong guarantee that either a returned provenance query is accurate and complete, or that a misbehaving node is identified with non-repudiable evidence against the node.

To demonstrate the capabilities of *NetTrails*'s temporal and security extensions, we describe a number of use cases of our system, as presented in [57].

Network Routing. The *Border Gateway Protocol* (BGP) used for interdomain routing over the Internet is plagued by a variety of attacks and malfunctions. We have applied *NetTrails* to the Quagga BGP daemon [45] and demonstrated how our solution enables a network administrator to determine why an entry from a routing table has disappeared. We also showed how *NetTrails* can be used to detect well-known BGP misconfigurations.

Distributed Hash Tables. We have applied *NetTrails* to a declarative implementation of the Chord [29] distributed hash table; no modifications are required to the Chord source code. We demonstrated *NetTrails'* ability to detect a well-known attack against Chord in which the attacker gains control over a large fraction of the neighbors of a correct node, and is then able to drop or reroute messages to this node and prevent correct overlay operation.

Hadoop MapReduce. Finally, we have applied *NetTrails* to Hadoop MapReduce [18]. We manually instrumented Hadoop to report provenance at the level of individual key-value pairs. We used Hadoop to encode the *WordCount* program that reports the number of occurrences of each word in a 1.2 GB Wikipedia dataset. In this scenario, we queried for the provenance of a given (unlikely) key-value pair in the output. *NetTrails* revealed that unexpected results might be attributed to a faulty or compromised map worker. More generally, *NetTrails* was able to identify the causes of suspicious MapReduce outputs.

6   Optimizing Distributed Systems

In distributed systems management, operators often configure system parameters that optimize performance objectives, given constraints in the deployment environment. In this section we present our recent work on a declarative optimization platform that enables constraint optimization problems (COP) to be declaratively specified and incrementally executed in distributed systems.

Traditional COP implementation approaches use imperative languages such as C++ or Java and often result in cumbersome and error-prone programs that are difficult to maintain and customize. Moreover, due to scalability and management constraints imposed across administrative domains, it is often necessary to execute COP in a *distributed* setting in which multiple *local* solvers must coordinate with one another. Each local solver handles a portion of the whole problem, and they together achieve a global objective.

Central to our optimization platform is the integration of a *declarative networking engine* [28] with an off-the-shelf constraint solver [1]. We highlight two use cases to which we have applied our platform:

6.1   Use Cases: PUMA and COPE

First, we have developed the *Policy-based Unified Multi-radio Architecture* (PUMA), a declarative constraint solving platform for optimizing wireless mesh networks. In PUMA, network operators can flexibly vary the choice of routing via adaptable *hybrid* routing protocols [24]. The hybrid technique combines several existing protocols (e.g., proactive, reactive, and epidemic) with specific criteria for determining when particular protocols are to be used. The hybrid compositional capabilities are particularly useful for routing in heterogeneous network settings in which application needs and network conditions keep changing over time. In addition, PUMA enables policies for *wireless channel selection* [23] to be declaratively specified and optimized; such policies may reduce network interference and maximize throughput while not violating constraints (for instance, refraining from channels owned exclusively by the primary users [43]).

Second, in our *Cloud Orchestration Policy Engine* (COPE) [25], we use our optimization framework to declaratively control the provisioning, configuration, management and decommissioning of cloud resource orchestration. COPE enables the automatic realization of customer service level agreements while simultaneously conforming to operational objectives of the cloud providers.

Beyond these two use cases, we envision that our platform has a wide-range of potential applications, including optimizing distributed systems for load balancing, robust routing, scheduling, and security.

6.2 *Colog* Language and Compilation

Our optimization platform uses the *Colog* declarative policy language. *Colog* allows operators to concisely model distributed system resources and formulate management decisions as declarative programs with specified goals and constraints. Compared to traditional imperative alternatives, *Colog* results in code that is smaller by orders of magnitude, and is easier to understand, debug and extend. Here, we present high level intuitions of *Colog*; a more comprehensive treatment of the language can be found in our earlier work [23,25].

Language extensions. Based on *NDlog*, *Colog* extends traditional *NDlog* with constructs for expressing goals and constraints. Two reserved keywords — goal and var — respectively specify the *optimization goal* and *variables* used by the constraint solver. *Constraint* rules of the form F1 -> F2, F3, ..., Fn denote that whenever F1 is true, then the rule body (F2 and F3 and ... and Fn) must also be true to satisfy the constraint. Unlike a Datalog rule which derives new values for a predicate, a constraint *restricts* a predicate's allowed values, hence representing an invariant that must be maintained at all times. These are used by the solver to limit the search space when computing the optimization goal. Using *Colog*, it is easy to customize policies simply by modifying the goals and constraints, and by adding additional derivation rules.

Distributed COP. *Colog* is extended for execution in a distributed setting. At a high level, multiple solver nodes execute a *local* COP, and then iteratively exchange COP results with neighboring nodes until a stopping condition is reached. Similar to *NDlog*, in the distributed COP program, a location specifier @ denotes the source location of each corresponding tuple. This allows us to write rules in which the input data span multiple nodes — a convenient language construct for formulating distributed optimizations.

One of the interesting aspects of *Colog*, from a query processing standpoint, is our integration of RapidNet (an incremental bottom-up distributed Datalog evaluation engine) and Gecode (a top-down goal-oriented constraint solver). This integration allows us to implement a distributed solver that can perform incremental and distributed constraint optimizations.

To execute distributed COP rules, *Colog* uses RapidNet, which already provides a runtime environment for implementing these rules. At a high level, each distributed rule or constraint (with multiple distinct location specifiers) is rewritten using a *localization* rewrite [28] step. This transformation results in rule bodies that can be executed locally and rule heads that can be derived and sent across nodes. The beauty of this rewrite is that even if the original program expresses distributed properties and constraints, the rewrite process will realize multiple local COP operations at different nodes, and have the output of COP operations via derivations sent across nodes.

Acknowledgments. Our work on declarative networking has been generously funded by NSF (CNS-0721845, CNS-0831376, IIS-0812270, CCF-0820208, CNS-0845552, CNS-1040672, CNS-1065130, and CNS-1117052), AFOSR MURI grant FA9550-08-1-0352, DARPA SAFER award N66001-11-C-4020, and DARPA Air Force Research Laboratory (AFRL) Contract FA8750-07-C-0169. We would also like to thank our collaborators listed on the NetDB@Penn site [39] for their contributions to the various research efforts described in this paper.

References

1. Gecode constraint development environment, http://www.gecode.org/
2. PVS Specification and Verification System, http://pvs.csl.sri.com/
3. RapidNet, http://netdb.cis.upenn.edu/rapidnet/
4. Alvaro, P., Condie, T., Conway, N., Elmeleegy, K., Hellerstein, J.M., Sears, R.: Boom Analytics: Exploring Data-Centric, Declarative Programming for the Cloud. In: Proceedings of Eurosys (2010)
5. Alvaro, P., Marczak, W., Conway, N., Hellerstein, J.M., Maier, D., Sears, R.C.: Dedalus: Datalog in time and space. Technical Report UCB/EECS-2009-173, EECS Department, University of California, Berkeley (December 2009)
6. Ameloot, T.J., Neven, F., Van den Bussche, J.: Relational Transducers for Declarative Networking. In: PODS (2011)
7. Application Aware Anonymity, http://a3.cis.upenn.edu/
8. Balakrishnan, H., Kaashoek, M.F., Karger, D., Morris, R., Stoica, I.: Looking Up Data in P2P Systems. Communications of the ACM 46(2) (2003)
9. Balbin, I., Ramamohanarao, K.: A Generalization of the Differential Approach to Recursive Query Evaluation. Journal of Logic Prog. 4(3), 259–262 (1987)
10. Chen, X., Mao, Y., Mao, Z.M., van der Merwe, J.: Declarative Configuration Management for Complex and Dynamic Networks. In: CoNEXT (2010)
11. Chu, D.C., Popa, L., Tavakoli, A., Hellerstein, J.M., Levis, P., Shenker, S., Stoica, I.: The Design and Implementation of a Declarative Sensor Network System. In: 5th ACM Conference on Embedded networked Sensor Systems, SenSys (2007)
12. DeTreville, J.: Binder: A logic-based security language. In: IEEE Symposium on Security and Privacy (2002)
13. Gelfond, M., Lifschitz, V.: The Stable Model Semantics For Logic Programming. In: ICLP/SLP, pp. 1070–1080 (1988)
14. Gill, H., Saeed, T., Fei, Q., Zhang, Z., Loo, B.T.: An Open-source and Declarative Approach Towards Teaching Large-scale Networked Systems Programming. In: SIGCOMM Education Workshop (2011)
15. Goldschlag, D., Reed, M., Syverson, P.: Onion Routing. Communications of the ACM 42(2), 39–41 (1999)
16. Griffin, T.G., Sobrinho, J.L.: Metarouting. In: ACM SIGCOMM (2005)
17. Gupta, A., Mumick, I.S., Subrahmanian, V.S.: Maintaining Views Incrementally. In: Proceedings of ACM SIGMOD International Conference on Management of Data (1993)
18. Hadoop, http://hadoop.apache.org/
19. Hellerstein, J.M.: Declarative imperative: Experiences and conjectures in distributed logic. SIGMOD Record 39(1) (2010)
20. Jim, T.: SD3: A Trust Management System With Certified Evaluation. In: IEEE Symposium on Security and Privacy (2001)

21. Kohler, E., Morris, R., Chen, B., Jannotti, J., Kaashoek, M.F.: The Click Modular Router. ACM Transactions on Computer Systems 18(3), 263–297 (2000)
22. Li, N., Grosof, B.N., Feigenbaum, J.: Delegation Logic: A logic-based approach to distributed authorization. ACM TISSEC (2003)
23. Liu, C., Correa, R., Gill, H., Gill, T., Li, X., Muthukumar, S., Saeed, T., Loo, B.T., Basu, P.: PUMA: Policy-based Unified Multi-radio Architecture for Agile Mesh Networking. In: 4th International Conference on Communication Systems and Networks, COMSNETS (2012)
24. Liu, C., Correa, R., Li, X., Basu, P., Loo, B.T., Mao, Y.: Declarative policy-based adaptive mobile ad hoc networking. IEEE/ACM Transactions on Networking, ToN (2011)
25. Liu, C., Loo, B.T., Mao, Y.: Declarative Automated Cloud Resource Orchestration. In: ACM Symposium on Cloud Computing, SOCC (2011)
26. LogicBlox Inc., http://www.logicblox.com/
27. Loo, B.T., Condie, T., Garofalakis, M., Gay, D.E., Hellerstein, J.M., Maniatis, P., Ramakrishnan, R., Roscoe, T., Stoica, I.: Declarative Networking: Language, Execution and Optimization. In: Proceedings of ACM SIGMOD International Conference on Management of Data (2006)
28. Loo, B.T., Condie, T., Garofalakis, M., Gay, D.E., Hellerstein, J.M., Maniatis, P., Ramakrishnan, R., Roscoe, T., Stoica, I.: Declarative Networking. Communications of the ACM, CACM (2009)
29. Loo, B.T., Condie, T., Hellerstein, J.M., Maniatis, P., Roscoe, T., Stoica, I.: Implementing Declarative Overlays. In: Proceedings of ACM Symposium on Operating Systems Principles (2005)
30. Loo, B.T., Hellerstein, J.M., Stoica, I.: Customizable Routing with Declarative Queries. In: ACM SIGCOMM Hot Topics in Networks (2004)
31. Loo, B.T., Hellerstein, J.M., Stoica, I., Ramakrishnan, R.: Declarative Routing: Extensible Routing with Declarative Queries. In: Proceedings of ACM SIGCOMM Conference on Data Communication (2005)
32. Mao, Y.: On the declarativity of declarative networking. In: ACM NetDB Workshop (2009)
33. Mao, Y., Loo, B.T., Ives, Z., Smith, J.M.: MOSAIC: Unified Platform for Dynamic Overlay Selection and Composition. In: CoNEXT (2008)
34. Marczak, W.R., Huang, S.S., Bravenboer, M., Sherr, M., Loo, B.T., Aref, M.: SecureBlox: Customizable Secure Distributed Data Processing. In: SIGMOD (2010)
35. Marczak, W.R., Zook, D., Zhou, W., Aref, M., Loo, B.T.: Declarative Reconfigurable Trust Management. In: Proceedings of Conference on Innovative Data Systems Research, CIDR (2009)
36. Liu, M., Taylor, N., Zhou, W., Ives, Z., Loo, B.T.: Recursive Computation of Regions and Connectivity in Networks. In: Proceedings of IEEE Conference on Data Engineering, ICDE (2009)
37. Muthukumar, S.C., Li, X., Liu, C., Kopena, J.B., Oprea, M., Correa, R., Loo, B.T., Basu, P.: RapidMesh: declarative toolkit for rapid experimentation of wireless mesh networks. In: WINTECH (2009)
38. Muthukumar, S.C., Li, X., Liu, C., Kopena, J.B., Oprea, M., Loo, B.T.: Declarative toolkit for rapid network protocol simulation and experimentation. In: SIGCOMM, demo (2009)
39. NetDB@Penn, http://netdb.cis.upenn.edu/
40. Network Simulator 3, http://www.nsnam.org/
41. Nigam, V., Jia, L., Loo, B.T., Scedrov, A.: Maintaining distributed logic programs incrementally. In: 13th International ACM SIGPLAN Symposium on Principles and Practice of Declarative Programming, PPDP (2011)
42. ORBIT - Wireless Network Testbed, http://www.orbit-lab.org/
43. Perich, F.: Policy-based Network Management for NeXt Generation Spectrum Access Control. In: DySPAN (2007)
44. PlanetLab. Global testbed, http://www.planet-lab.org/

45. Quagga Routing Suite, http://www.quagga.net/
46. Ramakrishnan, R., Ullman, J.D.: A Survey of Research on Deductive Database Systems. Journal of Logic Programming 23(2), 125–149 (1993)
47. RapidNet Declarative Networking Engine, http://netdb.cis.upenn.edu/rapidnet/
48. Ren, Y., Zhou, W., Wang, A., Jia, L., Gurney, A.J., Loo, B.T., Rexford, J.: FSR: Formal Analysis and Implementation Toolkit for Safe Inter-domain Routing. In: ACM SIGCOMM Conference on Data Communication, demonstration (2011)
49. Saccà, D., Zaniolo, C.: Stable Models and Non-Determinism in Logic Programs with Negation. In: PODS, pp. 205–217 (1990)
50. Secure BGP, http://www.ir.bbn.com/sbgp/
51. Sherr, M., Mao, A., Marczak, W.R., Zhou, W., Loo, B.T., Blaze, M.: A3: An Extensible Platform for Application-Aware Anonymity. In: Network and Distributed System Security (2010)
52. Singh, A., Das, T., Maniatis, P., Druschel, P., Roscoe, T.: BFT Protocols Under Fire. In: USENIX Symposium on Networked Systems Design and Implementation (2008)
53. Wang, A., Basu, P., Loo, B.T., Sokolsky, O.: Towards declarative network verification. In: 11th International Symposium on Practical Aspects of Declarative Languages, PADL (2009)
54. Wang, A., Jia, L., Zhou, W., Ren, Y., Loo, B.T., Rexford, J., Nigam, V., Scedrov, A., Talcott, C.: FSR: Formal analysis and implementation toolkit for safe inter-domain routing. University of Pennsylvania CIS Technical Report No. MS-CIS-11-10 (2011), http://repository.upenn.edu/cis_reports/954/
55. Yices, http://yices.csl.sri.com/
56. Zhou, W., Ding, L., Haeberlen, A., Ives, Z., Loo, B.T.: Tap: Time-aware provenance for distributed systems. In: 3rd USENIX Workshop on the Theory and Practice of Provenance, TaPP 2011 (2011)
57. Zhou, W., Fei, Q., Narayan, A., Haeberlen, A., Loo, B.T., Sherr, M.: Secure network provenance. In: Proceedings of ACM Symposium on Operating Systems Principles (2011)
58. Zhou, W., Fei, Q., Sun, S., Tao, T., Haeberlen, A., Ives, Z., Loo, B.T., Sherr, M.: Nettrails: A declarative platform for provenance maintenance and querying in distributed systems. In: SIGMOD, demonstration (2011)
59. Zhou, W., Mao, Y., Loo, B.T., Abadi, M.: Unified Declarative Platform for Secure Networked Information Systems. In: Proceedings of IEEE Conference on Data Engineering, ICDE (2009)
60. Zhou, W., Sherr, M., Tao, T., Li, X., Loo, B.T., Mao, Y.: Efficient querying and maintenance of network provenance at Internet-scale. In: Proc. SIGMOD (2010)
61. Zhou, W., Sokolsky, O., Loo, B.T., Lee, I.: Dmac: Distributed monitoring and checking. In: 9th International Workshop on Runtime Verification, RV (2009)

Make Things Now!
Pragmatic Functional Programming in Haskell

Don Stewart

Standard Chartered Bank
dons00@gmail.com

Abstract. For the past decade I've been building all kinds of software in Haskell: software for programming languages research; open source software as part of the Haskell.org project; and, more recently, commercial software for business and government.

This talk will look at the experience of delivering software written in Haskell, and how language features and tools can help you achieve a range of engineering goals. Beyond just technical issues though, we will look at how programmers that use Haskell and typed functional programming approach problems differently, and how small, skilled teams can do things faster and better.

C. Russo and N.-F. Zhou (Eds.): PADL 2012, LNCS 7149, p. 17, 2012.
© Springer-Verlag Berlin Heidelberg 2012

A Declarative Approach for Software Modeling

Mayer Goldberg[1] and Guy Wiener[2],[*]

[1] Dept. of Computer Science,
Ben-Gurion University of the Negev
gmayer@cs.bgu.ac.il
[2] Dept. of Computer Science & Applied Mathematics,
Weizmann Institute for Science
gwiener@weizmann.ac.il

Abstract. In this paper we describe a method for encoding software models as Prolog programs, and how to use these programs to support incremental development. Requirements, alternative designs, and implementation patterns are encoded as predicates in the program, and define a search routine, the solutions of which are possible implementations of the requirements. Under default operation, this routine validates that a given parsed code is compatible with one of these solutions. Additionally, the same search routine can be executed by special interpreters that provide traceability and code generation as well. Code generation may be complete or partial, allowing the user to combine hand-written and generated code. By customizing the interpreter, the user can generate an outline of the design or a tasks list, instead of code. We demonstrate these techniques using Java and SQL, but our approach is applicable to other programming languages and paradigms as well.

1   Introduction

What format will make requirements models, and models derived from them, most useful for developers? More generally, what functionality should modeling platforms provide to support the incremental development of long-term projects? These questions lead an ongoing discussion in the software engineering community. A survey of current approaches provides the following answers:

Compatibility. Developers should be able to validate that a given implementation conforms to the design and guidelines specified by the model. Works by Sefika et al. [13] and Jean-Marie Favre [4] describe implementations of this approach to validation based on logic programming. The validation process should also point out which parts of the model and code are incompatible, as described in works by the authors [6,19]. Following search-based approaches, as outlined by Clarke et al. [3], we observe that the validation should accept

---

[*] This research was supported in part by the John von Neumann Minerva Center for the Development of Reactive Systems at the Weizmann Institute of Science, and by an Advanced Research Grant from the European Research Council (ERC) under the European Community's Seventh Framework Programme (FP7/2007-2013).

C. Russo and N.-F. Zhou (Eds.): PADL 2012, LNCS 7149, pp. 18–32, 2012.

any program from a range of implementations, as there are often several possible realizations for a given specification.

Traceability. Winkler and Pilgrim define traceability as "the ability to follow the life of a software artifact" [20]. In the context of software development, "life" refers to the chain of design decisions that led from the original requirement to a specific implementation. Put otherwise, developers should be able to trace given implementation details to the requirements that they fulfill.

Code generation. It has become a common practice in software engineering to use models for code generation. Model-based approaches advocate code generation as a level of abstraction above third-generation programming languages (see Schmidt's review of MDE [12]). As with the first item, we observe that code generation should offer a range of generated programs, since there are often several implementation patterns for a given design. The user can select which program to generate, either explicitly, or by applying heuristics. To support incremental development, code generation must be incremental too, i.e., generate only specific parts of the code, and combine them with existing code. The opposite of *incremental* code generation is *complete* code generation, i.e., the entire application is generated automatically. Complete code generation is currently limited to specific application domains.

This work presents a declarative approach for modeling requirements and their implementations. In our approach, the requirements, the possible designs that derive from them, and the implementation patterns for these designs, are encoded as Prolog predicates. The patterns may describe implementations in another programming language, not necessarily Prolog. These predicates, together with the underlying Prolog interpreter, implement a search routine, in which design decisions are represented by predicates with multiple clauses. The solutions of the search are program fragments in the target language, that implement one of the possible designs, according to the given rules. Our current examples use the JTransformer framework (see Sect. 2.2) to read and write the abstract syntax tree (AST) of a Java program using Prolog. The method itself, however, is language-independent. The basic operation of the search routine is to find a solution, consisting of program fragments, and match these fragments against the given program, thus providing a compatibility check. We use logic programming meta-interpretation to provide for traceability and code generation as well. The resulting workflow is: (a) The developer encodes the software model. (b) The code is parsed into facts, representing its AST. (c) The code and model predicates are interpreted, for validation or traceability. (d) Code generation produces a partial AST, which is combined with the existing AST to update the program. (e) When the model or source code are updated, the process is repeated.

The rest of the paper is structured as follows. Section 2 provides the necessary background. Section 3 describes the model encoding method. Section 4 describes the usage of *explanatory interpretation* for traceability. Section 5 describes the usage of *partial evaluation* for code generation, where the generated code includes only unimplemented features. This section also describes how to generate a higher-level view, such as a summary of the design, or a list of tasks, using the same technique. Section 6 describes how to direct the code generation and prune undesired solutions by providing a heuristic function. Section 7 reviews related works. Section 8 discusses the limitations and possible extensions of this work. Section 9 summarizes. The appendixes provide code listings and explanations for the main Prolog predicates mentioned throughout this paper.

2 Background

2.1 Prolog

In the context of this work, Prolog serves as a generic platform for depth-first search programs, the results of which is an assignment of variables to terms. A Prolog program and a goal specify a search tree, where predicates with multiple clauses are OR-nodes, the bodies of rules are AND-nodes, and facts are leafs. We assume that the reader is reasonably familiar with Prolog. The material found in this paper is covered by most Prolog textbooks, e.g., *The Art of Prolog* [16].

2.2 JTransformer

JTransformer is a logic-based query and transformation engine for Java code, based on the Eclipse IDE. It is described in a survey by Kniesel, Hannemann and Rho on logic-based concerns detection [9,11]. In our work we use JTransformer to read the content of a Java program as Prolog facts, and to emit Java code that was generated by Prolog predicates. The JTransformer representation of AST nodes is as functors, whose arguments are a unique id of the node, the ids of parent and child nodes, and the content of the node itself. JTransformer provides a full AST, including method bodies and expressions, but in our examples, we use only two kinds of nodes:

(a) class declaration `classT(Id, ParentId, Name, Members)`, and
(b) field declaration `fieldT(Id, ClassId, Type, Name, Init)`, where `Type` is a functor `type(class, ClassId, Mult)`. The multiplicity is 0 for simple types and 1 for arrays.

Since node ids are not relevant to our examples, we replace the actual id with either an underscore or the name of the element, and omit them from diagrams.

3 Model Encoding

Our model encoding system is based on the following rules:

1. The model is encoded as a Prolog program, consisting of predicates that represent various model elements. The program entry point is a single predicate, named the *system predicate*. The body of the system predicate consists of goals representing top-level requirements. For example, the system predicate of a Content Management System `cms_system/0` is encoded as

   ```
   cms_system :- req₁, req₂, ... , reqₙ.
   ```

where req_1 ... req_n are goals invoking requirement predicates. The encoding of these predicates follow.

2. Hierarchy and composition are encoded as rules: the head is the containing element and the body consists of goals that invoke sub-elements. For example, if fulfilling the requirement present content requires implementing present summary and present full text, it is encoded as

```
present_content :- present_summary, present_full_text.
```

Similarly, if implementing an attribute in a database requires a table and a column, it is encoded as

```
attribute(Type, Attr) :- table(Type), column(Type, Attr).
```

3. Alternatives and decision points are encoded as multiple clauses of the same predicate. For example, if the requirement alert the user can be fulfilled by either a pop-up alert or a blinking alert, it is encoded as

```
alert_the_user :- pop_up_alert.
alert_the_user :- blinking_alert.
```

Similarly, if an association R between A and B can be implemented either as a pair of columns or as a single separate table, it is encoded as:

```
assoc(R, A, B) :- table(A), column(A, R), table(B), column(B, R).
assoc(R, A, B) :- table(R), column(R, A), column(R, B).
```

4. Dependencies between requirements are encoded similarly to sub-requirements. If choosing one option implies having to choose another option, the implied option is added as a sub-goal of the first option. For example, if payment method can be cash or credit, and communication can be plain or encrypted, and credit payment requires encryption, we add encrypted as a goal of credit.

5. Existing code and completed tasks are represented by facts. This part of the encoding depends on the format provided by the code parser. For Java code, facts are provided by the JTransformer framework, as explained in Sect. 2.2. Similarly, the fact that some requirement, e.g., redirect the user, is implemented, without explaining how, is encoded as:

```
redirect_the_user.
```

6. Optional requirements are encoded as predicates that consist both of a rule and a fact. If the rule is applied successfully, it means that the requirement is implemented. If the requirement is not implemented, invoking the predicate is still successful. The encoding pattern is:

```
opt_req :- goal1, goal2...
opt_req. % fact, always true
```

3.1   Encoding a Single Client-Story

To demonstrate our encoding rules, we provide a simplified example for encoding a single client-story as a set of predicates. The example discusses a blogging platform named weblog. The first client story for the system is: *As a writer, I can write a blog post, with a title, content and category.* We encode it using the following predicates: weblog/0 is the system predicate, and write_post/0 breaks the above client story into a list of requirements.

```
weblog :- write_post. % Version 1
write_post :- post_has_title, post_has_content, post_has_category.
```

For brevity, we discuss only the data scheme for these requirements. The predicate class_attr(Class, Attr, Type, Mult) specifies that the class Class exists, it has a field named Attr, with the type Type, and multiplicity Mult, which is either 0 for a single instance, or 1 for multiple instances.

The first two requirements are straightforward. We specify that they should be implemented by string attributes of the class Post. There are two options for implementing the third requirement: another attribute of Post, or a separate Category class that will aggregate all the posts of the same category. Since it is unclear which option is better, we encode both possibilities, resulting in a predicate with two clauses.

```
post_has_title :- class_attr('Post', title, 'String', 0).
post_has_content :- class_attr('Post', content, 'String', 0).
post_has_category :- class_attr('Post', category, 'String', 0).
post_has_category :- class_attr('Category', posts, 'Post', 1).
```

The class_attr/4 predicate specifies the structure of the code for an attribute in a class, using the underlying JTransformer framework:

```
class_attr(Class, Attr, Type, Mult) :-
  classT(Cid, _, Class, _),
  classT(Tid, _, Type, _),
  fieldT(_, Cid, type(class, Tid, Mult), Attr, _).
```

The system predicate weblog/0 succeeds in one of two cases: (a) The code that was parsed by JTransformer contains a class named Post with the three fields specified above. (b) The code contains both the class Post with two fields, and the class Category with an array of posts. Figure 1 lists matching code.

```
public class Post {
  public String title;
  public String content;
  public String category;
}
```

(a) Single class

```
public class Post {
  public String title;
  public String content;
}
public class Category {
  public Post[] posts;
}
```

(b) Two classes

Fig. 1. Possible implementations for the first client story, encoded as version 1 of the weblog/0 system predicate

3.2   Encoding Several Stories

To demonstrate the incremental nature of the model encoding, we extend the specifications of the system with another client story: *As a reader, I can browse from a post to other posts in the same category.* Adding a new requirement requires two steps: encode it as a predicate, and add to the system predicate (or to an encoded requirement that is already included in the model) a goal invoking it. In this example, we add the new requirement browse to other posts to the system predicate, as the listing below shows.

```
weblog :- write_post, browse_to_other_posts. % Version 2
browse_to_other_posts :-
  class_attr('Post', category, 'Category', 0),
  class_attr('Category', posts, 'Post', 1).
```

The specified implementation for the new requirement uses a bidirectional association between posts and their categories. This association is implemented as a pair of fields. Since a Java class cannot have two fields with the same name but different types, this requirement *constrains* the search: the validated program can not contain the string category field of the Post class. Therefore, there is only one acceptable solution, shown in Fig. 2.

```
public class Post {                 public class Category {
  public String title;                public Post[] posts;
  public String content;           }
  public Category category;
}
```

Fig. 2. A possible implementation for both client stories, encoded as version 2 of the weblog/0 system predicate

3.3   The Structure of the Model

As we can see from the above example, the model consists of several layers. The root of the model is the system predicate. The root is followed by the *requirements layer*, that consists of a hierarchy of requirements and sub-requirements. Leaf requirements are followed by design statements, that specify how the requirements should be implemented. These statements compose the *design layer*. The design statements are followed by patterns for coding the design elements in a programming language. These patterns compose the *implementation layer*. Implementation patterns for specific design statements can be re-used across projects, as libraries of patterns, e.g., libraries for mapping conceptual designs to Java or SQL code. Finally, the patterns in the implementation layer are matched against facts that represent an actual program, i.e., the *code layer*. In the above example, weblog is the system predicate; write_post, browse_to_other_posts, and the `post_has...` predicates are the requirements; the design layer consists of the `class_attr` predicate; the implementation layer consists of JTransformer predicates, such as `classT` and `fieldT`; the code layer includes concrete facts, such as `classT(12, 34, 'Post', [...])` (ids are made up).

We can view this model format as an extension of feature models (see [8]), that is not limited to requirements, but includes designs and implementations as lower-level features. When the search program is run, it solves the feature model using the depth-first search of Prolog, and matches the result with the parsed code. As described above, alternative and optional features are encoded as multi-clause predicates, and dependencies between features are encoded as goals. Figure 3 shows the above example as a layered features model.

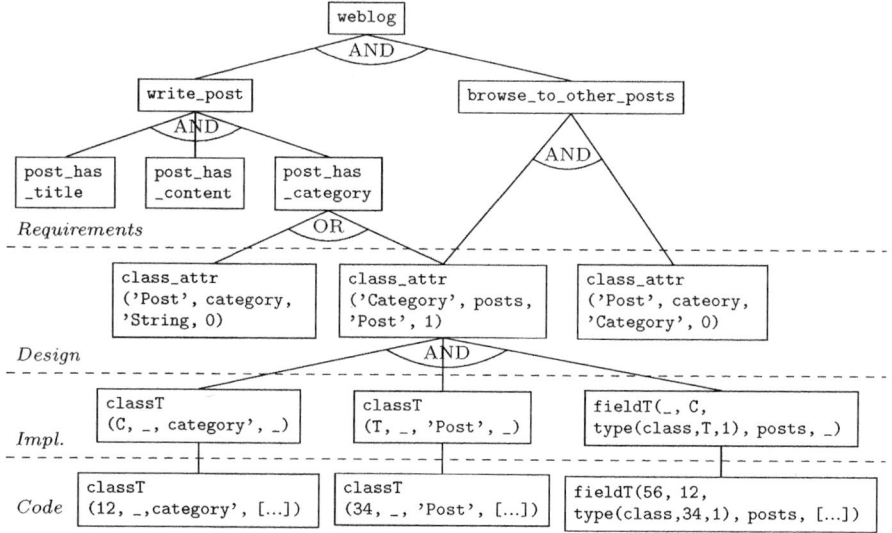

Fig. 3. Layers in a model. Some branches were omitted, for brevity.

4   Traceability

The encoding method described in Sect. 3 also allows developers to trace the sequence of design decisions that led to a specific code statement. This trace is obtained by using a variation of the *explanatory interpretation* technique, presented by Yoav Shoham [14, Chap. 3.4.1]. To trace the origin of a goal, we first generate a *proof tree* for the system predicate, by using `explain/2`, and then find the goal in it. The code for generating proof trees is listed in Appendix A. The path from the root of the proof tree to the goal is the trace. Since there may be more than one solution, and since a statement may implement more than one requirement, there may be more than one trace. Figure 4 shows the proof tree for `weblog/0` with the paths to the Category class marked.

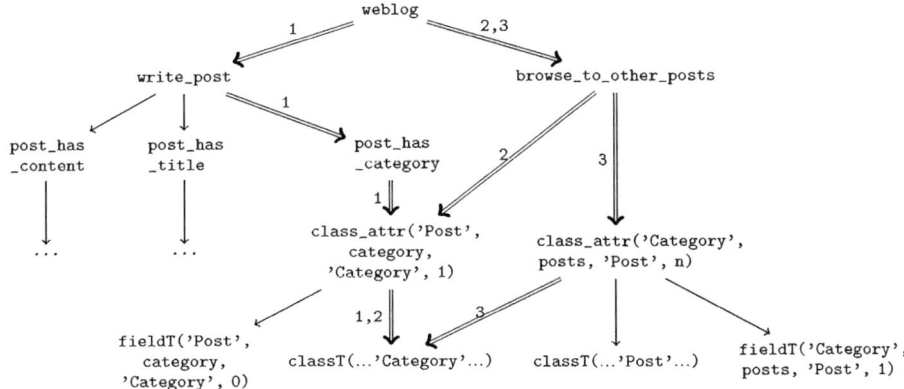

Fig. 4. Paths to the Category class in the proof tree. Redundant and alternative branches were omitted. Numbered double edges mark traces from the root to the implementation.

After gathering a proof tree, extracting the traces from the root to the goal is done by simple recursion. An example for finding traces is listed below. The different traces correspond to the paths in Fig. 4. We omitted the trivial code for the find/3 predicate.

```
?- explain(weblog, P), find(classT(_, _, 'Category', _), P, T).
T = [weblog, write_post, post_has_category,
class_attr('Post', category, 'Category', 0), classT(...'Category'...)];
T = [weblog, browse_to_other_posts, ...]; % The rest as above
T = [weblog, browse_to_other_posts,
class_attr('Category', posts, 'Post', 1), classT(...'Category'...)]
```

The technique described here also serves for finding *unspecified* code, i.e., code that cannot be linked to any specific requirement. For example, the predicate listed below finds unspecified classes. The second argument can be a variable. If we add the class Dummy to our project, unspecified_class(weblog, X) will return X = Dummy. In this way we can locate code that is either redundant, or requires specification. Locating unspecified code is particularly important after changes to the requirements, as some parts of the code may become unneeded.

```
unspecified_class(Pred, Class) :-
  explain(Pred, Proof),
  classT(Cid, _, Class, _), \+ externT(Cid)[1],
  \+ find(classT(Cid, _, Class, _), Proof, _).
```

---

[1] Types are considered *external* if they have no source code, e.g., are a part of the standard Java class library, or other imported libraries. \+ is the negation operator.

5   Code Generation

The validation and tracing techniques described above assume that calling the system predicate succeeds, i.e., all requirements are implemented. However, during most of the development process, this is not the situation. The common situation is that some of the requirements are implemented, and some are not. We would like to identify which requirements are still unimplemented, and generate the missing code for them, if possible. To this end, we use *partial evaluation* of the system predicate. According to Yoav Shoham, a partial evaluation of a Prolog goal is the set of facts that should be added to the program in order for the goal to succeed [14, Chap. 3.5]. For example, the partial evaluation of the rule a :-b,c, given the fact b, is [c]. In the context of software development, this set consists of the required code elements. To obtain this set, we use a variation of Shoham's partial evaluator. The modified code is listed in Appendix B.

The partial evaluation process requires some explanation. The partial evaluator interprets the given goal and looks for sub-goals that fail. If a rule fails, it tests the goals in the body of the rule, recursively. If a built-in predicate or a fact fails, it tries to add it to the results set. Built-in predicates are identified by the predicate builtin/1. Goal are added to the results set only if they they are not conflicting with other goals in the set. This restriction prevents the partial evaluator from finding impossible combinations. In our example, two fields in the same class having the same name, but a different type, are considered conflicting. In Java code, this conflict is detected by the compiler. Since the partial evaluator is not aware of the semantics of the programming language, it consults the user-defined predicate conflicting/2.

To demonstrate how partial evaluation can generate code, lets assume that the code contains only the Post class, with only the title and content fields. In this case, the weblog predicate fails. The partial evaluation will return a set with the following elements: (a) The Category class, (b) The posts array in the Category class, (c) The category field in the Post class, as shown below.

```
?- partial_eval(weblog, P).
P = [classT(_, _, 'Category', _),
 fieldT(_, Category, type(class, Post, 1), posts, _),
 fieldT(_, Post, type(class, Category, 0), category, _)]
```

This set provides sufficient information to generate the missing code.[2] As mentioned above, the partial evaluation may return several results, as there may be several possible ways to implement the given requirements — See, for example, Fig. 1 in Sect. 3. We discuss how to choose between these results in Sect. 6. An important advantage of using partial evaluation for code generation is that it generates only the part of the code, and ignores the rest. This property allows for *incremental* code generation. Code that becomes redundant after changes to the model can be located and removed, as described in Sect. 4.

---

[2] The actual code generation requires some more processing, due to the conditional transformations mechanism in JTransformer.

5.1 Changing the Granularity of the Interpreter

As explained above, the partial evaluator treats built-in predicates as atomic operations, i.e., even if the built-in predicate is a rule, its body is ignored. The evaluator uses the `builtin/1` predicate to identify built-ins. By default, it looks for predicates with the property `built_in` set by the Prolog environment. Developers can use this mechanism and add clauses to `builtin/1`, to set the threshold of the partial evaluation. For example, we can treat the class attribute design statements as built-ins, cutting off the code and implementations layers.

```
builtin(class_attr(_, _, _, _)). % Extending builtin/1
?- partial_eval(weblog, P).
P = [class_attr('Post', category, 'String', 0)] ;
P = [class_attr('Category', posts, 'Post', 1)]
```

We can raise the threshold further up, cutting off anything other than the requirements layer. In this case, the partial evaluation returns the unfulfilled requirements — `post_has_category` in the example above. Since distinguishing between the predicates from different layers depends on the structure of the model, we omit the exact implementation.

6   Heuristic Code Generation

A software model defines a range of possible implementations. Therefore, the code generator outlined in Sect. 5 provides a set of solutions. However, the model of an actual application may contain many options, and generate a large number of programs. To allow for limiting the number of solutions, we enhance the partial evaluator with a pruning mechanism, based on a given monotonic cost function. After each step of partial evaluation, the cost function is called. If the cost of the current solution exceeds a given bound, the evaluation backtracks. Therefore, the cost of the results of the enhanced evaluation is guaranteed to be lower than the bound. Running the bounded evaluator recursively, each time with the cost of the previous run as a bound, converges to a solution with a minimal cost. Design metrics can be used as cost functions, as suggested by Harman and Clark [7].

Since it is a part of the partial evaluation process, the cost function must consider both existing clauses and the current results set. To make this requirement transparent to the user, the cost function is not invoked directly, but interpreted. The interpreter, based on the classic Prolog meta-interpreter [14, Chap. 3.2], first checks if a goal is in the results set, before trying to invoke it. The complete code for the heuristic partial evaluator can be found at our web page [18].

6.1   An Example of Heuristics Code Generation

To demonstrate heuristics code generation, we present the following example, dealing with object-to-relational mapping. The model is based on Fowler's *accounting* analysis pattern [5, Chapter 6]. In an accounting system, there are two kinds of accounts: *detailed* and *summary*. A detailed account keeps track of entries , where each entry has an amount that is added to, or withdrawn from, the account. Each detailed account has an owner. A summary account aggregates several other accounts. Figure 5 is a class diagram for this model.

Our model uses the following possible designs, taken from the work of Blaha and Premerlani on object-oriented modeling for database applications [2, Chapters 13,14]: (a) a table that represents a type and includes its attributes as columns, (b) an extending table that contains the attributes of a sub-type and refers to a parent table, (c) embedding the attributes of a sub-type in the table of its super-type, and (d) a named relation, with the table and column names of each end as arguments. This example supports only one-to-many relations, and not the general case of many-to-many.

```
accounting :- account, entry, detailed, summary.
account :- table(account, [balance(int)]).
entry :- table(entry, [amount(int)]).

detailed :- % As a linked table
    extend(detailed, account, [owner(string)]),
    one_to_many(entries, detailed, account, entry, entry).
detailed :- % As embedded columns
    embed(account, [owner(string)]),
    one_to_many(entries, account, account, entry, entry).

summary :- % As a linked table
    extend(summary, account, []),
    one_to_many(components, summary, sum, account, sub).
summary :- % As embedded columns
    one_to_many(components, account, sum, account, sub).
```

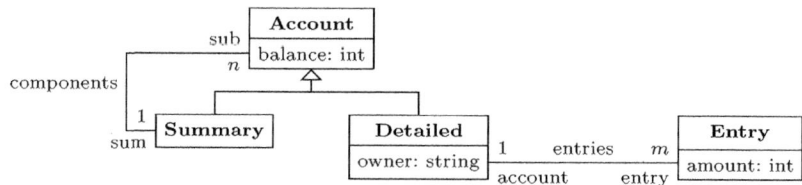

Fig. 5. Types in an accounting system

The following predicates encode implementation patterns mapping types and relations to a relational database schema. The code layer in this example includes a single predicate, col/4, whose arguments are the table name, the column name and type, and a list of properties. Possible column properties are being a primary key, or referring to a column in another table. The transformation of this predicate to SQL statements is trivial. We have encoded the designs listed above, with two alternatives for relations: (a) a reference column from the *many* side to the *one* side, and (b) a separate table with two reference columns.

```
table(Name, Attrs) :- col(Name, id, int, [key]), attrs(Name, Attrs).

extend(Name, Super, Attrs) :-
    col(Name, id, int, [key]), col(Name, parent, int, [ref(Super, id)]),
    attrs(Name, Attrs).

embed(Super, Attrs) :- attrs(Super, Attrs).

attrs(_, []).
attrs(Table, [Attr | Rest]) :-
  Attr =.. [Name, Type], col(Table, Name, Type, []),
  attrs(Table, Rest).

one_to_many(_, S, A, T, _) :- col(T, A, int, [ref(S, id)]).
one_to_many(R, S, A, T, B) :-
    col(R, A, int, [ref(S, id)]), col(R, B, int, [ref(T, id)]).
```

Since the model includes 4 choices, each with 2 alternatives, it matches, or generates, 16 different solutions. To choose between them, we use a cost function. For example, minimizing the number of tables results in the solution shown in Fig. 6a. Alternatively, penalizing tables with many columns gives Figs. 6b and 6c.

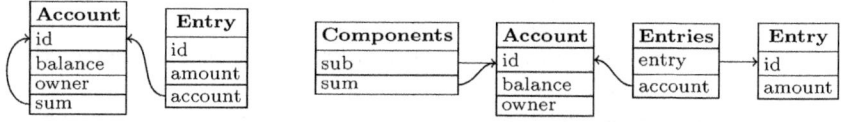

(a) All sub-types and relations embedded

(b) Embedded sub-types, relations in separate tables

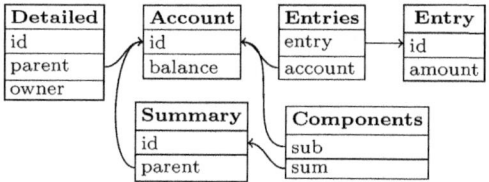

(c) All sub-types and relations in separate tables

Fig. 6. Few selected designs for an accounting system. Reference columns are connected to their destination columns by arrows.

7   Related Works

We aimed in this work at enabling gradual refinement of software models into code, while preserving traceability. There has been several efforts in this direction. Mainly, the architecture we propose can be viewed as a model-driven architecture, as described in [15], where Prolog replaces the OMG QVT language [10].

While the QVT work-flow consists of a series of transformations, Prolog rules will match any valid combination of given patterns. Similarly, our work does not rely on the bi-directionality property of transformations to support incremental changes (see Stevens' criticism on this topic [17]). Instead, we make use of known logic interpretation techniques, as discussed in Sects. 4 and 5.

Some formal methods, such as the B-method [1], discuss step-wise refinement of formal specifications into programs. This process both maintains traceability and assists in verifying the correctness of the code. In this work, however, we deliberately avoided limiting the modeling language to mathematical properties, in favor of free-form models. Adding formal contracts to code-generating patterns can be an interesting and non-trivial extension of our approach.

8   Limitations and Future Work

We have chosen to base this work on minimalistic and concise versions of the meta-interpreters we use. These versions, listed in the appendix, are short and simple enough for the interested reader to read and follow. However, the language that is accepted by these interpreters is limited. Cuts, negations and meta-predicates, are not a part of it. Extensions to Prolog, such as constraint solvers, are also not accepted. These limitations reduce the expressiveness of the modeling language, and makes it hard to write abstractions over models. There are two ways to overcome these limitations: (a) to enhance the interpreters, or (b) to use features that are specific to a Prolog implementation, such as programmable debugging. We leave extending the modeling language for future work.

We have selected to present our method using Prolog thanks to the availability of Prolog systems and textbooks. However, software modeling using a declarative programming language should not necessarily be limited to a specific language. Rule-based systems or theorem provers may also be adequate for our modeling method. We leave further explorations for future work as well.

9   Summary

In this work we presented a method for encoding software models as rules and facts in Prolog, and using queries to perform software engineering tasks. The encoded models consists of several layers: requirements, design, implementation patterns, and parsed code. The advantages of this encoding are: (a) It allows for validating that the code matches a possible implementation of the requirements, as specified by the given design patterns. (b) Additional specifications can be added incrementally, either widening or narrowing the search space. (c) Design considerations and alternatives are encoded explicitly, making them first-class elements of the model. (d) Interpreting the encoded model allows for tracing a program statement to its original requirement, or detecting unspecified statements. (e) Partial evaluation of the encoded model provides incremental code generation, suitable for incremental development.

The cost of using encoded models is the need to maintain the model as an auxiliary program. Our experience shows that implementation patterns requires the most effort to develop. However, this effort is amortized across projects. Once implementation patterns are encoded, they are re-used in the following models.

The current modeling language is limited to specifying a simple, choice-based depth-first search. We hope to lift this limitation in future works, and support a more expressive and intuitive model format.

A   Explanatory Interpretation

The `explain/2` predicate unifies the second argument with a list of proof trees for the query given as the first argument. The nodes in a tree are goals, and the branches are sub-goals of rules. Facts are leafs. The `clause/2` predicate, used in this code, unifies the second argument with the body of the clause whose head is the first argument, where the body of facts is true.

```
explain((A, B), Proof) :- % A is a sequence
  !, explain(A, AP), explain(B, BP), append(AP, BP, Proof).
explain(A, [A]) :- builtin(A), !, call(A). % A is a built-in
explain(A, [A]) :- clause(A, true), !. % A is a fact
explain(A, [tree(A, Proof)]) :- % A is a rule
  clause(A, B), explain(B, Proof).
```

B   Partial Evaluation

The `partial_eval/2` predicate takes a query as the first argument, and unifies the second argument with a list of facts, that had it been added to the program, would make the query successful. For a given query, there may be several possible partial evaluations. The `conflicting/2` let the user specify impossible combinations. The heuristic version of the partial evaluator is given in [18].

```
partial_eval(X, P) :- premises(X, [X], P).
premises(true, _, []) :- !. % a fact, no premise
premises((X, Y), Old, P) :- !, % combining two premises
  premises(X, Old, P1), append(P1, Old, New),
  premises(Y, New, P2), append(P1, P2, P).
premises(X, _, P) :- % built-in, ignore body
  builtin(X), !, ((callable(X), call(X)) -> P = [] ; P = [X]).
premises(X, Z, P) :- clause(X, Y), premises(Y, Z, P). % a clause
premises(X, Z, [X]) :- % no clause, not in current set
  \+ clause(X, _), \+ (member(Y, Z), conflicting(X, Y)), \+ member(X, Z).
premises(X, Z, []) :- % no clause, in current set
  \+ clause(X, _), member(Y, Z), \+ conflicting(X, Y), X = Y.
```

References

1. Abrial, J.: The B-book: assigning programs to meanings. Cambridge University Press (1996)
2. Blaha, M., Premerlani, W.: Object-oriented modeling and design for database applications. Prentice-Hall, Inc., Upper Saddle River (1997)
3. Clarke, J., Dolado, J., Harman, M., Hierons, R., Jones, B., Lumkin, M., Mitchell, B., Mancoridis, S., Rees, K., Roper, M., Shepperd, M.: Reformulating software engineering as a search problem. IEEE Software 150(3), 161–175 (2003)
4. Favre, J.M.: Towards a basic theory to model model driven engineering. In: 3rd Workshop in Software Model Engineering, WiSME (2004)
5. Fowler, M.: Analysis patterns: reusable objects models. Addison-Wesley Longman Publishing Co., Inc., Boston (1997)
6. Goldberg, M., Wiener, G.: Round-Trip Modeling using OPM/PL. In: International Conference on Software Science, Technology and Engineering, SwSTE (2010)
7. Harman, M., Clark, J.: Metrics are fitness functions too. In: 10th International Symposium on Software Metrics, pp. 58–69 (2004)
8. Kang, K.: Feature-oriented domain analysis (FODA) feasibility study. Technical report, Carnegie-Mellon University, Pittsburgh PA, USA (1990)
9. Kniesel, G., Hannemann, J., Rho, T.: A comparison of logic-based infrastructures for concern detection and extraction. In: 3rd Workshop on Linking Aspect Technology and Evolution, p. 6. ACM (2007)
10. Object Management Group: Meta Object Facility (MOF) 2.0 Query/View/Transformation Specification (2008), http://www.omg.org/spec/QVT/1.0/
11. ROOTS Group: The JTransformer project web page, http://sewiki.iai.uni-bonn.de/research/jtransformer/
12. Schmidt, D.: Guest editor's introduction: Model-driven engineering. Computer 39(2), 25–31 (2006)
13. Sefika, M., Sane, A., Campbell, R.: Monitoring compliance of a software system with its high-level design models. In: 18th International Conference for Software Engineering, ICSE, vol. 18, pp. 387–396 (1996)
14. Shoham, Y.: Artificial Intelligence Techniques in PROLOG. Morgan Kaufmann Publishers Inc., San Francisco (1993)
15. Soley, R.: The OMG Staff Strategy Group: Model-Driven Architecture. White paper (November 2000), http://www.omg.org/cgi-bin/doc?omg/00-11-05
16. Sterling, L., Shapiro, E.: The art of Prolog. MIT Press, Cambridge (1994)
17. Stevens, P.: Bidirectional model transformations in QVT: Semantic issues and open questions. Software and Systems Modeling 9(1), 7–20 (2010)
18. Wiener, G.: Heuristic partial evaluator source code, http://www.cs.bgu.ac.il/~gwiener/software/hpe/
19. Wiener, G.: Persistent Semantic Information. PhD thesis, Ben-Gurion University (March 2011) (to be published)
20. Winkler, S., Pilgrim, J.: A survey of traceability in requirements engineering and model-driven development. Software and System Modeling 9, 529–565 (2010)

Contracts and Specifications
for Functional Logic Programming

Sergio Antoy[1] and Michael Hanus[2]

[1] Computer Science Dept., Portland State University, Oregon, U.S.A.
antoy@cs.pdx.edu
[2] Institut für Informatik, CAU Kiel, D-24098 Kiel, Germany
mh@informatik.uni-kiel.de

Abstract. The expressive power of functional logic languages supports high-level specifications as well as efficient implementations of problems in the same language. If specifications are executable, they can be used both as initial prototypical implementations and as contracts for checking the reliable execution of implementations intended to satisfy the specification. In this paper, we propose a practical framework to support this general approach to coding. We discuss the notions of specifications and contracts for functional logic programming and present a tool that supports the development of declarative programs based on these notions.

1 Introduction

Functional logic programming languages [3,15] support a wide spectrum of programming styles. One can apply logic programming features like nondeterminism and logic variables to specify the basic knowledge about a problem and let the run-time system search for appropriate solutions. Or one can use a deterministic (functional) programming style to implement sophisticated and efficient algorithms [22].

The combination of both styles can be leveraged for increased reliability: high-level ("obviously correct") specifications can be formulated as functional logic programs. Since these specifications are executable, they can serve as initial prototypical implementations. Executable specifications are useful to run experiments which may expose defects and ultimately raise the confidence that a specification captures the intent. If the direct execution of the specification is too inefficient, one can choose more efficient data structures (e.g., balanced search trees instead of lists) and/or better algorithms for production software. In this case, the initial specification remains valuable since one can use it as an oracle to test the implementation on a large set of test data [8,13] or to check, via run-time assertions, that the implementation behaves as intended on particular executions.

In this paper we show the feasibility of this idea by formalizing specifications, contracts, and assertions, by showing some important relations between them, and by providing tools to support this approach to program design and development. The concrete language for our presentation is the multi-paradigm declarative language Curry [17]. We demonstrate that Curry can be used as a wide-spectrum language [5] for software

C. Russo and N.-F. Zhou (Eds.): PADL 2012, LNCS 7149, pp. 33–47, 2012.

development. In particular, we have implemented a tool that either transforms a specification into an executable program or, if the implementation of the specification is also
provided, into a contract attached to this implementation.

Although we assume familiarity with the general concepts of functional logic programming [3,15], we review in the next section the concepts crucial for this paper.
Section 3 presents the fundamental notions of our framework. The corresponding tool
support is sketched in Section 4 together with some examples.

2   Functional Logic Programming and Curry

The declarative multi-paradigm language Curry [17] extends non-strict functional programming languages such as Haskell [23] with logic programming features, e.g., non-
determinism and equational constraints. Consequently, Curry has a Haskell-like syntax[1]
extended by the possible inclusion of free (logic) variables in conditions and right-hand
sides of defining rules. The operational semantics is based on an optimal evaluation
strategy [1] which is a conservative extension of lazy functional programming and (concurrent) logic programming.

Expressions in Curry programs contain *operations* (defined functions), *constructors*
(introduced in data type declarations), and *variables* (arguments of operations or free
variables). The goal of a computation is to obtain a value of some expression, where
a *value* is an expression that does not contain any operation. Note that in a functional
logic language expressions might have more than one value due to nondeterministically
defined operations. For instance, Curry contains a *choice* operation defined by:

```
x ? _ = x
_ ? y = y
```

Thus, the expression "0 ? 1" has two values: 0 and 1. If expressions have more than
one value, these values are typically constrained by conditions in the rules defining
operations according to the program intent. A *rule* has the form "$f\ t_1 \ldots t_n\ |\ c = e$"
where c is a *constraint*, i.e., an expression of the built-in type Success. For instance,
the trivial constraint success is a value of type Success that denotes the always satisfiable constraint. An *equational constraint* $e_1 =:= e_2$ is satisfiable if both sides e_1 and
e_2 are reducible to unifiable values. Furthermore, if c_1 and c_2 are constraints, c_1 & c_2
denotes their concurrent conjunction (i.e., both constraints are concurrently evaluated)
and c_1 &> c_2 denotes their sequential conjunction (i.e., c_2 is evaluated after the successful evaluation of c_1).

Nondeterministic expressions could cause a semantical ambiguity when bound to
variables. Consider the operations

```
coin = 0 ? 1
double x = x + x
```

Standard term rewriting produces, among others, the derivation

```
double coin  →   coin + coin  →   0 + coin  →   0 + 1  →   1
```

---

[1] Variables and function names usually start with lowercase letters and the names of type and
data constructors start with an uppercase letter. The application of f to e is denoted by juxta-
position ("$f\ e$").

whose result is unintended. Therefore, González-Moreno et al. [14] proposed the rewriting logic CRWL as a logical foundation for declarative programming with non-strict and nondeterministic operations. This logic specifies the *call-time choice* semantics [18] where values of the arguments of an operation are determined before the operation is evaluated. In a lazy strategy, this is naturally obtained by sharing. For instance, the two occurrences of `coin` in the derivation above are shared so that "`double coin`" has only the results: 0 or 2. Since standard term rewriting does not conform to the intended call-time choice semantics, other notions of rewriting have been proposed to formalize this idea, like graph rewriting [11,12] or let rewriting [19]. For our purposes, it is sufficient to use a simple reduction relation that we sketch without giving all details (which can be found in [19]).

To cover non-strict computations, expressions can also contain the special symbol $\perp$ to represent *undefined or unevaluated values*. A *partial value* is a value containing occurrences of $\perp$. A *partial constructor substitution* is a substitution that replaces variables by partial values. A *context* $C[\cdot]$ is an expression with some "hole". Then the reduction relation we use throughout this paper is defined as follows (conditional rules are not considered for the sake of simplicity):

$$C[f \ \sigma(t_1)\ldots\sigma(t_n)] \ \rightarrow \ C[\sigma(r)] \quad f \ t_1\ldots t_n \rightarrow r \text{ program rule,}$$
$$\sigma \text{ partial constructor substitution}$$
$$C[e] \ \rightarrow \ C[\perp]$$

The first rule models the call-time choice: if a rule is applied, the actual arguments of the operation must have been evaluated to partial values. The second rule models non-strictness by allowing the evaluation of any subexpression to an undefined value (which is intended if the value of this subexpression is not demanded). As usual, $\xrightarrow{*}$ denotes the reflexive and transitive closure of this reduction relation. The equivalence of this rewrite relation and CRWL is shown in [19].

Sometimes we use `let`-expressions to enforce the call-time choice semantics. In order to avoid the explicit handling of `let`-expressions in the reduction relation (as proposed in [19]), we consider `let`-expressions as syntactic sugar for auxiliary functions. For instance, the definition

```
f x = let z = coin*x in z+coin
```

is syntactic sugar for

```
f x = g (coin*x)
g z = z+coin
```

where g is a fresh name.

In nondeterministic programming, it is sometimes useful to examine the set of all the values of some expression. A "set-of-values" operation applied to an arbitrary argument might produce results that depend on the degree of evaluation of the argument (see [6] for a detailed discussion). *Set functions* overcome this problem [2]. For each defined function f, f_S denotes the corresponding set function. f_S encapsulates the nondeterminism of f, but excludes the potential nondeterminism of the arguments to which f is applied. For instance, consider the operation `negOrPos` defined by:

```
negOrPos x = -x ? x
```

Then "negOrPos$_S$ 2" evaluates to the set $\{-2, 2\}$, i.e., the nondeterminism originating from negOrPos is encapsulated into a set. However, "negOrPos$_S$ (1?2)" evaluates to two different sets $\{-1, 1\}$ and $\{-2, 2\}$ due to its nondeterministic argument, i.e., the nondeterminism originating from the argument produces different sets. The type *set* is abstract, i.e., the implementation is hidden, but there are operations, e.g., to determine whether a set is empty, isEmpty, or an element belongs to a set.

3   Specifications and Contracts

Our framework to support the development of reliable declarative programs is based on the idea of using a single language for specifications, contracts, and implementations. Specifications differ from programs because they may be nondeterministic and/or refer to existentially quantified quantities. A functional logic language such as Curry is appropriate to express specifications because it is nondeterministic and it has equation-solving capabilities.

Using the same language makes specifications and implementations similar. In fact, a specification is like any other operation but with a specific tag so that the specification is more versatile:

- If there is only a specification but no implementation of an operation, the specification can be used as an initial implementation for this operation.
- If there are both a specification and an implementation of an operation, the specification can be used to check the implementation in two different ways:
   Dynamic checking: If the implementation computes some result when the operation is executed, test whether this result conforms to the specification.
   Static checking: If one formally proves that the implementation is correct w.r.t. the specification, run-time checking is not necessary.

We distinguish between a specification and a contract for an operation. A *specification* describes precisely the intended meaning of an operation. However, a *contract* describes conditions that must be satisfied by the implementation. These conditions can be weaker than a specification. Contracts have been introduced in the context of imperative and object-oriented programming languages [21] to improve the quality of software. Typically, a contract consists of both a pre- and a postcondition. The *precondition* is an obligation for the arguments of an operation application. The *postcondition* is an obligation for both the arguments of an operation application and the result of the operation application to those arguments. Intuitively, the application of or call to each operation must satisfy its precondition, and, if both the precondition is satisfied and the operation returns a result, this result must satisfy the postcondition. When a contract is checked at run-time, the pre- and postcondition are called *assertions*.

Specifications, preconditions, and postconditions are independent notions separately useful for software development. A precondition for an operation states general restrictions on arguments that must be satisfied in order to apply this operation. Hence, a specification is intended only for inputs satisfying the precondition. Likewise, a postcondition must only be satisfied for these inputs. In a strongly typed language, a type restriction on arguments can be considered a precondition. In general, one is interested in preconditions that are more expressive than a traditional type system. For instance, a precondition for a factorial function could require the argument to be non-negative. A postcondition is some requirement on all the results of an operation. It could be a type restriction, but it could also be much stronger. For instance, a postcondition for an operation to sort a list of values could state that the length of the output list is identical to the length of the input list. If a postcondition specifies all and only the intended results of an operation, it can be considered a specification. As we will see later, we can exploit the logic programming features of our language to execute a postcondition as a prototypical implementation by generating result values satisfying the postcondition.

The following definition fixes the notions discussed so far. For the sake of simplicity, we formally define our notions only for unary operations, but the extension to operations with several arguments is straightforward and, thus, it will be used in the subsequent examples.

Definition 1 (Specification, Contract). *Let f be an operation of type $\tau \to \tau'$. A specification for f is an operation f^{spec} of type $\tau \to \tau'$. A precondition for f is an operation f^{pre} of type $\tau \to$ Bool. A postcondition for f is an operation f^{post} of type $\tau \to \tau' \to$ Bool. A precondition and postcondition pair is also called a* contract *for the operation. If a precondition is not explicitly defined, the most general precondition "f^{pre} _ = True" is assumed.*

Similarly to other proposals for assertions or contracts for functional (logic) programs (e.g., [7,9,16]), we define pre- and postconditions as Boolean-valued functions. An exception is [4] where constraints are used as conditions which was motivated by the use of postconditions as specifications instead of an unequivocal specification as in this work.

As an example, consider an operation, sort, to sort a list of integers. The type of sort is:

```
sort :: [Int] → [Int]
```

Since we have no further requirements on arguments (apart from its type), our precondition for sort is the constant operation[2]

```
sort'pre :: [Int] → Bool
sort'pre _ = True
```

As an example for a postcondition, we require that the length of the input and output lists must be equal:

```
sort'post :: [Int] → [Int] → Bool
sort'post xs ys = length xs == length ys
```

However, an unequivocal specification states that the result of sort is a permutation in ascending order of its input:

```
sort'spec :: [Int] → [Int]
sort'spec xs | sorted ys = ys   where ys = perm xs
```

This specification requires the definition of permutations and sorted lists which are easily formalized in Curry ("<=:" denotes the less-than-or-equal-to constraint):

---

[2] Note that in the concrete syntax we use in our tool (see below) we write f'pre instead of f^{pre} (and similarly for postconditions and specifications).

```
perm []      = []
perm (x:xs) = ndinsert x (perm xs)
   where ndinsert x ys      = x : ys
         ndinsert x (y:ys) = y : ndinsert x ys
sorted []         = success
sorted [_]        = success
sorted (x:y:ys) = x<=:y & sorted (y:ys)
```

We can use the specification sort'spec to sort lists since it is a Curry program and, as such, executable. Obviously, it is inefficient for large lists, so we implement it more efficiently using the well-known quicksort algorithm:

```
sort :: [Int]  →  [Int]
sort []      = []
sort (x:xs) = sort (filter (<x) xs) ++ [x] ++ sort (filter (>x) xs)
```

If we apply our tool, DSDCurry, to this program, the specification is transformed into an additional postcondition and all existing pre- and postconditions are attached to the sort operation for dynamic assertion checking. The assertions checked during the execution of this transformed program reveal an error in our implementation:

```
SortC> sort [5,1,2,6,5,3]
ERROR: Postcondition of operation 'sort' violated for:
 [5,1,2,6,5,3]  →  [1,2,3,5,6]
```

If we correct the error, by replacing the condition (>x) with (>=x), the transformed program executes as intended and without error messages.

Before discussing some details of our tool, we have to define the precise meaning of correct implementations and violated assertions. In imperative or strict functional languages, this seems obvious. However, in a functional logic language like Curry, operations might have multiple results or reduce to infinite structures (i.e., their evaluation does not terminate). In order to support contract checking also in these situations, we have to prepare an appropriate setup.

First, we consider the possible violation of contracts. Obviously, a precondition f^{pre} is violated for some expression e if $f^{pre}\ e$ is reducible to False, since we want to avoid any calls on operations where the argument does not satisfy the precondition. For postconditions, the situation is less clear for nondeterministic functions. Consider a value v such that $f^{pre}\ v$ is reducible to True, $f\ v \xrightarrow{*} v_1$, $f\ v \xrightarrow{*} v_2$, and $f^{post}\ v\ v_1 \xrightarrow{*}$ True, but $f^{post}\ v\ v_2 \xrightarrow{*}$ False, i.e., one result, v_1, satisfies the postcondition but another result for the same input, v_2, does not satisfy the postcondition. In a complete implementation, all results of an operation could be produced. Therefore, we propose the strong view that *any* result that a function produces must satisfy the function's postcondition.

Definition 2 (Violation). *Let f be an operation of type $\tau \to \tau'$, f^{pre} and f^{post} be pre- and postconditions for f, and e an expression of type τ. A* violation of the precondition f^{pre} *of f at e is a derivation of $f^{pre}\ e$ to* False. *A* violation of the postcondition f^{post} *of f at e is a derivation of*

```
let x = e in not (f^{pre} x) || f^{post} x (f x)
```

to False, *where x is a fresh variable.*

The definition of a postcondition violation considers the fact that a violation should be reported only if the precondition holds for the given argument. Note that the `let`-expression is reasonable for nondeterministic arguments since the condition "not $(f^{pre}\ e)$ || $f^{post}\ e\ (f\ e)$" is different from the one given in the above definition if e is nondeterministic. For instance, consider

```
id'post x y = x==y
id x = x
e = 0 ? 1
```

Then "`id'post e (id e)`" reduces to both `True` and `False` whereas

```
let x = e in id'post x (id x)
```

cannot reduce to `False` due to the call-time choice semantics. The intent is that the postcondition should be satisfied for the same values used in the precondition; thus, our definition captures this demand.

Next we have to define the correctness of an implementation w.r.t. a given specification. A simple approach could require that the *values* of the specification are all and only the *values* of the implementation. However, this is not reasonable for non-strict languages. For instance, consider

```
nums'spec n = n : nums'spec (n+1)
```

Since `nums'spec` does not reduce to a value (its evaluation does not terminate), any other operation (of the same type) that does not reduce to a value would be correct w.r.t. this specification, e.g.:

```
nums n = n : nums n
```

Obviously, this is not intended. If we put the specification and the implementation in an identical context (e.g., by applying "`take 2`" to `nums'spec` and `nums`), then we might obtain different results. This motivates the following definition.

Definition 3 (Equivalence, Correctness). Let f_1, f_2 be operations of type $\tau \to \tau'$. f_1 is equivalent to f_2 iff, for any expression E_1, $E_1 \xrightarrow{*} v$ iff $E_2 \xrightarrow{*} v$, where v is a value and E_2 is obtained from E_1 by replacing any occurrence of f_1 with f_2. An implementation f is correct w.r.t. a specification f^{spec} iff f and f^{spec} are equivalent when applied to expressions satisfying f^{pre}.

The correctness of an implementation w.r.t. a specification imposes an equality of two sets of result values. The implementation could produce a value more or less times than the specification in the sense that the same expression has "substantially" distinct derivations to the same value. Furthermore, equivalent operations could differ in contexts that do not yield any result. For instance, the evaluation of one operation could diverge where an equivalent operation might terminate with a failure or some exception.

Intuitively, two operations are equivalent if it is impossible to detect any difference between them in any application context. If operations do not produce values or produce some values as well as failures, the consideration of an application context is important. For instance, consider the following alternative implementation of sorting a list based on an operation `idSorted` that is the identity on sorted lists:

```
sort' xs = idSorted (perm xs)
  where idSorted []  = []
        idSorted [x] = [x]
        idSorted (x:y:ys) | x<=y = x : idSorted (y:ys)
```

Although this implementation only returns values that are sorted lists, it is not correct w.r.t. the specification sort'spec. For instance, consider the operation head that returns the first element of the list. Then there is a derivation

head (sort' [2,3,1]) $\xrightarrow{*}$ head (idSorted [2,3,1])

$\xrightarrow{*}$ head (2 : idSorted [3,1])

$\xrightarrow{*}$ 2

whereas "head (sort'spec [2,3,1])" cannot be reduced to 2. The implementation sort' is incorrect with respect to the specification of sort: if we want to compute the minimum of a list by sorting the list and taking the first element, the previous derivation shows that we obtain an unintended result.

Specifications can be used to verify programs. This is a complex task that could be supported by proof systems. In this paper we exploit the property that specifications are executable so that we can use them to detect an incorrect execution of the implementation. For this purpose, we use a specification as a contract for an implementation. Thus, if we detect a violation at run-time, we can deduce that the implementation is not correct. This demands for a postcondition that is generated from a specification. In a naive approach, we could try to define such a postcondition as

$$f^{post} \ x \ y = y \in f_S^{spec} \ x$$

i.e., the postcondition checks whether the actual result is in the set of all the results according to the specification. Unfortunately, this simple definition does not work as intended due to the following problems:

1. For partially defined operations, this postcondition could be violated even though the implementation is correct. For instance, consider the simple example

   head'spec (x:_) = x
   head (x:_) = x

   Obviously, head is correct w.r.t. head'spec. However, the set head'spec$_S$ [] is empty so that the condition "head [] $\in$ head'spec$_S$ []" could reduce to False. Therefore, this condition should be checked only if the actual result is a value and not a failure. However, the implementation of "$\in$" may not require the evaluation of its left argument when its right argument is empty.[3]

2. The membership test requires the decision that two entities are equal. Since in functional logic languages, this test is evaluated by strict equality on (finite) values, the test will never be successful for operations delivering infinite structures.

The first problem can be handled by the addition of an equality test "y==y". Since the equality "==" compares *values*, the test is successful only if y is a value. This has the consequence that postconditions are not checked for failure cases. From a conceptual point of view, it would be better to exclude such cases by appropriate preconditions. Since the test for such an exclusion is undecidable in general, we add this sufficient condition to the postcondition.

The second problem can be handled in part by avoiding the comparison of complete results, and comparing only some computed parts, instead. For this purpose, we define a postcondition that is parametric w.r.t. some observation operation g.

---

[3] Although this problem can be avoided by excluding the application head [] using an appropriate precondition, in general it is difficult to avoid failing computations by preconditions.

Definition 4. *Let f^{spec} be a specification of type $\tau \to \tau'$ and g an operation of type $\tau' \to \tau''$. The postcondition f_g^{post} generated from f^{spec} w.r.t. g is defined by*

```
fₚᵒˢᵗ x y = let z = g y
                g' a = g (fˢᵖᵉᶜ a)
            in  z==z && z ∈ g'ₛ x
```

If we use $g = $ `id` (the identity function), the generated postcondition checks whether a result `y` is a value and it is contained in the set of all the results according to the specification. For instance, consider

```
f'spec = 0 ? 1
f = 1 ? 0
```

The generated postcondition f_{id}^{post} requires that each value of the implementation `f` is contained in the set $\{0, 1\}$.

If we know that a specification is deterministic, i.e., it yields at most one result for a given input, then we can provide a simpler postcondition without using an observation operation and set functions:

$$f^{post} \text{ x y = y == } f^{spec} \text{ x}$$

Although this definition does not support the detection of violations for failed computations (if the evaluation of `y` fails, the evaluation of f^{post} x y also fails so that it will never reduce to `False`), it might report violations when computing infinite structures, if the equality is checked in a demand-driven manner (e.g., the expression `[1..]==[2..]` evaluates to `False`). Hence, this optimized formulation is supported by our tool.

The use of a postcondition generated from a specification to check an implementation is justified by the following propositions. The first proposition shows that equivalent operations have the same violations.

Proposition 1. *Let f^{post} be a postcondition for f. If f is equivalent to f' and there is a violation of the postcondition f^{post} for f at e, then there is also a violation of the postcondition f^{post} for f' at e.*

The next proposition shows that any postcondition f^{post} derived from a specification f^{spec} cannot cause any violation when f^{post} is used to check an execution of f^{spec}.

Proposition 2. *If f_g^{post} is the postcondition generated from f^{spec} w.r.t. some operation g, then there is no e such that there is a violation of the postcondition f_g^{post} for f^{spec} at e.*

As a consequence, we can use the postcondition generated from f^{spec} to detect an incorrect implementation:

Corollary 1. *Let f_g^{post} be the postcondition generated from f^{spec} w.r.t. some operation g. If there is a violation of f_g^{post} for f at e, then f is not correct w.r.t. f^{spec}.*

Similarly to testing, the correctness of an implementation cannot be determined by individual executions of a program. Nevertheless, we can infer from a satisfied postcondition which is generated from f^{spec} and an observation operation g that the observed part of the computation is correct w.r.t. the specification:

Proposition 3. *Let f_g^{post} be the postcondition generated from f^{spec} w.r.t. some operation g and e an expression such that f_g^{post} e $(f$ $e)$ $\overset{*}{\to}$ True. Then there is a value s with g $(f$ $e)$ $\overset{*}{\to}$ s and g $(f^{spec}$ $e)$ $\overset{*}{\to}$ s.*

Now we are ready to put this theoretical framework into a tool to support the development of reliable declarative programs.

4   Tool Support

In this section we discuss a tool, DSDCurry[4], based on the ideas described in the previous sections. Basically, the tool transforms a Curry module M containing specifications, pre- and/or postconditions for some operations into a new Curry module MC providing the same interface, but where some operations are checked against the provided specifications and/or contracts. Providing specifications and/or contracts is not mandatory. However, when they are provided, they are used as follows in the transformed module:

- If there is a specification f^{spec}, then a corresponding postcondition is generated according to Definition 4 (if an observation operation is not provided by the programmer, the identity function id is used for g). If there is also a user-defined postcondition, it is combined with the generated postcondition by conjunction.
- If there is only a specification f^{spec} but no implementation[5] of operation f is provided, then an implementation for f is generated by the rule f = f^{spec}.
- If there is neither a specification nor an implementation but a postcondition f^{post} for some operation f, the postcondition is used as a (weak) specification for f, i.e., an initial implementation is generated for f by the following definition:

    `f x | ` f^{post} ` x y = y where y free`
- If there is a contract f^{pre}/f^{post} for some operation f, the implementation of f is replaced by

    `f x | checkPre "`f`" (`f^{pre}` x) &> checkPost "`f`" (`f^{post}` x y)`
    `    = y`
    `  where y = ` f' ` x`
    `        ` f' ` ...`

    where "f' ..." contains the original definition of f with every occurrence of f replaced by f'. Thus, the original interface of any function is preserved by DSD-Curry. The auxiliary operations checkPre and checkPost produce an error message if their second argument evaluates to False. For instance, checkPre is defined by:[6]

    `checkPre fname checkresult =`
    `  if checkresult then success else`
    `    error ("Precondition of operation ’"++fname++"’ violated!")`

---

[4] The tool together with more examples is available at:
http://www.informatik.uni-kiel.de/~pakcs/dsdcurry/.

[5] An operation defined by the rule "f = unknown" is considered as undefined. Such a vacuous definition might be necessary if f is referenced in the definition of other operations in M.

[6] The actual implementation provides more information, e.g., about the concrete arguments of the pre- and postcondition.

The postcondition checker, `checkPost`, is similarly defined. Note that the pre- and postcondition checkers are constraints rather than Boolean operations. This is useful for lazy assertion checking [16] since constraints can be concurrently evaluated.

We demonstrate the development of a simple program using DSDCurry. Consider the specification `sort'spec` and the contract `sort'pre/sort'post` for sorting a list as shown in Section 3. According to Definition 4, the specification and postcondition are combined into a new postcondition of the form

```
sort'post x y = sort'post'org x y && y == y && y ∈ sort'spec_S x
  where sort'post'org xs ys = length xs == length ys
```

where `sort'post'org` is the original, user-supplied postcondition. If we do not provide any implementation of the operation `sort`, an implementation is generated from its specification where contract checking is added:

```
sort x | checkPre "sort" (sort'pre x)
        &> checkPost "sort" (sort'post x y)
      = y
  where y = sort'spec x
```

In principle, postcondition checking should be superfluous for specifications since any user-defined postcondition should be a logical consequence of the specification. Nevertheless, it is included since this entailment is not checked at compile time by our tool.

This prototypical implementation is not efficient because it does not exploit any knowledge about sorting algorithms developed over decades of research in computer science. We improve the efficiency of this implementation by adopting one of these algorithms known as *straight selection sort*. Informally, a list is sorted by selecting its smallest element, sorting the remaining elements, and placing the smallest element in front of the sorted remaining elements. If we know how to select the smallest element of a list, the implementation of this sort method is straightforward by a case distinction on the form of the input list:

```
sort [] = []
sort (x:xs) = min : sort rest    where (min,rest) = minRest (x:xs)
```

Here, we assume that the essential operation of selecting the smallest element is encoded by the operation `minRest` that, for a non-empty input list, returns both the smallest element and the remaining elements. Since finding the smallest element is a non-trivial task, we define a contract for `minRest`:

```
minRest'pre = not . null
```

```
minRest'post xs (min,rest) = (min:rest) ∈ perm_S xs && all (>= min) xs
```

The precondition requires that `minRest` is only applied to non-empty lists. Since there might be different methods to select a minimal element and return the remaining ones, we do not put any requirements on the order of the remaining elements in the postcondition, hence `(min:rest)` is some permutation of the input list. This is also the reason why it would be too restrictive to provide a specification of `minRest`. However, we can use the postcondition as an initial implementation.[7] This implementation of `minRest` has the undesirable consequence of producing many values, i.e., the minimal element

---

[7] In this case, we slightly change the postcondition and replace the Boolean operation "∈" by a constraint since the equality test implicitly performed by "∈" suspends on free variables [17].

together with all permutations of the remaining elements. We can either restrict this implementation to return only one value and ignore the others (for this reason, DSDCurry has an option to enforce this behavior), or provide a more informed implementation of the operation `minRest` as follows.

A direct implementation of `minRest` could be obtained via two auxiliary operations, `min` and `del`, that return the minimal element of a list and delete an occurrence of an element in a list, respectively:

```
minRest (x:xs) = let m = min x xs
                   in (m, del m (x:xs))
   where min x [] = x
         min x (y:ys) = if x<=y then min x ys else min y ys

         del x (y:ys) = if x==y then ys else y : del x ys
```

If we transform this augmented program with DSDCurry, it works as intended without any contract violation. We observe that our implementation of `minRest`, in the worst case, performs two traversals of the input list, whereas it is possible to compute the minimal element and the remaining elements with a single traversal. To improve the performance, we re-code `minRest` as

```
minRest (x:xs) = mr x [] xs
   where mr m r [] = (m,r)
         mr m r (y:ys) = if m<=y then mr m (y:r) ys else mr y (m:r) ys
```

This implementation is more efficient, but also more complicated and its correctness is not as apparent as before. Thus, we apply again our transformation tool to integrate the contract into this implementation and execute the program to increase our confidence in its correctness. Now that we are satisfied with the implementation, we could attempt a formal correctness proof of this implementation. However, this is outside the scope of this paper.

As a further example, consider a program to compute the infinite list, `fibs`, of all the Fibonacci numbers. The specification maps the operation, `fib`, to compute the n-th Fibonacci number defined by the immediate recursive definition, onto the list of all naturals:

```
fibs'spec = map fib [0..]
   where fib n | n == 0    = 0
               | n == 1    = 1
               | otherwise = fib (n−1) + fib (n−2)
```

The application of DSDCurry immediately gives us a correct implementation of `fibs` from this specification, e.g., the expression "`take 10 fibs`" reduces to `[0,1,1,2,3,5,8,13,21,34]`. Since each number in the list is computed by applying operation `fib`, the implementation is quite inefficient due to the exponential complexity of `fib`. Hence, we improve the implementation and construct the list (in linear time) by creating the next element by adding the two previous ones:

```
fibs = fiblist 0 1   where fiblist x y = x : fiblist (x+y) y
```

When we execute "`take 10 fibs`" again after transforming our program with DSD-Curry, a violation is reported for the third element, 2, of the result list. We made a typical error in iterative definitions by swapping some arguments. If we correct the program to

```
fibs = fiblist 0 1  where fiblist x y = x : fiblist y (x+y)
```
and transform and run it again, no more violations are reported.

Contract checking in the presence of infinite structures requires the lazy evaluation of assertions. Thus, our simple implementation where the contract is completely checked in the condition of an operation would lead to an infinite loop in the transformed fibs operation. In general, the eager or strict checking of assertions might influence the execution behavior of a program. To avoid this problem, Chitil et al. [7] proposed *lazy assertions*. Lazy assertions do not evaluate their arguments, but check them when they become evaluated by the application program. Thus, as long as every assertion is satisfied, program executions with or without lazy assertion checking deliver the same results.

On the other hand, lazy assertion checking might not detect contract violations if the assertion arguments are not sufficiently evaluated by the main program. Thus, it is debatable whether full assertion checking should be avoided in order to preserve the behavior of programs [9,16]. Lazy assertions do not modify the behavior, but a lazily computed result cannot be trusted as long as some assertion has not been checked. As a compromise between these conflicting goals, *enforceable assertions* are proposed in [16]. These assertions behave like lazy assertions, but they can also be checked upon an explicit request of the programmer, e.g., at the end of a program execution or at key intermediate execution points.

Making the appropriate choice might be dependent on the application or require some sophisticated program analysis. Therefore, DSDCurry supports strict, lazy, and enforceable assertions by transformation options so that it can be easily adapted to future insights.

5   Conclusions and Related Work

We have discussed some notions that are essential for a methodology intended to develop reliable declarative programs. Specifications are executable so that they can be used as initial prototypes as well as contracts for implementations that might later be developed. We have shown some relationships between these notions that are the basis of a transformation tool to support this development. Our tool, DSDCurry, transforms a specification into an initial implementation, if an implementation is not provided, otherwise it transforms the specification into a contract that checks the results computed by the implementation. Furthermore, our tool supports various forms of contract checking, such as eager, lazy, or enforceable assertions.

In principle, our method and tool support can be seen as a proposal to use Curry as a wide-spectrum language. In contrast to a wide-spectrum language like CIP-L [5] that supports the development of correct programs by applying a stepwise transformation process to specifications, our approach is more flexible. It does not guarantee correct implementations, but it allows very efficient implementations. The correctness is only checked at each concrete program execution w.r.t. some observation operation.

The use of contracts or assertions to obtain more reliable programs has been proposed for many programming languages and paradigms. Concepts for assertions in strict languages, like imperative, logic, or strict functional languages, are easier to handle than in non-strict languages. For instance, [24] proposes an assertion language for (constraint) logic programming that is combined in [20] with a static verification framework. [10] considered a strict language with side effects and proposed the evaluation of assertions in parallel to the application program to exploit the power of multi-core computers. In non-strict languages, one has the option between lazy assertions [7], which do not change the meaning of a program (apart from reporting violated assertions) but might not report some violations, and strict assertions which could influence the evaluation order. Degen et al. [9] discussed the different approaches and came to the conclusion that there seems to be no way to satisfy both objectives, meaning preservation and violation reporting, in a non-strict language.

ESC/Haskell [25] is an approach to add pre- and postconditions to Haskell programs which are checked at compile time by sophisticated program transformations. Similarly to our approach, pre- and postconditions are arbitrary Boolean operations implemented in the source language. These conditions are considered as violated if the evaluation of an operation might fail due to incompletely defined operations (e.g., applying the operation head to the empty list). Such an interpretation of pre- and postconditions is too restrictive for functional logic languages where failures are used as a programming technique. Moreover, we distinguish between precise specifications and (weak) postconditions. For instance, [25] considers a sorting algorithm as verified if the output is a sorted list. We consider such a property as a weak postcondition whereas a precise specification should additionally require that the output is a permutation of the input list in order to exclude non-intended implementations.

An obvious challenge for future work is to provide proof support for contracts and specifications. If it can be shown at compile time that a contract is always satisfied by the corresponding implementation, its run-time checking can be omitted. This improves the efficiency of reliable software and reduces the need to test the developed software with large sets of test data [8,13]. Furthermore, a static proof guarantees the correctness of the implementation for all inputs rather than for particular executions.

References

1. Antoy, S., Echahed, R., Hanus, M.: A needed narrowing strategy. Journal of the ACM 47(4), 776–822 (2000)
2. Antoy, S., Hanus, M.: Set functions for functional logic programming. In: Proceedings of the 11th ACM SIGPLAN International Conference on Principles and Practice of Declarative Programming (PPDP 2009), pp. 73–82. ACM Press (2009)
3. Antoy, S., Hanus, M.: Functional logic programming. Communications of the ACM 53(4), 74–85 (2010)
4. Antoy, S., Hanus, M.: A transformation tool for functional logic program development. In: Proc. of the 24th Workshop on (Constraint) Logic Programming (WLP 2010), pp. 23–33. German University of Cairo (2010)
5. Bauer, F.L., Broy, M., Gnatz, R., Hesse, W., Krieg-Brückner, B., Partsch, H., Pepper, P., Wössner, H.: Towards a wide spectrum language to support program specification and program development. ACM SIGPLAN Notices 13(12), 15–24 (1978)
6. Braßel, B., Hanus, M., Huch, F.: Encapsulating non-determinism in functional logic computations. Journal of Functional and Logic Programming (July 2004)

7. Chitil, O., McNeill, D., Runciman, C.: Lazy Assertions. In: Trinder, P., Michaelson, G.J., Peña, R. (eds.) IFL 2003. LNCS, vol. 3145, pp. 1–19. Springer, Heidelberg (2004)

8. Christiansen, J., Fischer, S.: EasyCheck — Test Data for Free. In: Garrigue, J., Hermenegildo, M.V. (eds.) FLOPS 2008. LNCS, vol. 4989, pp. 322–336. Springer, Heidelberg (2008)

9. Degen, M., Thiemann, P., Wehr, S.: True lies: Lazy contracts for lazy languages (faithfulness is better than laziness). In: 4. Arbeitstagung Programmiersprachen (ATPS 2009), LNI. vol. 154, pages 370, 2946–2259. Springer (2009)

10. Dimoulas, C., Pucella, R., Felleisen, M.: Future contracts. In: Proceedings of the 11th ACM SIGPLAN International Conference on Principles and Practice of Declarative Programming (PPDP 2009), pp. 195–206. ACM Press (2009)

11. Echahed, R., Janodet, J.-C.: On constructor-based graph rewriting systems. Research report imag 985-i, IMAG-LSR, CNRS, Grenoble (1997)

12. Echahed, R., Janodet, J.-C.: Admissible graph rewriting and narrowing. In: Proc. Joint International Conference and Symposium on Logic Programming (JICSLP 1998), pp. 325–340 (1998)

13. Fischer, S., Kuchen, H.: Systematic generation of glass-box test cases for functional logic programs. In: Proceedings of the 9th ACM SIGPLAN International Conference on Principles and Practice of Declarative Programming (PPDP 2007), pp. 75–89. ACM Press (2007)

14. González-Moreno, J.C., Hortalá-González, M.T., López-Fraguas, F.J., Rodríguez-Artalejo, M.: An approach to declarative programming based on a rewriting logic. Journal of Logic Programming 40, 47–87 (1999)

15. Hanus, M.: Multi-paradigm Declarative Languages. In: Dahl, V., Niemelä, I. (eds.) ICLP 2007. LNCS, vol. 4670, pp. 45–75. Springer, Heidelberg (2007)

16. Hanus, M.: Lazy and Enforceable Assertions for Functional Logic Programs. In: Mariño, J. (ed.) WFLP 2010. LNCS, vol. 6559, pp. 84–100. Springer, Heidelberg (2011)

17. Hanus, M. (ed.): Curry: An integrated functional logic language, vers. 0.8.2 (2006), http://www.curry-language.org

18. Hussmann, H.: Nondeterministic algebraic specifications and nonconfluent term rewriting. Journal of Logic Programming 12, 237–255 (1992)

19. López-Fraguas, F.J., Rodríguez-Hortalá, J., Sánchez-Hernández, J.: A simple rewrite notion for call-time choice semantics. In: Proceedings of the 9th ACM SIGPLAN International Conference on Principles and Practice of Declarative Programming (PPDP 2007), pp. 197–208. ACM Press (2007)

20. Mera, E., Lopez-García, P., Hermenegildo, M.: Integrating Software Testing and Run-Time Checking in an Assertion Verification Framework. In: Hill, P.M., Warren, D.S. (eds.) ICLP 2009. LNCS, vol. 5649, pp. 281–295. Springer, Heidelberg (2009)

21. Meyer, B.: Object-oriented Software Construction, 2nd edn. Prentice Hall (1997)

22. Okasaki, C.: Purely Functional Data Structures. Cambridge University Press (1998)

23. Peyton Jones, S. (ed.): Haskell 98 Language and Libraries—The Revised Report. Cambridge University Press (2003)

24. Puebla, G., Bueno, F., Hermenegildo, M.: An Assertion Language for Constraint Logic Programs. In: Deransart, P., Małuszyński, J. (eds.) DiSCiPl 1999. LNCS, vol. 1870, pp. 23–62. Springer, Heidelberg (2000)

25. Xu, D.N.: Extended static checking for Haskell. In: Proc. of the 36th ACM SIGPLAN Workshop on Haskell (Haskell 2006), pp. 48–59 (2006)

The Environment as an Argument
Context-Aware Functional Programming

Pedro M. Martins*, Julie A. McCann, and Susan Eisenbach

Imperial College London
{pm1108,jamm,susan}@doc.ic.ac.uk

Abstract. Context-awareness as defined in the setting of Ubiquitous Computing [3] is all about expressing the dependency of a specific computation upon some implicit piece of information. The manipulation and expression of such dependencies may thus be neatly encapsulated in a language where computations are first-class values. Perhaps surprisingly however, context-aware programming has not been explored in a functional setting, where first-class computations and higher-order functions are commonplace. In this paper we present an embedded domain-specific language (EDSL) for constructing context-aware applications in the functional programming language Haskell.

1 Introduction

With widespread availability of mobile computing devices such as mobile phones and tablets, practical implementations of context-aware applications have started to appear. However, we observe a divide between the solutions proposed by researchers and the practical solutions adopted by implementers. We believe that this is because the former solutions are too heavyweight and rigid, and force developers to sacrifice some freedom in designing their applications, for little practical gain. As a result, practical implementations are typically based on bespoke implementations of context-aware behaviour. This prevents reusability of behaviour, but makes it easier for subtle bugs and programming errors to be repeated throughout implementations of the same behaviour. It has been argued that this is an inevitable consequence of context-awareness. Indeed, Lieberman and Selker [8] present a simple model for context-awareness and postulates that due to the dynamic nature of context-aware applications, it is hard to specify a module's behaviour in a way that will allow it to be reused at all.

In this paper we show that through a deeper embedding of context-awareness semantics into a programming language, we are able to specify this behaviour and provide natural programming language constructs for it. In addition to this, by being aware of the semantics of context-awareness, the compiler for our language is able to verify statically whether a certain number of properties that we believe should be true for this type of behaviour actually hold. This allows us to reuse

---

* Funded by FCT (Portugal) under grant SFRH/BD/61917/2009.

C. Russo and N.-F. Zhou (Eds.): PADL 2012, LNCS 7149, pp. 48–62, 2012.

context-aware behaviour in a controlled and automatically validated way, with minimal loss of expressivity.

Our contributions are as follows:

- A composable representation of context-aware computations that *automatically* derives the context dependencies needed at the type level (Section 3.1).
- An abstraction for knowledge bases which does not enforce any representation or reasoning procedure upon the knowledge base, over which we define all of our abstractions (Section 3.3).
- A *parameterized monad* [1] that encapsulates the adding context to a knowledge base, and statically verifies whether the required context information will be available at the call site of one of the previous context-aware computations (Section 3.5).
- A Haskell library that captures all of these abstractions in an *embedded domain specific language* (EDSL) (Section 3.6).

2   An Example Application

We present a simple implementation example of the declarative data-driven coding style for context-aware applications that we advocate in this paper. The syntax for the example is that of a pure declarative context-aware language with Haskell-like syntax, resembling the final syntax of our EDSL. Our simple scenario is one where a user is walking home from work and wishes to pick up something to eat on the way. The user does not want the food to get cold by the time they reach their home, so they wish to know where the nearest shops to their current location are, and how far each of these shops are from their home. Code listings 1.1 and 1.2 implement the main features needed for this functionality, namely a sorted list of shops and a routine that shows the user how close the nearest shop is from home. This example shows the definition of the domain of contextual information the application is going to manipulate, the relevant data types and the context-aware computation that is intrinsic in the given specification.

We begin by defining the domain of interesting contextual information for the application. Individuals are the entities of the domain that we are concerned with, in this case the user (1). Features are the properties of the individuals that we wish to inspect and manipulate, in this case where the user and their home are located at (3). The syntax i ▷ f is a type-level representation for feature f of individual i. We then define the normal data types that we will be manipulating in the application, namely shops (5). The connection between normal data and the contextual domain is provided in this case through a relevance relation. It states that locations are more relevant to the user the closer they are to them (10). We assume a data type Location is provided by some language library. Using the relevance relation, we sort a list of shops by contextual information, using the primitive sortC. In this case we are sorting the list of shops by their location field, using the applicable relevance relation with context (16). This

```
1   individual User
2
3   feature IsLocatedAt :: Location
4
5   data Shop = Shop { name :: String, location :: Location }
6
7   allShops :: [Shop]
8   allShops = ...
9
10  relevant Location (User ▷ IsLocatedAt) by distance
11
12  distance :: Location → Location → Double
13  distance = ...
14
15  nearestShops :: [Shop] ↓ { User ▷ IsLocatedAt }
16  nearestShops = sortC location allShops
17
18  main = loop do
19    loc ← fetchLocation
20    User ▶ IsLocatedAt := loc
21    print (take 10 nearestShops)
```

Listing 1.1. An application example

creates a computation that is context dependent, nearestShops. Its type reflects
the contextual dependencies that have to be satisfied in order for its value to
be computed. The type a ↓ c represents a value of type a, with contextual
dependencies c, where c is a set of context types.

In order to execute this computation we need to provide it with context.
The do keyword, similarly to Haskell, allows us to enter a sequential execution context. In this case the keyword will also provide a global knowledge base
for storing and retrieving context. Usage of the knowledge base will be tracked
and validated to ensure that contextual dependencies have been satisfied appropriately before context dependent values are used. In the main loop of the
application, we first fetch a location from the device's GPS (19) and add it to
the knowledge base with the primitive expression $i \blacktriangleright f := v$, which allows us
to assign the value of a feature f for the individual i as having value v. In this
case, we are assigning the IsLocatedAt feature for the individual User as the
location we have just retrieved (20). We then print the ten most relevant shops
to the screen. The usage of context in nearestShops is statically verified by the
compiler. Indeed, if we remove the line adding context to the knowledge base,
we will get a compiler error specifying that the context of the type we removed
is not available at the call site of nearestShops.

```
1   individual Home
2
3   distanceFromHome ::
4     Location → Double ↓ { Home ▷ IsLocatedAt }
5   distanceFromHome loc = distance loc (π (Home ▷ IsLocatedAt))
6
7   nearestShopDistanceFromHome ::
8     Double ↓ { User ▷ IsLocatedAt, Home ▷ IsLocatedAt }
9   nearestShopDistanceFromHome = distanceFromHome (head nearestShops)
10
11  exampleHomeDistance = loop do
12    loc ← fetchLocation
13    hloc ← askUserForHomeLocation
14    User ▶ IsLocatedAt := loc
15    Home ▶ IsLocatedAt := hloc
16    print nearestShopDistanceFromHome
```

Listing 1.2. Merging contextual information.

One of the main driving goals mentioned in the introduction was composability and code reuse. In that vein, we should be able to use our context dependent list in the same way that we would use a regular list. In the final line of the example, we use the standard library function take on the list of shops. This function is completely independent from the context library, and has the type:

```
take :: Int → [a] → [a]
```

We can use this function for both regular lists and context dependent lists. The application of this function to the sorted shops list will however push the contextual dependencies to the type of the return value:

```
take 2 nearestShops :: [Shop] ↓ { User ▷ IsLocatedAt }
```

The example so far shows that context-aware values are first-class and can interact naturally with standard library functions. Moreover, if we were to use two contextual values in a single expression, such as a value depending on the home location and another depending on the user location, those two context dependencies would be merged appropriately. This will be seen in the next example. The primitive π is provided by the library, and allows us to manually project context from the knowledge base by type. We have used it in listing 1.2 to calculate the distance to the user's home of the closest shop to them. Note how the type of nearestShopDistanceFromHome (7-8) reflects the contextual dependencies that we are required to satisfy, namely, User ▷ IsLocatedAt, coming from nearestShops and Home ▷ IsLocatedAt coming from distanceFromHome. The application semantics of this language collect the contextual dependencies we use, in the type of the resulting value. This allows us to validate the state of the global knowledge base. In exampleHomeDistance, if we removed either line 14 or 15, we would no longer be adding necessary context to the knowledge base, and we would get a compile time error. This shows the basic behaviour that our EDSL provides. The next sections describe our implementation, along with the compromises that we had to take to conform to the host language.

3   A DSL for Context-Aware Programming

The application example in section 2 shows that there are two main facets to context-awareness. Firstly, defining computations that depend on implicit values, without breaking composability and type safety. Secondly, managing a global knowledge base of context, that can be accessed to provide context to the previous computations. We approach the former in sections 3.1 through 3.3 and the latter in section 3.4. All of the following definitions are written in Haskell, with liberal use of extensions provided by its flagship compiler GHC.

3.1   Context-Aware Computations

We start by representing context-aware computations as pure functions from a contextual value to the desired output. Hinting at the fact that this input is implicit, we define a new type for these functions, which is isomorphic to the basic Haskell arrow type:

```
newtype ContextF a c = ContextF {runContextF :: c → a}
  deriving (Functor, Applicative, Monad)
type a :↓ c = ContextF c a
```

Semantically, $:\downarrow$ declares that a function's argument is contextual and should be considered implicit. `runContextF` then allows us to take this context-aware value and apply it to a context to return a pure value. However, context-aware values differ from regular functions in that we want to think about them as having the type of the return value. Indeed, when applying regular functions to these values, the argument of the context-aware value should be treated as implicit and become the implicit argument of the final value returned by the application. This effect can be achieved thus:

```
apply :: (a → b) → a :↓ c → b :↓ c
apply f ca = ContextF (λc → f (runContextF ca c))
```

This definition is that of `fmap` for the `Reader` functor. Extending this behaviour to accepting multiple arguments in a curried manner leads to the definition of ⊛ from the `Applicative` instance of `Reader` [9]:

```
(⊛) :: (a → b) :↓ c → a :↓ c → b :↓ c
ff ⊛ fa = ContextF (λc → (ff 'runContextF' c)
                        (fa 'runContextF' c))
```

However, this abstraction is exceedingly restrictive in the type of context it is able to deal with, as it forces c to be constant. In our case, this would require the definition of a "universe" product type for context types, which is impractical. We would like the product type to be *automatically derived* as we use more and more contexts. Effectively, what we want is to *parameterise* the applicative functor so that it is able to manage context dependencies appropriately. In this vein, let us define a new operator $\circledast_\times$ which combines the contextual dependencies of both the function and the argument in a product type:

```
(⊛ₓ) :: (a → b) :↓ c₁ → a :↓ c₂ → b :↓ (c₁ × c₂)
```

This is the operator we need to implement the application semantics we outlined in section 2. In the next paragraphs, we will describe its implementation.

3.2 Application over Context-Aware Values

For a constant type c, the existing `Applicative` instance for `Reader` would be enough to achieve the behaviour we want. To see how we might generalise this approach to define $\circledast_\times$, let us specialize the type of $\circledast$:

```
(⊛) :: (a → b) :↓ (c₁ × c₂) → a :↓ (c₁ × c₂) → b :↓ (c₁ × c₂)
```

It seems that the only thing that we need to do to unify this type with that proposed for $\circledast_\times$ is to provide functions that generate this "universe" type. All we need to do is to precompose both functions with an appropriate projection function; of type $c_1 \times c_2 \to c_1$ for the first one and $c_1 \times c_2 \to c_2$ for the second one. In this way, the type of a composite computation can emerge from its components in a canonical way. In order for this scheme to apply to n-ary functions, however, we need to be able to represent and handle cartesian products effortlessly in Haskell. We will use the HList library as presented by Kiselyov et al [6], which represents type-level lists as iterated products with a fixed structure, and provides utility functions and error handling. We use an extended version to obtain set semantics and operations. Other than the typical set operations we will use the `hProject` function, which allows us to retrieve subsets of context:

```
hProject :: (c₁ ⊆ c₂) ⇒ c₂ → c₁
```

In all other cases we will use regular set notation in the code listings and refer the reader to our online implementation for details [1]. We can thus rely on precomposition with `hProject` to derive the universe type that we referred to previously. Then, we can just use the classic applicative instance for $((\to)\ c)$, for all c, and we get the desired functionality. We can therefore generalize to get the $\circledast_\times$ operator:

```
(⊛ₓ) :: (a → b) :↓ c₁ → a :↓ c₂ → b :↓ (c₁ ∪ c₂)
af ⊛ₓ ax = ContextF ((runContextF af) . hProject) ⊛
           ContextF ((runContextF ax) . hProject)
```

This definition of $\circledast_\times$ has a more general principal type than the one we originally discussed, and generalizes to n-ary functions. We can also present a mapping between the "application" of an n-ary function to context-aware values and our combinators. Note that <$> is just infix `fmap`:

```
⟦ f x1 x2 .. xn ⟧ = f <$> x1 ⊛ₓ x2 ⊛ₓ ... ⊛ₓ xn
```

```
evalC :: (c₁ ⊆ c₂) ⇒ a :↓ c₁ → c₂ → a
evalC ca k = ca `runContextF` hProject k
```

```
mkC1 :: (c → a) → a :↓ { c }
mkC1 f = ContextF (f . hHead)
```

```
mkC :: (c → a :↓ cs) → a :↓ (cs ∪ { c })
mkC = comb . mkC1
```

---

[1] Available at http://www.doc.ic.ac.uk/~pm1108/hcontext

```
where comb :: (a :↓ c₁ :↓ c₂) → (a :↓ (c₁ ∪ c₂))
      comb cca = ContextF $ λk → (cca 'evalC' k) 'evalC' k
```

evalC allows us to evaluate a context dependent computation by providing it with the necessary context (or a superset). mkC and mkC1 allow us to build context-aware computations. mkC1 will have to be used when the return value of the function is not context dependent.

3.3   Abstract Knowledge Bases

We now turn to the issue of context representation. The abstractions that we have created clearly define semantics for context-aware values and ways to meaningfully combine them. However, we have not yet modelled access to context providers. In the sections that follow we assume that there is a language which is able to describe the full spectrum of context information that we might need. For the purposes of this paper we assume that all context information that we retrieve is encoded in the same language. Moreover, we will assume that all context providers will use the same ontology when describing concepts. This is a very strong assumption, however solving this issue is not the focus of this paper, and constitutes its own field of research [10]. To detach the current presentation from the previous semantics, we use a different syntax for HProject, k :▷ c, which is to be interpreted as a constraint that holds when we have a knowledge base of type k from which we can extract context information of type c, a set of context types. We also take this opportunity to add additional structure to our context information. We provide support for individuals and features through the following type:

```
type family FeatureType a :: *
data Feat a = a := (FeatureType a)
```

We then represent individuals as data types, and assign features to them with a new data type. The type family FeatureType allows us to embed the type system of features into that of Haskell. This is coupled with an arbitrary projection function, whose arguments serve solely as witnesses for the types corresponding to the individual/feature pair desired:

```
data individual ▷ feature = individual ▷ (Feat feature)
π :: a → f → FeatureType f :↓ { a ▷ f }
π _ _ = mkC1 $ λ(_ ▷ (_ := v)) → v
```

With these definitions, we have now implemented everything needed to produce the context-aware value nearestShopDistanceFromHome, we discussed in section 2:

```
data User = User
data Home = Home
data IsLocatedAt = IsLocatedAt
type instance FeatureType IsLocatedAt = Location

distanceFromHome loc = distance loc <$> (π Home IsLocatedAt)
nearestShopDistanceFromHome =
  distanceFromHome <$> (location . head <$> nearestShops)
```

In order to implement the example in section 2, the only feature missing in our context representation is a notion of relevance of a piece of data for a user, given a set of contextual information. Relevance is realised as a predicate, stating whether a contextual value is relevant to the sorting of another non-contextual value. We define a restriction of this notion in order to aid the type checker, where we constrain the relation $\mathcal{R}(c, k)$, to instead be a *function*. This is represented as the associated type $\mathcal{R}$, which behaves as a type function, assigning a relevant context type to a regular type:

```
class Relevant a where
    type R a :: *
    relevance :: a → R a → Double
```

The Location example in section 2 would become:

```
instance Relevant Location where
    type R Location = User ▷ IsLocatedAt
    relevance l1 (User ▷ (IsLocatedAt := l2)) = distance l1 l2
```

An example of this in action is the sortC function we introduced in section 2:

```
sortC :: (Relevant c) ⇒ (a → c) → [a] → [a] :↓ { R c }
sortC contextfn xs =
    let sortfn c x y = compare (relevance (contextfn x) c)
                               (relevance (contextfn y) c)
    in  ContextF (λc → sortBy (sortfn . hOccurs $ c) xs)
```

3.4 Managing a Global Knowledge Base

Our abstractions allow us to model context-aware computations and sources in a programming language. In order to make context truly implicit we would like to represent context as a shared knowledge base, that is populated by retrieving information from context sources and queried by context-aware computations. We should also be able to exploit all the typing information that we have been managing to make sure that this interaction is well-formed. It turns out that all of this is possible, using the formalism of parameterised monads. [1] First, we combine a context-aware computation and a contextual information producer into one single abstraction, that of stateful computations, which is a straightforward parameterisation of the State functor available in the Haskell libraries. By using the parameterised monad corresponding to this functor [1], we keep track of which knowledge is in the knowledge base at the type level. The approach of using parameterized monads to provide static guarantees over a DSL has been used before. Sackman and Eisenbach[11] show how to provide security guarantees for an imperative language embedded in Haskell. In Haskell, parameterised monads can be defined as a minor generalisation of the Monad type class:

```
class PMonad m where
    return :: a → m c c a
    (>>=) :: m c₁ c₂ a → (a → m c₂ c₃ b) → m c₁ c₃ b
```

GHC's support for rebindable syntax allows us to recover do notation for parameterized monads. Qualified importing of libraries may be used where traditional monadic behaviour is desired. The types for the parameterised context monad (and monad transformer) then become:

```
newtype ContextRuntime c₁ c₂ a =
  CR { runContextRuntime :: c₁ → (a, c₂) }
newtype ContextRuntimeT m c₁ c₂ a =
  CRT { runContextRuntimeT :: c₁ → m (a, c₂) }
```

```
liftCRT :: Monad m ⇒ m a → ContextRuntimeT m c c a
```

We omit the PMonad instances and transformer combinators as they are essentially the same as the ones provided by the regular state monad. Note that our parameterised "monad transformer" is not a fully general parameterised monad transformer as it only works for non-parameterised monads. However, this is enough for the purpose of interacting with most monads present in the Haskell libraries. We then need to define an injection from the parameterised applicative functor to the monad:

```
inContext :: (k :▷ cs) ⇒ ContextF cs a → ContextRuntime k k a
inContext cf = CR $ λk → (evalC cf k, k)
```

We must also provide combinators to add to and update the knowledge base, all whilst performing the required type-level updates. We define a function that operates on type-indexed products, which updates a value by type if it is in the product, and appends it otherwise, called hUpdateAtTypeOrAppend (the definition is ommitted for space reasons). Using this, updating a context value in the knowledge base simply becomes:

```
(▶) :: HUpdateAtTypeOrAppend (i ▷ f) c₁ c₂
     ⇒ i → Feat f → ContextRuntime c₁ c₂ ()
individual ▶ feat = CR $
  λc' → ((), hUpdateAtTypeOrAppend (individual ▷ feat) c')
```

We may now add context values to the knowledge base represented by an HList. Note that because of the constraints in the type of inContext, we can only use an injected function if the required contextual information is present in the knowledge base. The final step we must take before executing context-aware computations in this monad is enforcing an empty starting context. Thus, we now define a set of execution functions for the parameterised monad that enforce this restriction. These were inspired by the ones provided for the State monad in the Haskell standard library.

```
runCR :: ContextRuntime HNil k a → (a, k)
runCR ca = runContextRuntime ca hNil
```

evalCR and execCR are defined as the appropriate projections from the result of runCR. We also define evalCRT, execCRT and runCRT as the transformer versions of these combinators. Thus, the only way to run a context-aware computation is to start with the empty context. The compiler may track all context dependencies, and abort with a compile-time error if they are not satisfied. This characteristic is arguably one of the most interesting features of our EDSL, as we are able to reify into the type level the context dependencies of a particular computation, and thus statically guarantee that they will be fulfilled. This eliminates a whole class of potential bugs in context-aware applications, whereby the application attempts to use context when it is not stored in the knowledge base.

3.5 Automatically Satisfying Contextual Dependencies

Given that our EDSL is targeting situations where the domain of contextual information can have a type system imposed on it, that uniquely identifies the type of contextual information, it is not too far-fetched to think of satisfying these implicit dependencies automatically. That is, we can use the mechanisms outlined in the previous sections to collect contextual dependencies on the main program, and we can also create a library that adds specific portions of contextual information to a global knowledge base by querying device-specific sensors. We can then tie both of these together automatically, through the type system.

To achieve this, we introduce a new type class, the instances of which specify which types of contextual information we can retrieve under the IO monad, for the device we are currently using.

```
pushC :: (Monad m) ⇒ c → ContextRuntimeT m HNil c ()
pushC c = CRT . const . M.return $ ((), c)

class Realizable c where
    realize :: a :↓ c → ContextRuntimeT IO HNil c a
    fetch :: IO c
    realize x = liftCRT fetch >>= pushC >> inContextT x
```

This allows us to completely hide context from the programmer who is using the EDSL. For example, if the programmer had a main loop and a function called in every iteration that could benefit from contextual information, this dependency could be added to the code for the function, and lifted to the top-level using the mechanisms the EDSL provides. We can then provide the necessary instances of Realizable for the device in question, and selectively import the ones corresponding to the retrieval technique we wish to use.

4 Evaluation

In order to test the expressive power of our EDSL we implemented two context-aware applications, showcasing both the abstraction capabilities provided by the library as well as the ease of interaction with existing code.

4.1 Presence Board

Implementing a presence board application that keeps track of all people that have checked into a certain context (e.g. a building), has become the canonical application for evaluating context-aware libraries. This application is interesting because the presence information can then be used for more exciting context-aware applications, as will be seen. We assume an existing instance of Realizable for Location and an online service that can be used to match a location with the building that contains it, returning a circular area delimiting the range to be considered for that building/context:

```
locationToRange :: Location → IO (Location, Double)
```

The EDSL allows us to provide a reusable library for this device, fetching the contextual information under the IO monad. Through the realizable type class we ready this for easy use by the programmer of the final application. In our case, we simply supply an instance for Realizable, for presence information, in our own data type:

```
data User = ...
users :: [User]
fetchLocationForUser :: User → IO Location
fetchUsers :: IO [User]
newtype Presence x = Presence [(x, Bool)] deriving (Show, Eq)

instance Realizable Location where ...
instance Realizable (Presence User) where
  fetch :: IO (Presence User)
  fetch = do
    location ← fetch
    us ← fetchUsers
    ls ← mapM fetchLocationForUser us
    (l,d) ← locationToRange location
    return . Presence $ zip us (map ((<d) . distance l) ls)
```

With this we can define the application code easily:

```
displayPresence :: IO () :↓ { Presence User }
displayPresence = mkC1 $ λpresence → do -- ...
main = forever (realize displayPresence)
```

Which implements a simple presence board application. Note how the programmer writing the previous code did not need to worry about how to retrieve the presence information, as it was abstracted away into a library. Then, retrieving this contextual information from the point of view of the final presence board application is simply a matter of using it at the right type, and making it implicit, using the liftings.

4.2 Mailing List

In order to ascertain how easy it would be to add context-awareness to an existing application, we took one of the examples used by the context toolkit [4], a context-aware mailing list application. This application should forward emails to only those subscribers that are located in the specific context that the mailing list applies to, in our case, physically located in a building. We located a mailing list manager application implemented in Haskell, Mhailist, publicly available on the Hackage package database [12]. We then proceeded to implement this behaviour without using any EDSL for implicit information. At a high level this change corresponds to retrieving presence information for the mailing list subscribers and selectively forwarding emails depending on it.

```
...
(addressees, msg)    ← return $
    case action of
      SendToList  → (addresses, addHeader listIDHeader message)
...
main = do result ← runErrorT processMessage
...
```

The modification is fairly simple, we just have to pass in the presence information to the forwarding function, and calculate it in the main loop. However, this simple change implies adding an explicit argument at every call site of the forwarding function, all the way up to the main loop. This can result in fairly significant changes to the main program. Using the existent implicit arguments feature present in GHC, we are able to propagate this dependency in a more implicit way. However, we then need to satisfy these dependencies by name, and it would be rather hard to provide a EDSL that extracts from the implicit dependencies of a computation the exact fetching routine the program should undertake, as these are identified by name. Using types to identify implicit arguments however, we are able to do just that. We can, as before, propagate the implicit argument to the main loop in an easy way. Then, in order to satisfy the main loop's context requirements, we just need to call realize, and the Realizable type class will handle fetching the appropriate contextual information for the device and supplying it to the computation. We need to introduce the contextual dependency at the top level instead of using the lifting mechanisms presented, as otherwise we would have to fully desugar the do-notation and lift the binds. We also had to import the parameterized monad bind operator qualified as PM.>>= to allow us to use both monadic semantics.

```
mkC1 $ λpresence → do
...
  (addressees, msg)    ← return $
      case action of
        SendToList  →
          ( filter ((isJust . flip lookup $ presence) addresses)
          , addHeader listIDHeader message)
...
main = evalCRT $ realize processMessage PM.>>= λpm →
          liftCRT $ do result ← runErrorT pm
...
```

5   Related Work

Existing work in context-awareness has focused on creating flexible context representations as well as design patterns for developing context-aware applications within traditional programming languages. Context Toolkit [4] is a Java based toolkit that defines an architecture for developing context-aware applications, and provides the programming support for it. The central component of the context toolkit is the widget. It is defined by attributes and callbacks. There are several flaws with the widget abstraction, that are addressed with special components in the toolkit. Firstly, widgets appear to segment context information independently from the chosen context representation. This is accounted for with context servers that both aggregate contextual information and can choose an underlying widget depending on the request. In our representation, widgets would be an artificial abstraction. The typing information allows an application to precisely specify, at compile-time, what sort of information it is going to require. This allows us to define a universal context runtime that will produce widgets "on demand". The context runtime serves as a flexible universal context server. As pointed by Bardram [2], the context toolkit enforces a highly distributed structure for a context-aware application. This aids flexibility and allows for distribution of architectural components. However, it is also more demanding of the system where it is deployed. Through using a more lightweight solution, we are able to support a less distributed solution if required. Because of the data-driven approach that we take, we can exploit existing communication libraries if we need to distribute components. This is not as allows the user to pick the communication protocol and representation freely.

There has also been prior research done in modelling implicit arguments in a functional programming language, most notably that of Lewis et al [7], which is implemented in the Haskell compiler GHC as an extension. Our approach shares certain characteristics with this calculus, such as the implicit "floating out" of implicit arguments in composite computations. Our approach was designed from the ground up to be customised to the typical use cases in context-awareness, and that is reflected in our choice of identifying variables with their types, as there should only be one value of each type in the knowledge base. This allows us to make queries to the knowledge base more automatic, as only the typing information is required. In Lewis et al's solution [7] all implicit arguments have a name that identifies them, and it is up to the programmer to manage assignment of values to names and scoping of those names. In our approach, types identify implicit arguments, so no manual management of names is needed. The flexibility lost lies in the fact that we cannot have two values of the same type, which their calculus allows, but in our case is not necessary, as we have specified a type system that distinguishes all individual contextual data by type. This constraint however, allows us to extract more typing information statically and be able to manage the interaction between context sources and context consumers automatically. Also, it is possible to have multiple values of isomorphic types, and use the more sophisticated plumbing mechanisms of relevance and feature projection to manage these. An example of this was given with the user and their home's location, having types that are isomorphic in the haskell EDSL, but can conceptually be thought of as equal.

Another common way to introduce implicit global semantics is to use aspect-oriented programming. We can think of contextual dependencies as cross-cutting concerns, whereby the behaviours that would be injected would be both projections from the global knowledge base and retrieval and storage of contextual information. Using aspects for this purpose would make it much harder for us to provide safety guarantees in the knowledge base access. The manipulations performed by aspect-oriented programming are purely syntactical, and it is hard to work out which source code transformations are going to be applied to a piece of code without examining the whole application. For this same reason aspect-oriented programming is much more flexible. However, given that one of our main goals was to provide clearer semantics for context-awareness, the disadvantages of aspect-oriented programming would outweigh the advantages.

6   Future Work

We believe that the abstractions we presented are an interesting approach to modelling context-awareness and can indeed be used to develop practical applications that use context in more complex ways than we have seen to date. Our implementation in Haskell will hopefully encourage further experimentation with these abstractions in real-world scenarios, and serves as further proof that Haskell has become an extremely appropriate host language for DSLs even when the semantics are quite different from its. However, there are some quirks in the DSL that stem from the fact that our EDSL is being hosted in Haskell. For instance, the fact that creating a contextual value is not encapsulated in only one combinator, but is implemented as two separate functions mkC1 and mkC. This is because we have to deal with non context-aware types and interact naturally with them. If non context-aware types were considered equal to types that are dependent on a null context, mkC1 would be a special case of mkC. On the other hand, the fact that application of functions to context-aware values needs to be performed with special operators, makes this library slightly unnatural to use. Further, we have not provided abstractions for continuous retrieval of contextual information and modelling the retrieval-usage loop. We believe that we can use functional reactive programming [5] to manage context streams in a natural way. Thus, we believe it would be interesting to design a language from the ground up that is based around these concepts, as a purer exposition of these ideas, and maybe as a theory that can bring further insights into the nature of context-awareness and the interaction between context providers and consumers.

7   Conclusion

When integrating context into a system, programmers are presented with two options. To either conform to rigid frameworks or to build bespoke functions that represent contextual behaviour. The latter, though providing more freedom, is problematic in that it has been shown that these dynamical approaches limit the amount of reusability, and errors can be easily propagated where attempts to reuse are made.

   This is the first work that aims to overcome these problems by presenting an abstraction whereby context is deeply embedded into the programming language. In doing so, we are able to show that static verification can be achieved;

limiting the propagation of undesirable behaviours. Representing context-aware computations as functions with implicit arguments and inference rules, we are able to provide a composable type-safe system that provides static guarantees of well-formedness for context-aware applications. We also formalise the concept of a knowledge base and by using the type information we collected we are able to automatically satisfy contextual dependencies.

As proof of concept we implement our constructs in Haskell. It proved to be a good choice for a host language as both its type system and syntax are fairly programmable and allowed us to embed to provide an EDSL that presented significantly different semantics from those of vanilla Haskell.

In summary, our formal grounding for context-awareness, combined with its example implementation in Haskell, provides the abstractions to encourage the exploration of more complex context driven applications than have been seen to date.

References

1. Atkey, R.: Parameterised notions of computation. Journal of Functional Programming 19(3-4), 335 (2009)
2. Bardram, J.: The Java Context Awareness Framework (JCAF)–a service infrastructure and programming framework for context-aware applications. Pervasive Computing, 98–115 (2005)
3. Dey, A., Abowd, G.: Towards a better understanding of context and context-awareness. In: CHI 2000 Workshop on the What, Who, Where, When, and How of Context-Awareness, vol. 4, pp. 1–6. Citeseer (2000)
4. Dey, A., Abowd, G., Salber, D.: A conceptual framework and a toolkit for supporting the rapid prototyping of context-aware applications. Human-Computer Interaction 16(2), 97–166 (2001)
5. Elliott, C.: Push-pull functional reactive programming. In: Haskell Symposium (2009)
6. Kiselyov, O., Lämmel, R., Schupke, K.: Strongly typed heterogeneous collections. In: Haskell 2004: Proceedings of the ACM SIGPLAN Workshop on Haskell, pp. 96–107. ACM Press (2004)
7. Lewis, J.R., Launchbury, J., Meijer, E., Shields, M.B.: Implicit parameters: dynamic scoping with static types. In: Proceedings of the 27th ACM SIGPLAN-SIGACT Symposium on Principles of Programming Languages, POPL 2000, pp. 108–118. ACM, New York (2000)
8. Lieberman, H., Selker, T.: Out of context: Computer systems that adapt to, and learn from, context. IBM Systems Journal 39(3.4), 617–632 (2000)
9. McBride, C., Paterson, R.: Applicative programming with effects. Journal of Functional Programming 18(01), 1–13 (2007)
10. Pinto, H., Gómez-Pérez, A., Martins, J.: Some issues on ontology integration. In: IJCAI 1999 Workshop on Ontologies and Problem-Solving Methods (KRR5), Citeseer (1999)
11. Sackman, M., Eisenbach, S.: Safely Speaking in Tongues: Statically Checking Domain Specific Languages in Haskell. In: LDTA 2009 (March 2009)
12. Sampson, C., Kotthoff, L.: Mhailist: Haskell mailing list manager (April 2010), http://hackage.haskell.org/package/Mhailist-0.0

Weighted-Sequence Problem: ASP vs CASP and Declarative vs Problem-Oriented Solving

Yuliya Lierler, Shaden Smith, Miroslaw Truszczynski, and Alex Westlund

Department of Computer Science, University of Kentucky, Lexington, KY
40506-0633, USA

Abstract. Search problems with large variable domains pose a challenge to current answer-set programming (ASP) systems as large variable domains make grounding take a long time, and lead to large ground theories that may make solving infeasible. To circumvent the "grounding bottleneck" researchers proposed to integrate constraint solving techniques with ASP in an approach called *constraint* ASP (CASP). In the paper, we evaluate an ASP system CLINGO and a CASP system CLINGCON on a handcrafted problem involving large integer domains that is patterned after the database task of determining the optimal join order. We find that search methods used by CLINGO are superior to those used by CLINGCON, yet the latter system, not hampered by grounding, scales up better. The paper provides evidence that gains in solver technology can be obtained by further research on integrating ASP and CSP technologies.

1 Introduction

ASP [11,13] is a declarative programming formalism based on the answer-set semantics of logic programs [8]. It is oriented towards combinatorial search problems. Search problems with large variable domains pose a major challenge to the current generation of answer-set programming (ASP) systems, which require that the answer-set program representing the problem first be grounded by an ASP *grounder* and only then solved by an ASP *solver* [2]. The difficulty is that large variable domains make grounding take long, sometimes prohibitively long, time and result in large ground theories that often make solving infeasible, even though the problem may in fact be quite easy. Typical examples of problems with variables ranging over large domains are optimization problems, which require variables to represent possible values of goal function, and planning and scheduling problems that require variables to represent times when events can take place.

Constraint ASP [12,7,1] (CASP) integrates ASP with tools and techniques developed for constraint satisfaction problems (CSP). The goal of CASP systems is to address the grounding bottleneck of ASP. CASP solvers address the problem by performing partial grounding only, not grounding variables whose values range over large domains, but delegating the task of finding appropriate values for them to specialized algorithms such as constraint solvers.

C. Russo and N.-F. Zhou (Eds.): PADL 2012, LNCS 7149, pp. 63–77, 2012.

In the work we report here we experimentally evaluated ASP and CASP systems. For our study we selected the highly optimized ASP system CLINGO[1] [6] that is based on the ASP grounder GRINGO [5] and the ASP solver CLASP [6], and a CASP system CLINGCON[2] [7] that is based on modifications of GRINGO, CLASP, and the constraint solver GECODE[3]. To conduct the experiments we handcrafted a benchmark called a *weighted-sequence* problem. The key features of the problem are inspired by the important industrial problem of finding an optimal join order by cost-based query optimizers in database systems. When selecting and designing the problem, we were motivated by the fact that it involved variables with large domains of integers, which made it well suited for our study. We were also motivated by the practical relevance of that problem and its hardness. Current query optimizers attempt to find an optimal join order only for joins consisting of relatively few tables (five tables in the case of the ORACLE optimizer [9, Page 416]). We modified the problem by introducing additional complexities to enrich its structure and create possibilities for non-trivial modeling enhancements requiring a deeper understanding of problem properties.[4]

In our experiments we aimed to understand relative advantages of sophisticated search procedures involving conflict-driven clause learning and backjumping of the ASP solver CLINGO (which implements learning and backjumping following CLASP [6]) versus the idea of limiting grounding and delegating some constraint solving tasks to a specialized constraint solver employed by CLINGCON – an idea central to CASP. We experimented with two sets of instances: a SMALL set of 30 instances, where the integer parameters were quite small, and a LARGE set also of 30 instances, where the integer parameters were substantially larger. Our key findings are that: the effectiveness of the search procedure used by CLINGCON lags behind that of CLINGO; and that circumventing the grounding bottleneck makes CLINGCON scale up substantially better.

The former finding is demonstrated by the running times we observed on instances in the SMALL set, where the integer parameters are low and grounding is not a major factor. On these instances, CLINGO in general performed better. Further evidence in support of that claim came from experiments with several encodings of the weighted-sequence problem, one of which represented the problem requirements literally as they appeared in the problem statement, while others also included constraints not given explicitly but derived from those stated directly. CLINGO was much less sensitive to modeling enhancements, suggesting that its learning techniques could infer at least some of the derived constraints. However, including these "derived" constraints had a major positive effect on CLINGCON, suggesting its search methods are not yet powerful enough to infer useful constraints when they are not given explicitly.

---

[1] http://potassco.sourceforge.net/

[2] http://www.cs.uni-potsdam.de/clingcon/

[3] http://www.gecode.org/

[4] The benchmark was submitted to and used in the Third Answer Set Programming Competition (https://www.mat.unical.it/aspcomp2011/OfficialProblemSuite). It was referred to as benchmark number 28, *Weight-Assignment Tree*.

The latter key finding concerning the scalability was evidenced by the results concerning the LARGE set of instances showing that when the parameters get larger, large sizes of grounded programs slow down CLINGO dramatically, while even less sophisticated search methods of CLINGCON are capable to find solutions quickly.

Our results strongly suggest the validity of the CASP approach but also point out that there is still much room for improvement in the way CASP systems do learning.

2   Problem Statement

In the weighted-sequence problem we are given a set of leaves (nodes) and an integer m — *maximum cost*. Each leaf is a pair $(weight, cardinality)$ where *weight* and *cardinality* are integers. Every sequence (permutation) of leaves is such that all leaves but the first are assigned a color. A colored sequence is associated with the *cost*. The task is to find a colored sequence with the cost at most m.

For a set S of leaves and an integer m, we denote the corresponding weighted-sequence problem by $[S, m]$. We say that an integer m is *optimal* with respect to a set S of leaves if m is the least integer u such that the weighted-sequence problem $[S, u]$ has a solution.

Let M be a sequence of n leaves $l_0, \ldots, l_{n-1}$. For each leaf l_i, $0 \leq i \leq n-1$, by $w(l_i)$ and $c(l_i)$ we denote its weight and cardinality, respectively. We color each leaf l_i, $1 \leq i \leq n-1$, *green, red,* or *blue*; the leaf l_0 is not colored. We define the costs of leaves as follows. For the leaf l_0, we set

$$cost(l_0) = w(l_0).$$

For every colored leaf l_i, $1 \leq i \leq n-1$, we set

$$cost(l_i) = \begin{cases} w(l_i) + c(l_i) & \text{if } l_i \text{ is green} \\ cost(l_{i-1}) + w(l_i) & \text{if } l_i \text{ is red} \\ cost(l_{i-1}) + c(l_i) & \text{if } l_i \text{ is blue.} \end{cases}$$

The cost of the sequence M is the sum of the costs of its colored leaves:

$$cost(M) = cost(l_1) + \cdots + cost(l_{n-1}).$$

3   ASP: Generate and Test Methodology

Answer set programming [11,13] is a declarative programming formalism based on the answer set semantics of logic programs [8]. The idea of ASP is to represent a given computational problem by a program whose answer sets correspond to solutions. A common methodology to solve a problem in ASP is to design two main parts of a program: GENERATE and TEST [10]. The former defines a larger collection of answer sets that could be seen as potential solutions. The latter consists of rules that eliminate the answer sets that do not correspond to solutions. Often a third part of the program, DEFINE, is also necessary to express auxiliary concepts that are used to encode the conditions of GENERATE and TEST. Thus, when we represent a problem in ASP, two kinds of rules have a special role: those that *generate* many answer sets corresponding to possible solutions, and those that can be used to *eliminate* the answer sets that do not correspond to solutions.

A typical logic programming *rule* has a form

$$a_0 \leftarrow a_1, \ldots, a_m, \ not \ a_{m+1}, \ldots, \ not \ a_n, \tag{1}$$

where each a_i $(0 \leq i \leq n)$ is an atom of the underlying language. We call the left-hand side (right-hand side) of the arrow symbol in a rule (1) the rule's *head* (*body*, respectively). Rules are used to describe relations between concepts represented by their atoms. Together, as a program, they specify a class of special models for the program. These models are called *answer sets*. Informally speaking, answer sets are those models of a program that are in some very precise way "justified" by the program. We refer for the formal definition to the overview by Brewka et al. [2].

For instance, the program

$$p.$$
$$q \leftarrow p, \ not \ r.$$

is composed of two rules. The first rule is often called a *fact* since its body is empty and it represents the fact p. The second rule justifies the derivation of q, as we have p and the program has no way to justify r (no rule has r as its head). Consequently, by a form of the closed-world assumption, *not* r is true and the rule "fires." In this case, $\{p, q\}$ is the only model "justified" by the program, that is, the only answer set, even though the program has additional models.

In addition to rules of the form (1), GRINGO also accepts rules of other kinds. Two important examples are *choice rules* and *constraints*. For example, the rule

$$\{p, q, r\}.$$

is a choice rule (in this case, with the empty body). Informally, it justifies any (even empty) subset of $\{p, q, r\}$. Thus, any subset of $\{p, q, r\}$ is an answer set the program consisting of this rule only. As this example demonstrates, choice rules generate sets of models and are typically members of the GENERATE part of the program.

Constraints often form the TEST section of a program. Syntactically, a *constraint* is the rule with an empty head. It encodes the constraints of the problem that answer sets must have. For instance, the constraint

$$\leftarrow p, \ not \ q.$$

eliminates answer sets that include p and do not include q. When this constraint and the constraint $\leftarrow r$, which eliminates answer sets containing r, are conjoined with the choice rule above, the resulting program has three answer sets: $\emptyset$, $\{q\}$ and $\{p, q\}$.

The input language of CLINGO (CLINGCON) allows the user to specify large programs in a compact fashion, using rules with schematic variables and other abbreviations. We refer the reader to the manual of CLINGO [5] for more details.

When processing, programs are first grounded by a grounder (a program like GRINGO). Afterwards, a solver program (for instance, CLASP; these programs share much similarity with propositional SAT solvers) searches for the answer sets of the propositional output of the grounding phase.[5] The problem is that the output of the grounder may be large. By exploiting constraint (CSP) solvers for some search tasks, one can get by with a smaller grounding. This is the idea behind CASP, which we compare here experimentally to the standard ASP solving method.

4   Encodings

ASP encodings of the weighted-sequence problem represent it as a logic program so that answer sets of the program correspond to sequences of leaves with the cost less than or equal to the given bound. Below we present several encodings. One of them simply represents literally the requirements as they appear in the problem statement. The remaining ones expand it by imposing additional constraints derived by analyzing the problem statement. All these encodings can be systematically transformed into the corresponding CLINGCON programs that take advantage of a special feature of CLINGCON, *constraint atoms*. We use the resulting CLINGCON programs in our experiments with CLINGCON.

There are several concepts that are common to all the encodings. Let n and m be integers giving the number of leaves in a weighted-sequence and the bound on the total cost of a solution (maximum cost), respectively. Then each encoding contains the following facts

$$num(n)$$
$$maxCost(m).$$

The weight and cardinality of each leaf is specified by facts of the form

$$leafWeightCard(i, w, c)$$

where i is an integer that ranges from 1 to n and stands for an *id* of a leaf, and w and c are the weight and cardinality of this leaf, respectively.

In addition, the DEFINE part of every encoding presented here contains the rules

$$position(X) \leftarrow X = 0..N - 1, num(N)$$
$$coloredPos(X) \leftarrow X = 1..N - 1, num(N),$$

which specify that there are n positions $0 \ldots n - 1$ in the sequence, and that the positions $1 \ldots n - 1$ are colored and the position 0 is not.

---

[5] CLINGO, the program we study in this paper, simply combines the two programs into one.

Declarative Encoding: The GENERATE part of a *declarative* encoding, DECL, consists of two components. The first one generates a sequence by assigning each leaf its position. It is formed by the following two rules:

$$1\{leafPos(L, P) : position(P)\}1 \leftarrow leaf(L)$$
$$1\{leafPos(L, P) : leaf(L)\}1 \leftarrow position(P).$$

Intuitively, the first rule says that each leaf is assigned exactly one position. The second rule ensures that each position holds exactly one leaf.

The second component of the GENERATE part assigns exactly one color to every colored position in a sequence (positions $1, \dots, n - 1$). To this end, it uses the rule

$$1\{posColor(P, C) : color(C)\}1 \leftarrow coloredPos(P). \tag{2}$$

The DEFINE part of the program DECL includes the rules that specify the cost of each colored leaf in a sequence. For instance, the two rules

$$
\begin{aligned}
posCost(0, Cost) &\leftarrow leafWeightCard(L, Cost, C), leafPos(L, 0) \\
posCost(P, Cost) &\leftarrow coloredPos(P),\ posColor(P, red),\ leafPos(L, P), \\
&\quad leafWeightCard(L, W, C),\ posCost(P - 1, Cost'), \\
&\quad Cost = Cost' + W
\end{aligned}
\tag{3}
$$

state that (i) the cost of the leaf in position 0 is its weight, and (ii) the cost of the leaf in position P that is colored *red* is the sum of its weight and the cost of the preceding node. Similar rules specify costs of leaves when they are colored *green* or *blue*. The DEFINE part of DECL also contains rules that define the cost of a sequence:

$$
\begin{aligned}
seqCost(1, Cost) &\leftarrow posCost(1, Cost) \\
seqCost(P, Cost) &\leftarrow coloredPos(P),\ P > 1,\ seqCost(P - 1, C), \\
&\quad posCost(P, C'),\ Cost = C + C'.
\end{aligned}
\tag{4}
$$

Consequently, an answer set contains the ground atom $seqCost(n - 1, c)$ if and only if c is the number that corresponds to the cost of the sequence determined by other ground atoms in this answer set (we recall that n is the number of leaves).

Finally, DEFINE includes the rule that introduces an auxiliary predicate *exists*:

$$exists \leftarrow seqCost(N - 1, Cost),\ num(N),\ Cost \leq M, maxCost(M) \tag{5}$$

which affirms that the sequence determined by an answer set has total cost within the specified bound m.

The TEST part of DECL contains a single constraint:

$$\leftarrow\ not\ exists$$

It tests whether an answer set contains the atom *exists* and eliminates those that do not. In this way only answer sets determining sequences with the total cost within the specified bound remain. If no such sequence exists the program has no answer sets.

We note that the rules in (3) and   (4) may be augmented by additional conditions in the bodies

$$Cost \leq M, \ maxCost(M).$$

This modification is crucial for making grounded instances of programs smaller and is incorporated in our encodings.

Sequence Encoding: For a leaf l, we define its *value* $val(l)$ as the smaller of the two numbers, the weight and the cardinality, associated with l. That is,

$$val(l) = \begin{cases} w(l) & \text{if } w(l) \leq c(l), \\ c(l) & \text{otherwise.} \end{cases}$$

Let l and l' be two leaves in a sequence so that l immediately precedes l'. We define the *color number* of the leaf l' to be

$$colorNum(l') = min(w(l') + c(l'), cost(l) + val(l')).$$

Let us assign a color to every leaf l' in a colored position according to the formula:

$$color(l') = \begin{cases} green & \text{if } colorNum(l') = w(l') + c(l') \\ red & \text{otherwise, if } colorNum(l') = cost(l) + w(l') \\ blue & \text{otherwise, if } colorNum(l') = cost(l) + c(l') \end{cases}$$

where l precedes l' in the sequence.

Observation 1: Any color assignment different from the one defined above results in a colored sequence with the same or higher cost.

Observation 1 represents a property of the weighted-sequence problem that is not explicitly present in the problem statement and so, it is not a part of the DECL encoding. It is the basis for the *sequence* encoding SEQ that builds upon the DECL encoding by replacing the "non-deterministic" color-choice rule (2) with a set of "deterministic rules." For instance,

$$\begin{aligned} posColor(P, green) \leftarrow \ & P > 1, \ coloredPos(P), \ leafPos(L, P), \\ & leafWeightCard(L, W, C), \ leafValue(L, V), \\ & posCost(P - 1, Cost), \ W + C < Cost + V \end{aligned}$$

is one of the rules in this set (for a leaf l, $leafValue(l, v)$ is defined to hold precisely when $v = val(l)$).

Intuitively, the advantage of the encoding SEQ over DECL is a reduced search space as color assignment requires no choices. However, by Observation 1, no optimal solutions are lost while some suboptimal ones are pruned. We note that an additional (minor) simplification results from the fact that in the DECL encoding, three cases are considered when a position is colored *green*, *red*, and *blue*. In the encoding SEQ, with the use of *leafValue* predicate, it is sufficient to consider two cases only: when position is colored green and when it is not.

Sequence Encoding+:

Observation 2: Let l and l' be two consecutive elements in a sequence M (in that order), neither being a green-colored leaf. It is easy to see that if $val(l') < val(l)$ then the sequence M' constructed from M by changing the order of l and l' has a smaller cost than M, i.e., $cost(M') < cost(M)$.

Observation 2 allows us to add the constraint

$$\begin{aligned}
\leftarrow &\ coloredPos(P; P-1), \\
&\ not\ posColor(P, green),\ not\ posColor(P-1, green), \\
&\ leafPos(L, P-1),\ leafPos(L', P), \\
&\ leafValue(L, V),\ leafValue(L', V'), V > V'.
\end{aligned} \qquad (6)$$

to the SEQ encoding. We denote the resulting program by SEQ+.

The idea behind extending the SEQ encoding with (6) is that it reduces the search space. Observation 2 implies that no optimal solutions to the weighted-sequence problem are lost because of the additional constraint, some suboptimal ones will in general be pruned.

Sequence Encoding++:

Let $g_1, \ldots, g_k$ be a set of all green nodes in a sequence M, that is,

$$M = M_0\, g_1\, M_1 \ldots g_k\, M_k \qquad (7)$$

where each M_i, $0 \le i \le k$, is a sequence of non-green leaves. We call M_0 the $0th$ *partition* of (7) and each $g_i\, M_i$, $1 \le i \le k$, a *green partition* of (7).

Observation 3: The fact that the cost of a green node only relies on its own weight and cardinality makes it evident that the cost of the sequence (7) is the same as the cost of the sequence $M_0\ P$, where P is any permutation of the set of green partitions of (7), $\{g_1\, M_1, \ldots, g_k\, M_k\}$.

Observation 3 allows us to add a constraint

$$\begin{aligned}
\leftarrow &\ leafPos(L, P),\ leafPos(L', P'), \\
&\ posColor(P, green),\ posColor(P', green), \\
&\ L < L',\ P > P'
\end{aligned}$$

to the SEQ+ encoding. We denote the resulting program by SEQ++. Intuitively, the last rule "breaks the symmetry" by enforcing that any answer set to the program has the green leaves in the corresponding solution sequence sorted according to their costs.

Clingcon Encodings: The CASP language of CLINGCON extends the ASP language of CLINGO by introducing "constraint atoms". These atoms are interpreted differently than "typical" ASP atoms. The system CLINGCON splits the task of search between two programs: an ASP solver (CLASP) and a CSP solver (GECODE). The ASP solver incorporated in CLINGCON treats constraint atoms as boolean atoms and assigns them some *truth* value. The CSP solver, on the other hand, is used to verify whether the assignments given to the constraint atoms by the ASP solver of CLINGCON hold based on their "real" meaning.

Let us note that *posCost* and *seqCost* predicates used in all CLINGO encodings are "functional". In other words, when this predicate occurs in an answer set its first argument uniquely determines its second argument. Often, functional predicates in ASP encodings can be replaced by constraint atoms in CASP encodings. Indeed, this is the case in the weighted-sequence problem domain. This allows us to create alternative encodings for DECL, SEQ and the extensions of SEQ.

We note that only the rules containing functional predicates *posCost* and *seqCost* were changed in DECL and SEQ and its extensions to produce CLINGCON programs. For instance, the rules in (4) and (5) have the following form in the CLINGCON encodings

$$seqCost(1) =^\$ posCost(1) \leftarrow coloredPos(1)$$
$$seqCost(P) =^\$ posCost(P) + seqCost(P-1) \leftarrow P > 1, \ coloredPos(P)$$
$$exists \leftarrow seqCost(N-1) \leq^\$ M, \ num(N), \ maxCost(M),$$

where

$$seqCost(1) =^\$ leafCost(1), \ seqCost(P) =^\$ leafCost(P), \ seqCost(N-1) \leq^\$ M$$

are constraint atoms. The rules defining *posCost*, such as (3), are rewritten in a similar manner:

$$posCost(0) =^\$ Cost \leftarrow leafWeightCard(L, Cost, C), leafPos(L, 0)$$
$$posCost(P) =^\$ posCost(P-1) + W \leftarrow coloredPos(P), \ posColor(P, red),$$
$$leafPos(L, P), \ lwc(L, W, C)$$

where $posCost(0) =^\$ Cost$ and $posCost(P) =^\$ posCost(P-1) + W$ are constraint atoms.

We may benefit from the CLINGCON encodings when weights, cardinalities, and maximum cost of a given weighted-sequence problem are "large" integers. In such cases, any CLINGO encoding (that we were able to come up with) faces the *grounding bottleneck*. The size of the grounded CLINGO program heavily depends on the integer values provided by the problem specification. On the other hand, the size of the corresponding grounded CLINGCON program is only affected by these integer values to a small degree or, even, not affected at all.

5   Experimental Analysis

We first describe hardware specifications, the instance generation method, and the procedures used to perform all experiments. Then we discuss the experimental results reported.

Experiments were performed concurrently on several identical machines, each with a single-core 3.60GHz Pentium 4 CPU and 3Gb of RAM, and running Ubuntu Linux version 10.04. Experiments were performed with CLINGO version 3.0.3 and CLINGCON version 0.1.2.

Instance generation is driven by two inputs: the number of leaves in the instance, n, and the maximum value of a weight and cardinality of a single leaf, v. First, the set S of n leaves is created by generating random weights $w_0, \ldots, w_{n-1}$ and cardinalities $c_0, \ldots, c_{n-1}$ so that $0 \leq w_i, c_i \leq v$. For all instances in SMALL we used $v = 12$ and $n = 10$. For all instances in LARGE we used $v = 100$ and $n = 8$.

As leaves are created they are assigned a unique position in a sequence M. Positions 1 through $n - 1$ in M are then randomly assigned colors *green*, *red*, or *blue*. We calculate the total cost m of the resulting colored sequence M and use it, together with S, as an instance to the weighted-sequence problem, denoted by $[S, m]$.

Thirty random problem instances generated in the way described above form the first set of instances, called *easy*, in the SMALL and in the LARGE sets, respectively. Clearly, all of these instances are satisfiable.

To create harder instances required an encoding and a solver. We chose the encoding SEQ++ along with CLINGCON. We proceeded by starting with an instance $[S, m]$ in the set of easy instances. We used CLINGCON to solve it, and if the instance was satisfiable, we calculated the tree cost for the solution found, $\hat{m}$, (clearly, $\hat{m} \leq m$). We then repeated the process for the instance $[S, \hat{m}-1]$. When $[S, \hat{m} - 1]$ was found unsatisfiable, it indicated that $\hat{m}$ was optimal with respect to S, and $\hat{m} - 1$ made the set S "barely" unsatisfiable (to be more precise, we used a version of binary search here to speed the process up). Instances obtained in this way from the *easy* instances formed the sets of *optimal* and *unsatisfiable* instances, respectively. The instances $[S, \hat{m} + 5]$ formed the set of *hard* instances in the SMALL SET, and the instances $[S, \hat{m} + 50]$ formed the set of *hard* instances in the LARGE SET. As before, we constructed groups of thirty hard, optimal and unsatisfiable instances for both SMALL and LARGE sets.

We used each instance with all encodings we considered. A time limit of 1500 seconds (25:00 minutes) was enforced for each instance. From each solve the grounding time, solving time, solution, the number of choices and the sizes of ground theories were recorded for further study.

We now present and discuss the results of our experiments. Due to space limits only summary results are presented here. For the encodings we used and the complete results, we refer to http://www.csr.uky.edu/WeightedSequence/. The first two tables, Table 1 and Table 2, concern SMALL and LARGE sets of instances, respectively. In the case of each set we considered its easy, hard, optimal and unsat subsets, and for each subset included a row in the table. There are two groups of columns in each table, one for CLINGO and the other one for CLINGCON. The columns in each group represent encodings DECL, SEQ, SEQ+ and SEQ++. Each entry in the table contains either the average running time of CLINGO or CLINGCON, respectively, for the set of 30 instances in the corresponding easy, hard optimal and unsat subset. However, if for at least one instance in the group we had a timeout, instead of the average running time we report the number of timeouts in the group.

Table 1. SMALL Instances

	CLINGO				CLINGCON			
Instance	DECL	SEQ	SEQ+	SEQ++	DECL	SEQ	SEQ+	SEQ++
Easy	0.88	0.75	0.81	0.86	0.02	0.06	0.05	0.15
Hard	4.01	1.19	1.77	2.97	to=7	9.50	4.34	5.04
Optimal	26.28	15.75	20.41	15.04	to=27	253.30	203.75	34.57
Unsat	180.62	193.79	162.88	27.88	to=30	to=25	to=17	128.63

Table 2. LARGE Instances

	CLINGO				CLINGCON			
Instance	DECL	SEQ	SEQ+	SEQ++	DECL	SEQ	SEQ+	SEQ++
Easy	21.76	15.38	15.35	16.73	0.01	0.07	0.07	0.08
Hard	22.75	13.96	14.41	23.36	to=4	1.76	1.18	0.72
Optimal	to=1	97.38	to=1	101.95	to=24	46.58	23.49	5.07
Unsat	to=12	to=12	to=10	248.81	to=30	189.38	92.29	10.43

Before we discuss the results as they pertain to comparisons of CLINGO versus CLINGCON, and to the role of explicit modeling of additional domain knowledge, we note that both tables show the increasing hardness of our instances as we move from easy to hard to optimal and, finally, to unsat ones. That is, the tables support the soundness of our approach to generate increasingly harder instances by lowering the bound for the total weight.

Effectiveness of search. We consider first the SMALL set of instances. When run on easy instances in that group, CLINGCON outperforms CLINGO. However, already on hard instances, the situation reverses. CLINGCON running times are worse and it times out on seven instances under the encoding DECL. The trend continues when we move on to optimal and unsat instances — CLINGCON performance deteriorates. The results suggest that for problems in that group, due to relatively small integer parameters used, neither the time needed for the compete grounding nor the size of the ground theory seem to have much negative effect on CLINGO, whose efficient and highly optimized search techniques more than compensate for that. On the other hand, worse (and, in the case of optimal and unsat instances, significantly worse) performance of CLINGCON suggests its search techniques lag behind those of CLINGO.

Our results provide also support to the claim of the importance of constraint learning while solving. CLINGO exploits sophisticated conflict-driven clause learning algorithm. The encodings we considered differ in that they represent progressively more and more problem constraints. The encoding used has very limited effect on the performance of CLINGO, when it is run on instances from the SMALL set. The only exception comes from the SEQ++ encoding resulting in a much better performance of CLINGO when run on the group of unsat instances. On the other hand, the choice of the encoding has a major effect on CLINGCON. The results concerning instances in the LARGE set (Table 2), show a similar behavior. The effect of extra domain knowledge on the performance of CLINGO (while no longer negligible) is still much smaller that the effect it has on CLINGCON.

Thus, it seems that search techniques of CLINGO can learn some or even a major portion of the missing constraints, while CLINGCON search methods are not effective enough in that respect, as they benefit greatly when the constraints are provided explicitly.

Next, we note that instances in SMALL set where generated for $n = 10$ leaves (tables in the join problem), while in the LARGE set for $n = 8$. The problems in the LARGE set turn out to be easier for CLINGCON than those in the SMALL set. This suggests that CLINGCON handles increasing weights well but is more sensitive to changes in other parameters (line n). This observation is yet another indication of CLINGCON's weaker search techniques on the ASP side.

Lastly, we note briefly that while the additional constraints modeled explicitly in SEQ and SEQ+ encodings do help CLINGCON, it is the symmetry-breaking constraint used in SEQ++ that is particularly beneficial. In fact, it also seems to have a significant positive effect on CLINGO, as evidenced by the performance of CLINGO on unsat instances in the set LARGE (cf. Table 2).

In summary, our discussion above shows that there seem to be much room for improvement as concerns overall performance of search in CASP tools such as CLINGCON. It shows that sophisticated search techniques can compensate for some of the "derived" constraints not explicitly present in the problem statement, but also that some types of constraints, such as symmetry-breaking, make a difference even if solvers use a sophisticated constraint-learning algorithms.

Scalability: The results from Tables 3 and 4 provide evidence that CLINGCON scales up better than CLINGO as weights go up. To argue that we recall (cf. Table 1) that for the instances in the SMALL set, CLINGCON performs worse than CLINGO (except for instances that are easy). However when we move to instances in the LARGE set, the situation changes (cf. Table 2). Except for the encoding DECL, where it timed out frequently and much more often than CLINGO (as we argued above, due to its inability to learn useful constraints), CLINGCON completed the computation for every instance under SEQ, SEQ+ and SEQ++ encodings. CLINGO, on the other hand, times out on 23 instances under these three encodings (12 unsat instances under SEQ, one optimal and 10 unsat under SEQ+) and when it does not time out, its running times are much worse than those of CLINGO (one order of magnitude difference for the encoding SEQ++.

These results suggest that CLINGCON successfully addresses the grounding bottleneck resulting from large integer domains. To see this let us consider the sizes of ground theories (measured as the numbers of clauses and reported as averages over 30 instances that form each group).

First, we note that the sizes of CLINGCON encoding do not vary as we move from easy down to unsat instances. It is because these CLINGCON instantiates only non-weight, non-cardinality variables (such as the number of leaves and the number of colored positions) and they do not change. The only parameter that distinguishes between the encodings, the bound on the weight, m, does not affect CLINGCON grounding size as, unlike in the CLINGO encodings, no "groundable" variable in CLINGCON encodings ranges over the domain $[0..m]$.

Table 3. Sizes of ground programs: SMALL Instances

	CLINGO				CLINGCON			
Instance	DECL	SEQ	SEQ+	SEQ++	DECL	SEQ	SEQ+	SEQ++
Easy	75268	62739	63099	64719	575	539	899	2519
Hard	29326	26588	26948	28568	575	539	899	2519
Optimal	26842	24495	24855	26475	575	539	899	2519
Unsat	26350	24077	24437	26057	575	539	899	2519

Table 4. Sizes of ground programs: LARGE Instances

	CLINGO				CLINGCON			
Instance	DECL	SEQ	SEQ+	SEQ++	DECL	SEQ	SEQ+	SEQ++
Easy	1546714	1162451	1162619	1163207	383	358	526	1114
Hard	434237	377120	377288	377876	383	358	526	1114
Optimal	350933	308383	308551	309139	383	358	526	1114
Unsat	349336	307052	307220	307808	383	358	526	1114

This brings us to the second observation, directly relevant for our study. Grounded CLINGCON encodings are much smaller than those resulting from the CLINGO ones. For instances in the LARGE set, the ground programs considered by clingo are quite large (hundreds of thousands of ground rules) and when constraints become tight (for optimal and unsat problems), very hard for CLINGO to process successfully within the time bounds set.

Next, we note that, not surprisingly, it is not only the size of the grounded program that matters. Easy instances result, after grounding, in much larger programs than unsat ones but as the constrains are not tight, the search process can terminate quickly. It is the combination of a large size and tight constraints that slows CLINGO down. Tight constraints are clearly a problem for CLINGCON, too (cf. the tables reporting the running times). But since the size of the ground theory it has to deal with is low, it does not hamper its performance on the ASP side of search, and the types of constraint problems CLINGCON delegates to GECODE are handled well (at least for our instances) by that CSP solver.

6   Conclusions and Future Work

Our experimental findings suggest several observations. Highly tuned ASP search algorithms (specifically, CLINGO) display a similar behavior on both "literal" (DECL) and "sophisticated" (SEQ, SEQ+ and SEQ++) encodings of a weighted-sequence problem (although, as the instances get larger, symmetry-breaking incorporated into SEQ++ seems to start showing a noticeable benefit). The sophisticated encodings impose a number of restrictions on the problem's search space in comparison with the literal encoding and, our results show, for hybrid systems such as CLINGCON (that combines both ASP and CSP techniques in its search), it is of importance. Reduced search space that results can have a significant positive effect on their performance. Thus, our results suggest that the effectiveness of the search procedure used by CLINGCON lags behind that of CLINGO. They show that the problem seems to be with lack of strong learning techniques in CLINGCON. Including extra domain knowledge explicitly into problem representations greatly improves CLINGCON performance.

In the same time, we observed that CLINGCON scales up better than CLINGO and we attribute it to the fact that search in CLINGCON has to process smaller search spaces due to limiting the scope of grounding. Thus, CASP promises to become a milestone in declarative problem solving by providing the means of solving ASP grounding bottleneck. However, based on our work, we believe that to reach its full potential, CASP search methods need to incorporate learning to a much larger degree than they do so now. Certainly, other factors may be of importance, too, such as the enhanced communication between ASP and CSP processes while solving. The effect of those factors still needs to be evaluated.

We also stress that when we claim better scalability of CLINGCON we have in mind scalability with the size of weights (and cardinalities) going up. When we increase the number of leaves (and keep weight small) we expect the picture most likely would be different simply because of stronger search methods implemented in CLINGO.

This research focused on a single problem. In order to study the degree to which our findings are generizable, in the future work we will consider additional problems with large integer parameters and subject them to a similar study. On the other hand, we will also consider in more depth the problem that inspired the benchmark we considered here, the optimal join order problem, and study the effectiveness of ASP/CASP/CSP tools in solving it. This work is already under way.

The integration of ASP and CSP has received significant attention. Much of that research focused on ideas developed in constraint logic programming (CLP) [4,3,14], with the last of these papers presenting a comparison of CLP and ASP systems. CLP tools show significant promise in solving search and optimization problems. In particular, a CLP system B-Prolog[6], was the best solver for the Weight-Assignment Tree benchmark in the Third Answer Set Programming Competition[7]. We intend to extend our study to include CLP systems such as B-Prolog. However, taking directly advantage of the B-Prolog encoding used in the competition is not possible as there are minor differences between the problem that underlies the benchmark and the one we studied here.

Acknowledgments. We are grateful to Philip Cannata for bringing the problem of finding an optimal join order to our attention, to Vladimir Lifschitz and Yuanlin Zhang for useful discussions related to the topic of this work, and to Max Ostrowski for suggestions on CLINGCON encodings. We thank the reviewers for suggesting relevant references. Yuliya Lierler was supported by a CRA/NSF 2010 Computing Innovation Fellowship, Miroslaw Truszczynski by the NSF grant IIS-0913459, and Shaden Smith and Alex Westlund by the NSF REU Supplement to that grant.

---

[6] http://www.probp.com/

[7] The winning B-Prolog encoding can be found at
http://www.sci.brooklyn.cuny.edu/~zhou/asp11/weightAssign.pl

References

1. Balduccini, M.: Representing constraint satisfaction problems in answer set programming. In: Proceedings of ICLP 2009 Workshop on Answer Set Programming and Other Computing Paradigms, ASPOCP 2009 (2009)
2. Brewka, G., Eiter, T., Truszczynski, M.: Answer set programming at a glance. Communications of the ACM (2011), to appear in December 2011
3. Dovier, A., Formisano, A., Pontelli, E.: A Comparison of CLP(FD) and ASP Solutions to NP-Complete Problems. In: Gabbrielli, M., Gupta, G. (eds.) ICLP 2005. LNCS, vol. 3668, pp. 67–82. Springer, Heidelberg (2005)
4. Elkabani, I., Pontelli, E., Son, T.C.: Smodels with CLP and Its Applications: A Simple and Effective Approach to Aggregates in ASP. In: Demoen, B., Lifschitz, V. (eds.) ICLP 2004. LNCS, vol. 3132, pp. 73–89. Springer, Heidelberg (2004)
5. Gebser, M., Kaminski, R., Kaufmann, B., Ostrowski, M., Schaub, T., Thiele, S.: A User Guide to gringo, clasp, clingo and iclingo (2010), http://cdnetworks-us-2.dl.sourceforge.net/project/potassco/potassco _guide/2010-10-04/guide.pdf
6. Gebser, M., Kaufmann, B., Neumann, A., Schaub, T.: Conflict-driven answer set solving. In: Proceedings of 20th International Joint Conference on Artificial Intelligence (IJCAI 2007), pp. 386–392. MIT Press (2007)
7. Gebser, M., Ostrowski, M., Schaub, T.: Constraint Answer Set Solving. In: Hill, P.M., Warren, D.S. (eds.) ICLP 2009. LNCS, vol. 5649, pp. 235–249. Springer, Heidelberg (2009)
8. Gelfond, M., Lifschitz, V.: The stable model semantics for logic programming. In: Kowalski, R., Bowen, K. (eds.) Proceedings of International Logic Programming Conference and Symposium, pp. 1070–1080. MIT Press (1988)
9. Lewis, J.: Cost-Based Oracle Fundamentals. Apress (2005)
10. Lifschitz, V.: Answer set programming and plan generation. Artif. Intell. 138(1-2), 39–54 (2002)
11. Marek, V., Truszczyński, M.: Stable models and an alternative logic programming paradigm. In: The Logic Programming Paradigm: a 25-Year Perspective, pp. 375–398. Springer, Heidelberg (1999)
12. Mellarkod, V.S., Gelfond, M., Zhang, Y.: Integrating answer set programming and constraint logic programming. Annals of Mathematics and Artificial Intelligence (2008)
13. Niemelä, I.: Logic programs with stable model semantics as a constraint programming paradigm. Annals of Mathematics and Artificial Intelligence 25, 241–273 (1999)
14. Dal Palù, A., Dovier, A., Pontelli, E., Rossi, G.: Answer Set Programming with Constraints Using Lazy Grounding. In: Hill, P.M., Warren, D.S. (eds.) ICLP 2009. LNCS, vol. 5649, pp. 115–129. Springer, Heidelberg (2009)

Practical and Methodological Aspects
of the Use of Cutting-Edge ASP Tools

Marcello Balduccini[1] and Yuliya Lierler[2]

[1] Eastman Kodak Company
marcello.balduccini@gmail.com
[2] University of Kentucky
yuliya@cs.utexas.edu

Abstract. In the development of practical applications of answer set programming (ASP), encodings that use well-established solvers such as CLASP and DLV are sometimes affected by scalability issues. In those situations, one can resort to more sophisticated ASP tools exploiting, for instance, incremental and constraint ASP. However, today there is no specific methodology for the selection or use of such tools. In this paper we describe how we used such cutting-edge ASP tools on challenging problems from the *Third Answer Set Programming Competition*. We view this paper as a first step in the development of a general methodology for the use of advanced ASP tools.

Keywords: answer set programming, solvers, constraint ASP, incremental ASP.

1 Introduction

The *Third Answer Set Programming Competition – 2011* [1] (ASPCOMP) included a *Model and Solve* track. Within this track the teams were free to choose a specific declarative solver and modeling technique for each problem. Answer set programming (ASP) solvers were the primary focus. Nowadays, there are a number of well-established ASP solvers such as CLASP [6], DLV [8], and cutting-edge solvers based on constraint and incremental ASP (resp., CASP, IASP), such as EZCSP [3] and ICLINGO [5]. Well-established solvers are robust and their use relies on a well-understood programming methodology. On the other hand, in some circumstances the encodings for these systems have scalability issues. The extensions of ASP implemented by the solvers for CASP and IASP aim at overcoming some of these issues. However, today there is no specific methodology for the formalization of knowledge with such new tools, or even for the selection of a suitable tool given the features of a domain.

In this paper we describe how we used CASP and IASP tools to tackle four challenging ASPCOMP benchmarks (*Weight-Assignment, Reverse-Folding, Hydraulic-System-Planning, and Airport-Pickup*). Throughout our description, we provide methodological considerations, both from the perspective of tool selection and of knowledge representation. Although the discussion in this paper is still oriented towards the specific problems we solved, we view this effort as a first, necessary step towards a general methodology for the use of advanced ASP tools.

C. Russo and N.-F. Zhou (Eds.): PADL 2012, LNCS 7149, pp. 78–92, 2012.
© Springer-Verlag Berlin Heidelberg 2012

Our decisions with respect to tool selection and modeling techniques were based on problem statement analysis and performance assessments that we conducted on the training instances available before the competition. Because the number of training instances was rather small – ranging from 5 to 7 – we could not carry out a thorough pre-competition performance assessment. Nonetheless, the evaluation gave us some evidence [4] of the performance yielded by our encodings. After the competition we conducted a post-competition performance assessment described in Section 7.

The structure of this paper is as follows. We begin with a short introduction on ASP, CASP and IASP. Sections 3, 4, 5, and 6 provide the problem statements and the specifications of the encodings for the Weight-Assignment, Reverse-Folding, Hydraulic-System-Planning, and Airport-Pickup benchmarks, respectively. In Section 7 we discuss performance. In the final section we draw conclusions.

2 Background

Because of space considerations, in this section we only provide a short introduction on ASP, CASP and IASP, and refer the reader to [7], [3] and [5], respectively for the syntax and semantics of the corresponding languages.

ASP is a declarative programming paradigm based on the answer set semantics of logic programs [7]. The idea of ASP is to represent a given problem by a program whose answer sets correspond to solutions. A common programming methodology is to design two main parts of a program: *generate* and *test*. The former defines a collection of answer sets, seen as potential solutions. The latter consists of the rules that remove the non-solutions. To distinguish the language in [7] from its extensions, we talk about *pure* ASP, programs, and rules.

CASP extends the syntax and semantics of ASP with constraint processing elements. It allows for new modeling features and novel computational methods that combine traditional ASP procedures with constraint satisfaction (CSP) and constraint logic programming (CLP) algorithms. CASP is especially useful in domains that pose constraints over large numerical values. In such cases, grounding often becomes a bottleneck in the pure ASP approach. EZCSP is an inference engine for CASP that allows a lightweight integration of ASP and constraint programming. In the EZCSP terminology, an *extended answer set* of a CASP program Π, is a pair consisting of an answer set of Π where some of the atoms encode CSP constraints, and of a solution to these CSP constraints. Given a program Π, the EZCSP solver computes one or more of Π's extended answer sets. The solver combines off-the-shelf ASP (e.g., CLASP) and CLP solvers (e.g., BPROLOG, http://www.probp.com/). The architecture is such that first the ASP solver is used to find an answer set A of a given CASP program Π. Then the CSP constraints encoded by A are evaluated by the constraint solver. If the solver determines that the constraints from A are not satisfiable, another answer set is computed and the process repeats. Otherwise, A and a solution found by the constraint solver form an extended answer set. If Π is a pure ASP program then EZCSP behaves as its underlying ASP solver. Conversely, Π may also be a direct encoding of a CSP theory, and in this case EZCSP behaves as its underlying constraint solver.

In certain domains, a numerical parameter can be identified that reflects the size or complexity of a candidate solution. IASP extends pure ASP by allowing one to take advantage of such a parameter (the *growth parameter*). The programmer is given means to denote rules that are independent of the growth parameter (the *base*), rules whose grounding should be computed incrementally in dependence of the value of the parameter (the *cumulative part*), and rules that should be grounded anew for each different value of the parameter considered (the *volatile part*). An incremental answer set solver such as ICLINGO first attempts to find a solution for a minimum value of the growth parameter. If unsuccessful, it iteratively (1) increments this value, incrementally grows the grounding of the cumulative part of the program, (2) re-grounds the volatile part, and (3) checks again for a solution.

3 Weight-Assignment Benchmark

In the Weight-Assignment Benchmark, a binary tree with n leaves is considered, such that (1) the leaves are pairs of integers $\langle weight, cardinality \rangle$; (2) the right child of an inner node is a leaf; (3) each inner node is a pair $\langle color, weight \rangle$, where *color* is green, red, or blue; (4) the inner nodes are numbered from 1 to $n - 1$; node $n - 1$ is the root node; the left child of each inner node i is inner node $i - 1$. The weight of an inner node k is computed as follows: (1) if the color of k is green, then $weight(k)$ is the sum of the weight and cardinality of k's right child; (2) if the color of k is red, then its weight is the sum of the weight of its right and left children; (3) if the color of k is blue, then its weight is the sum of the cardinality of its right child and of the weight of its left child. The task is to verify that there is a tree formed by the given leaves in accordance with (1-4) so that the total weight of this tree – the sum of the weights of its inner nodes – is less than or equal to a given integer *maximum weight*. Problem instances are specified by the relations of the form $leafWeightCard(l, w, c)$, $num(n)$, and $maxWeight(mv)$, where l is a name of the leaf $\langle w, c \rangle$, n is a number of leaves, and mv is a maximum weight. More detailed descriptions of the Weight-Assignment benchmark and also of other benchmarks discussed in this paper are given on the ASPCOMP website [1].

Because of the abundance of constraints over numerical values, i.e., weights and cardinalities of the leaves and inner nodes, this benchmarks lends itself to being solved using EZCSP.

Hybrid ASP-CSP Encoding: let n and mv denote a number of leaves and a maximum weight in a given weight-assignment problem instance, respectively. We say that a leaf l occurs at position $1 \leq p < n$ in the tree if it is the right child of an inner node p. Furthermore, a position of an inner node is identified with a number associated with it, i.e., $1 \dots n - 1$. A leaf occurs at position 0 if it is the left child of an inner node 1. We model the assignment of a leaf to position p by the relation $assignedLeafPos(l, p)$ that denotes that a leaf with the name l is assigned a position p. Set of rules (1) below states that each leaf is assigned a unique position. Relation $innerNodeColor(k, c)$ denotes the fact that inner node k is assigned a color c. Rule (2) states that each inner node (identified by its position) is assigned a single color.

$$1\{assignedLeafPos(L, P) : position(P)\}1 \leftarrow leafWeightCard(L, W, C). \qquad (1)$$
$$\leftarrow assignedLeafPos(L, P), \; assignedLeafPos(L', P), \; L \neq L'.$$

$$1\{innerNodeColor(P, C) : color(C)\}1 \leftarrow position(P), P \neq 0. \qquad (2)$$

The weight of an inner node k is modeled by a CSP variable $weight(k)$, whose value ranges from 0 to mv. In order to simplify the encoding of the constraints, we use CSP variable $weight(0)$ to denote the weight of the leaf at position 0. The corresponding rules are:

$cspvar(weight(K), 0, MV) \leftarrow num(N), K = 0..N - 1, maxWeight(MV).$
$required(weight(0) = W) \leftarrow assignedLeafPos(L, 0), leafWeightCard(L, W, C).$

The first rule declares the CSP variables of the form $weight(k)$. The other rule encodes a CSP constraint that determines the value of variable $weight(0)$ to be the weight of the leaf assigned position 0. The constraints on the weights of the inner nodes are encoded by statements such as:

$$required(weight(P) = W + weight(P')) \leftarrow$$
$$position(P), P \neq 0, P' = P - 1, innerNodeColor(P, red), \quad (3)$$
$$assignedLeafPos(L, P), leafWeightCard(L, W, C).$$

To compute the total weight of a tree, we introduce a set of auxiliary CSP variables of the form $innerWeight(k)$, where k ranges from 1 to $n - 1$. For every k in that range, variable $innerWeight(k)$ equals $weight(k)$:

$cspvar(innerWeight(K), 0, MV) \leftarrow num(N), K = 1..N - 1, maxWeight(MV).$
$required(innerWeight(K) = weight(K)) \leftarrow num(N), K = 1..N - 1.$
$required(sum([innerWeight/1], \leq, MV)) \leftarrow maxWeight(MV).$

The last rule encodes a CSP constraint stating that the sum of the weights of the inner nodes of the tree must be less than or equal to mv. We denote the program consisting of the rules discussed so far by $\Pi_1(WA)$.

Encoding Analysis: in program $\Pi_1(WA)$, the generate part consists of the rules in (1) and (2). The rest of the rules form the test part. Note that generation is formed by pure ASP rules whereas testing is formulated using rules that contain CSP variables. Recall the general architecture of the EZCSP system discussed in Section 2. It is not difficult to see that in the worst-case scenario (for instance, when the problem is unsatisfiable) EZCSP will generate and evaluate every possible combination of leaf-position/inner node-color assignments during its search process. To avoid such behavior we restate the generate part of the program so that the CSP solver of the EZCSP system is responsible for both generate and test. Thus the encoding we discuss next can be viewed as a CSP formalization of the weight-assignment problem by means of a CASP language. We denote this encoding by $\Pi_2(WA)$.

CSP Formalization by Means of CASP: we begin by modeling the assignment of a leaf to a position p by the CSP variable $assignedLeaf(p)$. Since CSP variables have numerical values, we map the name l of a leaf $\langle w, c \rangle$ (given by $leafWeightCard(l, w, c)$) to an integer id ranging from 1 to n and add an auxiliary fact $leafId(l, id)$ to a program. The EZCSP declaration of $assignedLeaf(p)$ is:

$$cspvar(assignedLeaf(P), 1, N) \leftarrow position(P), num(N). \quad (4)$$

The fact that a leaf can only be assigned one position is compactly enforced by means of a global constraint $all\_different$, encoded by

$$required(all\_different([assignedLeaf/1])). \quad (5)$$

where the expression $[assignedLeaf/1]$ denotes the list of the CSP variables formed by function symbol $assignedLeaf$ with arity 1. Rules (4) and (5) are the counterparts of (1) in $\Pi_1(WA)$. The statement

$$cspvar(innerNodeColor(P), 0, 2) \leftarrow position(P). \tag{6}$$

declares a CSP variable $innerNodeColor(k)$ for each inner node k; the value of the variable denotes the color assigned to k that ranges between 0 (representing color red) and 2 (representing blue). The association between a color and its identifier is encoded by a set of facts of the form $colorId(c, id)$, where c is red, blue or green, and id is its identifier. The declaration of $innerNodeColor(k)$ is the counterpart of rule (2). As in $\Pi_1(WA)$, the weight of an inner node k is modeled by a CSP variable $weight(k)$. The variable declaration remains the same, but the encoding of the requirements on $weight(k)$ is different. For instance, rule (3) becomes:

$$required((innerNodeColor(P) = REDID \wedge assignedLeaf(P) = ID) \rightarrow$$
$$weight(P) = W + weight(P')) \leftarrow$$
$$position(P),\ P \neq 0,\ P' = P - 1,$$
$$colorId(red, REDID),\ leafId(L, ID),\ leafWeightCard(L, W, C).$$

The rules for $innerWeight$ are reformulated similarly. In order to improve performance, the encoding also contains constraints that provide bounds for the value of the weight of an inner node *independently of the color of the node*, such as:

$$required(assignedLeaf(P) = ID \rightarrow weight(P) \geq$$
$$min(W + C, min(W + weight(P'), C + weight(P')))) \leftarrow$$
$$position(P),\ P \neq 0,\ P' = P - 1,\ leafId(L, ID),\ leafWeightCard(L, W, C).$$

4   Reverse-Folding Benchmark

In the Reverse-Folding benchmark, one manipulates a sequence of n pairwise connected segments located on a 2D plane in order to take the sequence from the initial configuration to the goal configuration specified. The ordering of the sequence and the fact that the segments are connected to each other allows one to label each end point of a segment either as a starting point or as an ending point. All segments have unary length, and are parallel either to the x-axis or to the y-axis. In the initial configuration, the segments are parallel to the y-axis and oriented so that the sequence extends in the direction of the positive y-axis. The sequence is manipulated by rotating a segment around its starting point by 90 degree (in either direction). This action is called pivot move. A pivot move on a segment causes the segments that follow it to rotate around the same center of rotation. Concurrent pivot moves are prohibited. At the end of a pivot move, the segments in the sequence must not intersect. In the Reverse-Folding problem, one is given the number n of segments (relation $length$), the goal configuration (relation $fold(i, x, y)$, where $1 \leq i \leq n$ and x, y are the coordinates of the ith starting point, or of the ending point of the last segment for $i = n$), and an integer t (relation $time$). The task is to find a sequence of exactly t pivot moves, which produces the goal configuration from the initial configuration, satisfying the constraints cited above. A solution is encoded as a set of atoms of the form $pivot(t, i, r)$, saying that the tth pivot move rotates the ith segment either clockwise ($r = clock$) or counterclockwise ($r = anticlock$).

Simple Encoding: In writing an encoding that solves this benchmark, the first thing that became apparent is that a minimum number of necessary pivot moves can be inferred directly by observing the structure of the goal configuration. If two segments are at an angle in the goal configuration, it is not difficult to prove that every solution to the problem instance must contain a pivot move that rotates the second segment of the pair. In order to infer such moves, we first define a relation $segDirection(i, d, o)$, which intuitively states that the ith segment in the goal sequence has direction d and orientation o. For example, the rules for the segments parallel to the x-axis are:

$$segDirection(I, horiz, plus) \leftarrow X2 > X1, \; fold(I, X1, Y), \; fold(I + 1, X2, Y).$$
$$segDirection(I, horiz, minus) \leftarrow X2 < X1, \; fold(I, X1, Y), \; fold(I + 1, X2, Y).$$

Next, we define relation $foldDirection(i, d)$, intuitively saying that in the goal configuration the ith segment is aligned with its predecessor ($r = none$), or rotated clockwise or counterclockwise with respect to it ($r = clock$ and $r = anticlock$, respectively). The rules for $r \in \{none, clock\}$ are:

$$foldDirection(I, none) \leftarrow segDirection(I - 1, D, O), \; segDirection(I, D, O).$$
$$foldDirection(I, clock) \leftarrow clockFold(D1, O1, D2, O2),$$
$$segDirection(I - 1, D1, O1), \; segDirection(I, D2, O2).$$
$$clockFold(vert, plus, horiz, plus). \; clockFold(horiz, plus, vert, minus). \; \ldots$$

Finally, relation $requiredFold(i, r)$ says that the ith segment must be rotated clockwise or counterclockwise:

$$requiredFold(I, R) \leftarrow R \neq none, \; foldDirection(I, R).$$

In most cases, performing the pivot moves beginning from the end of the sequence produces a solution. In this case, the pivot moves can be determined by the rules:

$$pivot(1, I, R) \leftarrow first(I), \; requiredFold(I, R).$$
$$pivot(T1, I1, R1) \leftarrow pivot(T, I2, R2), \; T1 = T + 1, \; next(I1, I2)$$
$$requiredFold(I1, R1), \; requiredFold(I2, R2).$$

where $first(i)$ and $next(i_1, i_2)$ enumerate the segments that are to be rotated, beginning from the one closest to the end of the sequence. Because a solution to the Reverse-Folding problem is required to contain exactly the specified number of moves, it may happen that extra, irrelevant moves need to be generated. This can be achieved by alternating clockwise and counterclockwise rotations of segment 1:

$$pivot(T1, 1, clock) \leftarrow numRequiredFolds(R), \; time(T),$$
$$T1 > R, \; T1 \leq T, \; (T1 - R) \bmod 2 = 1.$$

Relation $numRequiredFolds(r)$ says that r required folds were identified in the goal configuration. The rule for $anticlock$ is similar. Next, we ensure that there are no overlapping segments during the execution of the moves. To achieve this, we project the effects of each move on the segments and check for an overlap. To reduce the size of the grounding, we consider separately the effects of the rotations on the x and y coordinates of the end points of the segments. The information is encoded by $foldx(t, i, p)$ and $foldy(t, i, p)$, saying that the x (resp., y) coordinate of the ith end point before move t is p. The effect of a move on the x coordinate of a segment is encoded by:

$$foldx(T1, I, Y - Y1 + X1) \leftarrow foldy(T, I, Y), \; pivot(T, I1, clock), \; I \geq I1,$$
$$T1 = T + 1, \; foldx(T, I1, X1), \; foldy(T, I1, Y1).$$

$$foldx(T1, I, Y1 - Y + X1) \leftarrow foldy(T, I, Y), \; pivot(T, I1, anticlock), \; I \geq I1, \qquad (7)$$
$$T1 = T + 1, \; foldx(T, I1, X1), \; foldy(T, I1, Y1).$$

$$foldx(T1, I, X) \leftarrow foldx(T, I, X), \; pivot(T, I1, R), \; I < I1, \; T1 = T + 1.$$

The first two rules state the effect of clockwise and counterclockwise rotations on the segments that follow the point where the rotation is applied. The last rule states that the x coordinate of the other end points is unchanged. The definition of $foldy$ is similar. The following denial states that overlaps are not allowed to occur:

$$\leftarrow foldx(T, I1, X1),\ foldy(T, I1, Y1),\ foldx(T, I2, X1), foldy(T, I2, Y1),$$
$$I1 < I2,\ pivot(T-1, I3, R),\ I2 > I3.$$

The two inequalities in the denial are aimed at reducing the size of the grounding, the former by exploiting symmetry considerations, and the second by preventing the denial from considering segments that were not affected by the pivot move. Finally, relations $foldx$ and $foldy$ are used to ensure that the goal configuration is eventually reached:

$$\leftarrow time(T),\ T1 = T+1,\ X1 \neq X2,\ foldx(T1, I, X1),\ fold(I, X2, Y2). \qquad (8)$$
$$\leftarrow time(T),\ T1 = T+1,\ Y1 \neq Y2,\ foldy(T1, I, Y1),\ fold(I, X2, Y2).$$

The program consisting of the rules discussed so far will be denoted by $\Pi_1(RF)$.

Encoding Analysis: Unfortunately, the presence of the pivot moves identified by $\Pi_1(RF)$ is a necessary, but not always sufficient, condition to find a solution. In some cases, executing the pivot moves beginning from the end of the sequence of segments causes some segments to overlap, but the moves can be re-ordered so that no overlap exists. In particular, it is often possible to find a solution by postponing one (suitable) pivot move to the end of the sequence of moves. We call this the *delayed-move* case. (To keep this presentation simple, other cases are not discussed.)

The delayed-move case can be handled by adding a choice rule for the selection of one delayed move and modifying the definition of relation $pivot$ so that the delayed move is executed at the end of the sequence of moves. One such choice rule is:

$$0\{\ delayed(I) : requiredFold(I, D)\ \}1.$$

Let $\Pi_2(RF)$ denote the modified program. The computation for $\Pi_2(RF)$ is substantially slower than the computation for $\Pi_1(RF)$, with the performance of the grounding process particularly affected. In $\Pi_2(RF)$ the grounder does not handle efficiently the rules involving $foldx$ and $foldy$, whose arguments have rather large numerical domains. Recall that the definitions of $foldx$ and $foldy$ rely on relation $pivot$, whose definition in $\Pi_2(RF)$ differs from the one in $\Pi_1(RF)$. Hence, we created a variant $\Pi_3(RF)$ of $\Pi_2(RF)$ that takes advantage of CASP capabilities of EZCSP by encoding constraints on $foldx$ and $foldy$ using CSP, such as:

$$required(foldx^\gamma(T1, I) = foldy^\gamma(T, I) - foldy^\gamma(T, I1) + foldx^\gamma(T, I1)) \leftarrow$$
$$pivot(T, I1, clock),\ T1 = T+1,\ I \geq I1.$$

5   Hydraulic-System-Planning Benchmark

In the Hydraulic-System-Planning benchmark, a hydraulic system is viewed as a directed graph G. The nodes of G represent tanks, jets, and junctions. Tanks are either empty or full. Each link between nodes is labeled by a valve. A valve can be opened (by action *switchon*). Valves that are *stuck* cannot be opened. A node of G is called *pressurized* in state S if it is a full tank or if there exists a path from some full tank to this node such that all valves on the edges of this path are open. Furthermore, no path connecting two tanks exists and every jet is connected to at least one tank. An input for this benchmark consists of a graph G, a specification of which tanks are full and which valves are stuck (all valves are initially closed), and a set of *goal jets*. The goal is to find a shortest sequence of *switchon* actions to pressurize the goal jets. In the sequence, no actions can be executed concurrently.

The challenge in this benchmark is that the length of the sequence of actions must be minimized. From a methodological standpoint, we approached the problem by first writing a pure ASP encoding, and then addressing its performance by transforming it into an ICLINGO program. For later reference, we label various sets of rules as we introduce them. We define an important notion of *viable path* as a path in G such that no valve along the path is stuck. Relation $viablePath(j, n)$ formalizes this notion recursively, restricting it to the goal jets for efficiency:

$$viablePath(J, J) \leftarrow goal(J).$$
$$viablePath(J, N') \leftarrow goal(J), \; viablePath(J, N), \; link(N', N, V), \; not \; stuck(V).$$

The following rules ensure that there is a viable path to a full tank for every goal jet:

$$canPressurize(J) \leftarrow goal(J), \; full(T), \; viablePath(J, T).$$
$$\leftarrow goal(J), \; not \; canPressurize(J).$$

Let $\Pi_1(HP)$ denote all of the rules above. Next, we address the planning task in two steps. In the first step we find the length of the shortest viable paths between each goal jet and a full tank, and in the second step we determine a sequence of actions that opens the paths of the given length. We begin by defining the notion of reachability in a given number of steps, which again we restrict to goal jets for performance:

$$reachable(J, J, 0) \leftarrow goal(J).$$
$$reachable(J, N', S) \leftarrow$$
$$goal(J), \; reachable(J, N, S - 1), \; link(N', N, V), \; not \; stuck(V). \tag{9}$$

Using this relation, we can now define the notion of a *pressure path* of length k between goal jet j and full tank t, i.e. a viable path of length k between j and t:

$$pressurePath(J, T, S) \leftarrow goal(J), \; full(T), \; reachable(J, T, S). \tag{10}$$

We denote the set of rules (9) and (10) by $\Pi_2(HP)$. Next we describe the set of rules that form $\Pi_3(HP)$. The length of the shortest paths from goal jet j to any full tank is defined by:

$$shortestPath(J, Len) \leftarrow$$
$$goal(J), \; Len = \# min[\, pressurePath(J, T, L) = L : full(T)\,].$$

Note that there may be multiple shortest paths for a goal jet. Therefore, we determine a single shortest path for each jet. We begin by defining the notion of valves that *can be possibly* used to open a shortest path for a given jet. We encode this notion recursively using relation $poss\_use\_valve(j, n, v, s)$, which states that at the end of the path from j to node n of length s, valve v can be possibly used:

$$poss\_use\_valve(J, N, V, S - 1) \leftarrow goal(J), \; shortestPath(J, S), \; full(T), link(T, N, V),$$
$$reachable(J, T, S), \; reachable(J, N, S - 1).$$
$$poss\_use\_valve(J, N2, V2, S - 1) \leftarrow goal(J), \; poss\_use\_valve(J, N1, V1, S),$$
$$reachable(J, N2, S - 1), \; link(N1, N2, V2).$$

The recursion intuitively enumerates the valves moving from a tank towards a goal jet. The first rule encodes the base case and says that if the shortest paths for jet j have length s and a full tank t is reachable from j in s steps, then for any node n connected to t and reachable from j in $s - 1$ steps, the connecting valve v can be used at the end of the path from j to n. The second rule states that, if valve v_1 can be possibly used at the end of the path from j to n_1 of length s, then for any node n_2 reachable from j in $s - 1$ steps and directly connected to n_1 by valve v_2, v_2 can be possibly used at the end of the path to n_2 of length $s - 1$.

The selection of valves to be used is also performed recursively. We begin by considering, for each jet j, all paths of length 0. We select exactly one valve among the valves that can be possibly used at the end of each of those paths:

$$1\{ \ use\_valve(J, N, V, 0) : poss\_use\_valve(J, N, V, 0) \ \}1 \leftarrow goal(J).$$

Next, given the decision to use valve v at the end of the path from j to n of length s, we identify the node, n', connected to n by v, and select exactly one valve among the ones that can be possibly used at the end of the path from j to n':

$$1\{ \ use\_valve(J, N2, V2, S + 1) : poss\_use\_valve(J, N2, V2, S + 1)$$
$$: link(N2, N1, V1) \ : not \ tank(N2) \ \}1 \leftarrow$$
$$goal(J), \ shortestPath(J, MS), \ use\_valve(J, N1, V1, S), \ S < MS - 1.$$

Finally, we generate the corresponding $switchon$ actions. Because the actions cannot be executed concurrently, we produce a global ordering of the actions. This is achieved by, first, ordering the goal jets (in lexicographic order according to their name). Second, we schedule the execution of the actions for the first jet, followed by the actions for the second jet, and so on. We define relation $num\_prevActions(j, n)$, which states that n is the number of actions to be executed before the first action for goal jet j takes place:

$$num\_prevActions(J, NP) \leftarrow goal(J),$$
$$NP = \#sum[\ shortestPath(J1, N) = N : J1 < J\ ].$$

At this point, the $switchon$ actions for a jet j are scheduled to progressively open the path beginning from the tank that has been selected to feed j:

$$switchon(V, S - LS - 1 + NP) \leftarrow goal(J), \ shortestPath(J, S),$$
$$num\_prevActions(J, NP), \ use\_valve(J, N, V, LS).$$

This concludes the description of $\Pi_3(HP)$.

Encoding Analysis: It is not difficult to see that the program $\Pi(HP)$ consisting of $\Pi_1(HP) - \Pi_3(HP)$ may not scale well. As the size of the graph grows, the number of possible paths of arbitrary length may grow dramatically, leading to an explosion in the grounding. However, because the goal is to find a shortest path for each goal jet, the search performed by $\Pi(HP)$ could be intuitively done in an incremental fashion. Among the ASP tools available, ICLINGO[5] offers a simple way to deal with programs that involve an incremental search, and program $\Pi(HP)$ lends itself to being extended to exploit the features of ICLINGO.

IASP Encoding: First, we identify the set $\Pi_b'(HP)$ of rules that define the base of the program. $\Pi_b'(HP)$ consists of $\Pi_1(HP)$ together with the first rule in (9). The presence of $\Pi_1(HP)$ is particularly important from the point of view of performance, because it allows to identify a problem instance that has no solution without performing any iteration of the search. Let s denote the growth parameter. The cumulative part, $\Pi_c'(HP)$, of the program includes a number of elements. First, $\Pi_c'(HP)$ includes a modification of the second rule in (9) and rule (10) where these two rules contain an additional condition $S = s$. This allows us to restrict the grounding of the rules to only the paths of the length considered by the current iteration of the search. *The semantics of the rules changes so that now they define, respectively, reachability in exactly s steps and the presence of a pressure path of length s. The overall meaning of the relations remains unchanged because the cumulative part of an ICLINGO program is implicitly quantified over all of the possible values of the growth parameter.*

Next, we add to $\Pi_c'(HP)$ rules aimed at detecting when the length of the shortest paths for all goal jets can be computed. This detection was not needed in the pure ASP program, but is used here to terminate the iterations of the search process:

$$\neg orphan(J, s) \leftarrow goal(J),\ S \leq s,\ pressurePath(J, T, S).$$
$$orphans(s) \leftarrow goal(J),\ \text{not } \neg orphan(J, s).$$
$$all\_jets\_fed(s) \leftarrow \text{not } orphans(s).$$

The key notion defined by the above rules is that of an *orphan* goal jet. A goal jet j is orphan of rank s if no pressure path of length s or less exists for j. The second rule determines if there are still orphans of rank s. The last rule states that $all\_jets\_fed(s)$ holds if no orphans of rank s exist.

Finally, $\Pi_c'(HP)$ includes $\Pi_3(HP)$ modified by adding to each rule the condition $all\_jets\_fed(s)$. This modification ensures that the rules are considered only if pressure paths of length s or less exist for every goal jet.

The volatile part $\Pi_v'(HP)$ of the program contains the denial $\leftarrow orphans(s)$, which states that it is impossible for the iterative search to terminate at step s if orphans of rank s exist. This constraint forces the iterative search to continue until pressure paths have been found for every goal jet. Once these have been found, the rules in $\Pi_c'(HP)$ select a shortest path for each goal jet and determine a suitable sequence of *switchon* operation. By $\Pi'(HP)$ we denote the union of $\Pi_b'(HP)$, $\Pi_c'(HP)$, and $\Pi_v'(HP)$. Answer sets of $\Pi'(HP)$ encode solutions to the problem instances.

6   Airport-Pickup Benchmark

In the Airport-Pickup benchmark, one must solve resource-based planning problems that involve objects moving between locations. More precisely, a city is represented by a weighted undirected graph G. The nodes of G represent locations where exactly two of them are airports. Some locations may contain gas stations. The arcs of G represent direct connections between the locations and are labeled with an integer corresponding to the amount of gas required to travel between them. The problem also involves a set of vehicles and a set of passengers. A vehicle can initially be at any location, and can travel from its current location, l, to any location connected to l as long as it has enough gas. A problem instance specifies the amount of gas in each vehicle originally. Each passenger is initially located at an airport, and his goal is to reach the other airport. Passengers can move between locations only by vehicle. Vehicles can pick up and drop off passengers, but only one passenger at a time can ride a vehicle. Finally, vehicles can fill their tanks at a gas station. The goal is to find a sequence of actions that takes each passenger to its goal destination.

This benchmark is interesting because the large size of the corresponding search space makes it difficult to solve it efficiently using a single call to a solver. In our initial evaluation we could not find any such "monolithic" encoding that would scale to the training instances provided for ASPCOMP. For this reason, we decided to adopt an approach in which the problem is divided into sub-problems, and multiple calls to solvers are used. It is important to stress that this approach, although not frequently discussed in the literature, can be extremely useful in practical applications of ASP.

Our solution of the Airport-Pickup benchmark is based on an architecture consisting of a main module, tackling the overall search problem, and of a number of auxiliary modules, to which the main module delegates the solution of various sub-problems. This allows us to limit the size of the grounding of the programs, and at the same time makes it possible to use the language/solver best suited for each module. The main module, $\Pi_1(AP)$, employs an extension of ASP developed for controlling the interactions among modules [2]. To keep the presentation simple we abstract from the technical details of the control structure, and describe $\Pi_1(AP)$ as a pure ASP program.

The first task performed by the main module is a preliminary check to ensure that, in the initial state of the domain, each passenger can be reached by at least one vehicle, and that the vehicle can then reach the passenger's destination. (Reachability also takes into account the amount of gas initially in the vehicle and the amount of gas needed to travel between locations.) This check is done by formulating a sub-problem $\Pi_2(AP, p)$ for each passenger p, so that $\Pi_2(AP, p)$ is consistent if-and-only-if p can be reached by some vehicle and then driven to his destination. The main module's task is then reduced to verifying whether all $\Pi_2(AP, p)$'s are consistent. The passenger that is to be considered is specified by an atom of the form $selected(p)$. The main rules of $\Pi_2(AP, p)$ are:

$$1\{\ assigned(P, V) : vehicle(V, M)\ \}1 \leftarrow selected(P).$$
$$\leftarrow not\ pass\_reachable\_from\_start.$$
$$\leftarrow not\ destination\_reachable\_from\_passenger.$$

$$pass\_reachable\_from\_start \leftarrow p\_location(S),\ reach\_from\_start(S, G).$$

The first rule states that exactly one vehicle should be assigned to drive the selected passenger. The two denials require that the assigned vehicle can reach the passenger from its initial location and can subsequently drive the passenger to his destination. As a result, $\Pi_2(AP, p) \cup \{selected(p)\}$ has an answer set if and only if passenger p can be reached by at least one vehicle that satisfies these requirements. The last rule defines reachability of the passenger in general terms of reachability of a location from the vehicle's initial location (with a certain amount of gas left at the end of the trip). Relation $destination\_reachable\_from\_passenger$ is defined in a similar way. Relation $reach\_from\_start(s, g)$ is defined by the rules:

$reach\_from\_start(S, G) \leftarrow start(S), gas(G).$
$reach\_from\_start(Y, G - C) \leftarrow reach\_from\_start(X, G), connected(X, Y, C), G \geq C.$
$reach\_from\_start(X, T) \leftarrow reach\_from\_start(X, G), gasstation(X), tank(T).$
$start(S) \leftarrow assigned(P, V), vehicle\_at(V, S).$

The relation is formalized recursively. The first rule encodes the base case, and states that the start is reachable without using any gas. The next rule encodes the recursive step, and says that any location connected to the current location is reachable if enough fuel is left in the vehicle's tank; the amount of fuel in the tank at the end of the leg takes into account the cost of driving to the new location. The third rule considers the availability of a gas station and states that, if the current location is reachable from the start and has a gas station, then it is reachable from the start with a full tank left at the end of the trip. The last rule determines the start location of the vehicle currently assigned to the passenger; the rules for relations gas and $tank$ are similar.

If the preliminary test implemented by $\Pi_2(AP, p)$ succeeds, then $\Pi_1(AP)$ proceeds with the next phase of the search. In this phase, $\Pi_1(AP)$ maintains the current locations of passengers and vehicles and the gas level in the tank of each vehicle. The program selects one passenger p and assigns to him a vehicle v capable of taking him to his destination. The state of the domain is then updated according to the effects of driving p to his destination using v. Note that at this stage of the search we are only concerned with final locations of the objects and gas levels, and abstract from the low-level actions that need to be performed to drive p to his destination. At this point, the process repeats: $\Pi_1(AP)$ selects another passenger, assigns him a vehicle, and the search continues.

Whenever no vehicle can be found for driving a currently selected passenger, the search backtracks. To improve performance, the selection of passengers and vehicles is guided by a heuristic that prefers to use vehicles that are already at a passenger's current location. This is implemented by the rules:

$1\{ use\_at\_passenger, \neg use\_at\_passenger \}1 \leftarrow \neg all\_at\_destination.$
$\leftarrow use\_at\_passenger, \text{not } some\_already\_at\_passenger.$
$\#minimize[use\_at\_passenger = 1, \neg use\_at\_passenger = 2].$

The first rule states that if not all passengers are at their destinations, then it is possible to select between using vehicles that are at a passenger's location and vehicles that are not. The second rule states that it is impossible to require the use of a vehicle that is at a passenger's location if no vehicle is at this location. The last rule (from a language extension of CLASP) states that choosing to use vehicles that are not at a passenger's location has a penalty. The selection of a passenger and a vehicle is performed by the rules:

$1\{ assigned(P, V) : passenger(P) : \text{not } at\_destination(P)$
$: vehicle(V, M) : good(V, P) : already\_at\_passenger(V, P) \}1 \leftarrow$
$\neg all\_at\_destination, use\_at\_passenger.$

$1\{ assigned(P, V) : passenger(P) : \text{not } at\_destination(P) : vehicle(V, M)$
$: good(V, P) \}1 \leftarrow \neg all\_at\_destination, \neg use\_at\_passenger.$

Both rules state that exactly one pair $\langle p, v \rangle$ must be selected. In the first rule, the selection is among the pairs for which p and v are at the same location. In the second rule, this restriction is lifted. Next, $\Pi_1(AP)$ verifies the reachability of p from v's location (if necessary) and of p's destination after v has picked up p. The rules for the definition of reachability are the same as used in $\Pi_2(AP)$. Note that multiple paths may exist that allow v to drive p to his destination. For this reason, we consider only *best* paths, i.e. those that leave the largest amount of gas in v's tank at the end of the path. Note that if a solution to the main problem cannot be found by using best paths, then no solution can be found even if the condition is lifted. Considering explicitly multiple paths, in general, involves an amount of backtracking that would make performance unacceptable.

At this stage of the search, we focus on finding the amount of gas left that characterizes the best path. The amount is determined in two steps. First, relation $best\_d1\_gas(g)$ says that bg is the largest amount of gas left in v's tank after it has reached p's location:

$$best\_d1\_gas(BG) \leftarrow p\_location(D), \ BG = \#\max[\ reach\_from\_start(D, G) = G\ ].$$

It should be noted that in the definition of $destination\_reachable\_from\_passenger$ used in $\Pi_2(AP, p)$, the amount determined by $best\_d1\_gas$ is used as the initial gas level for the trip to the passenger's goal location. We then define the similar relation $best\_dest\_gas(g)$:

$$best\_dest\_gas(BG) \leftarrow destination(D), \ BG = \#\max[\ reach\_from\_d1(D, G) = G\ ].$$

The value g for which $best\_dest\_gas$ holds is the amount of gas left in v's tank after driving p to the airport along the best path.

Once $\Pi_1(AP)$ has determined a sequence of passenger-vehicle selections that successfully takes all passengers to their respective destinations, the sequence of actions to be performed for each passenger-vehicle pair is determined by means of another program, $\Pi_3(AP)$. The program $\Pi_3(AP)$ (i) takes as an input a pair $\langle p, v \rangle$ and the current state of the domain, and (ii) finds the sequence of actions corresponding to the best path for $\langle p, v \rangle$. The program is called iteratively for each passenger-vehicle assignment determined earlier by $\Pi_1(AP)$. Between calls, $\Pi_1(AP)$ updates the state of the domain according to the sequences generated by $\Pi_3(AP)$.

As in the Hydraulic-System-Planning benchmark, $\Pi_3(AP)$ is written in the language of ICLINGO, using the maximum length of the paths considered as the growth parameter. The search revolves around the notion of *extension of input graph G for vehicle v*: a directed graph whose nodes are pairs $\langle l, g \rangle$, where l is a location and g is an integer specifying an amount of gas. A pair $\langle l, g \rangle$ belongs to the extension E of G if l can be reached from the current location of v (in the current state of the domain) with an amount of gas g left in the tank. In $\Pi_3(AP)$, we consider paths in E of increasing length until we find the best path. The paths are represented by $arc(l, lg, n, ng, i)$, stating that the ith element of a path is the arc from $\langle l, lg \rangle$ to $\langle n, ng \rangle$. The base of $\Pi_3(AP)$ is:

$$arc(S, SG, X, SG - C, 1) \leftarrow start(S), \ gas(SG), \ connected(S, X, C), \ SG \geq C.$$
$$arc(S, SG, S, T, 1) \leftarrow start(S), \ gas(SG), \ gasstation(SG), \ tank(T).$$

The rules define the first arc of each path in E, with the second rule dealing with the case in which the vehicle is refueled at the start. The cumulative part of $\Pi_3(AP)$ determines the ith arc in each path, where i is the growth parameter:

$arc(X, G1, Y, G1 - C, i + 1) \leftarrow arc(Z, G0, X, G1, i), connected(X, Y, C), G1 \geq C.$
$arc(X, G1, X, T, i + 1) \leftarrow arc(Z, G0, X, G1, i), gasstation(X), tank(T).$

The cumulative part also includes the definition of relation $at\_dest(i)$, saying that there exists a path of length i that leads v to the destination location (after picking up p) in such a way that the intended amount of gas is left in v's tank:

$$at\_dest(i) \leftarrow arc(X, G, D, BG, i), destination(D), best\_dest\_gas(BG).$$

Relation at_dest is the key to detecting when the best path has been found. Finally, the volatile part of $\Pi_3(AP)$ contains a denial $\leftarrow$ not $at\_dest(i)$. which intuitively forces the iterations to continue until the best path has been found. Once that occurs, the corresponding sequence of actions is generated by re-tracing the best path from its end, with the same approach used in the Hydraulic-System-Planning benchmark. By $\Pi(AP)$ we denote $\Pi_1(AP)$-$\Pi_3(AP)$.

7   Performance Assessment

In order to evaluate how well our tool selection and modeling techniques fared in the competition, we conducted a series of experiments on the competition instances (made publicly available after the end of ASPCOMP). All experiments were performed on a computer with an Intel i7 processor running at 3 GHz, 4 GB RAM and FedoraCore 11. The systems used were GRINGO 3.0.3, CLASP 1.3.7, ICLINGO 3.0.3 (with CLASP 1.3.5), BPROLOG 7.4 and EZCSP 1.6.20b33. Our goal was to compare the performance of our encodings with that of the pure ASP encodings made available by the ASPCOMP organizers[1] [1] and run using CLASP. Below, we label the pure ASP encodings by $\Pi_b(\cdot)$ (e.g. $\Pi_b(WA)$ is the pure ASP encoding for the Weight-Assignment benchmark). For Reverse-Folding benchmark no pure ASP encoding was available. We use $\Pi_2(RF)$ as the baseline. The timeout for each run was 600 seconds. The average times were computed by considering only the instances that did not time out.

Table 1. Performance comparison (T/O stands for number of timeouts)

	WA		RF		HP		AP	
	$\Pi_2(WA)$	$\Pi_b(WA)$	$\Pi_3(RF)$	$\Pi_2(RF)$	$\Pi'(HP)$	$\Pi_b(HP)$	$\Pi(AP)$	$\Pi_b(AP)$
Total	3.49	2158.44	88.61	9000.00	2.07	47.25	302.71	7077.21
T/O	0	0	0	15	0	0	0	7
Avg	0.23	143.90	5.91	–	0.16	3.63	20.18	359.65

The results (see Table 1) show that the encodings developed in this paper are substantially faster than the baseline encodings. In no case our encodings timed out, whereas the baseline encodings timed out a total of 22 times. The time taken by our encodings was between 1 and 3 orders of magnitude better than that of the baseline encodings, which is even more impressive considering that the instances that timed out

---

[1] In these encodings we replaced all disjunctive rules by suitable choice rules.

were not used in computing the average times. We believe that the post-competition results clearly demonstrate the superior performance and scalability yielded by the encodings we developed. Detailed tables can be found on the EZCSP web page (http://marcy.cjb.net/ezcsp) together with the encodings described in this paper.

8 Conclusions

In this paper we have described our solutions to four challenging ASPCOMP problems. The solutions involved non-trivial use of solvers for CASP and IASP – selected out of concerns for the scalability of the pure ASP solutions. Currently no programming methodology exists for these tools. We hope that our description has provided an outline of the methodology we followed and that this, albeit being expressed at this point in problem-specific terms, may constitute a first step in the development of a general methodology for the use of such advanced ASP solvers.

Acknowledgments. The idea to use irrelevant moves in the Reverse-Folding benchmark is by Selim Erdogan, who also gave valuable suggestions on this paper and was a member of the EZCSP team at ASPCOMP. Yuliya Lierler was supported by a CRA/NSF 2010 Computing Innovation Fellowship.

References

1. Third answer set programming competition (2011),
   https://www.mat.unical.it/aspcomp2011/
2. Balduccini, M.: A General Method To Solve Complex Problems By Combining Multiple Answer Set Programs. In: ICLP 2009 Workshop on Answer Set Programming and Other Computing Paradigms (ASPOCP 2009) (July 2009)
3. Balduccini, M.: Representing Constraint Satisfaction Problems in Answer Set Programming. In: ICLP 2009 Workshop on Answer Set Programming and Other Computing Paradigms (ASPOCP 2009) (July 2009)
4. Balduccini, M., Lierler, Y.: ASP-Based Problem Solving with Cutting-Edge Tools. In: ICLP 2011 Workshop on Answer Set Programming and Other Computing Paradigms (ASPOCP 2011), pp. 14–28 (July 2011)
5. Gebser, M., Kaminski, R., Kaufmann, B., Ostrowski, M., Schaub, T., Thiele, S.: Engineering an Incremental ASP Solver. In: Garcia de la Banda, M., Pontelli, E. (eds.) ICLP 2008. LNCS, vol. 5366, pp. 190–205. Springer, Heidelberg (2008)
6. Gebser, M., Kaufmann, B., Neumann, A., Schaub, T.: Conflict-Driven Answer Set Solving. In: Veloso, M.M. (ed.) Proceedings of the Twentieth International Joint Conference on Artificial Intelligence (IJCAI 2007), pp. 386–392 (2007)
7. Gelfond, M., Lifschitz, V.: Classical Negation in Logic Programs and Disjunctive Databases. New Generation Computing 9, 365–385 (1991)
8. Leone, N., Pfeifer, G., Faber, W., Eiter, T., Gottlob, G., Perri, S., Scarcello, F.: The DLV System for Knowledge Representation and Reasoning. ACM Transactions on Computational Logic 7(3), 499–562 (2006)

Efficient Tabling of Structured Data Using Indexing and Program Transformation

Christian Theil Have and Henning Christiansen

Research group PLIS: Programming, Logic and Intelligent Systems
Department of Communication, Business and Information Technologies
Roskilde University, P.O. Box 260, DK-4000 Roskilde, Denmark
{cth, henning}@ruc.dk

Abstract. Tabling of structured data is important to support dynamic programming in logic programs. Several existing tabling systems for Prolog do not efficiently deal with structured data, but duplicate part of the structured data in different instances of tabled goals. As a consequence, time and space complexity may often be significantly higher than the theoretically optimal. A simple program transformation is proposed which uses an indexing of structured data that eliminates this problem, and drastic improvements of time and space complexity can be demonstrated. The technique is demonstrated for dynamic programming examples expressed in Prolog and in PRISM.

1 Introduction

Tabling in logic programming systems is an established technique which can give a significant speed-up of program execution and make it easier to write efficient programs in a declarative style. Basically, tabling means that the system maintains a table of calls and their answers and each time a new call is entered, it is checked if it (or a perhaps more general call, cf. [15]) is stored in the table already; if so, there is no need to execute it again and a previously found solution is used. It is included in several recognized Prolog systems such as B-Prolog [17], XSB [13] and YAP [7].

However, we can demonstrate that these systems may waste unnecessary time and space for copying and matching structures in situations where operations on single pointers could have been used instead. This can be the case when a program is called with a huge, ground structure as one of its arguments, and this argument is decomposed into sub-structures which are tabled independently.

In addition to pointing out the problem, we can show how it can be bypassed by a straightforward program transformation and a few auxiliary predicates that can be written in plain Prolog. A significant speed-up is demonstrated for selected test programs. In a longer perspective, we advocate such techniques be incorporated into logic programming systems with tabling such as those mentioned, where it can be implemented at a lower level where machine address pointers are available rather that using a high-level "simulation" of pointers as we do here.

C. Russo and N.-F. Zhou (Eds.): PADL 2012, LNCS 7149, pp. 93–107, 2012.

Our own background for working with this problem is work on analysis of biological sequence data using the probabilistic-logic system PRISM [8] which is implemented on top of B-Prolog and which is heavily dependent on its tabling mechanism. Together with another general program transformation based technique that we have developed [2], which improves the performance of tabling in the presence of non-discriminatory arguments, the technique described in the present paper increases significantly the size of sequences that can be meaningfully analyzed by means of PRISM programs.

Section 2 introduces the problem with tabling of structured data through an example. Section 3 describes an indexed representation of structured data that circumvents the problem, and section 4 demonstrates the effect for two problems, a dynamic programming problem in Prolog in section 4.1 and a PRISM program in section 4.2. Section 5 describes a general and automatic program transformation. Section 6 discuss limitations of our approach. Section 7 describes related work and section 8 sums up and discuss future work.

2   The Trouble with Tabling Structured Data

In this section we empirically demonstrate that all major Prolog tabling systems have a problem with structured data. Through the benchmarking of an implementation of the last/2 predicate — which traverses a list to find the last element — we observe that when this predicate is tabled, time and space complexity is far worse than without tabling.

The following is a straight-forward implementation of the last/2 predicate.

```
last([X],X).
last([_|L],X) :-
    last(L,X).
```

If last/2 is called with a list L of length N, e.g. last(L,_), then the expected time-complexity of this implementation is clearly $O(N)$. However, if the predicate is tabled, then the tabling system may have to store N partial copies of the list, e.g. the first copy will be the full list, the second copy will just store $N-1$ elements, and so on until every possible tail down to the last element of the list has been tabled. This results in $O(N^2)$ tabled list elements.

Naive copying of the lists hence make the tabled version of last/2 (at least) quadratic — with regard to both time and space consumption — rather than linear as in the non-tabled version. Tabling systems do employ some advanced techniques to avoid the expensive copying and which may reduce memory consumption and/or time complexity. For instance, B-Prolog uses hashing of goals [18], XSB uses a trie data structure [13] and Yap [7] uses a trie structure, which in [6] is refined into a so-called global trie which applies a sharing strategy for common subterms whenever possible. This can reduce space consumption, but since there is no sharing between the trie and the actual arguments of an active call, each execution of a call may typically involve a full traversal of its arguments.

Nevertheless, as can be witnessed from Figure 1, all tabling systems pay a price for structured data in either time or space. The figure shows time and space consumption for last(L,_) with varying sizes of L, where L is either a list of consecutive ones or a list of random numbers generated using the following simple random number generator.

```
random_list(0,_,[]).
random_list(N,Prev,[X|L]):-
    B is (9381*Prev + 12345) mod 32768,
    X is B mod 12,
    N1 is N-1,
    random_list(N1,B,L).
```

The nature of the data seems highly relevant. For instance, YAP and XSB performs better with repeated data and B-Prolog performs better with random data. As can be observed from Figure 1 plots a and c, time complexity is larger than linear in all cases, but varies depending the type of data. Space consumption is linear for repeated data in XSB and YAP, but for B-Prolog it is linear regardless of the type of data. The best time complexity is observed for B-Prolog with random data but as can be observed in plot c it is still super-linear. XSB and YAP show a different pattern where the time complexity seems to be more closely coupled to space complexity. For repeated data they are more time-efficient than B-Prolog but still significantly slower than B-Prolog with random data and still distinctively super-linear.

3   A Workaround and Its Implementation in Prolog

We present here a workaround that results in $O(1)$ time and space complexity for table lookups for programs with arbitrarily large ground structured data as input arguments. A term is represented as a set of facts, each representing a subterm which is referenced by a unique integer serving as an abstract pointer. Matching related to tabling is done solely by comparison of such pointers, independently of the underlying system. The representation is given by the following predicates which all together can be understood as an abstract datatype.

store_term(+*ground-term*, *pointer*)
    The *ground-term* is any ground term, and the *pointer* returned is a unique reference (an integer) for that term.
retrieve_term(+*pointer*, ?*functor*, ?*arg-pointers-list*)
    Returns the functor and a list of pointers to representations of the substructures of the term represented by *pointer*.
full_retrieve_term(+*pointer*, ?*ground-term*)
    Returns the term represented by *pointer*.

More precisely, it must hold for any ground term s, that the query

```
store_term(s, P), full_retrieve_term(P, S),
```

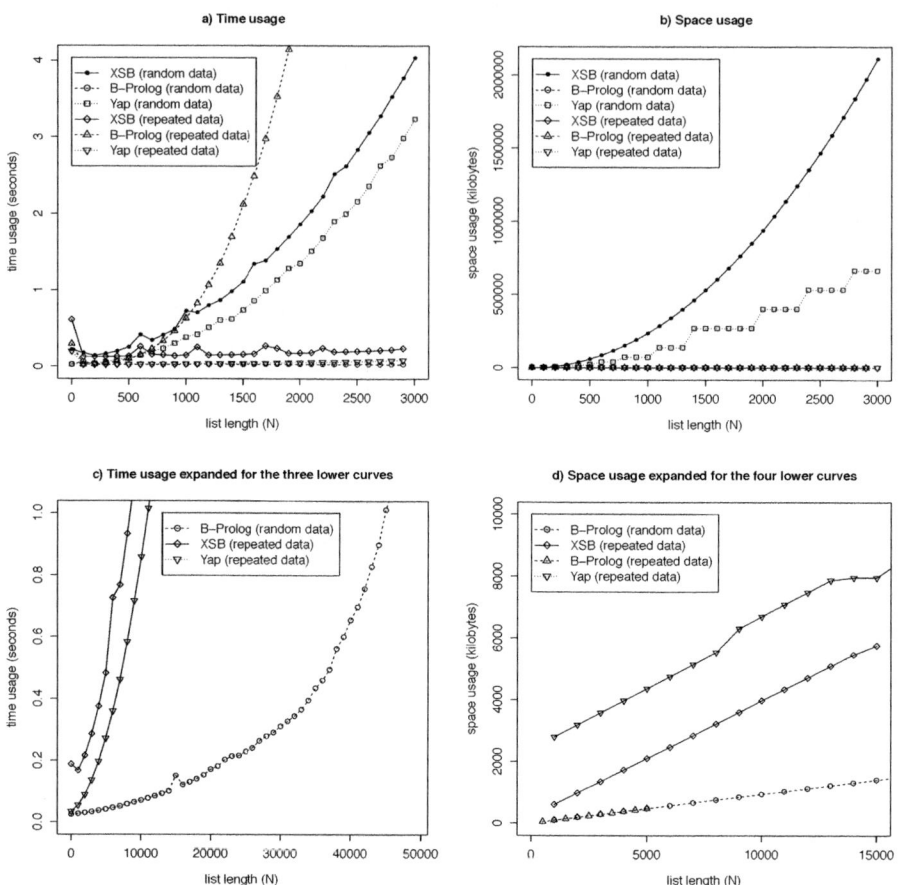

Fig. 1. Plot a) shows the time consumption of different Prolog engines for running tabled `last/2` with lists of length N and plot b) shows the table space usage. Table space usage is measured using the `statistics/1` predicate (which is different for each Prolog). In Yap it includes no specific measurement of "table space" and we measure instead the "program space" which is taken to include the table space. *Random data* means that the list contained random integers and in the *repeated data* means that the lists containing the same integer repeated N times. Plot c) and d) shows time and table space usage for the curves in a) and b) that looks flat because of the scale, but expanded for larger values of N. The curve of B-Prolog for repeated data in plot d) is truncated at 5000 due to its long running time for larger values.

assigns to the variable S a value identical to s. Furthermore, it must hold for any ground term s of the form $f(s_1, \ldots, s_n)$ that

```
store_term(s, P), retrieve_term(P, F, Ss),
```

assigns to the variable F the symbol f, and to Ss a list of ground values $[p_1, \ldots, p_n]$ such that additional queries

```
full_retrieve_term(p_i, S_i), i = 1, ..., n
```

assign to the variables S_i values identical to s_i.

Example 1. The following call converts the term `f(a,g(b))` into its internal representation and returns a pointer value in the variable P.

```
store_term(f(a,g(b)),P).
```

After this, the following sequence of calls will succeed.

```
retrieve_term(P,f,[P1,P2]),
retrieve_term(P1,a,[]),
retrieve_term(P2,g,[P21]),
retrieve_term(P21,b,[]),
full_retrieve_term(P,f(a,g(b))).
```

Example 2. One possible way of implementing the predicates introduced above is to have `store_term/2` asserting facts for the `retrieve_term/3` predicate using increasing integers as pointers. Then the call `store_term(f(a,g(b)),P)` considered in example 1 may assign the value 100 to P and as a side-effect assert the following facts.

```
retrieve_term(100,f,[101,102]).
retrieve_term(101,a,[]).
retrieve_term(102,g,[103]).
retrieve_term(103,b,[]).
```

Notice that Prolog's indexing on first arguments ensures a constant lookup time.

Example 3. In an application for which large numbers of identical subterms are expected, the representation can exploit this for sharing, so for example the term `h(very(large,sub(term)), very(large,sub(term)))` may be represented by the pointer value 200 and the following facts.

```
retrieve_term(200,g,[201,201]).
retrieve_term(201,very,[...]).
...
```

This will increase the time complexity for `store_term/2` but the advantages are *i)* storage consumption is reduced, and more importantly *ii)* an additional – and for the right sort of application programs drastic – speed-up may be obtained from the improved utilization of tabling that this automatically implies.

Finally we introduce a utility predicate which may simplify the use of the representation in application programs. It utilizes a special kind of terms, called *patterns*, which are not necessarily ground and which may contain subterms of the form lazy(*variable*).

lookup_pattern(+*pointer*, +*pattern*)
> The *pattern* is matched in a recursive way against the term represented by the pointer p in the following way.
> - lookup_pattern(p,X) is treated as full_retrieve_term(p,X).
> - lookup_pattern(p,lazy(X)) unifies X with p.
> - For any other *pattern* =.. [F,X$_1$,...,X$_n$] we call
>   retrieve_term(p, F, [P$_1$,...,P$_n$])
>   followed by lookup_pattern(P$_i$,X$_i$), $i = 1,\ldots,n$.

Example 4. Continuing example 2, we get that

    lookup_pattern(100, f(X,lazy(Y)))

leads to X=a and Y=102.

The lookup_pattern/2 predicate simplifies the program transformation introduced in section 5 although further efficiency can be gained by compiling it out for each specific pattern.

4   Examples

The impact of indexing for ground arguments with tabled execution is evaluated through two experiments. Firstly, we compare the performance of existing Prolog systems with tabling for a simple edit distance problem. The second experiment is related to our driving motivation – biological sequence analysis in PRISM, exemplified for probabilistic inference with Hidden Markov Models. All experiments were run on a MacBook Pro with a 2.53 GHz Intel core 2 Duo processor, 4 GB memory and Mac OS X version 10.6.8 (Snow Leopard).

4.1   Example: Edit Distance

We consider a minimal edit-distance algorithm written in Prolog which is dependent on tabling for any non-trivial problem. Time and space consumption are measured for increasing problem sizes in the three major tabling systems with and without our indexed representation.

Edit-distance is the textbook example dynamic programming. In the classic imperative formulation of the problem, a matrix with N^2 values is calculated, such that the calculation of the value for each cell is a constant time operation that depends on at most three other cells. The theoretical best time complexity of edit distance has been proven to be $O(N^2)$ [16]. Dynamic programming problems exhibit *optimal sub-structure* which implies that partial solutions can be reused rather than recomputed [1]. Tabling supports dynamic programming since resolved goals are kept in a table and reused rather than re-derived if the tabled goals are called again. The following Prolog program implements *minimal edit distance* between two lists; given two lists L_1 and L_2, the call `edit`(L_1, L_2,D) will return the minimal number of edits (substitutions,insertions and deletions) needed to change one of the lists into the other.

```
:- table edit/3.

edit([],[],0).

edit([],[Y|Ys],Dist) :-
    edit([],Ys,Dist1),
    Dist is 1 + Dist1.

edit([X|Xs],[],Dist) :-
    edit(Xs,[],Dist1),
    Dist is 1 + Dist1.

edit([X|Xs],[Y|Ys],Dist) :-
    edit([X|Xs],Ys,InsDist),
    edit(Xs,[Y|Ys],DelDist),
    edit(Xs,Ys,TailDist),
    (X==Y ->
        Dist = TailDist
        ;
        % Minimum of insertion, deletion or substitution
        sort([InsDist,DelDist,TailDist],[MinDist|_]),
        Dist is 1 + MinDist).
```

Without tabling the `edit/3` predicate, the same subgoals are derived again and again leading to exponential blowup, but it can be shown that the number of distinct calls are quadratic, which is the actual complexity we may hope for with optimal tabling.

The program has been transformed manually for this experiment based on the pointer based representation shown in example 2 above, simplified slightly for lists. The `retrieve_term` predicate is applied to resolve pointers during program execution. For completeness, we include a suitable implementation of `store_term/2` and `retrieve_term/2`.

```
store_term([],Index) :- assert(retrieve_term([],Index)).

store_term([X|Xs],Idx) :-
    Idx1 is Idx + 1,
    assert(retrieve_term(Idx,[X,Idx1])),
    store_term(Xs,Idx1).
```

The transformed version of the edit distance program is now as follows.

```
:- table edit/3.

edit(XIdx,YIdx,0) :-
    retrieve_term(XIdx,[]),
    retrieve_term(YIdx,[]).

edit(XIdx,YIdx,Dist) :-
    retrieve_term(XIdx,[]),
    retrieve_term(YIdx,[_,YIdxNext]),
    edit(XIdx,YIdxNext,Dist1),
    Dist is Dist1 + 1.

edit(XIdx,YIdx,Dist) :-
    retrieve_term(YIdx,[]),
    retrieve_term(XIdx,[_,XIdxNext]),
    edit(XIdxNext,YIdx,Dist1),
    Dist is Dist1 + 1.

edit(XIdx,YIdx,Dist) :-
    retrieve_term(XIdx,[X,NextXIdx]),
    retrieve_term(YIdx,[Y,NextYIdx]),
    edit(XIdx,NextYIdx,InsDist),
    edit(NextXIdx,YIdx,DelDist),
    edit(NextXIdx,NextYIdx,TailDist),
    (X==Y ->
        Dist = TailDist
        ;
        sort([InsDist,DelDist,TailDist],[MinDist|_]),
        Dist is 1 + MinDist).
```

The program is tested for randomly generated sequences of increasing lengths.
We measure the total time for the different Prolog engines to load the program
file, generate two different random sequences of a particular length, assert these
lists using store_term/2 and compute edit distance between these sequences, as
follows.

```
run(N) :-
    random_list(N,117,L1), % Generate random list L1 with seed 117
    random_list(N,42,L2),  % Generate random list L1 with seed 42
    store_term(L1,P1),
    store_term(L2,P2),
    edit(P1,P2,_Dist).
```

The results, shown in Figure 2, demonstrate that all tested Prolog systems use
more time for the unmodified tabled edit distance program than for the transformed program when applied to large data instances. For XSB and Yap the
major factor impacting time complexity seems to be space consumption. The

transformation has a positive impact space complexity regardless of the underlying tabling strategy. For B-Prolog, space consumption is much closer to the theoretical $O(N^2)$. Even though B-Prolog is very space efficient, the transformed program still uses less memory.

For larger problem instances the transformation has a significant impact on time complexity. XSB seems to benefit greatly from the transformation, although it starts out the slowest, it catches up for longer sequences, where it outperforms the two other Prologs in time efficiency. Yap seems to gain a modest boost from the transformation strategy and still seems to have a rather high time complexity although it is significantly faster than without the transformation. For B-Prolog, the two versions perform more or less the same for sequences of length up to 350, but for longer sequences (not shown in the figure) the transformed version is significantly faster: for example, with length 1000, the execution times are 7.5 seconds for the transformed and 21.5 seconds for the original version.

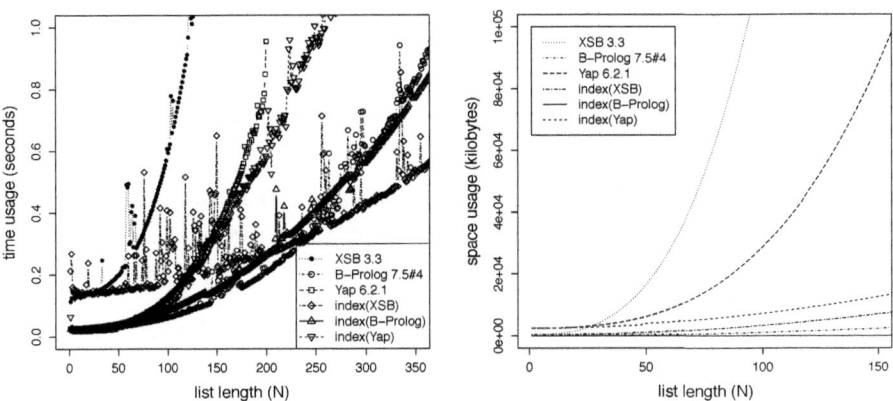

Fig. 2. The first plot shows the time consumption of different Prolog engines for edit distance with two lists of length N. The second is a plot of the space consumption for the same calls. The plots for both normal tabled in execution and execution of a transformed program that uses indexing as described in section 3 are shown, e.g. the plot $index(X)$ shows the performance of the transformed version for Prolog implementation X.

4.2   Example: Hidden Markov Model in PRISM

PRISM [8] is an extension of Prolog with special goals representing random variables. A global declaration such as values(coin, [head,tail]) introduces a so-called multivalued switch which means that an occurrence of the subgoal msw(coin,C) represents a probabilistic choice of assigning either head or tail to C. The semantics of PRISM is defined in terms of probabilistic Herbrand models, which means that a program specifies a probability of any goal G to be true determined from the possible combinations of msw outcomes that happen to make G true.

The PRISM system supports various probabilistic inferences, such as finding an optimal derivation, computing the probability for a goal or deriving msw probabilities by learning from a set of goals. The algorithms behind these inferences are dynamic programming algorithms and PRISM is implemented in B-Prolog [17], relying heavily on tabling for the efficiency of the probabilistic inferences.

We consider the example of a Hidden Markov Model (HMM) in PRISM taken from the PRISM manual [10] and adapted here to accommodate variable length sequences. In general, an HMM is a probabilistic model for sequential phenomena based on a finite automaton, which chooses state transitions and emissions by probabilistic choices; see [5] for a general introduction to HMMs and [3] for an account on how different HMMs are expressed in PRISM. Our example program is the following.

```
values(init,[s0,s1]).              hmm(_,[]).
values(out(_),[a,b]).
values(tr(_),[s0,s1]).             hmm(S,[Ob|Y]) :-
                                       msw(out(S),Ob),
hmm(L):-                               msw(tr(S),Next),
    msw(init,S),                       hmm(Next,Y).
    hmm(S,L).
```

The init, out(−) and tr(−) switches determine initial state, state transitions and emissions. Notice that two last ones are parameterized meaning that they define a switch for whatever value is substituted in for the parameter, which in this program always is the present state.

Using the same list encoding as in the previous example, the recursive predicate is rewritten as follows.

```
hmm(S,ObsPtr):-
    retrieve_term(ObsPtr,[]).

hmm(S,ObsPtr) :-
    retrieve_term(ObsPtr,[Ob,Y]),
    msw(out(S),Ob),
    msw(tr(S),Next),
    hmm(Next,Y).
```

The rewritten program can be shown to be semantics preserving wrt a standard Prolog semantics as well as PRISM's probabilistic semantics, and thus running PRISM's utilities for probability calculations should yield the same results.

When calculating the probability of a given goal, PRISM iterates over all possible ways to execute the goal using tabling to avoid enumerating the exponential number of different derivations. The same principle applies for PRISMs version of the Viterbi algorithm which is a dynamic programming algorithm that finds the most probable derivation. Assuming optimal execution of tabling, these algorithms should in principle run in linear time.

We measured running times of probability calculations (prob in PRISM lingo) for both the original and the transformed version of the PRISM HMM program with sequences of increasing lengths from 100 to 5000. The actual sequences used are instances of the pattern [a,b] repeated a number of times. The results are shown in Figure 3. It is apparent from the figure that indexed lookups results in approximately linear running time while the running time is at least quadratic for the unmodified program. The reported times are measured using prism_statistics(infer_time,Time), which is a PRISM built-in predicate.

We did not measure running times of sequences longer than 5000 for the unmodified program, but the transformed program scales up to sequences much longer than this, for instance, the time for probability calculation for a sequence of length 100000 takes less than 5 seconds.

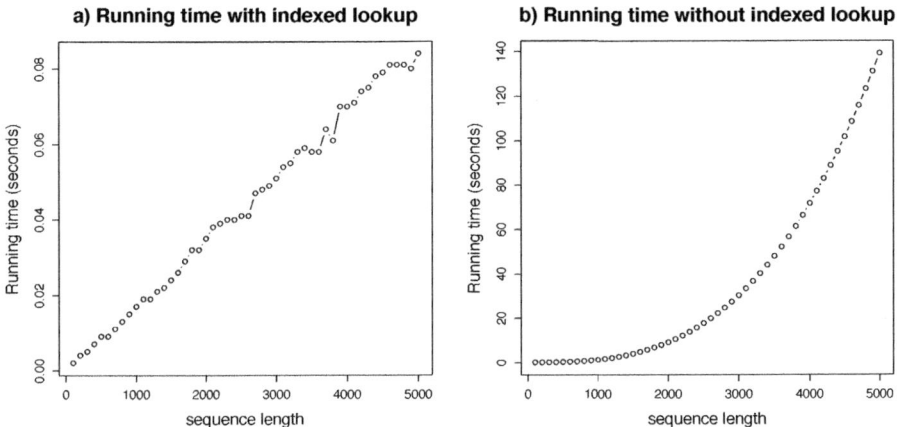

Fig. 3. The running time of the a) the transformed PRISM program and b) the unmodified PRISM program. While a) shows a linear development as function of sequence length, the development in b) is a higher-degree polynomial. Notice also the different scales on the vertical axes.

5   Automatic Program Transformation

The indexed versions of the example programs shown in section 4 can be produced automatically by a straightforward program transformation. The user must declare modes for which arguments predicate arguments that should be indexed. For the HMM program of section 4.2 this may look as follows; plus means transform the argument, minus means keep it unchanged.

```
table_index_mode(hmm(+))
table_index_mode(hmm(-,+))
```

The correctness of the transformation depends on the following properties of the program.

- The arguments indicated for indexing must be called with ground data only.
- Variables that occur in an indexed argument in the head of a clause, cannot occur in the body of that clause in both an indexed and a non-indexed argument.
- Any argument of a goal within a clause body which is declared to be indexed, must be given as a variable that also occurs in an indexed argument in the head of that clause.

Each clause whose head predicate is covered by a table mode declaration is transformed using the procedure outlined in algorithm 1, and all other clauses are left untouched. The transformation moves any term appearing in an indexed

> **for** *each* clause H:-B *in* original program **do**
> **if** table_index_mode *(M) matching* H **then**
>   **for** *each* argument $H_i \in H, M_i \in M$ **do**
>   **if** $M_i = {'+'}$ **then**
> $H_i' \leftarrow$ MarkLazy(H_i, B)
> $B \leftarrow (lookup\_pattern(V_i, H_i'), B)$
> $H_i \leftarrow V_i$
>   **end**
> **end**
>
> where MarkLazy is defined as
>
> MarkLazy(H_i,B) :
> $PotentialLazy =$ variables in all goals $G \in B$
>   where G has table_index_mode declaration
> $NonLazy =$ variables in all goals $G \in B$
>   where G has no table_index_mode declaration
> $Lazy = PotentialLazy \setminus NonLazy$
> **for** *each* variable $V \in H_i$ **do**
>   **if** $V \in Lazy$ **then**
> $V \leftarrow lazy(V)$
> **end**

Algorithm 1: Program transformation

position in the head of a clause into a call to the lookup_pattern predicate, which is added to the body. Variables in such terms are marked lazy when they do not occur in any non-indexed argument inside the clause. This transformation can be shown to be semantics preserving for programs satisfying the requirements given above.

The translation can be further enhanced by an unfolding of lookup_pattern calls into specialized calls to retrieve_term as shown in the examples in the previous section. This last step gave a speed-up of a factor of 5 for these examples when comparing with implementations using lookup_pattern directly.

6   Limitations

Our transformation assumes ground input arguments. As illustrated by the examples, this has applications to a lot of interesting problems, in particular dynamic programming problems. With regard to PRISM, our transformation is useful for ordinary probability calculation, Viterbi decoding and supervised learning. For other probabilistic inferences such as sampling, posterior decoding, unsupervised and semi-supervised learning, arguments containing variables are required. Sampling is of minor concern, since this can be done in linear time using the original program.

We currently have no optimization for structured terms in output arguments – they must be handled by the usual tabling mechanism. Structured terms in output arguments have the same consequences for complexity, which can be observed for instance with the well-known `append/3` predicate. Suppose that `append/3` is tabled and transformed using our approach, e.g. with `table_index_mode(+,+,-)`. Using our workaround, the space complexity for the input lists will be kept linear rather than quadratic, but the answers for the third list is tabled in the usual way which leads to quadratic space complexity nevertheless. Output arguments that do not contain structured data — as in the case of edit distance — do not present such a problem since the output argument is of constant size.

A drawback of our transformation is that it, by replacing the patterns in the head of rules with pointers, circumvents Prolog own indexing mechanism. As result, indexing cannot use the pattern of the arguments to determine which clauses to try. Instead, when multiple clauses with same name and arity exist, Prolog will have to try each of them in order and creates a choice point each time it tries a clause. This adds a constant factor — corresponding to the number of such clauses — to the running time of the program. It most practical programs it is realistic to assume that this factor will be fairly low, e.g. in the edit distance program only four such clauses exist.

7   Related Work

The hashing employed by B-Prolog and the global trie of YAP [6] address a related problem. Both methods reduce space consumption and this may lead to reductions in running time since less copying is needed. However, even with these mechanisms complexity is sub-optimal as shown in section 2. Furthermore, the methods have the drawback that the running time depends on the type of data. In comparison, our approach is data invariant and yields optimal complexity.

Due to restrictions in the Mercury language, input arguments are always ground, and the tabling system provides an option which identifies arguments by their pointers [11] (see also more detailed explanations in the reference manual [4]). This yields constant time storing and comparison of tabled arguments, similar to how any standard tabling mechanism will work for the programs produced by our program transformation.

The problem with tabling of structured data has addressed in applications with methods similar to our approach. In particular, in chart-parsing with DCGs supported by tabling, position indexed facts has been used [12]. A similar approach has been applied to PCFG parsing in PRISM [9]. This works by splitting the input list, $t_1 \ldots t_N$ into facts, $\{\texttt{pos}(1, t_1, 2), \ldots, \texttt{pos}(N-1, t_n, N)\}$. XSB Prolog have special constructions for tabled DCGs, where the standard 'C'/3' predicate is replaced by a special version that instead of using difference lists, utilize position indexed facts constructed from the original input list [14]. The position indexed difference list approach is quite similar to our approach, but is specific for difference lists. Our approach is more generally applicable and can be used with various kinds of structured data.

8   Conclusion

We have demonstrated that major Prolog implementations do not efficiently handle tabling of structured data and we have provided a program transformation that ensures $O(1)$ time and space complexity of tabled lookups of goals with structured data in input arguments and is applicable regardless of inefficiencies with structured data in the underlying tabling implementation. We have demonstrated the applicability of our transformation using examples from dynamic programming in Prolog and PRISM. The transformation makes it possible to scale to much larger problem instances.

Our program transformation should be seen as workaround, until such optimizations find their way into the tabling systems. We hope that Prolog implementors will pick up on this and integrate such optimizations directly in the tabling systems, so that the user does not need to transform his program, and need not worry about the underlying tabled representation and its implicit complexity.

Acknowledgements. This work is supported by the project "Logic-statistic modelling and analysis of biological sequence data" funded by the NABIIT program under the Danish Strategic Research Council.

We would like to thank Neng-Fa Zhou and Yoshitaka Kameya for their encouraging comments on a very early draft of this paper. We would also like to thank to the anonymous reviewers for insightful and constructive reviews.

References

1. Bellman, R.: Dynamic Programming. Princeton University Press (1957)
2. Christiansen, H., Gallagher, J.P.: Non-discriminating Arguments and Their Uses. In: Hill, P.M., Warren, D.S. (eds.) ICLP 2009. LNCS, vol. 5649, pp. 55–69. Springer, Heidelberg (2009)
3. Christiansen, H., Have, C.T., Lassen, O.T., Petit, M.: Taming the zoo of discrete HMM subspecies & some of their relatives. In: Biology, Computation and Linguistics, New Interdisciplinary Paradigms. Frontiers in Artificial Intelligence and Applications, vol. 228, pp. 28–42. IOS Press (2011)

4. Henderson, F., Conway, T., Somogyi, Z., Jeffery, D., Schachte, P., Taylor, S., Speirs, C., Dowd, T., Becket, R., Brown, M., Wang, P.: The Mercury Language Reference Manual. Version 11.01 (2011),
http://www.mercury.cs.mu.oz.au/information/documentation.html
5. Rabiner, L.R.: A tutorial on Hidden Markov Models and selected applications in speech recognition. Proceedings of the IEEE 77(2), 257–286 (1989)
6. Raimundo, J., Rocha, R.: Global Trie for Subterms. In: Abreu, S., Costa, V.S. (eds.) Proceedings of the 11th Colloquium on Implementation of Constraint and Logic Programming Systems, CICLOPS 2011, Lexington, Kentucky, USA, pp. 34–48 (July 2011)
7. Rocha, R., Silva, F., Costa, V.S.: A tabling engine for the Yap Prolog system. In: Proceedings of the 2000 APPIA-GULP-PRODE Joint Conference on Declarative Programming (AGP 2000), La Habana, Cuba (December 2000)
8. Sato, T., Kameya, Y.: PRISM: A language for symbolic-statistical modeling. In: IJCAI, pp. 1330–1339 (1997)
9. Sato, T., Kameya, Y.: New advances in logic-based probabilistic modeling (2007)
10. Sato, T., Zhou, N.-F., Kameya, Y., Izumi, Y.: PRISM User's Manual, Version 2.0 (2010)
11. Somogyi, Z., Sagonas, K.F.: Tabling in Mercury: Design and Implementation. In: Van Hentenryck, P. (ed.) PADL 2006. LNCS, vol. 3819, pp. 150–167. Springer, Heidelberg (2005)
12. Swift, T.: Design Patterns for Tabled Logic Programming. In: Abreu, S., Seipel, D. (eds.) INAP 2009. LNCS, vol. 6547, pp. 1–19. Springer, Heidelberg (2011)
13. Swift, T., Warren, D.S.: XSB: Extending prolog with tabled logic programming. Theory and Practice of Logic Programming (to appear, 2011)
14. Swift, T., Warren, D.S.: The XSB Programmer's Manual. Version 3.3 (June 2011)
15. Tamaki, H., Sato, T.: OLD Resolution with Tabulation. In: Shapiro, E. (ed.) ICLP 1986. LNCS, vol. 225, pp. 84–98. Springer, Heidelberg (1986)
16. Wong, C.K., Chandra, A.K.: Bounds for the string editing problem. J. ACM 23(1), 13–16 (1976)
17. Zhou, N.-F.: The language features and architecture of B-Prolog. Theory and Practice of Logic Programming (to appear, 2011)
18. Zhou, N.-F., Shen, Y.-D., Yuan, L.-Y., You, J.-H.: Implementation of a Linear Tabling Mechanism. In: Pontelli, E., Santos Costa, V. (eds.) PADL 2000. LNCS, vol. 1753, pp. 109–123. Springer, Heidelberg (2000)

Optimizing Inequality Joins in Datalog with Approximated Constraint Propagation

Dario Campagna[1], Beata Sarna-Starosta[2], and Tom Schrijvers[3]

[1] Dept.of Mathematics and Computer Science, University of Perugia, Italy
dario.campagna@dmi.unipg.it
[2] LogicBlox Inc., Atlanta, Georgia, USA
bss@logicblox.com
[3] Dept. of Applied Mathematics and Computer Science, UGent, Belgium
tom.schrijvers@ugent.be

Abstract. Datalog systems evaluate joins over arithmetic (in)equalities as a naive generate-and-test of Cartesian products. We exploit aggregates in a source-to-source transformation to reduce the size of Cartesian products and to improve performance. Our approach approximates the well-known propagation technique from Constraint Programming.

Experimental evaluation shows good run time speed-ups on a range of non-recursive as well as recursive programs. Furthermore, our technique improves upon the previously reported in the literature constraint magic set transformation approach.

1 Introduction

Datalog [13,1] is a syntactic subset of Prolog introduced in the 1980s for database processing. By supporting a limited, safe form of recursion, Datalog considerably extends the expressive power of traditional database query languages like SQL. At the same time, unlike Prolog, Datalog allows SQL's set-at-a-time evaluation. Also similarly to SQL, the programs in Datalog are guaranteed to terminate. Hence, extra-logical constructs such as Prolog's cut ('!') operator are not needed.

After its original introduction as a smarter version of SQL, Datalog lost the interest of researchers for a time, until recently re-gaining attention in applications falling outside of the realm of traditional database reasoning, which include: program analysis [8], networks [12], security protocols [10], knowledge representation [9], robotics [2] and gaming [19]. Our industrial partner, LogicBlox Inc. [11], uses a variant of Datalog, called Datalog^{LB}, as the basis for implementing decision automation and business planning systems.

Many of the above application domains rely on processing numerical data with arithmetic operations, in Datalog available as built-in relations (predicates). We focus in particular on built-in arithmetic (in)equality predicates ($>$, $<$, etc.) which we also refer to as *(arithmetic) constraints*. Existing Datalog compilers do not exploit the constraining properties of arithmetic predicates, but rather implement them as ordinary tests. As a result, evaluation of programs with arithmetic constraints follows the naive *generate-and-test* approach, where ordinary

C. Russo and N.-F. Zhou (Eds.): PADL 2012, LNCS 7149, pp. 108–122, 2012.

predicates act as generators, and the entire search space they produce is enumerated before the constraints can be applied to prune the candidate solutions. In database terminology, the full $\mathcal{O}(n^2)$ Cartesian product of two tables is computed. This is in stark contrast with $\mathcal{O}(n \log n)$ equality-based joins, for which current Datalog systems are optimized.

The research area of Constraint Programming (CP) offers approaches that prune the search space more eagerly, e.g., *constrain-and-generate*, as well as the constraint implementation technique, called *constraint propagators*, which allows to prune the domains of the variables involved in the constraints to narrow down the sets of candidate values even before the values are enumerated.

We adapt the CP constraint propagator technique to filter the individual Datalog generators in $\mathcal{O}(n)$ time before they are used in, potentially much smaller, Cartesian products. For this purpose we extended the Datalog^{LB} system with an automatic program transformation framework. Experimental evaluation shows that our technique enables good run-time improvements for a variety of test programs.

2 Datalog^{LB}

LogicBlox is a commercial Datalog-based platform for building enterprise-scale corporate planning and pricing applications. LogicBlox is currently used in several commercial decision automation applications, including retail supply-chain management [14] and software program analysis [3,4,16]. A typical LogicBlox application involves computational analyses that require aggregation across very large data sets combined with simulation and modeling techniques. The platform accommodates these features by means of its custom query language Datalog^{LB}, a type-safe variant of Datalog, based on incremental evaluation, with trigger-like functionality and support for dynamic updates, declarative specification of functional dependencies, non-deterministic choice, stratified negation, meta-programming, and a wide range of extra-logical computations, including aggregation utilized by our optimization approach. In the following paragraphs we outline the main features of Datalog^{LB} and the LogicBlox run-time system. A more exhaustive description of Datalog^{LB} can be found in [21]. Readers familiar with Datalog may want to use this section as a reference when reading the remainder of the paper.

The Datalog^{LB} Language. Figure 1 shows a Datalog^{LB} encoding of the cryptarithmetic puzzle LP+FP=PL, the goal of which is to find an assignment of digits to letters that satisfies the equation LP+FP = PL.

The basic programming construct in Datalog^{LB} is the implication '<-', denoting derivation rules of the form:

```
Head <- Body.
```

where Head and Body are conjunctions of *atoms*. An atom can be either a predicate with variable or constant arguments, a comparison expression, an arithmetic

```
1    digit(_) ->.
2    digit(d), val(d:v) -> uint[8](v), v<=9.
3
4    solution(l,p,f) -> digit(l), digit(p), digit(f).
5    solution(l,p,f) <-
6        digit(l), val(l:vl),
7        digit(p), val(p:vp),
8        digit(f), val(f:vf),
9        vl != 0, vp != 0, vf != 0,
10       vl != vp, vl != vf, vp != vf
11       10*vl+vp + 10*vf+vp = 10*vp+vl.
```

Fig. 1. The Datalog^{LB} encoding of the LP+FP=PL cryptarithmetic puzzle

expressions, or a negated atom. The above rule means that the atoms constituting Head can be derived from the atoms constituting Body. The example program in Figure 1 contains only one rule (lines 5-11), which derives the facts of the predicate solution based on the facts of the predicates digit and val, and the constraints represented as comparisons and arithmetic expressions on their arguments.

Datalog^{LB} extends Datalog with the notion of an *integrity constraint* of the form:

$$Lhs \; \text{->} \; Rhs.$$

Informally, the above constraint means that if Lhs is true, then Rhs must also be true, where Lhs and Rhs are conjunctions of atoms. The difference between a constraint and a rule is that a rule derives data for the atoms in its head, whereas a constraint checks that for the existing data matching its left-hand side, the right-hand side holds. The integrity constraints constitute the basis of Datalog^{LB}'s static type system, which guarantees at compile-time that certain kinds of constraints always hold for all possible instantiations of a given schema. Our approach uses integrity constraints to declare *filter types* which allow to reduce the domains of predicates subjected to arithmetic constraints.

Datalog^{LB} types are represented as unary predicates. Custom types may be defined using *entity predicates*. For instance, in Figure 1, the constraint in line 1 declares the entity predicate digit. The constraint in line 4 is a *type declaration* for the predicate solution, which states that for every tuple solution(l,p,f), the arguments l, p, and f must be digit entities. An entity predicate P may be associated with a *reference mode predicate*, which uniquely identifies each element in P with a value of a primitive type, thus allowing to access the specific entity elements from user applications. For instance, line 2 of Figure 1 declares a reference mode predicate val, which associates each entity element d in digit with v, an 8-bit unsigned integer value no greater than 9, thus binding the digit type to represent single-digit integers. The syntactic form val(d:v) denotes the one-to-one functional relation between d and v, and is reserved for declaring reference mode predicates. The decision to express digits as entities is dictated by one of the mechanisms contributing to Datalog^{LB}'s termination guarantee, which restricts the use of primitive types as arguments to built-in predicates such as arithmetic operations.

The extra-logical operations supported by LogicBlox, including aggregation computations, are represented by special-syntax rules of the form:

```
result[x1,...,xn]=v <- Op<<v=Method>> Body.
```

The head of the rule uses Datalog^{LB}'s shorthand notation for declaring functional dependencies: `result[x1,...,xn]=v` declares the predicate `result` to be a function from `x1,...,xn` to `v`. The notation also allows declaring singleton (constant) values: `p[]=v` declares the predicate `p` to be a singleton that contains only the value `v`. The value can be retrieved through `p[]`. The right-hand side of the above rule, in addition to the conjunction of atoms in `Body`, includes a directive which specifies the type of the operation to be performed (e.g., aggregation), and the particular method (e.g., finding the minimum value) to be used. For instance, in Section 3.1 we show the following rule which finds the lower bound for the `val` predicate:

```
lb_digit[]=n <- agg<<n=min(v)>> digit(d), val(d:v).
```

Above, `agg` states that the rule computes an aggregation, and `min` names the specific operation to be applied to the values referenced by `v`.

3 The Filter Predicates Transformation

This section describes the details of our transformation, beginning with non-recursive programs, and then considering the impact of recursion.

3.1 Non-recursive Programs

Recall the LP+FP=PL program from the previous section. Our goal is to reduce the number of different candidate values that are used for producing answers. Thus, we exploit the equality constraint

$$10 * v_l + v_p + 10 * v_f + v_p = 10 * v_p + v_l$$

from the program rule to filter candidate values in the generator predicate `digit`. Specifically, for each generator predicate atom appearing in the constraint, we consider the value generated by this atom in the context of the upper and lower bounds of the values produced by other generator atoms.

For instance, for the generator atom `digit(1)`, the original constraint, which is equivalent to the pair of inequalities:

$$\begin{cases} 10 * v_l + v_p + 10 * v_f + v_p \leq 10 * v_p + v_l \\ 10 * v_l + v_p + 10 * v_f + v_p \geq 10 * v_p + v_l \end{cases}$$

yields the pair of inequalities:

$$\begin{cases} 10 * v_l + l_d + 10 * l_d + l_d \leq 10 * u_d + v_l \\ 10 * v_l + u_d + 10 * u_d + u_d \geq 10 * l_d + v_l \end{cases}$$

where u_d and l_d represent the upper and lower bound of the generator predicate digit, respectively. We use these inequalities in the Datalog definition of the filter predicate for digit(1), which is linear in the size of the digit set.

```
digit_filtered_l(l) <-
    digit(l),
    val(l:vl),
    lb_digit[]=ld,
    ub_digit[]=ud,
    10*vl+ld+10*ld+ld <= 10*ud+vl,
    10*ld+vl <= 10*vl+ud+10*ud+ud.
```

Similar filter predicates are generated for the remaining generator atoms.

The bounds for the generator predicates are computed in separate aggregate predicates, again adding only linear overhead, and reused in all filter predicates:

```
lb_digit[]=n <- agg<<n=min(v)>> digit(d), val(d:v).
ub_digit[]=n <- agg<<n=max(v)>> digit(d), val(d:v).
```

In the last step of the transformation we replace the generator predicate atoms in the body of the solution/3 rule by atoms representing corresponding filter predicates:

```
solution(l,p,f) <-
    digit_filtered_l(l),
    digit_filtered_p(p),
    digit_filtered_f(f),
    ... % rest of the original LP+FP=PL program
```

As the transformation adds only linear overhead, the overall worst-case time complexity is not increased. Moreover, the filtered generator sets are potentially much smaller than the original sets, thus resulting in a Cartesian product much smaller than the original one. In this small example the filtered generator sets for 1, p and f are all reduced from $[0, 9]$ to respectively $[1, 8]$, $[2, 9]$ and $[1, 8]$.

Our approach is inspired by the well-known *bounds consistency* technique [5], in CP implemented by finite-domain constraint propagators. We simplify constraint propagation in two ways: (1) by computing filtered domains on the original domains rather than as a fixed point of the filtering process, and (2) by filtering only at the beginning of the evaluation rather than repeatedly after every enumeration step (in CP terminology known as *labeling*). As a consequence of these simplifications, (1) we cannot encode unbounded fixpoint computations, and (2) computing and storing many successively filtered tables for the same variable adds considerable time and space overhead. Nevertheless, our approach

```
p(t,w) -> string(t), int[64](w).
s(t,w) -> string(t), int[64](w).

e(t,w) -> string(t), int[64](w).
e(t,w) <- p(t,w).
e(t,w) <- s(t,w),
          e(tp,wp),
          w - wp <= 100,
          w + wp >= 19500.
```

Fig. 2. The Engine program

```
e(t,w) <- p(t,w).                         s_filtered(t,w) <-
e(t,w) <- s_filtered(t,w),                  s(t,w),
          e_filtered(tp,wp),                w-ub_e[] <= 100,
          w-wp <= 100,                      19500 <= w+ub_e[].
          w+wp >= 19500.
                                          e_filtered(tp,wp) <-
                                            e(tp,wp),
lb_s[]=n <- agg<<n=min(v)>> s(_,v).         lb_s[]-wp <= 100,
ub_s[]=n <- agg<<n=max(v)>> s(_,v).         19500 <= ub_s[]+wp.
ub_e[]=n <- agg<<n=max(v)>> e(_,v). % ERROR
```

Fig. 3. Ill-formed Engine program after naive transformation

yields a light-weight technique that is easily provided on top of the existing Datalog implementations, offering a satisfactory compromise between the anticipated speed-up and the overhead.

3.2   Recursive Programs

Recursion considerably complicates our transformation. Consider the Engine program listed in Figure 2. The program selects suitable engines for an engine yard. In the predicates p(t,w), s(t,w) and e(t,w), t corresponds to the engine type and w to the produced wattage. The predicate p represents the primary engines, and the predicate s represents the potentially spare engines. A suitable engine for the engine compound e(t,w) is either a primary engine, or a spare engine that can assist another engine in the compound. The difference in wattage between the assisting engine and the assistee should not exceed 100, and the total wattage of the compound should be no less than 19,500.

The naive application of our technique yields the ill-formed program shown in Figure 3. The program involves recursion through aggregation: in order to compute the set of e/2 we need to know the upper bound of e/2. Such recursion is not supported by Datalog[LB] (nor by any other LP system we are aware of).

Since it is not possible to effectively compute the *exact* upper bound on e/2, we approximate it as the upper bound of the approximated upper bounds of the two rules defining e/2. For the first, non-recursive rule, such an approximated (and exact) upper bound is ub_p[]. A crudely approximated upper bound for the second, recursive rule, is ub_s[]. Hence:

ub_e[]=n <- n=max(ub_p[],ub_s[]).

where

ub_p[]=n <- agg<<n=max(v)>> p(_,v).

We may attempt to tighten the upper bound of the second rule, based on the observation that it is bounded from above by ub_e[]+100:

ub_e[]=n <- n=max(ub_p[],min(ub_s[],ub_e[]+100)).

Alas, this step reintroduces recursion through aggregation. We eliminate it in the same way as before, by substituting the cruder approximation derived earlier:

ub_e[]=n <- n=max(ub_p[],min(ub_s[],max(ub_p[],ub_s[])+100)).

We further simplify the above expression by noticing that

$$\forall x, y, c \in \mathbb{N}. \min(x, \max(y, x) + c) = x$$

This step brings us back to the first approximation, thus proving that the refinement attempt was unsuccessful. Nevertheless, as we show in Section 5, our approximation is still quite effective at pruning the predicate domains and improving the performance of the programs.

4   Implementation

Most of the Datalog^{LB} syntax is compatible with the term syntax of standard Prolog. The discrepancies in the particular notations, such as the functional dependency syntax, can be easily accommodated by simple processing steps. Hence, we chose Prolog (specifically, SWI-Prolog [20]) to implement the transformations of Datalog^{LB} programs. Our analyzer consists of three Prolog modules, for the total of about 1,500 lines of Prolog code, including comments.

4.1   LogicBlox/SWI-Prolog Interface

Figure 4 shows the LogicBlox compilation scheme and outlines the communication between the LogicBlox engine and the SWI-Prolog analyzer.

The LogicBlox compiler rewrites a source Datalog^{LB} program into a core representation, which is then encoded using Google's protocol buffers (GPBs) interface for further use by a number of tools, including an interpreter. GPBs [7] is a platform-independent, extensible mechanism for serializing structured data

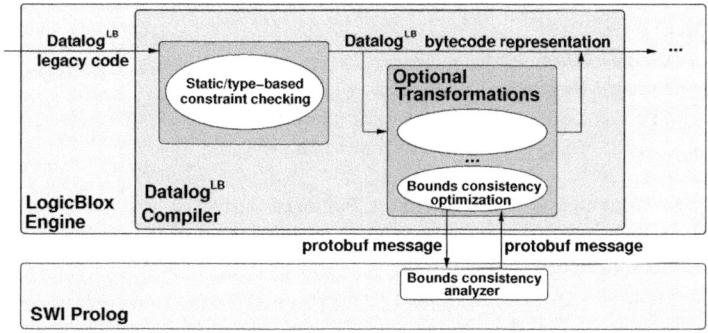

Fig. 4. LogicBlox Compiler and its communication with SWI-Prolog

to binary form. GPBs allow the programmers to determine how to structure their data by defining simple data structures (messages) in a dedicated specification language, and then to compile those data structures into the language and platform of their choice. As shown in Figure 4, the core program representation generated by the LogicBlox compiler is either passed directly to the subsequent phase of run-time processing, or subjected to one or more optional transformations aimed at optimizing the compiled code or collecting information to be used in further evaluation steps. This infrastructure makes the GPBs the medium of choice for interfacing LogicBlox with external analysis modules. The interface for our application comprises three Prolog modules for the total of about 1,700 lines of code (including comments), and five new modules in the LogicBlox code, for the total of 1,800 lines.

The interface on the SWI-Prolog side is based on SWI-Prolog's native GPBs library [15]. We extended the library with the capability to represent recursively structured data (which is essential to encode $Datalog^{LB}$ programs), and optimized it to linear run-time complexity. Our version of the library is available in a dedicated branch of the SWI-Prolog code repository.

The communication between LogicBlox and SWI-Prolog proceeds as follows. The output of the $Datalog^{LB}$ compiler is received by a new LogicBlox module which extracts from it the information relevant to our analysis, encodes it as a collection of GPBs messages, and opens a socket connection with SWI-Prolog. Once the connection is established, the messages are supplied to our analyzer. The analyzer decodes the messages into a program representation, applies the transformation, encodes the resulting program, and sends it back to the LogicBlox side, where another dedicated module retrieves the transformation results and updates the core representation of the program accordingly.

We illustrate the use of GPBs on $Datalog^{LB}$ rule bodies. A rule body is a formula defined as an atom, a disjunction, a conjunction, or a negation. LogicBlox serializes and deserializes formulas with GPBs messages of the following form:

```
message Formula {
    optional Atom atom = 1;
    optional Negation negation = 2;
    optional Conjunction conjunction = 3;
    optional Disjunction disjunction = 4;
}
message Conjunction { repeated Formula formula = 1; }
...
```

Note the mutually recursive nature of the `Formula` and `Conjunction` definitions. On the SWI-Prolog side, the messages are defined in `message/2` clauses:

```
protobufs:message(formula, [ optional(1,message(atom))
                           , optional(2,message(negation))
                           , optional(3,message(conjunction))
                           , optional(4,message(disjunction)) ]).

protobufs:message(conjunction, [ repeated(1,message(formula)) ]).
```

The predicate `message/2`, which we added to the SWI-Prolog GPBs library, enables naming message templates. It is essential for recursive and repeated embedded messages. The `protobuf_message/2` predicate serializes and deserializes messages to and from binary form, like the representation of the single-atom formula `digit(d)`.

```
?- protobuf_message(message(formula,
       [ optional(1, message(atom,
                      [ string(1,"digit")
                      , repeated(2,[ /* variable d */ ],term) ]))
       ]),Bytes).
```

4.2   The Transformation

Given a representation of a Datalog^{LB} program, our transformation processes in turn each of its rules. For every rule with one or more arithmetic constraints, it identifies the generator predicate atoms, exploits the constraints to produce corresponding filter predicates, and replaces the generator atoms accordingly. It also extends the program with the definitions for the auxiliary predicates performing bounds computations.

Implementation of the code that generates the bounds-computing predicates turned out to be one of the more involved aspects of our project. The numerical data appearing in the arithmetic constraints pertinent to our transformation is often represented as the values of the Datalog^{LB} reference mode predicates where the keys are the entities produced by the predicates serving as generators. To access these data, it is necessary to reconstruct the chain of functional dependencies connecting each value with the appropriate entity generator. For instance, to compute predicate bounds for the atom set:

```
p(x), val_1(x:vx), q(y), val_2(y:vy), vx > vy
```

we need to reconstruct the chain connecting `vx` with `p` and `vy` with `q`. Additional complications arise when the reference mode predicates (and the corresponding generators) have non-unary keys, in which case the reconstructed dependencies are trees with the functional dependencies as nodes and the generators as leaves.

As mentioned in Section 2, Datalog^{LB}'s static type system relies on the type information in the form of the integrity constraints. To ensure completeness of the type information in the transformed programs, we need to provide type declarations for the predicates generated by the analyzer (i.e., filter and aggregate predicates). It turns out that we can conveniently derive these directly from the original predicates, with no additional bookkeeping during the transformation.

5   Evaluation

We now present the results of applying our transformation to a variety of programs. All experiments were performed on a machine with a 2.83 GHz Intel® Core™ 2 Quad CPU and 4 GB of RAM, running Ubuntu 10.10 (Linux kernel 2.6.35-24-server). For each experiment we show the run times, in seconds, for the original programs (*Original* column), and the relative performance change after the filter predicates transformations (*FP* column).

For LogicBlox (v 3.7), in the *Opt* column, we additionally measure the impact of the system's optimizer [17] aimed at improving the performance of equality-based joins by reordering the goals and applying a variant of magic-set rewrite.

In order to have a point of reference, we also report the results of tabled top-down evaluation of our test suites using XSB Prolog 3.3.1. The changes required to accommodate Datalog^{LB} programs in XSB are minimal and mainly syntactic in nature: we omit type declarations, replace '<-' arrows with ':-', capitalize variable names, change functional dependencies to ordinary arguments, and provide Prolog implementations for aggregates. To guarantee termination, we declare all predicates as tabled.

5.1   Non-recursive Programs

Cryptarithmetic Puzzles.   Table 1 shows the evaluation run times for a set of cryptarithmetic puzzles building on the idea of the LP+FP=PL program from Section 2. In almost all cases the transformation yields drastic performance improvements ($3\times$ to $10\times$) over both original and optimized LogicBlox evaluation. There are two exceptions. In the first case, the overhead of the auxiliary predicates introduced by the transformation dominates the extremely short run time of the original program. In the second case, the transformed program prunes very few values from the initial domains, and consequently shows performance similar to that of the original program.

The XSB evaluation yields similar results both in terms of the original program performance, and the benefits from the transformation.

Table 1. Benchmark results for cryptarithmetic puzzles

Puzzle	Datalog^{LB}			XSB	
	Original	Opt	FP	Original	FP
Puzzle 1	0.01 sec.	100.00 %	140.90 %	0.01 sec.	100.00 %
LP+FP=PL	0.01 sec.	100.00 %	100.00 %	0.01 sec.	100.00 %
Puzzle 2	0.80 sec.	72.50 %	14.02 %	0.65 sec.	15.38 %
Puzzle 3	3.10 sec.	25.16 %	11.42 %	2.60 sec.	11.92 %
Puzzle 4	2.67 sec.	104.49 %	12.79 %	2.73 sec.	12.09 %
Puzzle 5	6.39 sec.	114.71 %	15.02 %	7.70 sec.	12.60 %
Puzzle 6	3.90 sec.	82.56 %	27.05 %	8.75 sec.	25.26 %
Puzzle 7	17.54 sec.	50.85 %	105.01 %	17.20 sec.	107.62 %
Puzzle 8	20.63 sec.	92.05 %	11.71 %	19.99 sec.	52.53 %

Table 2. Benchmark results for the Production problem

Tons range	Datalog^{LB}			XSB	
	Original	Opt	FP	Original	FP
[1,500]	0.60 sec.	101.67 %	103.64 %	0.29 sec.	96.55 %
[1,1000]	2.81 sec.	46.26 %	100.75 %	1.10 sec.	98.18 %
[1,2500]	12.37 sec.	42.52 %	40.60 %	5.01 sec.	92.41 %
[1,5000]	13.71 sec.	43.69 %	41.27 %	5.90 sec.	88.30 %

The Production Problem. The Production program[1] models the mathematical programming problem of optimizing the profit from manufacturing several types of products, subject to a set of constraints such as production costs and maximum number of items to be manufactured for each product type, or the availability of the factory line. From a technical point of view this program is interesting because it contains multi-key functional dependencies that drive the filter predicates. Another non-standard feature is the use of the aggregates for computing the optimized profit.

Table 2 reports the results of evaluating the original and transformed program with four data sets differing in the range of the generator predicate indicating the number of tons of products being manufactured. Clearly, for LogicBlox evaluation, the transformation has no significant effect on the program for the small tons ranges, but enables a lot of pruning, and thus considerable performance improvement, when the tons ranges are large. On XSB the effects of the transformation are more uniform across the different data sets, with slightly better performance improvements for the larger tons ranges.

5.2 Recursive Programs

The Engine Program. To evaluate the effects of our transformation on the recursive Engine program from Figure 2, we used four different data sets. Each

---

[1] We refer to http://users.ugent.be/~tschrijv/Datalog for the source code.

Table 3. Benchmark results for the Engine program

| Data set | Datalog^{LB} | | | XSB | |
	Original	Opt	FP	Original	FP
Set_1	26.87 sec.	106.43 %	21.41 %	43.40 sec.	6.11 %
Set_2	9.82 sec.	106.92 %	4.65 %	8.29 sec.	0.84 %
Set_3	172.47 sec.	100.93 %	84.18 %	119.82 sec.	64.91 %
Set_4	53.61 sec.	100.39 %	104.75 %	20.30 sec.	97.93 %

data set defines the sets of couples produced by p/2 (denoted P in the following), and s/2 (denoted S). Let

$$\mathcal{T} = \{\text{Steam engine}, \text{Internal combustion engine}, \text{Gas Turbine}\}$$

The four data sets define the sets P and S as follows.

- Set_1: $\begin{cases} P = \mathcal{T} \times [1100, 11500] \\ S = \mathcal{T} \times [1, 10000] \end{cases}$ - Set_3: $\begin{cases} P = \mathcal{T} \times [500, 16000] \\ S = \mathcal{T} \times [1000, 14000] \end{cases}$

- Set_2: $\begin{cases} P = \mathcal{T} \times [500, 5000] \\ S = \mathcal{T} \times [1, 6000] \end{cases}$ - Set_4: $\begin{cases} P = \mathcal{T} \times [10000, 16000] \\ S = \mathcal{T} \times [8, 12000] \end{cases}$

The results of the evaluation are shown in Table 3. There is a visible correlation between the particular data set and the effects of the transformation. With little pruning comes modest speed-up or even a slow-down, whereas considerable pruning yields large performance improvements. Again our transformation achieves drastic improvements where the LogicBlox optimizer does not.

Multi-Legged Flights Program. The Flights program (Figure 5) models multi-legged flights and their travel distance. More abstractly, it captures the transitive closure of a directed weighted graph. The Datalog^{LB} encoding consists of the basic variant of the program, based on that studied by Stuckey and Sudarshan [18], together with a sample query to compute all possible destinations no further than 10,000 miles from Sydney.

Predicate e(x,y,d) (line 1) denotes a flight leg, i.e., a direct connection between cities x and y with the distance d. The data of this predicate are given as facts. The predicate f (lines 3-7) defines a multi-legged flight as the transitive closure of the predicate e. Since the second rule for f contains recursion, to be expressible in Datalog^{LB}, it needs to be bounded. Hence, we have added the constraint 'd <= 10000' (line 7), which is not present in the encoding of [18]. Lines 9-10 define the query predicate.

It turns out that our transformation has no significant effect on the performance of the Flights program; it does not provide additional pruning. Fortunately, to our aid comes the *constraint magic set transformation* [18]. Not only is the constraint magic set rewritten (CMR) variant of the program (Figure 6) faster than the original, but also it is amenable to our transformation.

```
1   e(x,y,d) -> string(x), string(y), int[64](d).
2
3   f(x,y,d) -> string(x), string(y), int[64](d).
4   f(x,y,d) <- e(x,y,d), d >= 0.
5   f(x,y,d) <- e(x,z,d1), d1 >= 0,
6                 f(z,y,d2), d2 >= 0,
7                 d = d1 + d2, d <= 10000.
8
9   query(x,y,d) -> string(x), string(y), int[64](d).
10  query("Sydney",y,d) <- f("Sydney",y,d), d >= 0, d <= 10000.
```

Fig. 5. The Datalog^{LB} encoding of the Flights program

```
answer_f(x,y,d) -> string(x), string(y), int[64](d).
answer_f(x,y,d) <- x = "Sydney", f_a(x,y,d), d >= 0, d <= 10000.

f_a(x,y,d) -> string(x), string(y), int[64](d).
f_a(x,y,d) <- query_f_a(x,ld,ud), ld <= ud,
              e(x,y,d), d >= 0, d >= ld, d <= ud.
f_a(x,y,d) <- query_f_a(x,ld,ud), ld <= ud,
              e(x,z,d1), d1 >= 0,
              f_a(z,y,d2), d2 >= 0,
              d = d1 + d2, d >= ld, d <= ud.

query_f_a(x,ld,ud) -> string(x), int[64](ld), int[64](ud).
query_f_a("Sydney",0,10000).
query_f_a(y,ld2,ud2) <- query_f_a(x,ld,ud), ld <= ud,
              e(x,y,d), d >= 0,
              ud2 = ud - d, ld2 = max(ld-d,0).

e(x,y,d) -> string(x), string(y), int[64](d).
```

Fig. 6. Constraint magic rewritten variant of the Flights program

Table 4 shows the results of evaluating the CMR variant of the Flights program without (CMR) and with (CMR+FP) filter predicate transformation for a collection of 19 different data graphs, with different structures.

For the LogicBlox evaluation, Table 4 reports performance decrease for three transformed programs with corresponding original run times below 0.1s, and visible improvement for all other benchmarks. The speed-up varies roughly between 2× for the original programs with the shorter run times and 8× for those with longer run times. Interestingly, the performance in XSB is very different. First, we observe that the run times for programs without the transformation are considerably shorter than in LogicBlox. Furthermore, applying the transformation has no effect on the three programs with the shortest original run

Table 4. Benchmark results for the `Flights` program

Graph	Datalog^{LB}		XSB	
	CMR	**CMR+FP**	**CMR**	**CMR+FP**
Graph 1	0.01 sec.	191.1 %	0.01 sec.	100.0 %
Graph 2	0.03 sec.	162.0 %	0.01 sec.	100.0 %
Graph 3	0.02 sec.	117.2 %	0.01 sec.	100.0 %
Graph 4	0.19 sec.	54.5 %	0.02 sec.	250.0 %
Graph 5	4.47 sec.	21.2 %	0.51 sec.	468.6 %
Graph 6	0.24 sec.	63.5 %	0.04 sec.	925.0 %
Graph 7	0.76 sec.	41.7 %	0.12 sec.	2266.7 %
Graph 8	2.91 sec.	22.1 %	0.31 sec.	442.8 %
Graph 9	65.79 sec.	13.3 %	5.28 sec.	988.8 %
Graph 10	5.76 sec.	42.0 %	1.26 sec.	504.8 %
Graph 11	1.94 sec.	21.3 %	0.19 sec.	163.1 %
Graph 12	2.40 sec.	38.0 %	0.39 sec.	2761.5 %
Graph 13	2.83 sec.	22.1 %	0.29 sec.	320.7 %
Graph 14	4.99 sec.	25.5 %	0.73 sec.	291.8 %
Graph 15	66.93 sec.	13.0 %	5.14 sec.	1010.9 %
Graph 16	1.92 sec.	22.9 %	0.17 sec.	170.6 %
Graph 17	2.85 sec.	21.5 %	0.27 sec.	340.7 %
Graph 18	1.92 sec.	21.4 %	0.16 sec.	181.2 %
Graph 19	67.60 sec.	13.3 %	5.06 sec.	1030.0 %

times, whereas it significantly slows down the evaluation of all other programs. We attribute this negative effect to the ordering of constraints—imposed by our transformation when introducing filter predicates—which forces overhead computations in the order-sensitive XSB.

6   Conclusion and Future Work

We presented a technique exploiting Datalog with aggregates to improve the performance of Datalog^{LB} programs with arithmetic (in)equalities. Our approach employs a source-to-source program transformation that approximates the propagation technique from Constraint Programming. The experimental evaluation of the approach shows good run time speed-ups on a range of non-recursive as well as recursive programs. Furthermore, our technique improves upon the constraint magic set transformation approach proposed by Stuckey and Sudarshan.

In the future we plan to investigate ways to integrate finite domain solvers with the Datalog's semi-naive bottom-up evaluation mechanism to enable further benefits from constraint propagation. We would also like to compare our transformation-based approach to the tabled constraint programming approach proposed by Cui and Warren [6], applied to a finite domain constraint solver.

References

1. Abiteboul, S., Hull, R., Vianu, V.: Foundations of Databases. Addison-Wesley (1995)
2. Ashley-Rollman, M.P., De Rosa, M., Srinivasa, S.S., Pillai, P., Goldstein, S.C., Campbell, J.D.: Declarative Programming for Modular Robots. In: Workshop on Self-Reconfigurable Robots/Systems and Applications at IROS (2007)
3. Bravenboer, M., Smaragdakis, Y.: Exception Analysis and Points-To Analysis: Better Together. In: ISSTA, pp. 1–12 (2009)
4. Bravenboer, M., Smaragdakis, Y.: Strictly Declarative Specification of Sophisticated Points-To Analyses. In: OOPSLA, pp. 243–262 (2009)
5. Choi, C., Harvey, W., Lee, J., Stuckey, P.: Finite Domain Bounds Consistency Revisited. In: Sattar, A., Kang, B.-h. (eds.) AI 2006. LNCS (LNAI), vol. 4304, pp. 49–58. Springer, Heidelberg (2006)
6. Cui, B., Warren, D.S.: A System for Tabled Constraint Logic Programming. In: Palamidessi, C., Moniz Pereira, L., Lloyd, J.W., Dahl, V., Furbach, U., Kerber, M., Lau, K.-K., Sagiv, Y., Stuckey, P.J. (eds.) CL 2000. LNCS (LNAI), vol. 1861, pp. 478–492. Springer, Heidelberg (2000)
7. Google's Protocol Buffers, http://code.google.com/apis/protocolbuffers/
8. Lam, M.S., Whaley, J., Livshits, V.B., Martin, M.C., Avots, D., Carbin, M., Unkel, C.: Context-sensitive program analysis as database queries. In: PODS, pp. 1–12 (2005)
9. Leone, N., Pfeifer, G., Faber, W., Eiter, T., Gottlob, G., Perri, S., Scarcello, F.: The DLV system for knowledge representation and reasoning. ACM Trans. Comput. Logic 7(3), 499–562 (2006)
10. Li, N., Mitchell, J.C.: DATALOG with Constraints: A Foundation for Trust Management Languages. In: Dahl, V. (ed.) PADL 2003. LNCS, vol. 2562, pp. 58–73. Springer, Heidelberg (2002)
11. LogicBlox, http://logicblox.com/
12. Loo, B.T., Condie, T., Garofalakis, M.N., Gay, D.E., Hellerstein, J.M., Maniatis, P., Ramakrishnan, R., Roscoe, T., Stoica, I.: Declarative networking: language, execution and optimization. In: SIGMOD, pp. 97–108 (2006)
13. Maier, D., Warren, D.S.: Computing with Logic: Logic Programming with Prolog. Benjamin/Cummings (1988)
14. Predictix, http://www.predictix.com/
15. Rosenwald, J.: SWI-Prolog Google's Protocol Buffers library, http://www.swi-prolog.org/pldoc/package/protobufs.html
16. Semmle, http://semmle.com/
17. Sereni, D., Avgustinov, P., de Moor, O.: Adding magic to an optimising Datalog compiler. In: SIGMOD, pp. 553–565 (2008)
18. Stuckey, P.J., Sudarshan, S.: Compiling query constraints (extended abstract). In: PODS, pp. 56–67 (1994)
19. White, W., Demers, A., Koch, C., Gehrke, J., Rajagopalan, R.: Scaling games to epic proportions. In: SIGMOD, pp. 31–42 (2007)
20. Wielemaker, J.: SWI-Prolog 5.10 Reference Manual (April 2010), http://www.swi-prolog.org
21. Zook, D., Pasalic, E., Sarna-Starosta, B.: Typed Datalog. In: Gill, A., Swift, T. (eds.) PADL 2009. LNCS, vol. 5418, pp. 168–182. Springer, Heidelberg (2008)

Symbolic Execution
of Concurrent Objects in CLP

Elvira Albert, Puri Arenas, and Miguel Gómez-Zamalloa

DSIC, Complutense University of Madrid, Spain

Abstract. In the *concurrent objects* model, objects have conceptually dedicated processors and live in a distributed environment with unordered communication by means of asynchronous method calls. Method callers may decide at runtime when to synchronize with the reply from a call. This paper presents a CLP-based approach to *symbolic execution* of concurrent OO programs. Developing a symbolic execution engine for concurrent objects is challenging because it needs to combine the OO features of the language, concurrency and backtracking. Our approach consists in, first, transforming the OO program into an equivalent CLP program which contains calls to specific builtins that handle the concurrency model. The builtins are implemented in CLP and include primitives to handle asynchronous calls synchronization operations and scheduling policies, among others. Interestingly, symbolic execution of the transformed programs then relies simply on the standard sequential execution of CLP. We report on a prototype implementation within the PET system which shows the feasibility of our approach.

1   Introduction

Increasing performance demands, application complexity and multi-core parallelism make distribution and concurrency omnipresent in today's software applications. There is thus a renewed interest in investigating techniques that help in simulating, debugging, testing, verifying, etc., distributed and concurrent programs. The focus of this paper is on developing a CLP-based framework for the symbolic execution of concurrent *object-oriented* (OO) imperative programs. Symbolic execution of a program consists in executing it "a la Prolog", i.e., using as arguments free (logic) variables. It allows thus reasoning about all the inputs that take the same path through the program. Symbolic execution is at the core of software verification [14] and testing tools [15,18,23]. In the latter case, by incorporating coverage and termination criteria, symbolic execution allows automatically obtaining test-inputs ensuring a certain degree of code coverage.

Within the OO paradigm, there are two main approaches to concurrency: (1) thread-based concurrency models (like those of Java and C#) are based on threads which share memory and are scheduled preemptively, i.e., they can be suspended or activated at any time. To prevent threads from undesired interleavings, low-level synchronization mechanisms such as locks have to be used.

C. Russo and N.-F. Zhou (Eds.): PADL 2012, LNCS 7149, pp. 123–137, 2012.

Experience has shown that software written in the thread-based model is error-prone, difficult to debug, verify and maintain [20]. (2) In order to overcome these problems, the *active-objects* model [6,13,17,20,21] aims at providing programmers with simple language extensions which allow programming concurrent applications with relatively little effort. Active (also called concurrent) objects operate similar to Actors [1] and Erlang processes [5].

In this paper, we consider the imperative OO language ABS [12] which is based on the active-objects concurrency model. A concurrent object, conceptually, has a dedicated processor and it encapsulates a local heap which is not accessible from outside the object. The language supports asynchronous method calls, which trigger activities in other objects without transferring control from the caller. The method caller may decide at runtime when to synchronize with the reply from a call. In general, an object may have many method activations competing to be executed. Among these, at most one process (or *task*) is active and the other processes are suspended in a process pool. Process scheduling is non-deterministic, but controlled by processor release points in a *cooperative* way. Cooperative scheduling means that switching between tasks of the same object happens only at specific scheduling points during program execution, which are explicit in the source code and can be syntactically identified.

The goal of this paper is to design (and implement) a *CLP-based symbolic execution* engine for concurrent ABS programs. This is a challenging problem as one needs to combine the OO and concurrent aspects of the ABS language with the backtracking mechanism required to perform symbolic execution. For *sequential* programs, we have seen in [7, 8, 9, 16] that, as symbolic execution is the standard evaluation mechanism of CLP, symbolic execution of imperative programs can be performed in a natural and efficient way by: (1) first, translating the imperative program into an equivalent CLP program and, (2) then, relying on the execution mechanism of CLP which performs symbolic execution natively.

The main contribution of this paper is to lift such CLP-based framework from the sequential to the concurrent OO setting. In particular, we first propose an automatic transformation of concurrent imperative programs into CLP programs which include specific builtin operations to handle the concurrency aspects of the language. The global state is made explicit in the translation as an additional argument of clauses. It includes the set of concurrent objects with their fields values and corresponding queues of pending tasks. We then provide an implementation in CLP of the builtins to treat all concurrency aspects of the language: (a) *asynchronous* calls are handled by adding corresponding pending tasks to the queues of the remote objects on which the calls are performed, (b) *synchronization* operations can be performed to suspend the execution of a task in an object until certain condition holds, (c) *future variables* become part of the state and allow synchronizing with the reply from a call, and (d) different *scheduling policies* can be easily integrated in our symbolic execution engine. We report on a prototype implementation of our proposal within the PET system [8] (a generic platform for CLP-based testing) and evaluate it on a series of small applications which are classical examples of concurrent programming.

$T ::= B \mid I \mid D \mid D\langle \bar{T} \rangle$	$A ::= N \mid T \mid D\langle \bar{A} \rangle$
$Dd ::= \textbf{data}\ D[\langle \bar{A} \rangle] = Cons[\ \mid\ Cons]$	$Cons ::= Co[(\bar{A})]$
$F ::= \textbf{def}\ A\ fn[\langle \bar{A} \rangle](\overline{A\ x}) = e$	$p ::= x \mid t \mid Co[(\bar{p})]$
$e ::= b \mid x \mid t \mid \textbf{this} \mid Co[(\bar{e})] \mid fn(\bar{e}) \mid \textbf{case}\ e\ \{\overline{p \Rightarrow e}\}$	$t ::= Co[(\bar{t})] \mid \textbf{null}$

$IF ::= \textbf{interface}\ I\ [\textbf{extends}\ \bar{I}]\ \{\ \overline{Sg}\ \}$	$Sg ::= T\ m\ (\overline{T\ x})$
$CL ::= \textbf{class}\ C\ [(\overline{T\ x})]\ [\textbf{implements}\ \bar{I}]\ \{\ \overline{T\ x};\ \overline{M}\ \}$	$M ::= Sg\ \{\overline{T\ x};\ s\ \}$
$s ::= s\ ;\ s \mid x = rhs \mid \textbf{await}\ g \mid \textbf{return}\ e$	$g ::= b \mid e? \mid g \wedge g$
$\qquad \mid \textbf{if}\ (b)\ \{\ s\ \}\ [\textbf{else}\ \{\ s\ \}] \mid \textbf{while}\ (b)\ \{\ s\ \} \mid \textbf{skip}$	
$rhs ::= e \mid \textbf{new}\ C[(\bar{e})] \mid e\ !\ m(\bar{e}) \mid e.m(\bar{e}) \mid x.\textbf{get}$	

Fig. 1. ABS Syntax for Functional (top) and Concurrent Object Level (bottom)

2   An Overview of Concurrent Objects

Our method is presented for the core of the ABS language [12], a successor of Creol [13, 6]. ABS is an OO language for distributed concurrent systems whose concurrency model is based on *concurrent objects*. An ABS *program* defines interfaces, classes, datatypes, and functions, and has a main block to configure the initial state. The *functional sub-language* allows abstracting from implementation details: abstract data types are used to specify internal, sequential computations, while concurrency is handled in the imperative part.

Fig. 1 gives the syntax of ABS programs. In the functional level (top), ground types T consist of basic types B (Bool, Int, etc.), names for interfaces I and data types D. In contrast to T, types A may contain type variables named N. Dd stands for data type declarations, where D has at least one constructor $Cons$. Function declarations F consist of a return type A, a function name fn, a list of variable declarations $\bar{x}$ of types $\bar{A}$, and an *expression* e. Expressions e include Boolean expressions b, variables x, (ground) terms t, the special read-only variable **this** which refers to the identifier of the object, constructor expressions of the form $Co[(\bar{e})]$, function applications of the form $fn(\bar{e})$, and case expressions of the form **case** $e\{\overline{p \Rightarrow e}\}$, where p is a *pattern*, as defined in the grammar.

In the *concurrent object level of* ABS (bottom), an interface IF has a name I and method signatures Sg, and it can extend other interfaces $\bar{I}$. A class has a name C, implements a list of interfaces, may contain class parameters and state variables $\bar{x}$ of type $\bar{T}$, and methods $\bar{M}$. The *fields* of the class are both its parameters and state variables. Objects are instances of classes; their declared fields are initialized to arbitrary type-correct values. A method signature Sg declares the return type T of a method m and formal parameters $\bar{x}$ of types $\bar{T}$. M defines a method with signature Sg, a list of local variable declarations $\bar{x}$ of types $\bar{T}$, and a statement s. All methods return a value (Unit plays the role of void in sequential programming). Statements may access fields of the *current class*, locally defined variables, and the method's formal parameters. Right hand side expressions rhs include object creation, method calls, and expressions e. Statements are standard for assignment $x = rhs$, sequential composition $s_1\ ;\ s_2$, **skip, if**, **while**, and **return** constructs. In **await** g, the guard g controls processor

```
data List⟨A⟩=Nil | Cons(A,List⟨A⟩);        def Bool contains⟨A⟩(Set⟨A⟩ s,A e)=
data Set⟨A⟩=EmptyS | Insert(A,Set⟨A⟩);       case s {
data Pairs⟨A,B⟩=Pair(A,B);                     EmptyS ⇒ False;
data Map⟨A,B⟩=EmptyM |                          Insert(e, _) ⇒ True;
      Assoc(Pairs⟨A,B⟩,Map⟨A,B⟩);              Insert(_, xs) ⇒ contains(xs, e);}
type FN, Packet=String;                    def Node findServer(FN f,Catalog c)=
type FNs=Set⟨String⟩;                         case c {
type File=List⟨Packet⟩;                        Nil ⇒ null;
type Catalog=List⟨Pairs⟨Node,FNs⟩⟩;            Cons(Pair(s, fs), r) ⇒
def B lookup⟨A,B⟩(Map⟨A,B⟩ ms, A k)=             case contains(fs, f) {
  case ms {Assoc(Pair(k,y),_) ⇒ y;               True ⇒ s;
           Assoc(_,tm) ⇒ lookup(tm,k);}          False ⇒ findServer(f, r); };}
```

Fig. 2. (Fragment of) Functional Sequential Part of ABS P2P Network

release and consists of Boolean conditions b, return tests x? and conjunctions. If g evaluates to false, the processor is released, the current process is *suspended* and the processor becomes idle. When the processor is idle, any enabled process from the object's pool of suspended processes may be scheduled.

Example 1. Our running example is a peer-to-peer (P2P) distributed application borrowed from [13]. Fig. 2 shows a fragment of the functional program which includes type definitions (*String* and *Int* are predefined) and three functions which are executed using strict evaluation. Fig. 3 shows the most relevant part of the imperative concurrent program (interfaces and the implementation of class Network are not shown). Calls to functions and functional data appear in italics. Function *nth* returns the n-th element of a list and *appr* concatenates two lists. A P2P network is formed by a set of interconnected peers which can act as clients and servers. Peers make the files stored in their database (an object of type DB) available to other peers, without central coordination. The only coordination is by means of an object of class Network. It is enough to know that nodes learn who their neighbors are by invoking getNeighbors implemented in this class. A node acting as client triggers computations with searchFile, which first finds a neighbor node s that can provide the file and then requests the file using reqFile.

Communication in ABS is based on asynchronous method calls, denoted $o\,!\,m(\bar{e})$, and future variables ($Fut\langle\cdot\rangle$). Method calls may be seen as triggers of concurrent activity, spawning new tasks (so-called *processes*) in the called object. After asynchronously calling $x=o\,!\,m(\bar{e})$, the caller may proceed with its execution without blocking on the call. Here x is a future variable, o is an object (typed by an interface), and $\bar{e}$ are expressions. A future variable x refers to a return value which has yet to be computed. There are two operations on future variables, which control external synchronization in ABS. First, a return test x? evaluates to false unless the reply to the call can be retrieved. Second, the return value is retrieved by the expression x.**get**, which blocks all execution in the object until the return value is available. A *synchronous call*, abbreviated as $v=o.m(\bar{e})$, is internally transformed into the statement sequence $x=o\,!\,m(\bar{e})$; $if(o==this)$ **await** x?; $v=x$.**get**.

```
class DBImp(Map⟨FN,File⟩ db)          Int getLength(FN fId) {
implements DB {                          Fut⟨Int⟩ lth; lth=db ! getLength(fId);
  File getFile(FN fId) {                 await lth?; return lth.get;}
    return lookup(db, fId);}          Packet getPack(FN fId, Int pNbr) {
  Int getLength(FN fId) {                File f=Nil; Fut⟨File⟩ ff;
    return length(lookup(db,fId));}       ff=db ! getFile(fId);
  Unit storeFile(FN fId, File file) {     await ff?; f=ff.get;
    db=Assoc(Pair(fId,file), db);}        return nth(f, pNbr);}
  FNs listFiles() {                    Catalog availFiles (List⟨Peer⟩ sL) {
    return keys(db);}                     Catalog cat=Nil; FNs fNs=EmptyS;
}                                         Fut⟨FNs⟩ fN; Catalog catL=Nil;
class Node(DB db,FN file)                 Fut⟨Catalog⟩ cL;
implements Peer {                         if (sL != Nil) {
  Catalog cat=Nil;                          fN=head(sL) ! enquire();
  List⟨Peer⟩ myN=Nil;                       cL=this ! availFiles(tail(sL));
  Network admin=null;                       await fN? & cL?;
  Unit run() {                              catL=cL.get; fNs=fN.get;
    Fut⟨Catalog⟩ c; Fut⟨List⟨Peer⟩⟩ f;      cat=appr(catL,Pair(head(sL),fNs));
    Server server ;                       }
    await admin != null;                  return cat;}
    f=admin ! getNeighbors(this);      Unit reqFile(Server sId, FN fId) {
    await f?; myN=f.get;                  Fut⟨Int⟩ l1; Fut⟨Packet⟩ l2;
    c=this ! availFiles(myN);             l1=sId ! getLength(fId);
    await c?; cat=c.get;                  await l1?; Int lth=l1.get;
    server=findServer(file, cat);         while (lth > 0) {
    if (server != null) {                   lth=lth - 1;
      this.reqFile(server,file);}}          l2=sId ! getPack(fId, lth);
  Unit setAdmin(Network admin) {            await l2?; Packet pack=l2.get ;
    this.admin=admin;}                      file=Cons(pack, file);}
  FNs enquire() {                         db ! storeFile(fId, file);}
    Fut⟨FNs⟩ f; f=db ! listFiles();     }
    await f?; return f.get;}
```

Fig. 3. Concurrent Part of ABS Implementation of P2P Network

Observe that checking if $o==this$ is necessary to avoid that the execution of the current object blocks when a synchronous local call is performed.

Example 2. The following fragment of code corresponds to a possible main method for the P2P example.

$Map\langle FN, File\rangle$ dataBase $= Assoc(Pair("file_0", Cons("a", Cons("b", Cons("c", Nil)))),$
$\qquad\qquad\qquad Assoc(Pair("file_1", Cons("d", Cons("e", Nil))), EmptyM));$
DB $db_1 = $ **new** DBImp($EmptyM$); DB $db_2 = $ **new** DBImp(dataBase);
Peer $n_1 = $ **new** Node($db_1, "file_0"$); Peer $n_2 = $ **new** Node($db_1, "file_1"$);
Peer $n_3 = $ **new** Node($db_2, "file_1"$); NetWork admin $= $ **new** NetWork(n_1, n_2, n_3);
n_1 ! setAdmin(admin); n_2 ! setAdmin(admin); n_3 ! setAdmin(admin);
n_1 ! run(); n_2 ! run();

The network configuration consists of three nodes, two databases and one Network object (admin). Nodes n_1 and n_2 are neighbors of n_3. Such six objects become distinct concurrent entities which communicate with each other by means of asynchronous calls and use *future* variables to eventually return/retrieve the results. Any concurrent object has its own heap, its queue of pending tasks and an active task (if any).

3   CLP-Translated Programs

The translation of *sequential* imperative programs into equivalent CLP programs has been subject of previous work (see, e.g., [3,7]). Intuitively, for each method (or function), the translation represents the method (or function) as well as the intermediate blocks within the method (e.g., loops, conditionals) by means of predicates in the CLP program. The fact that the imperative program works on a global state is simulated by representing the state using additional arguments of all predicates. We will not go into details of how the transformation of the sequential part is formalized (see [3,7]). Instead, we focus on the syntactic extensions of the ABS translated concurrent programs.

3.1   Syntax of CLP-Translated Programs

An ABS *CLP-translated program* is made up of a set of predicates, each of them defined by one or more *mutually exclusive clauses*, which adhere to the following grammar:

$$
\begin{aligned}
Clause ::=\ & Pred(Args, Args, S, S) : -[\bar{G},]\bar{B}. \\
G ::=\ & Num^* \, Op_R \, Num^* \mid Ref_1^* \backslash == Ref_2^* \mid Var = FTerm^* \mid \\
& diff(Var, FTerm^*) \mid \mathsf{type}(S, Ref^*, C) \\
B ::=\ & Var \, \#= \, Num^* \, Op_A \, Num^* \mid Pred(Args, Args, S, S) \mid Var{=}FTerm \mid \\
& \mathsf{new}(C, Ref^*, S, S) \mid \mathsf{gctField}(Ref^*, FSig, Var, S) \mid \mathsf{async}(Ref^*, Call, S, S) \mid \\
& \mathsf{setField}(Ref^*, FSig, Var^*, S, S) \mid \mathsf{await}(Call, Call, S, S) \mid \\
& \mathsf{get}(Var, Var, Call, S, S) \mid \mathsf{return}(Var^*, Var, S, S) \mid \mathsf{futAvail}(Var, Var) \\
Call ::=\ & Pred(Args, Args) \qquad\qquad Ref ::= null \mid Var \\
Pred ::=\ & BlockN \mid MethodN \mid FuncN \quad Op_R ::= \#> \mid \#< \mid \#>= \mid \#=< \mid \#= \mid \#\backslash = \\
Args ::=\ & [\,] \mid [Data^*|Args] \qquad\qquad Op_A ::= + \mid - \mid * \mid / \mid mod \\
Data ::=\ & Num \mid Ref \mid FTerm \qquad\quad S ::= Var
\end{aligned}
$$

We use *FuncN*, *MethodN*, *FSig* to denote the set of functions names, methods and field signatures. Clauses can define methods and functions which appear in the original source program (*MethodN*, *FuncN*) and additional predicates which correspond to intermediate blocks in the program (*BlockN*). *Num* is a number, *Var* is a Prolog variable and *FTerm* is a term that represents a corresponding functional data (namely p in Fig. 1). An asterisk on any element denotes that it can be either as defined by the grammar or a variable. Each clause receives as input a possibly empty list of parameters (1st argument) and a global state (3rd argument), and returns an output (2nd argument) and a final global state

(4th argument). The body of a clause may include a sequence of guards followed by a sequence of instructions, including: arithmetic operations, calls to other predicates, builtins to create objects and to write and read on object fields, and builtins to handle the concurrency.

We use three different kinds of inequalities in guards, namely, "$\backslash$==", "=" and *diff* to represent, resp., arithmetic comparisons, comparisons of references and pattern matchings in ABS functions. Virtual method invocations in the OO language are resolved at compile-time and translated into a choice of type builtins followed by the corresponding method invocation for each runtime instance. As expected, the builtin new(C, R, S_1, S_2) creates a new object of class C in state S_1 and returns its assigned reference R and the updated state S_2; getField($R, FSig, V, S$) retrieves in variable V the value of field $FSig$ of the object referenced by R in the state S; setField($R, FSig, V, S_1, S_2$) sets the field $FSig$ of the object referenced by R in S_1 to V and returns the modified state S_2.

In the translation of concurrent programs, when a concurrency construct appears (namely an asynchronous call, an **await** or **get** statement), we introduce a call to a corresponding builtin predicate that will simulate the concurrent behaviour. Besides, an important point to notice is that, for all **await** and **get** statements, we introduce a *continuation* predicate which allows us to suspend the current task (if needed) and then be able to resume its execution at this precise point. Also, we introduce in the translation *return* statements in order to syntactically identify in the CLP-translated program when the execution of a task finishes and thus another task from the queue can be scheduled.

Example 3. The following code shows the CLP-translated program for method reqFile of class Node.

```
'Node.reqFile'([This, SId, FId], [Out], S1, S2) :-
    async(SId,'Node.getLength'([SId, FId], [L1]), S1, S3),
    await(awguard1([L1], [_]), cont1([This, SId, FId, L1], [Out]), S3, S2).
awguard1([L1], [V]) :- futAvail(L1, V).
cont1([This, SId, FId, L1], [Out], S1, S2) :-
    get(L1, Lth, cont2([This, SId, FId, Lth], [Out]), S1, S2).
cont2([This, SId, FId, Lth], [Out], S1, S2) :- File ='Nil',
    while([This, SId, FId, File, Lth], [Out], S1, S2).
while([This, SId, FId, File, Lth], [Out], S1, S2) :- # <= (Lth, 0),
    getField(This,'Node.db', Db, S1),
    async(Db,'DBImp.storeFile'([Db, FId, File], [_], S1, S3),
    return([' Unit'], [Out], S3, S2).
while([This, SId, FId, File, Lth], [Out], S1, S2) :- # > (Lth, 0), # = (Lth1, Lth - 1),
    async(SId,'Node.getPack'([SId, FId, Lth1], [L2]), S1, S3),
    await(awguard2([L2], _), cont3([This, SId, FId, File, L2, Lth1], [Out]), S3, S2).
awguard2([L2], [V]) :- futAvail(L2, V).
cont3([This, SId, FId, File, L2, Lth], [Out], S1, S2) :-
    get(L2, Pack, cont4([This, SId, FId, File, Pack, Lth], [Out]), S1, S2).
cont4([This, SId, FId, File, Pack, Lth], [Out], S1, S2) :- File1 ='Cons'(Pack, File),
    while([This, SId, FId, File1, Lth], [Out], S1, S2).
```

The main features that can be observed from the translation are: **(1)** Methods (like reqFile), intermediate blocks (like $cont_1$) and functions are uniformly represented by means of predicates and are not distinguishable in the translated program. The input arguments list of all rules includes: the *this* reference, the list of input parameters of the ABS method from which the rule originates, and, in the case of predicates corresponding to intermediate blocks, their local variables. The output arguments list is always a unitary list with the return value. **(2)** Conditional statements and loops in the source program are transformed into guarded rules and recursion in the CLP program, resp., e.g., rules for *while*. **(3)** Additional rules are produced for the continuations after await and get statements. The calls to such continuation rules are included within the arguments of the await and get builtins (see e.g. rules '*Node.reqFile*' for the case of await or $cont_1$ for get). This allows the symbolic execution engine to suspend the execution at this point and resume it later. **(4)** A global state is explicitly handled. Observe that each rule includes as arguments an input and an output state. The state is carried along the execution being used and transformed by the corresponding builtins as a black box, therefore it is always a variable in the CLP program.

3.2   The Global State

In a sequential OO language, the global state carried along by the CLP-translated program only contains the data stored in the heap. Instead, in our concurrent setting, it has to include the set of existing concurrent objects, each of them with its associated internal state. The internal state of an object includes two pieces of information: (1) its heap (set of fields) which is not accessible from outside the object and (2) the queue of pending tasks. Formally, the syntax of the global state is as follows:

$$
\begin{aligned}
State &::= [\,] \mid [(Num, Object)|State] & Object &::= object(C, Fields, Q) \\
Fields &::= [\,] \mid [field(f, Data)|Fields] & Q &::= [\,] \mid [Task|Q] \\
Fut &::= ready(Data)|Var & Task &::= call(Call) \mid await(Call, Call) \mid \\
& & & \quad get(Fut, Var, Call)
\end{aligned}
$$

The state is represented as a list of pairs, where *Num* is a unique reference to the object *Object*. Each object is a term which includes its class *C*, a list of fields *Fields* and a queue *Q* of pending tasks. Each element in *Fields* is a term containing a field name and its associated data. The meaning of the different kinds of tasks *Task* and the syntax of future variables *Fut* is related to the symbolic execution of the translated programs and will be explained in detail in the next section.

Example 4. Consider an execution of the main method in Ex. 2 which starts from an initial state [ ]. After creating the objects of type DBImp, the state takes the form $[o_{db_1}, o_{db_2}]$, where $o_{db_1} = (1, object('DBImp', [field(db,'EmptyM')], [\,]))$ and $o_{db_2} = (2, object('DBImp', [field(db, dataBase)], [\,]))]$. Here, *1* and *2* are the references for db_1 and db_2, respectively. Similarly, the next three new instructions add three new elements to the state, resulting in $[o_{db_1}, o_{db_2}, o_{n_1}, o_{n_2}, o_{n_3}]$, where:

$$
\begin{aligned}
o_{n_1} = (&3, object('Node', [\, field(db, 1), field(file, "file_o"), field(cat,'Nil'), \\
& field(myN,'Nil'), field(admin, null)], [\,]))
\end{aligned}
$$

```
async(Ref,Call,S₁,S₂) :- addTask(S₁,Ref,call(Call),S₂).
await(Cond,Cont,S₁,S₃) :-
       Cond =..[_,[This|_],[Ret]], buildCall(Cond,S₁,S₂,CondCall), CondCall,
       (Ret = 'False' -> addTask(S₁,This,await(Cond,Cont),S₂), switchContext(S₂,S₃)
                       ; buildCall(Cont,S₁,S₃,ContCall), ContCall).
get(FV,V,Cont,S₁,S₃) :- Cont =..[_,[This|_],_],
           (var(FV) -> addTask(S₁,This,get(FV,V,Cont),S₂), switchContext(S₂,S₃)
                     ; FV = ready(V), buildCall(Cont,S₁,S₃,ContCall), ContCall).
return([Ret],[ready(Ret)],S₁,S₂) :- switchContext(S₁,S₂).
futAvail(FV,'False') :- var(FV), !.
futAvail(ready(_),'True').

addTask(S₁,Ref,T,S₂) :- getCell(S₁,Ref,object(C,Fs,Q₁)),
                        insert(Q₁,T,Q₂), setCell(S₁,Ref,object(C,Fs,Q₂),S₂).
switchContext(S₁,S₃) :- S₁ = [(Ref,_)|_], firstToLast(S₁,S₂),
                        switchContext_(S₂,S₃,Ref).
switchContext_(S,S,Ref₁) :- S = [(Ref₂,object(_,_,[]))|_], Ref₁ == Ref₂, !.
switchContext_(S₁,S₃,Ref) :-
       (extractTask(S₁,Task,S₂) -> runTask(Task,S₂,S₃)
                                   firstToLast(S₁,S₂), switchContext_(S₂,S₃,Ref)).
runTask(call(ShortCall),S₁,S₂) :- buildCall(ShortCall,S₁,S₂,Call), Call.
runTask(await(Cond,Cont),S₁,S₂) :- await(Cond,Cont,S₁,S₂).
runTask(get(FV,V,Cont),S₁,S₂) :- get(FV,V,Cont,S₁,S₂).
buildCall(ShortCall,S₁,S₂,Call) :- ShortCall =..[RN,In,Out], Call =..[RN,In,Out,S₁,S₂].
```

Fig. 4. Implementation of Concurrency builtins

and o_{n_2}, o_{n_3} are similar to o_{n_1} except for the object identifiers (4 and 5 respectively) and the value of field *file* (which is "*file₁*" in both objects). Field db has value *1* for o_{n_2}, and value *2* for o_{n_3}.

4   Symbolic Execution of Concurrent Objects

In dynamic (or concrete) execution, the initial state must be a ground term (e.g., if execution starts from a main, it is an empty list). Objects must be created using new/4 before their fields can be read or written. In symbolic execution, the intuitive idea proposed in [8] is that the state contains two parts: the known part (beginning of the list) with the objects that have been explicitly created during symbolic execution, and the unknown part which is a logic variable (tail of the list) in which new data can be added by producing the corresponding bindings. Therefore, the state starts being a free variable, and the implementation of get-Field/4 and setField/5 invokes predicates getCell/3 and setCell/4 which, if the object whose fields are going to be read or written is not in the known part, they instantiate the unknown part of the heap to be able to assume the previous allocation of the object and access its fields. Figure 4 shows the CLP implementation of the builtins to handle concurrency. They rely on the above getCell/3 and setCell/4 operations (whose implementation is in [8]) to symbolically access the heap. The following sections explain the behavior of the different builtins.

4.1 Asynchronous Calls

Predicate async(Ref,Call,S_1,S_2), given the current state S_1 adds the asynchronous call Call to the queue of tasks of the receiver object Ref producing the updated state S_2. The call to addTask/4 searches the state for the object pointed to by reference Ref by means of getCell/3, adds the task to its queue and updates the state with the updated object. As explained above, if the object pointed to by Ref is not in the known part of the state, getCell/3 produces a corresponding instantiation on the unknown part so that after this operation the object is in the state.

Example 5. Let us consider the symbolic execution of method reqFile, i.e., we run in CLP the goal *'Node.reqFile'*(In, Out, S_0, S_1). After the first call to async/4 the following instantiations are produced:

$S_0 = [(SId, object('Node', [field('Node.db', DB), \ldots]), [\,])]$
$S_1 = [(SId, object('Node', [field('Node.db', DB), \ldots]), [call('Node.getLength'(\ldots))])]$

Observe that, as expected, asynchronous calls do not transfer control from the caller, i.e., they are not executed when they occur but rather added as pending tasks on the receiver objects that will eventually schedule them for execution.

4.2 Implementation of Distribution and Concurrency

The fact that objects do not share memory ensures that their execution states (and thus the global state) are not affected by how distribution is realized. Therefore, symbolic execution can simulate distribution in any convenient way. We implement it in the following specific way: each object executes its scheduled task as far as possible and, when a task finishes or gets blocked, simulation proceeds circularly with the *next* object in the state (which could be running in parallel in an actual deployment configuration). In contrast, *concurrency* occurs at the level of object in the sense that tasks in the object queue are executed concurrently. Cooperative scheduling of the ABS language only specifies that the execution of the current task must proceed until a call to return/4, await/4 or get/5 is found. The scheduling policy which decides the task that executes next (among those ready for execution) is left unspecified.

Predicate switchContext/2 is used when the execution of the current task can no longer proceed. It gives the turn of execution to the first task (according to the scheduling policy) of the following object (the next one in the state). This is implemented by always keeping the current object in the head of the state, and moving it to the last position when its current task finishes or gets blocked, as it can be observed in the implementation of switchContext/2. If the current object has some pending task in its queue, the task is run (calling runTask/3). Otherwise (predicate extractTask/3 fails), the following object is tried. The execution of the whole application finishes when there is no pending task in any object (see first rule of switchContext_/3). Observe that there are three different types of tasks, call, await and get, whose behaviour is explained below.

One can implement different scheduling policies by providing concrete implementations of predicates insert/3 and extractTask/3. For instance, a FIFO scheduling policy is implemented by 1) inserting at the end of the queue, and 2) extracting always the first task. One can also use priority queues. The implementation becomes parametric on the scheduling policy by just asserting the selected policy and adding a parameter to predicates insert and extractTask to apply the selected policy. Furthermore, the language allows that different objects apply different scheduling policies. Thus, one can also select the desired policy per object. In this case, when scheduling a new task, we first read the asserted information which indicates the scheduling policy at the object level and, then, invoke the appropriate implementation of insert and extractTask for the current object. Having parametric scheduling policies is interesting in the application of symbolic execution to regression testing, as one then wants to save the selected policy within the test-cases in order to be able to replay them.

4.3   Synchronization: Future Variables, Await, Get and Return

Await. Predicate await(Cond,Cont,S_1,S_3) first checks its condition Cond by means of the meta-call CondCall. If the condition holds (Ret gets instantiated to 'True'), a meta-call to the continuation Cont is made (meta-call ContCall). Otherwise (Ret is 'False'), an await task is added to the queue of the involved object and we switch context. Let us observe that the calls wrapped within asyncs, awaits and gets as well as those stored in object queues, do not include states but just input and output arguments (see grammars in Sect. 3). This is because when a task is to be executed the current state must be used (and not the one that was current when the task was first created). Predicate buildCall/4 builds a *full* call from a call without states and the two states involved.

Future variables. The evaluation of await conditions can involve return tests on future variables. This is represented in our CLP programs by a call to the futAvail/2 builtin. Future variables occur in the global state in the output arguments of call tasks, and are available when they get instantiated. Since, in the context of symbolic execution, the return value of a method can be a variable V, we use the special term ready(V) to know whether the execution has finished (see the global state grammar in Sect. 3.2). Predicate futAvail/2 then just has to check whether the future variable is a CLP variable or is instantiated to ready(_) and returns, resp., 'False' or 'True'.

Example 6. Let us continue with the symbolic execution of method reqFile right after the execution of the first async (see Ex. 5). The call to await first produces a call to *awguard*$_1$ which checks whether the return value L_1 (future variable) of the call to *getLength* is already available (by means of the call to futAvail/2). Since it is not the case (i.e, a 'False' is returned) the execution of the current task cannot proceed, therefore the await task is added to the current object (so that it is re-tried later on) and context is switched (see

Table 1. Statistics about the Analysis Process

Benchmark	D=50			D=75			D=100		
	#I	#S	T	#I	#S	T	#I	#S	T
ProducerImpl.loop	1175	29	30	8028	134	140	35291	437	630
ConsumerImpl.loop	35	2	10	159	4	20	254	5	20
BoundedBuffer.append	2751	77	10	10494	198	30	24840	360	40
DistHT.lookupNode	319	11	20	697	17	10	1219	23	10
DistHT.getAllData	6	1	10	1406	21	40	9466	111	130
DistHT.getAllKeysAux	96	3	10	849	14	60	15622	173	360
DistHT.getAllKeys	22	1	11	160	3	30	1177	14	119
DistHT.putData	2220	50	10	14608	242	30	47532	612	70
DBImp.getLength	9108	253	61	30940	595	160	78208	1128	359
Node.run	0	0	10	51241	720	240	14219536	148466	45640
Node.getLength	3731	91	40	20475	351	150	55081	741	360
Node.getPack	1736	42	20	9919	169	40	26961	361	60
Node.reqFile	0	0	10	1988	28	110	16530	190	390
SessionImp.order	0	0	30	0	0	110	5647	59	320
AgentImp.free	616	22	10	1435	35	10	2491	47	10
DBImp.confirmOrder	95568	2167	599	4863238	71277	21230	-	-	-

the calls to addTask/4 and switchContext/2). This, in turn, produces a call to
runTask(call('Node.getLength'(...)),S_2,S_3) where the current state is now

$$S_2 = [(SId, object('Node', [field('Node.db', DB_1), \ldots]), [\ ]),$$
$$(This, object('Node', [field('Node.db', DB_2), \ldots]), [await(awguard_1(\ldots), cont_1(\ldots))])]$$

Return. When a method finishes its execution, we reach a return statement which
instantiates the future variable V associated to the current task to ready(V). This
allows that, if the task that requested the execution of this one was blocked await-
ing on this future variable, it can proceed its execution when it is re-scheduled.

Get. Predicate get first checks if the task can resume execution because the
future variable that is blocking it has become instantiated. In such case, the
continuation of the get is executed (meta-call ContCall). Otherwise, the current
task is added to the queue and context is switched.

5   Experimental Results in aPET

PET [8] is a test-case generation tool which aims at being a generic platform
for CLP-based test-case generation of different languages. This work implements
the core part of aPET, an extension of PET to generate test-cases from concurrent ABS programs. Currently, we have implemented the automatic translation
of ABS programs into CLP equivalent programs and extended the symbolic execution engine of PET with the concurrency primitives of ABS described along
the paper. Experimental evaluation has been carried out using several typical
concurrent applications: BBuffer, a classical bounded-buffer for communicating several producers and consumers, DistHT which implements a distributed

hash-table, PeerToPeer, our running example; BookShop, which implements a web shop client-server application. The code of the examples can be found in http://costa.ls.fi.upm.es/pet/apet.

Table 1 summarizes our experiments. Each set of rows contains the results of symbolically executing methods which belong to the above benchmarks. Symbolic execution for all methods works properly but, in the table, we have only showed the results for the methods which have more complex code and whose symbolic execution takes longer. As methods contain loops or recursion, symbolic execution does not terminate unless we introduce some termination criteria. In our case, we limit the length of the branches of the symbolic execution tree to a constant D (i.e., the depth of the tree to D). For each experiment, we show three sets of columns with the results of setting D to 50, 75 and 100 steps. Then, column $\#I$ shows the total number of instructions that have been executed including all branches, $\#S$ shows the number of solutions (branches) in the resulting symbolic execution tree, and T the total time (in milliseconds) required to build the tree. Experiments have been performed on an Intel Core i5 at 3.2GHz with 3.1GB of RAM, running Linux. All times have been computed as the average of 5 runs. When time is negligible, the system gives $T = 10$. As expected, when allowing larger values for the depth of the tree, the number of branches grows exponentially and thus the total time. This is not a problem related to our approach, but rather inherent to symbolic execution. Methods Node.run and DBImp.confirmOrder have larger times (and number of instructions) because the size of the code reachable from them is much larger (they contain many calls to other methods). For the last one, no result is computed in a reasonable time for $D=100$. In order to alleviate this problem, testing tools often limit the number of iterations on loops to a small number. Otherwise, the process can become quite expensive and too many test-cases can be obtained, as it can be observed from the large number of solutions obtained.

6   Conclusions and Related Work

We have presented the first CLP-based approach to symbolic execution of concurrent objects. The main idea is that concurrent distributed imperative programs can be translated into equivalent CLP programs which contain calls to builtin operations that simulate the concurrent behavior of the active objects paradigm. A unique feature of our approach is that, as the builtin operations can be fully implemented in logic programming, symbolic execution boils down to standard sequential execution of the CLP transformed program.

Process scheduling in concurrent objects has some similarities with the *dynamic scheduling* available in Prolog systems. However, the behavior is not the same and it cannot be directly used. This is because synchronization using dynamic scheduling can resume the execution of a task as soon as the await condition is satisfied, while cooperative scheduling only allows switching between tasks at specific scheduling points. As concurrent objects do not share memory, one could think of using Prolog's parallelism [11] to simulate the distributed execution by running each object as a parallel task. However, there is no support to simulate the fact that one object receives requests from another one by means of asynchronous calls. Some systems, like SWI, implement parallelism using threads with associated queues and synchronization is achieved by means of asserted variables. Indeed, for concrete execution, we have a working implementation using SWI Prolog parallelism in which tasks communicate by means of global variables (asserted in Prolog's database). However, the use of impure features does not allow the backtracking required in symbolic execution. Recent years are witnessing a wealth of research in testing concurrent programs. Symbolic execution is the central part of most static test-case generation tools, which typically obtain the test-cases from the branches of the symbolic execution tree. There is previous related work on using Creol for modeling and testing systems against specifications [2], though the problem of symbolic execution is not studied there. Later, [10] studies dynamic symbolic execution of Creol programs which combines concrete and symbolic execution. A fundamental difference with our approach is that they use an interpreter of Creol to perform symbolic execution, while in our case, we transform the ABS program into an equivalent CLP which does not require any interpretation layer, rather it is executed natively in CLP. Simulation tools for ABS programs that perform concrete execution [4] are only tangentially related to our work. This is because dynamic execution does not require backtracking and hence the use of CLP has less interest.

Recent work on testing thread-based languages studies ways to improve scalability [19] which could also be adapted to our context. Likewise, [22] proposes new coverage criteria in the context of concurrent languages that could be studied in our CLP-based setting. As future work, we plan to integrate our symbolic execution mechanism within a test-case generation tool in order to generate unit tests for ABS programs in a fully automatic way.

Acknowledgments. This work was funded in part by the Information & Communication Technologies program of the European Commission, Future and Emerging Technologies (FET), under the ICT-231620 *HATS* project, the UCM-BSCH-GR35/10-A-910502 *GPD* Research Group, the Madrid Regional Government under the S2009TIC-1465 *PROMETIDOS-CM* project and by the Spanish Ministry of Science (MICINN) under the TIN-2008-05624 *DOVES* project.

References

1. Agha, G.A.: Actors: A Model of Concurrent Computation in Distributed Systems. MIT Press, Cambridge (1986)
2. Aichernig, B.K., Griesmayer, A., Schlatte, R., Stam, A.: Modeling and Testing Multi-Threaded Asynchronous Systems with Creol. ENTCS 243, 3–14 (2009)
3. Albert, E., Arenas, P., Genaim, S., Puebla, G., Zanardini, D.: Cost Analysis of Java Bytecode. In: De Nicola, R. (ed.) ESOP 2007. LNCS, vol. 4421, pp. 157–172. Springer, Heidelberg (2007)
4. Albert, E., Genaim, S., Gómez-Zamalloa, M., Johnsen, E.B., Schlatte, R., Tarifa, S.L.T.: Simulating Concurrent Behaviors with Worst-Case Cost Bounds. In: Butler, M., Schulte, W. (eds.) FM 2011. LNCS, vol. 6664, pp. 353–368. Springer, Heidelberg (2011)

5. Armstrong, J., Virding, R., Wistrom, C., Williams, M.: Concurrent Programming in Erlang. Prentice Hall (1996)
6. de Boer, F.S., Clarke, D., Johnsen, E.B.: A Complete Guide to the Future. In: De Nicola, R. (ed.) ESOP 2007. LNCS, vol. 4421, pp. 316–330. Springer, Heidelberg (2007)
7. Gómez-Zamalloa, M., Albert, E., Puebla, G.: Decompilation of Java Bytecode to Prolog by Partial Evaluation. JIST 51, 1409–1427 (2009)
8. Gómez-Zamalloa, M., Albert, E., Puebla, G.: Test Case Generation for Object-Oriented Imperative Languages in CLP. TPLP, ICLP 2010 Special Issue (2010)
9. Gotlieb, A., Botella, B., Rueher, M.: A CLP Framework for Computing Structural Test Data. In: Palamidessi, C., Moniz Pereira, L., Lloyd, J.W., Dahl, V., Furbach, U., Kerber, M., Lau, K.-K., Sagiv, Y., Stuckey, P.J. (eds.) CL 2000. LNCS (LNAI), vol. 1861, pp. 399–413. Springer, Heidelberg (2000)
10. Griesmayer, A., Aichernig, B.K., Johnsen, E.B., Schlatte, R.: Dynamic Symbolic Execution of Distributed Concurrent Objects. In: Lee, D., Lopes, A., Poetzsch-Heffter, A. (eds.) FMOODS 2009. LNCS, vol. 5522, pp. 225–230. Springer, Heidelberg (2009)
11. Gupta, G., Pontelli, E., Ali, K., Carlsson, M., Hermenegildo, M.: Parallel Execution of Prolog Programs: a Survey. ACM TOPLAS 23(4), 472–602 (2001)
12. Johnsen, E.B., Hähnle, R., Schäfer, J., Schlatte, R., Steffen, M.: ABS: A Core Language for Abstract Behavioral Specification. In: Proc. of FMCO 2010. Springer, Heidelberg (to appear, 2011)
13. Johnsen, E.B., Owe, O.: An Asynchronous Communication Model for Distributed concurrent objects. Software and Systems Modeling 6(1), 35–58 (2007)
14. Khurshid, S., Păsăreanu, C.S., Visser, W.: Generalized Symbolic Execution for Model Checking and Testing. In: Garavel, H., Hatcliff, J. (eds.) TACAS 2003. LNCS, vol. 2619, pp. 553–568. Springer, Heidelberg (2003)
15. King, J.C.: Symbolic Execution and Program Testing. Commun. ACM 19(7), 385–394 (1976)
16. Meudec, C.: Atgen: Automatic Test Data Generation using Constraint Logic Programming and Symbolic Execution. Softw. Test., Verif. Reliab. 11(2), 81–96 (2001)
17. Meyer, B.: Object-Oriented Software Construction, 2nd edn. Prentice-Hall, Inc., Upper Saddle River (1997)
18. Müller, R.A., Lembeck, C., Kuchen, H.: A Symbolic Java Virtual Machine for Test Case Generation. In: IASTED Conf. on Software Engineering, pp. 365–371 (2004)
19. Rungta, N., Mercer, E.G., Visser, W.: Efficient Testing of Concurrent Programs with Abstraction-Guided Symbolic Execution. In: Păsăreanu, C.S. (ed.) SPIN 2009. LNCS, vol. 5578, pp. 174–191. Springer, Heidelberg (2009)
20. Schäfer, J., Poetzsch-Heffter, A.: Jcobox: Generalizing Active Objects to Concurrent Components. In: D'Hondt, T. (ed.) ECOOP 2010. LNCS, vol. 6183, pp. 275–299. Springer, Heidelberg (2010)
21. Srinivasan, S., Mycroft, A.: Kilim: Isolation-Typed Actors for Java. In: Ryan, M. (ed.) ECOOP 2008. LNCS, vol. 5142, pp. 104–128. Springer, Heidelberg (2008)
22. Takahashi, J., Kojima, H., Furukawa, Z.: Coverage based Testing for Concurrent Software. In: ICDCS Workshops, pp. 533–538. IEEE Computer Society (2008)
23. Tillmann, N., de Halleux, J.: Pex–White Box Test Generation for.NET. In: Beckert, B., Hähnle, R. (eds.) TAP 2008. LNCS, vol. 4966, pp. 134–153. Springer, Heidelberg (2008)

A Segment-Swapping Approach for Executing Trapped Computations[*]

Pablo Chico de Guzmán[1], Amadeo Casas[2],
Manuel Carro[1,3], and Manuel V. Hermenegildo[1,3]

[1] School of Computer Science, Univ. Politécnica de Madrid, Spain
[2] Samsung Research, USA
[3] IMDEA Software Institute, Spain
pchico@clip.dia.fi.upm.es, {mcarro,herme}@fi.upm.es,
amadeo.c@samsung.com

Abstract. We consider the problem of supporting goal-level, independent and-parallelism (IAP) in the presence of non-determinism. IAP is exploited when two or more goals which will not interfere at run time are scheduled for simultaneous execution. Backtracking over non-deterministic parallel goals runs into the well-known trapped goal and garbage slot problems. The proposed solutions for these problems generally require complex low-level machinery which makes systems difficult to maintain and extend, and in some cases can even affect sequential execution performance. In this paper we propose a novel solution to the problem of trapped nondeterministic goals and garbage slots which is based on a single stack reordering operation and offers several advantages over previous proposals. While the implementation of this operation itself is not simple, in return it does not impose constraints on the scheduler. As a result, the scheduler and the rest of the run-time machinery can safely ignore the trapped goal and garbage slot problems and their implementation is greatly simplified. Also, standard sequential execution remains unaffected. In addition to describing the solution we report on an implementation and provide performance results. We also suggest other possible applications of the proposed approach beyond parallel execution.

Keywords: Parallelism, Logic Programming, Trapped Computations, Backtracking, Performance.

1 Introduction

Extracting parallelism from sequential programs has become a key point for the practical exploitation of multicore technology. However, writing parallel application has shown to be a difficult, time-consuming, and error-prone process for developers. Consequently, the design of new language constructs that aim at easing the task of writing parallel applications and the development of language tools to uncover the parallelism intrinsic in sequential applications have drawn the interest of the research community. Traditionally, declarative languages have received much attention for both expressing and exploiting parallelism due to their comparatively clean semantics and expressive power. In particular, a large amount of effort has been invested by the community in the area of parallel

---

[*] Work partially funded by EU project IST-215483 *S-Cube*, MICINN project TIN-2008-05624 *DOVES*, and CAM project S2009TIC-1465 *PROMETIDOS*. Pablo Chico is also funded by a MEC FPU scholarship.

C. Russo and N.-F. Zhou (Eds.): PADL 2012, LNCS 7149, pp. 138–152, 2012.

execution of logic programs [1], where two main sources of parallelism have been iden-tified and exploited. Or-parallelism, efficiently exploited by systems such as Aurora [2] and MUSE [3], aims at executing different branches of the execution in parallel. On the other hand, and-parallelism schedules the literals of a resolvent to be executed in parallel. As an alternative to execution models specifically designed for executing and-parallel programs, efficient models to exploit and-parallelism based on the WAM were developed. The latter have the advantage of retaining the many optimizations present in the WAM which improve performance in the sequential execution parts — and, conse-quently, improve the overall performance. &-Prolog [4] (the first fully described such system) and DDAS [5] are among the best-known proposals in that class. In addition, other systems such as (&)ACE [6], AKL [7], Andorra [8] and the Extended Andorra Model (EAM) [9,10] have tackled the challenge of increasing performance of applica-tions by providing solutions that combine both kinds of parallelism. In this paper we will focus on *goal-level, independent and-parallelism*, a subclass of and-parallelism in which parallelism is exploited among goals which do not compete for resources (bindings to variables, I/O, databases, and others) at run-time.

Although previous systems that have exploited independent and-parallelism excelled at speeding up the execution of programs in multiprocessor systems [1], the difficulty of the machinery required to execute nondeterministic programs in parallel hindered their widespread availability. In particular, one of the most delicate aspects that these systems need to address is the management of trapped goals and stack unwinding, which are nec-essary to free garbage slots left by the nondeterministic parallel execution, resulting in a complex interaction between goal age, scheduling, and memory management [11,12]. Dealing with these issues required low-level, complex engineering, such as special stack frames in the stack sets [4,13].

Notwithstanding, non-determinism is an essential concept that arises in many core areas of computer science, such as artificial intelligence and constraint-based optimiza-tion, and is necessary in general problem-solving patterns, such as generate-and-test. In order to avoid complexity, recent approaches to independent and-parallelism focus more on simplicity than on ultimate performance, abstracting core components of the imple-mentation out to the source level. In [14], a high-level implementation of goal-level IAP was proposed that showed reasonable speedups despite the overhead added by the high level nature of the implementation. Other recent proposals [15], with a different focus from traditional approaches, concentrate on providing machinery to take advantage of underlying thread-based OS building blocks. Unfortunately, these implementations have not completely removed to date the need for low-level machinery in order to solve the trapped goal and garbage slot problems or are only appropriate for coarse-grain paral-lelism.

In line with this trend towards simplicity, we propose in this paper a novel solution for trapped goals and garbage slots that is based on reordering the stack to generate a stack state that could have been generated by a sequential SLD execution. Although the implementation of this solution is involved, in return it does not impose constraints on the scheduler for parallel execution which can remain unchanged. As a result, the scheduler and the rest of the run-time machinery can safely ignore the trapped goal and garbage slot problems and as a result their implementation and maintenance are greatly simplified. Finally, it is worth mentioning that our approach does not affect the performance of standard sequential execution.

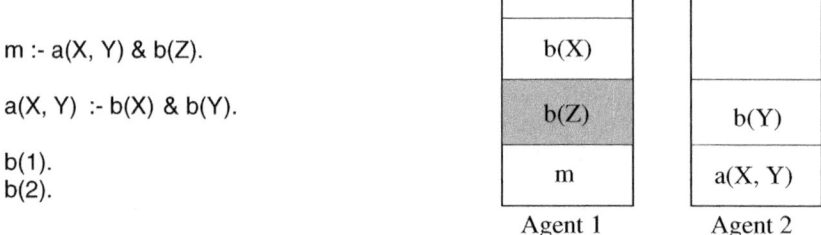

m :- a(X, Y) & b(Z).

a(X, Y) :- b(X) & b(Y).

b(1).
b(2).

Fig. 1. Example of execution state in IAP with trapped goals

In Section 2, we provide a brief introduction to the trapped goal problem and review some of the classical solutions that have been proposed to work around it. Section 3 focuses on the design and low-level details of our approach. Section 4 shows how this solution can be applied as well to solving the garbage slot problem. In Section 5, we present a performance evaluation of our approach, together with some data on the frequency of trapped goals in our implementation. Section 6 discusses how our technique can be applied to the implementation of execution strategies other than and-parallelism. Finally, Section 7 presents some conclusions.

For brevity, we assume the reader is familiar with the WAM [16,17] and the RAP-WAM [4] architectures.

2 The Trapped Goal Problem

As mentioned before, one of the main challenges in IAP implementation is how to deal correctly with backtracking. The problem stems from the fact that in principle any of the available parallel goals can be selected for execution, and therefore they can be piled on the execution stacks in an order which differs from the one which would be generated by sequential execution. Since IAP implementations have been traditionally required to follow a right-to-left backtracking order, this clearly leads to a problem: it is possible that a goal to be backtracked over is *trapped* under a logically older goal which would hinder the application of the usual right-to-left backtracking order [11,12]. We illustrate this with an example.

Figure 1 shows a possible state of the execution of a call to m using two agents.[1] When the first agent starts computing the first answer, goals a(X, Y) and b(Z) are scheduled to be executed in parallel. Let us assume that goal b(Z) is executed locally by the first agent and that goal a(X, Y) is stolen by the second agent for execution. Then, the second agent schedules goals b(X) and b(Y) to be executed in parallel, which results in goal b(Y) being locally executed by the second agent and goal b(X) taken by the first agent after finishing the computation of an answer for goal b(Z). In order to obtain another answer for predicate m, right-to-left backtracking requires computing additional answers for goals b(Z), b(Y), and b(X), in that order. However, goal b(Z) cannot be directly backtracked over since the execution of goal b(X) is stacked on top of it. Goal b(Z) has become a trapped goal.

Several solutions have been proposed to solve this problem. One of the original proposals makes use of *continuation markers* [4,13] to *skip* over stacked goals. Even though

---

[1] Herein we use agent to refer to an executing thread attached to its own stack set.

this solution deals correctly with the trapped goal problem, it leads to a quite complex implementation, having to cope with a relatively large number of cases. In addition, it needs to store a good amount of additional information, which increases memory overhead. Another solution (also suggested in [4,5,18] and developed further and studied in [13]) is to allow public backtracking, i.e., to let an agent perform backtracking over a choicepoint that belongs to the stack set of a different agent. Unfortunately, this solution creates a difference between logical and physical views of the stacks, and adds the complexity of having to manage parallel accesses to the private stacks of each of the agents. More recently, a further solution to the problem was presented in [14], which is based on moving the execution of the trapped goals to the top of the stack before the agent starts to compute a new answer of the parallel goal. This solution simplifies the implementation, reducing the need for low-level machinery in comparison to previous approaches. However, garbage slots may still appear in the stacks. A common disadvantage of these approaches is that the parallel scheduler is forced to directly manage trapped goals. Also, they all share a relatively complex marker architecture. All of this keeps the complexity of these approaches still relatively high, affecting overall system maintenance, extensibility, and portability, as well as affecting standard sequential execution.

A completely different approach to solving the trapped goal and garbage slot problems is *restricted scheduling*: to keep track of goal execution order dependencies in order to restrict the set of goals that an agent is allowed to execute to only those that ensure that no goal under them will become trapped or garbage [11,12]. An agent will not execute a goal G on a stack set if that stack set already contains a goal which could be backtracked over before goal G. While this solution shares with our approach the advantage of keeping stacks ordered, it complicates scheduling, adds overhead, and, above all, it comes at the cost of limiting the degree of parallelism in the system. In Section 5.2 we present a preliminary performance evaluation that shows that this effect can be quite significant in practice.

Finally, other systems with support for parallelism, such as Erlang [19], opted to create a new small stack set for each parallel goal. Note that Erlang, unlike Prolog, does not have support for backtracking. Therefore the problem we are tackling in this paper simply does not exist and the shape of the stacks is much simpler. The creation of multiple stacks (as needed) has also been suggested in the context of Prolog (as early as [11]), but the WAM multi-stack structure makes creating fresh stacks more expensive in time and memory.

Note that, while we have discussed so far approaches which keep the sequential solution order, trapped computations also appear in approaches to and-parallelism which give up on maintaining sequential execution solution order [20]. Therefore this paper is not as much a quest for efficiency as an attempt to find a simple solution (which minimizes changes to the scheduler while keeping the performance of the sequential execution) to a problem which seems unavoidable in and-parallel execution.

3   Reordering Stacks to Free Trapped Goals

In classical WAM implementations [16,17], the order of the choicepoints corresponds to the chronological order in which backtracking has to be performed. This strong correspondence between the logical and the physical view of the choicepoint stack (and the corresponding heap and trail segments) is exploited to perform backtracking efficiently, to reclaim all storage in the process in a very simple and fast way, and to pave

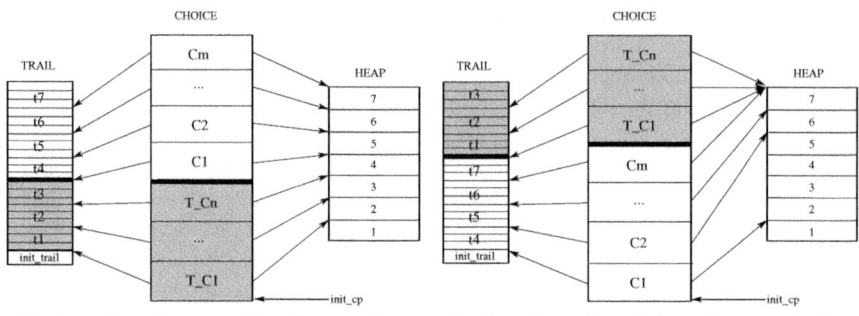

(a) Snapshot of a trapped goal execution.   (b) Snapshot after choicepoints reordering.

Fig. 2. Example of choicepoint reordering before executing a trapped goal

the way to other optimizations. Unfortunately, trapped goals break this correspondence between logical and physical views and therefore some of the WAM assumptions do not hold anymore. As we saw before, this lack of correspondence appears in most previous approaches, in which the logical and physical views are separated. We propose to force this correspondence by explicitly reordering the stacks. The advantage is that this will maintain all the invariants of the sequential execution, which will in turn facilitate maintenance and make sequential optimizations easier to adopt.

3.1 An Example of Stack Reordering

Figure 2(a) shows the stack state of an agent which needs to compute a new answer of a goal that is currently trapped. $T_C_1, \ldots, T_C_n$ correspond to the choicepoints generated by the previous execution of such trapped goal. $C_1, \ldots, C_m$ correspond to the choicepoints that belong to computations younger than the one of the trapped goal. Pointers on the left of each choicepoint indicate the corresponding trail section associated to each choicepoint (`trail(choice_point)`), and show the limits of the logical effects that need to be undone when backtracking over each of the choicepoints. Pointers on the right of each choicepoint indicate the corresponding heap section of each of the choicepoints (`heap_top(choice_point)`), and show the limit of heap memory that can be reclaimed on backtracking.[2] In this case, it is possible to reinstate the correspondence between the logical and physical views by reordering the choicepoints in the stack. Figure 2(b) shows the stack set after reordering, which involves moving the choicepoints of the trapped goal $T_C_1, \ldots, T_C_n$ to the top of the stack, therefore creating a new backtracking execution order. Note that reordering the choicepoints needs a trail cell reordering in order to remove those logical effects generated by previous goal executions.

In addition, this choicepoint reordering operation requires updating the heap top pointers $\mathtt{heap\_top}(T_C_1), \ldots, \mathtt{heap\_top}(T_C_n)$ of each choicepoint to the current heap top of the agent's stack set, in order to protect the heap positions which belong to the trapping computations from backtracking over the trapped goal.[3] If these pointers are not reallocated, backtracking over the previously trapped goal (now on top) would

---

[2] Similar pointers for the environment stack have been omitted from Figure 2(a).

[3] A similar idea was proposed in the context of tabling [21].

set the H (heap) pointer to a location under the trapping goal heap area and forward execution would run over the heap area used by the trapping goal. For example, if heap_top(T_C$_n$) were still pointing to cell 4, backtracking over T_C$_n$ would set H = 4 and forward execution could overwrite heap cell 5, which belongs to another computation. By setting all heap pointers from heap_top(T_C$_1$) to heap_top(T_C$_n$) to point to the heap top, trapped cells remain protected and heap construction happens at the top of the heap. Given that younger heap cells point to older heap cells (i.e., top points to bottom in this figure), dangling pointers will not appear.

After reallocating pointers as shown in the previous paragraph, the heap section corresponding to the old trapped computation becomes unreachable. This is taken care of by updating the heap top pointer heap_top(C1) associated with choicepoint C1. It is made to point to the cell where the first choicepoint of the initially trapped computation was pointing (heap_top(T_C1)). This will reclaim the unused section on backtracking as backtracking over C$_1$ will set the heap pointer to the start of the heap area.

A similar operation needs to be performed for the environment stack to protect the environments of the trapping computation from backtracking. Note that it is not necessary to reorder the heap or the environment frame stack, and that the choicepoint stack reordering operation can be executed without requiring the agents to compete for mutual exclusion since this operation only affects locally the stack set of each agent.

3.2 Stack Reordering Algorithm

Figure 3 presents the algorithm that allows restarting the computation of a particular trapped goal. The procedure move_exec_top is supplied with a *handler* h as argument, which corresponds to a structure that is associated to the execution of each parallel goal, and stores the execution state of such computation. Let us use the example shown in Figure 2 to understand this procedure.

Fields initCP(h) and lastCP(h) of a particular handler h return the initial and the last choicepoint of the parallel computation associated with h. Lines 4 and 5 initialize local variables to point to the first choicepoint and the first trail cell of the trapped goal.

The first step in the algorithm (line 7) is to check whether the goal execution that needs to be restarted is currently trapped or not. If that is the case then the choicepoints of the trapped goal execution need to be moved to the top of the stack and the corresponding trail sections to the top of the trail (Section 3.1). In the case of the example shown in Figure 2, lines 8 to 12 of the algorithm copy the choicepoints T_C$_1$, ..., T_C$_n$ to an auxiliary memory location denoted by tg_cp and, similarly, the choicepoints C$_1$, ..., C$_m$ are copied over to yg_cp, the trail sections t1 to t3 are copied onto tg_trail, and finally trail sections t4 to t7 are copied over to yg_trail.[4]

We maintain a handler stack, HandlerStack, keeping the chronological order in which goals are executed. It is used by lines 14 to 18 to update the pointers initCP and lastCP of those handlers representing goals younger than the trapped one.[5] Lines 19 and 20 update the pointers initCP and lastCP of the trapped handler. Line 21 moves the trapped handler to the top of the handler stack, corresponding with the new stack order.

---

[4] The amount of necessary auxiliary memory is usually negligible w.r.t. heap memory. Its size is the maximum between that of the trail/choicepoint stack section of the trapped goal and the trapping computations.

[5] Note that the complexity of this traversal is never worse than the choicepoint stack reordering.

```
 1  void move_exec_top(Handler h)
 2  begin
 3
 4      init_cp   = initCP(h);
 5      init_trail    = trail(initCP(h));
 6
 7      if (IS_YOUNGER_CP(CP(wam), lastCP(h))) then
 8          MEM_ALLOC_COPY(tg_cp, init_cp, lastCP(h));
 9          MEM_ALLOC_COPY(yg_cp, ONE_YOUNGER_CP(lastCP(h)), CP(wam));
10          MEM_ALLOC_COPY(tg_trail, init_trail,
11                          ONE_OLDER_TRAIL(trail(ONE_YOUNGER_CP(lastCP(h)))));
12          MEM_ALLOC_COPY(yg_trail, trail(ONE_YOUNGER_CP(lastCP(h))), trail(wam));
13
14          for all  handler OnTop(handler, h, HandlerStack) do
15          begin
16              initCP(handler) := initCP(handler) − sizeof(tg_cp);
17              lastCP(handler) := lastCP(handler) − sizeof(tg_cp)
18          end for;
19          initCP(h) := initCP(h) + sizeof(yg_cp);
20          lastCP(h) := lastCP(h) + sizeof(yg_cp);
21          MoveToTop(h, HandlerStack);
22
23          MEM_COPY(init_cp, yg_cp);
24          MEM_COPY(init_cp + sizeof(yg_cp), tg_cp);
25          MEM_COPY(init_trail, yg_trail);
26          MEM_COPY(init_trail + sizeof(yg_trail),   tg_trail);
27
28          for all  cp in yg_cp do
29          begin
30              trail(cp)   := trail(cp)   − sizeof(tg_trail);
31          end for;
32
33          heap_top(CP(init_cp)) := heap_top(initCP(h));
34          frame_top(CP(init_cp)) := frame_top(initCP(h));
35
36          for all  cp in tg_cp do
37          begin
38              trail(cp)   := trail(cp)   + sizeof(yg_trail);
39              heap_top(cp) := heap_top(wam);
40              frame_top(cp) := frame_top(wam);
41          end for;
42      end if
43  end;
```

Fig. 3. Algorithm to perform choicepoints reordering in an agent's stack set

The next step in the algorithm is to copy the choicepoints and trail sections back from the auxiliary memory locations tg_cp, yg_cp, tg_trail and yg_trail to the agent's stack and trail. This is performed in lines 23 to 26, which first move the choice-points $C_1, \ldots, C_m$ back to the stack, followed by choicepoints $T\_C_1, \ldots, T\_C_n$, and then move trail sections t4 to t7 over to the trail, followed by trail sections t1 to t3.

Lines 28 to 31 iterate over the trail pointers of each of the initially trapping choice-points `trail(C_1),..., trail(C_m)` to ensure that they point to the updated location of their corresponding trail sections. Lines 33 and 34 update the heap and frame top pointers of the first trapping choicepoint in the stack C_1 to point to the original value of the heap and frame top pointers of the first choicepoint of the initially trapped computation T_C_1, to allow a proper release of the trapped goal memory when the execution backtracks over choicepoint C_1. After executing lines 23 to 26, `init_cp` is now point-ing to C_1.

The algorithm then continues in lines 36 to 41 updating the trail pointers `trail(T_C_1),..., trail(T_C_n)` for each of the choicepoints of the initially trapped computation to point to the new location of their corresponding trail sections, as well as their heap top and frame top pointers to point to the current heap top of the agent's stack set, and therefore protect the heap and the environment frame of choicepoints $C_1,...,C_m$ from backtracking over the initially trapped goal. Now, the trapped goal is ready to be backtracked over using standard WAM machinery, after the auxiliary memory allocated in `tg_cp`, `yg_cp`, `tg_trail` and `yg_trail` is released.

Note that this algorithm assumes that choicepoints are not linked, but just stacked one over the previous one. In implementations where each choicepoint points to the previous one, reordering can boil down to pointer updating. Also, even for the case of memory reallocation, as will be shown in Section 5, backtracking over trapped goals does not occur very often, which reduces the impact of the overhead of the `move_exec_top` algorithm so that it does not significantly impact performance during execution of IAP.

3.3 Some Low Level Details

Our solution for the trapped goals problem requires considering two particular situations which have to be managed at a low level. The first one involves considering the *environment trimming* optimization, and the second one is related to "spurious" trail cells that may appear after the execution of the Prolog `cut/0` operator.

Environment Trimming. The *environment trimming* optimization reclaims, during for-ward execution, variables of the current environment when it is known that they are not going to be accessed again during forward execution. This is determined by comparing the ages of the current environment and the environment pointed to by the current choi-cepoint (using the `environment_cp` field of the choicepoint). In general, choicepoints protect local variables which have been created prior to the creation of the choicepoint. Under IAP execution, environment trimming may occur after a parallel call is performed. However, remote agents may generate choicepoints that protect some of these local vari-ables. Unfortunately, environment trimming is not aware of the existence of these remote choicepoints, and unsafe environment trimming operations may then be performed. The simplest way to solve this problem is to insert a "void" choicepoint before any parallel call in order to protect all current local variables. A lighter solution would involve mod-ifying the `environment_cp` field of the last choicepoint to protect all current local variables. The trail may be used to reinstall the original value of the `environment_cp` field before backwards execution is performed over this choicepoint.

Spurious trail cells. Trail entries keep track of the cells with *conditional bindings*: those made to variables which appeared before a given choicepoint was pushed and bound after that choicepoint is pushed. These cells will not be reclaimed after backtracking over the last choicepoint of a goal execution, but their bindings need to be undone on backtracking. After executing a `cut/0` operator, some of these bindings become unconditional (because the choicepoint which was pushed between cell creation and cell binding is no longer active), and therefore they should not be part of the trail. Some Prolog systems remove these bindings as soon as a `cut/0` is executed. However, other systems (such as Ciao, on which our implementation is based) do not do so because these "spurious" trail cells do not affect the standard sequential execution: they always point to reclaimed memory. Unfortunately, spurious trail cells become a problem after the execution of the `move_exec_top` procedure, since the order of cells in the trail changes. In the case of environment frame variables, environment trimming or *last call* optimizations could make these spurious trail cells point to new, live environment stack sections. Using again the example in Figure 2, referencing a spurious trail cell belonging to choicepoint T_C_n could affect the environment frame of C_1. The problem is solved by invalidating those trail cells of choicepoints $T\_C_1, \ldots, T\_C_n$ which do not belong to the heap and the environment frame segments of these choicepoints (because they are not conditional).

4   Dealing with Garbage Slots

In addition to the trapped goal problem, unused sections of the stack may appear when executing nondeterministic parallel programs under IAP. Let us consider the goal `g :- a, (b & c), d.`. Let us assume that all goals in the body of `g/0` can return several solutions. There are several scenarios that may occur depending on which subgoal fails:

- If subgoal `a/0` fails, sequential backtracking is performed.
- Since subgoals `b/0` and `c/0` are mutually independent, if either one of them fails without a solution, backwards execution must proceed over subgoal `a/0`, because subgoals `b/0` and `c/0` do not affect each other's search space.
- If subgoal `d/0` fails, backwards execution must proceed over the right-most choicepoint of the parallel conjunction `b & c`, which could be trapped, and recompute the answers for all subgoals to the right of that choicepoint. Thus, backtracking within a conjunction of parallel subgoals occurs only if initiated by a failure from outside of the subgoals conjunction (also known as *outside backtracking*). Instead, if the backwards execution is initiated from within the subgoals in the parallel conjunction, backtracking proceeds outside of all these subgoals, i.e., to the left of the conjunction (also known as *inside backtracking*).

Inside backtracking requires canceling the execution of the parallel goals that belong to the same parallel goal conjunction. These goals could be trapped and they would then produce *garbage slots* in the trail, choicepoint stack, and heap. Traditionally, IAP implementations have solved this problem with methods closely related to those used to solve the trapped goal problem, with similar drawbacks, including complexity in the implementation of the parallel scheduler, as well as impacting its performance.

The solution for trapped goals that we have presented in Section 3.2 can be reused to avoid leaving garbage slots in the stack by executing the procedure `move_exec_top` before canceling the execution of a trapped goal. By doing so, the corresponding trail cells and choicepoints of the canceled goal would be immediately reclaimed. The heap and environment frame stack would be reclaimed by garbage collection or upon backwards execution over the first choicepoint above the choice points of the canceled goal (choicepoint C1 following the example in Figure 2). In our set of benchmarks, the trapped heap memory increases the memory use by 1% in the worst case.

5   Performance Evaluation

We present in this section some of the performance results obtained with the implementation of our proposed solution in the Ciao [22,23] system. Such implementation is based on a previous high-level implementation of IAP [14], whose functionality has been augmented with the support to manage trapped goals and garbage slots.

All the benchmarks that are shown in this section were automatically parallelized with CiaoPP [24], using the annotation algorithms described in [25,26,27]. Finally, the actual performance results for each of the benchmarks were obtained after averaging ten different runs on a Sun UltraSparc T2000 (known as *Niagara* architecture) machine with eight 4-thread cores and 8Gb of memory running Solaris 10u1.

As we stated before, the aim of this paper is not so much to evaluate raw performance gains as it is to clarify up to which point the proposed technique is advantageous. In order to measure this, we will evaluate, on one hand, how often trapped goals appear in typical and-parallel computations and how much overhead the stack reorganization operations impose on the execution and, on the other hand, what speedups can be expected from executions which respect goal dependencies in order to avoid trapped computations.

We have used some deterministic and non-deterministic benchmarks selected from [28,20], listed in Table 1. All these benchmarks can produce trapped goals (i.e., goals stacked out of order w.r.t. the sequential execution). Note that even if some of these benchmarks only return one solution, they are forced to fail in order to backtrack and explore all the search tree. For deterministic benchmarks, this means that backtracking is attempted on all parallel goals which are piled out-of-order in the stacks following the logical dependencies across the execution tree, even if they do not produce additional solutions.

5.1   Deterministic and Non-deterministic Benchmarks

Table 2 presents the ratio of trapped goals vs. total parallel goals in the execution of each benchmark (column *Trapped*) and the percentage of the parallel execution time that is spent on the move_exec_top operation (column *Lost*). While this of course depends on the particular scheduling performed, it has been found to be quite stable in our current implementation. The evaluation is performed only up to 8 agents in order to make sure that every agent receives the full computing power of a core (threads in a core compete for shared resources, such as arithmetic units). The cases for one and two agents are also omitted since they do not generate trapped goals.

The first conclusion is that trapped goals do not appear very often in general, and their behavior depends largely on the nature of the benchmark itself. This scarcity favors our approach, whose cost grows with the number of trapped goals that need to be moved but otherwise does not pose overhead. This explains that the overhead imposed by the move_exec_top operation is very small in all of the benchmarks. These benchmarks create between 200 and 6000 choicepoints, and the precise number is related to the

Table 1. Benchmark descriptions

Program	Description
fft	Fast Fourier transform.
fibo	22nd Fibonacci number, executed sequentially from the 12th downwards.
hanoi	Towers of Hanoi of size 14, executed sequentially from the 7th downwards.
hanoi_dl	Towers of Hanoi with difference lists.
mmat	Multiplication of two 50×50 matrices.
pal	Recursively generates a palindrome of 2^{15} elements, switching to sequential execution when generating palindromes of length 2^7.
qsort	Use QuickSort to sort a list of 10000 elements, switching to sequential execution when the list to be sorted has 300 elements.
qsort_dl	QuickSort with difference lists.
iqsort	QuickSort with an irregular input list which makes the subgoals to be very different in size and favours the occurrence of trapped goals.
iqsort_dl	QuickSort with difference lists, sorting an irregular input list.
tak	Takeuchi function with arguments tak(14, 10, 3).
qsort_nd	Non-deterministic QuickSort (gives topological sortings) with an input list size 4000 elements, switching to sequential execution on 50 elements.

Table 2. Trapped goal statistics

Program	3 Trapped	Lost	4 Trapped	Lost	5 Trapped	Lost	6 Trapped	Lost	7 Trapped	Lost	8 Trapped	Lost
fft	0.03	0.00	0.00	0.00	0.05	0.00	0.09	0.00	0.10	0.00	0.15	0.00
fibo	0.00	0.00	0.02	0.01	0.03	0.00	0.03	0.01	0.04	0.01	0.06	0.02
hanoi	0.00	0.00	0.00	0.00	0.02	0.00	0.02	0.00	0.04	0.00	0.04	0.00
hanoi_dl	0.00	0.02	0.00	0.03	0.03	0.05	0.04	0.05	0.03	0.05	0.04	0.07
mmat	0.00	0.00	0.00	0.00	0.00	0.00	0.00	0.00	0.02	0.01	0.00	0.00
pal	0.00	0.00	0.00	0.00	0.00	0.00	0.02	0.00	0.01	0.00	0.03	0.00
qsort	0.02	0.00	0.02	0.00	0.07	0.00	0.11	0.00	0.06	0.00	0.09	0.00
qsort_dl	0.03	0.00	0.03	0.00	0.06	0.00	0.13	0.01	0.11	0.01	0.11	0.01
iqsort	0.03	0.00	0.09	0.01	0.18	0.02	0.26	0.02	0.27	0.02	0.35	0.03
iqsort_dl	0.03	0.00	0.08	0.01	0.15	0.02	0.20	0.02	0.28	0.03	0.36	0.03
tak	0.00	0.00	0.08	0.00	0.01	0.00	0.13	0.00	0.07	0.00	0.05	0.00
qsort_nd	0.02	0.00	0.07	0.00	0.14	0.00	0.21	0.00	0.33	0.01	0.39	0.01

amount of work that move_exec_top operation has to perform. The highest overhead (7%) is in hanoi_dl, which appears as an exceptional case. These results appear to support our thesis that it is debatable whether providing a very efficient but complex solution to the trapped goals problems is worth the effort. Instead, the proposed solution seems more practical since it greatly simplifies the parallel scheduler (with the added advantage, discussed later, that it can be reused for other purposes). This is even more so if we take into account that the frequency of trapped goals can be largely reduced by out-of-order backtracking with answer memoization [20], in which the traditional right-to-left order in backtracking is not maintained on parallel goal conjunctions. In this case the stack reorganization operation, although still necessary, is used even less frequently.

Table 3. Speedup comparison: dependence analysis vs. trapped goals

Program	2 Trap	2 Prec	3 Trap	3 Prec	4 Trap	4 Prec	5 Trap	5 Prec	6 Trap	6 Prec	7 Trap	7 Prec	8 Trap	8 Prec
fft	1.75	1.74	2.06	1.75	2.69	2.68	2.68	2.69	2.87	2.68	2.97	2.67	3.02	2.68
fibo	1.91	1.72	2.62	2.51	3.18	2.50	3.98	4.10	4.51	3.98	5.48	5.14	5.98	5.13
hanoi	1.81	1.81	1.94	1.91	2.93	1.91	3.24	3.24	3.41	3.21	3.74	3.23	4.11	3.42
hanoi_dl	1.41	1.41	1.41	1.41	1.86	1.40	2.95	2.76	3.06	2.75	3.59	2.75	3.75	2.67
mmat	1.52	1.53	2.24	2.23	2.95	2.91	3.72	3.67	4.35	4.11	4.97	4.68	5.63	5.42
pal	1.81	1.82	2.27	1.83	2.59	1.82	3.18	1.82	3.29	3.17	3.60	3.18	3.96	3.03
qsort	1.79	1.78	2.25	1.78	2.51	2.27	2.69	2.29	2.84	2.29	3.42	2.29	3.73	2.29
qsort_dl	1.73	1.71	2.23	1.71	2.44	2.19	2.65	2.19	3.13	2.19	3.25	2.19	3.32	2.16
iqsort	1.33	1.33	1.33	1.33	1.67	1.33	2.27	1.33	2.43	1.33	2.80	1.33	3.02	1.33
iqsort_dl	1.29	1.29	1.30	1.29	1.64	1.29	2.13	1.29	2.68	1.29	2.88	1.29	3.19	1.29
tak	0.89	0.89	1.77	1.77	2.38	2.38	3.50	3.50	3.54	3.54	4.47	3.54	4.25	4.40
qsort_nd	1.53	1.53	1.59	1.58	1.92	1.59	1.93	1.59	2.01	1.59	2.34	1.59	2.54	1.66

5.2 Avoiding Trapped Goals: The Impact of Goal Precedence

As mentioned in Section 2, a valid approach [12] to solving the trapped goal problem is to respect a notion of goal precedence during forward execution to completely avoid trapped goals. The low frequency of trapped goals previously found seems to suggest that this approach might be effective in practice.

In order to assess whether this is the case, we have developed a prototype implementation of IAP which schedules goals according to their precedence. Table 3 presents some of the speedups we obtained w.r.t. the Ciao sequential execution using this prototype (column *Prec*) and the speedups of our approach to handle trapped goals (column *Trap*), but adding the overhead of determining precedences: precedence dependencies are calculated but not used. The reason is that our dependency calculation algorithm may be suboptimal, and by applying it to both cases we obtain a conservative comparison.[6]

From the experimental results, the speedups obtained with a goal-precedence scheduler are in general reduced, with some benchmarks having a bigger difference (e.g., iqsort and iqsort_dl, probably due to an initial imbalanced split of the input list). In addition, the execution based on goal precedence of our prototype has been shown to be quite sensitive to the order in which the parallel goals are taken by remote agents, which makes the overall speed of the parallel execution less predictable. Finally, this solution is intended to match the behavior of standard sequential execution and is of no use in the case of strategies which use less strict execution strategies to increase the amount of search performed in parallel [20]. Therefore, we believe that avoiding trapped goals based on goal precedence has drawbacks which makes it not advantageous in practice.

6 Other Applications for Stack Reordering

So far, we have used move_exec_top to arrange the stack order so that it could have been generated by the standard sequential execution. However, other execution algorithms for logic programs can also benefit from this approach and take advantage of

---

[6] Note that the observed overhead of the precedence analysis is rarely above 1%.

the move_exec_top operation. We show two examples: *swapping evaluation* [29] and *intelligent backtracking* [30].

Swapping Evaluation. Swapping evaluation originates in the context of tabling [31]. Tabling records calls to goals to reuse their solutions and also to break infinite loops: repeated calls (which generate loops) are suspended and other clauses for the looping predicate are tried in order to generate answers which allow the suspended computation branch to continue. The first call to a tabled predicate is named the *generator* and subsequent calls are named the *consumers*. Consumers read answers from a table where the generator inserted them. If the generator returns answers on demand, consumers can appear out of the scope of the generator execution. These consumers, named *external consumers*, suspend waiting for the generator to compute more answers, and fail when there are no more available answers.

External consumers change the standard SLD execution order. Assume t/1 is tabled and has two solutions, t(1) and t(2). In the query ?- t(X), t(Y) goal t(X) is a generator and t(Y) is an external consumer. In an SLD execution, the answer sequence would be: {X=1, Y=1}, {X=1, Y=2}, {X=2, Y=1} and {X=2, Y=2}. Under tabled evaluation, t(Y) suspends and more answers of t(X), the generator, are generated on backtracking. In this case, under tabled execution, the sequence of answers would be: {X=1, Y =1}, {X=2, Y=1}, {X=2, Y=2} and {X=1, Y=2}. With standard scheduling strategies (e.g., batched scheduling), the suspension of an external consumer can lead to massive memory consumption.

Swapping evaluation exchanges the role of the external consumer and its generator to avoid external consumer suspension. When t(Y) consumes the first answer, the execution tree of t(X), which is trapped in the stack, is moved to the top of the stack so it can generate more answers. Swapping evaluation was originally implemented in XSB [32] and it is currently being ported to Ciao Prolog using the move_exec_top operation in order to untrap the execution tree of the generator.

Intelligent Backtracking. Intelligent backtracking strategies are based on the idea of performing backtracking directly on the goal which generated the bindings that caused a failure. In the following example:

```
p(X,Y) :- a(X), b(Y), c(X).
a(1). a(2). b(1). b(2). c(2).
```

the execution of c(X) fails because a(X) unified X with 1. Standard backtracking would retry b(Y) in a purposeless attempt to execute c(X) with a new binding for Y. Intelligent backtracking would change the backward execution order to allow backward execution over a(X) before backtracking over b(X). Intelligent backtracking needs to keep track of the point where bindings were produced in order to safely detect the closest useful backtracking point. Intelligent backtracking could make use of the move_exec_top operation to change the backtracking order.

7   Conclusions

We have presented a new algorithm to solve the trapped goal problem in which the stack is reordered to generate an execution state that could have been generated by the sequential execution. Using this algorithm simplifies the implementation of the scheduler for parallelism and does not affect the performance in case of standard sequential execution. Our approach has been implemented in the Ciao system, and we have performed an experimental evaluation of its effectiveness. We have also compared our approach to that based on keeping track of goal dependencies in order not to generate trapped goals and found that the restriction in the degree of parallelism brought about by the dependency-based approach makes this solution less advantageous. On the other hand, the use of the `move_exec_top` operation imposes only a limited overhead and does not restrict parallelism. Finally, the stack reordering operation presented in this paper represents semantically a change in the backtracking execution order, which we believe could be successfully applied to the implementation of tabling, swapping evaluation, or intelligent backtracking.

References

1. Gupta, G., Pontelli, E., Ali, K., Carlsson, M., Hermenegildo, M.: Parallel Execution of Prolog Programs: a Survey. ACM Transactions on Programming Languages and Systems 23(4), 472–602 (2001)
2. Lusk, E., Butler, R., Disz, T., Olson, R., Stevens, R., Warren, D.H.D., Calderwood, A., Szeredi, P., Brand, P., Carlsson, M., Ciepielewski, A., Hausman, B., Haridi, S.: The Aurora Or-parallel Prolog System. New Generation Computing 7(2/3), 243–271 (1988)
3. Ali, K.A.M., Karlsson, R.: The Muse Or-Parallel Prolog Model and its Performance. In: 1990 North American Conference on Logic Programming, pp. 757–776. MIT Press, Cambridge (1990)
4. Hermenegildo, M., Greene, K.: The &-Prolog System: Exploiting Independent And-Parallelism. New Generation Computing 9(3,4), 233–257 (1991)
5. Shen, K.: Overview of DASWAM: Exploitation of Dependent And-parallelism. Journal of Logic Programming 29(1-3), 245–293 (1996)
6. Pontelli, E., Gupta, G., Hermenegildo, M.: &ACE: A High-Performance Parallel Prolog System. In: International Parallel Processing Symposium IEEE Computer Society Technical Committee on Parallel Processing, pp. 564–572. IEEE Computer Society (April 1995)
7. Janson, S.: AKL. A Multiparadigm Programming Language. PhD thesis, Uppsala University (1994)
8. Santos-Costa, V.M.: Compile-Time Analysis for the Parallel Execution of Logic Programs in Andorra-I. PhD thesis, University of Bristol (August 1993)
9. Warren, D.: The Extended Andorra Model with Implicit Control. In: Jansson, S. (ed.) Parallel Logic Programming Workshop, Box 1263, S-163 13 Spanga, Sweden. SICS (June 1990)
10. Lopes, R., Santos Costa, V., Silva, F.: A Novel Implementation of the Extended Andorra Model. In: Ramakrishnan, I.V. (ed.) PADL 2001. LNCS, vol. 1990, pp. 199–213. Springer, Heidelberg (2001)
11. Hermenegildo, M.: An Abstract Machine Based Execution Model for Computer Architecture Design and Efficient Implementation of Logic Programs in Parallel. PhD thesis, U. of Texas at Austin (August 1986)
12. Hermenegildo, M.: Relating Goal Scheduling, Precedence, and Memory Management in AND-Parallel Execution of Logic Programs. In: 4th. ICLP, pp. 556–575. MIT Press (1987)
13. Pontelli, E., Gupta, G.: Backtracking in independent and-parallel implementations of logic programming languages. IEEE Transactions on Parallel and Distributed Systems 12(11), 1169–1189 (2001)
14. Casas, A., Carro, M., Hermenegildo, M.V.: A High-Level Implementation of Non-deterministic, Unrestricted, Independent And-Parallelism. In: Garcia de la Banda, M., Pontelli, E. (eds.) ICLP 2008. LNCS, vol. 5366, pp. 651–666. Springer, Heidelberg (2008)

15. Moura, P., Crocker, P., Nunes, P.: High-Level Multi-threading Programming in Logtalk. In: Hudak, P., Warren, D.S. (eds.) PADL 2008. LNCS, vol. 4902, pp. 265–281. Springer, Heidelberg (2008)

16. Warren, D.: An Abstract Prolog Instruction Set. Technical Report 309, Artificial Intelligence Center, SRI International, 333 Ravenswood Ave, Menlo Park CA 94025 (1983)

17. Ait-Kaci, H.: Warren's Abstract Machine, A Tutorial Reconstruction. MIT Press (1991)

18. Shen, K., Hermenegildo, M.: Flexible Scheduling for Non-Deterministic, And-parallel Execution of Logic Programs. In: Fraigniaud, P., Mignotte, A., Robert, Y., Bougé, L. (eds.) Euro-Par 1996. LNCS, vol. 1124, pp. 635–640. Springer, Heidelberg (1996)

19. Ericsson, A.B.: Erlang Efficiency Guide. 5.8.5 edn. (October 2011), http://www.erlang.org/doc/efficiency_guide/users_guide.html

20. Chico de Guzmán, P., Casas, A., Carro, M., Hermenegildo, M.: Parallel Backtracking with Answer Memoing for Independent And-Parallelism. In: Theory and Practice of Logic Programming, 27th Int'l. Conference on Logic Programming (ICLP 2011) Special Issue, vol. 11(4–5), pp. 555–574 (July 2011), http://arxiv.org/abs/1107.4724

21. Demoen, B., Sagonas, K.: CHAT: the copy-hybrid approach to tabling. Future Generation Computer Systems 16, 809–830 (2000)

22. Bueno, F., Cabeza, D., Carro, M., Hermenegildo, M., López-García, P., Puebla, G. (eds.): The Ciao System. Ref. Manual (v1.13). Technical report, School of Computer Science, T.U. of Madrid, UPM (2009), http://www.ciaohome.org

23. Hermenegildo, M.V., Bueno, F., Carro, M., López, P., Mera, E., Morales, J., Puebla, G.: An Overview of Ciao and its Design Philosophy. Theory and Practice of Logic Programming (2012), http://arxiv.org/abs/1102.5497

24. Hermenegildo, M., Puebla, G., Bueno, F., López-García, P.: Integrated Program Debugging, Verification, and Optimization Using Abstract Interpretation (and The Ciao System Preprocessor). Science of Computer Programming 58(1-2), 115–140 (2005)

25. Muthukumar, K., Bueno, F., de la Banda, M.G., Hermenegildo, M.: Automatic Compile-time Parallelization of Logic Programs for Restricted, Goal-level, Independent And-parallelism. Journal of Logic Programming 38(2), 165–218 (1999)

26. Cabeza, D.: An Extensible, Global Analysis Friendly Logic Programming System. PhD thesis, Universidad Politécnica de Madrid (UPM), Facultad Informatica UPM, 28660-Boadilla del Monte, Madrid-Spain (August 2004)

27. Casas, A., Carro, M., Hermenegildo, M.: Annotation Algorithms for Unrestricted Independent And-Parallelism in Logic Programs. In: King, A. (ed.) LOPSTR 2007. LNCS, vol. 4915, pp. 138–153. Springer, Heidelberg (2008)

28. Casas, A.: Automatic Unrestricted Independent And-Parallelism in Declarative Multiparadigm Languages. PhD thesis, University of New Mexico (UNM), Electrical and Computer Engineering Department, University of New Mexico, Albuquerque, NM 87131-0001 (USA) (September 2008)

29. Chico de Guzmán, P., Carro, M., Warren, D.S.: Swapping Evaluation: A Memory-Scalable Solution for Answer-On-Demand Tabling. In: Theory and Practice of Logic Programming, 26th Int'l. Conference on Logic Programming (ICLP 2010) Special Issue, vol. 10(4-6), pp. 401–416 (July 2010)

30. Pereira, L., Porto, A.: Intelligent backtracking and sidetracking in horn clause programs - the theory. Report 2/79, Departamento de Informatica, Universidade Nova de Lisboa (October 1979)

31. Warren, D.S.: Memoing for logic programs. Communications of the ACM 35(3), 93–111 (1992)

32. Sagonas, K., Swift, T.: An Abstract Machine for Tabled Execution of Fixed-Order Stratified Logic Programs. ACM Transactions on Programming Languages and Systems 20(3), 586–634 (1998)

Palovca: Describing and Executing
Graph Algorithms in Haskell

Michael Lesniak

University of Kassel
Research Group Programming Languages / Methodologies
Wilhelmshöher Allee 73
Kassel, Germany
mlesniak@uni-kassel.de

Abstract. Graph algorithms have fundamental applications in the real world but can be both cumbersome to implement in traditional languages and difficult to execute efficiently on modern multicore hardware. The Bulk Synchronous Parallel model of computation has recently been used to define vertex-centric computations on graphs. We describe an embedded domain specific language (using Haskell as the underlying host language) for specifying such algorithms, and show an implementation of an execution platform that allows to execute them on multicore systems in parallel. For several benchmarks varying in algorithm, graph size and edge distribution, we achieved speedups ranging from 9 up to 11 for 16 threads.

1 Introduction

Graph algorithms such as finding shortest paths, clustering or matching have fundamental applications in the real world. It can be quite challenging for non-experts to write and optimize them, in particular on multicore hardware [1].

A new approach to implement graph algorithms is based on Valiant's Bulk Synchronous Parallel (BSP) model of computation [2,3]. BSP models a concurrent computation as a set of independent processing nodes with local state that communicate solely by explicit message passing. This model has recently been adapted to support a new *vertex-centric* approach for graph algorithms called *Pregel* [4]. In Pregel, an algorithm performs *local* (sub)computations for each vertex: these computations do not have direct access to the whole graph structure but only to the local vertex state, the vertex' neighbors and received messages. Pregel uses C++ as the underlying description language and defines a class `Vertex` which is inherited to implement the actual vertex behavior. In our opinion, the usage of C++ has drawbacks for both users and implementators of the system. For users, concepts like iterators and inheritance are rather unintuitive in the context of graph algorithms. For implementators, problem-specific optimizations are difficult, since the vertex-centric C++-code can use arbitrary functions. A solution to both problems is to restrict the description of graph algorithms to a small sublanguage.

C. Russo and N.-F. Zhou (Eds.): PADL 2012, LNCS 7149, pp. 153–167, 2012.

Domain specific languages (DSLs) are a well-known software-engineering concept to describe solutions or problems in a restricted domain. Successful examples of DSLs are Verilog for hardware design [5] and SQL for databases [6]. For DSL users, the reduced vocabulary is more intuitive and makes development less error-prone. For implementators, DSLs offer potential for efficient implementation, since boundary conditions and particular features of the problems are known in advance and can be used for optimizations such as parallelization on shared-memory multicore machines. Although DSLs have both theoretical and practical advantages, e.g. are easier to prove for correctness and are self-documenting, they are seldom developed from scratch. The implementation of a compiler and the whole ecosystem that a modern language offers (debuggers, profilers and libraries) is rarely justified. Instead, modern DSLs are typically *embedded* into a host language, which provides the underlying infrastructure, and called Embedded Domain Specific Language (EDSL). The functional programming language Haskell is well-suited as a host language due to its high degree of abstraction [7] such as support for higher-order functions and monads. Successful Haskell EDSLs have been developed for hardware design [8], programming GPUs [9], describing graphics [10] and financial contracts [11].

In our work we combine the advantages of an EDSL and the ideas of the bulk synchronous parallel model and Pregel. We call our combination of the language and its execution platform *Palovca* for PArallel LOcal Vertex Calculations in hAskell. The full source code of our implementation, as well as the shell scripts for benchmarking and the raw benchmark results can be found at the author's software repository [12]. Our contributions in this paper are

- The definition of an embedded domain specific language to describe vertex-centric graph algorithms and an evaluation of Haskell's suitability as a host language for this purpose.
- The implementation of an execution platform that runs on shared-memory multicore systems. It is based on explicit concurrency, i.e. manual synchronization and explicit thread control.
- An experimental investigation of the platform with various benchmarks.

To summarize our results, the expressiveness of the EDSL is high and allows a concise and comprehensible formulation of vertex-centric algorithms. Our experiments have shown that the implementation scales very well. Depending on the particular graph, its edge distribution and the computational load per vertex, we achieve speedups between 9 and 11 with 16 threads.

The rest of the paper is structured as follows. Section 2 describes Palovca's underlying computational model. Section 3 shows its syntax and examples of vertex-centric algorithms. Section 4 describes the implementation in detail. Section 5 explains our benchmarks and discusses the experimental results. Section 6 reviews related work and Section 7 concludes and gives an outlook to future work.

2   Palovca's Computational Model

The BSP model that Palovca is based on uses independent processing nodes and messages. The computation is divided into a sequence of discrete steps called supersteps: In each superstep, all nodes work independently and are allowed to 1) perform computations on their local data 2) receive messages sent in the previous superstep, and 3) send messages to other nodes. The messages are delivered by the beginning of the next superstep, after all computations of the current superstep have finished. An advantage of BSP is its simplicity. By restricting communication to message passing, problems with concurrent synchronization, e.g. race conditions and deadlocks, do not occur. Since messages are only delivered between supersteps, developing and reasoning about algorithms is easier.

The central idea behind Pregel and Palovca is adapting BSP to graph problems. Vertices correspond to nodes and graph edges define the source and destination for messages. A sent message is delivered to all vertices which are connected to the source vertex by an edge (see Figure 1). Termination is handled as follows. In addition to the user-defined local state each vertex is in one of two states, active or inactive. Initially all vertices are active and run the algorithm. After each superstep, a node can switch to inactive state and is only reactivated by receiving new messages. When all vertices are inactive, the algorithm terminates.

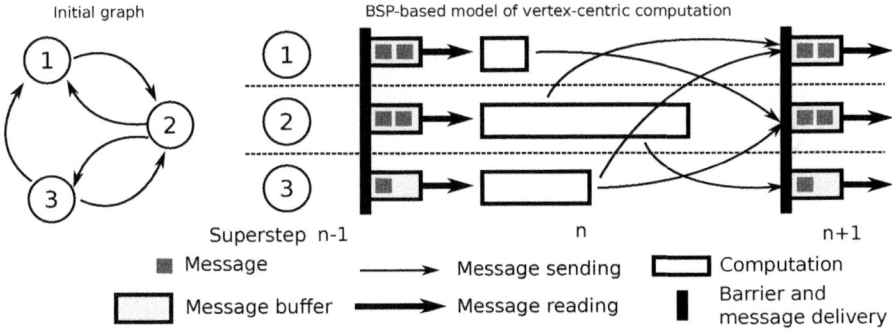

Fig. 1. Source graph and part of the computation of a vertex-centric algorithm showing message passing, buffering and local computations

With this approach, graph algorithms can be expressed quite elegantly, in particular with the Palovca language, as will be shown in Section 3.2. Moreover, we show in Section 5 that it allows for an efficient parallelization.

3   An EDSL for Vertex-Centric Graph Algorithms

In the following sections we describe the syntax and core functions of the EDSL. Two examples illustrate that the syntax is concise but easy to understand.

3.1 The Palovca Language

A major design requirement for the Palovca language was to allow a concise yet understandable formulation of vertex-centric algorithms. Therefore many functions typical for graph algorithms and BSP are part of the language, e.g. `size` to get the number of vertices in the graph, or `step` to get the number of the current superstep, numbered $0, 1, \ldots$

The language is internally based on a type that describes graphs (`Graph`), and a custom monad (`GraphM`) that handles the global and local states. Both have type parameters v, e and m for the local vertex state, the value of the edges and the value of the messages, respectively. All types need to be instances of `NFData` (see Section 4) but we omit that in nearly all type signatures for conciseness. An initial graph is typically created by calling one of the file-based input functions mentioned below. Palovca only supports directed graphs, although undirected graphs can easily be created by inserting symmetrical edges. A calculation with a graph is expressed with the function `run :: Graph v e m -> GraphM v e m () -> IO ()`. It receives a graph and a function working in the `GraphM` monad. The function is executed for each active vertex (in accordance with the computational model mentioned in the last section) until all vertices are inactive.

Table 1. Overview of core functions in Palovca

```
-- Graph query
size              :: GraphM v e m Int
step              :: GraphM v e m Int

-- Vertex modifications
modifyVertices :: Graph v e m -> GraphM v e m () -> IO ()

-- Vertex local state
identifier        :: GraphM v e m Int
get               :: GraphM v e m v
set               :: v -> GraphM v e m ()
halt              :: GraphM v e m ()

-- Message passing
messages          :: GraphM v e m [m]
send              :: m -> GraphM v e m
sendEdges         :: (e -> m) -> GraphM v e m ()
neighbors         :: GraphM v e m Int
```

Table 1 gives an overview of core functions. The local vertex state is accessible and modifiable by the `get` and `set` functions, respectively. A graph-wide unique identifier for each vertex is obtained by `identifier`. A vertex switches to inactive by calling `halt`. The number of neighbors is obtained by `neighbors`. Messages sent in the previous superstep are obtained by calling `messages`, messages for the next superstep are sent by `send` and `sendEdges`. While `send` sends the same message to all connected vertices (neighbors), sendEdges allows to modify the message with respect to the edge value of each particular neighbor.

For file-based input we defined a data format that specifies the vertex value, its neighbors and their possible edge values. Parsers for typical types are predefined in Palovca. Moreover, adding own parsers to support arbitrarily complex graphs is easily possible.

Some algorithms use a global convergence criterion to check for termination or want to collect statistical data. Therefore, Palovca supports *aggregators* (see Table 2): in each superstep a vertex can aggregate a value with aggregate; to reduce the number of type parameters, the aggregated value must *currently* have the same type as the vertex state. All aggregated values of a superstep are combined using a previously defined aggregator function [v] -> v. The new value is available in the next superstep and accessible by calling aggregator. Some algorithms, e.g. clustering or matching, need to change the graph topology. Our current version of Palovca supports adding and removing edges, and adding new vertices. Moreover, Palovca contains various functions that ease the formulation of vertex-centric graph algorithms such as selective sends and random neighbor selection. Many of these functions use higher-order functions or partial evaluation similar to sendEdges which was an argument for using Haskell as our host language.

Table 2. Aggregator functions for global communication between supersteps

```
setAggregator  ::  Graph v e m -> ([v] -> v) -> IO ()
aggregate      ::  v -> GraphM v e m ()
aggregator     ::  GraphM v e m v
```

3.2   Examples

In the following we describe two examples of vertex-centric algorithms and show their concise and understandable implementation in our EDSL. More examples of Palovca can be found in the source repository [12].

Pagerank. The pagerank algorithm [13] is widely known for being the foundation of the Google search engine: the pagerank of a webpage is a numerical value that is the higher the more pages point to it. In our modeling of this scheme vertices stand for pages, and edges denote links. The formulation of this algorithm is shown in Figure 2. Both vertices and messages are of type Double and edges are of type None (a synonym for ()), i.e. do not store any value. Each vertex state is initialized with $\frac{1}{N}$ where N denotes the size of the graph. In each superstep the new pagerank for each vertex is computed and distributed: First, a vertex collects all weights from its incoming neighbors with the messages function. Second, it accesses the graph size with size and updates its new pagerank with the shown formula using set. Third, the vertex distributes its updated value to its outgoing neighbors. The calculation stops after a given number of calculation steps. A nice property of having a lazy host language is shown at (*): we do not need to check that **n** is zero. In this case, no messages are sent and the division is never evaluated.

```
pagerank  :: GraphM Double None Double ()
pagerank = do
    msgs <- messages
    s    <- size
    let value = 0.15 / (toEnum s) + 0.85 * (sum msgs)
    set value

    s <- step
    if s < 30
        then do
            n <- neighbors
            send (value / toEnum n)  -- (*)
        else halt
```

Fig. 2. The pagerank algorithm in the Palovca EDSL

Single-source shortest path. Finding the shortest path between different vertices in a graph is one of the most important real-world applications of graph theory. In the single-source shortest-path (SSSP) problem we want to find the shortest path between a single source and every other vertex. The vertex-centric formulation of this algorithm is shown in Figure 3 and works as follows. Vertex state, edges and messages are of type **Double**. The state defines the distance from the source and is initially set to $1e30$ (denoting infinity). In an initialization phase that precedes the execution of the **run**-function, all vertices except the source (here the vertex with identifier 0) are set inactive using **modifyVertices**. In each superstep all active vertices receive messages from their incoming neighbors that denote the minimal distances of these neighbours. The minimal value of the distances is compared to the currently stored one: if it is smaller, the stored one is updated and sent to each outgoing neighbor, which reactivates them. When all vertices are inactive, the calculation is finished.

4   Implementation

In this section we describe the implementation of the EDSL and its parallelization using explicit concurrent programming. The presentation is occasionally simplified for conciseness; further details can be found in the documentation of the source code [12].

4.1   Implementing Palovca in Haskell

Language features of Haskell are not only useful in the Palovca language (e.g. lazy evaluation in Section 3.2), but in the Palovca implementation as well. We use monads to hide the underlying local and global state and higher-order functions to make the code reusable and maintainable.

```
sssp  :: GraphM Double Double Double ()
sssp = do
  i <- identifier
  let dist = if i == 0 then 0 else 1e30  -- 1e30 as infinity

  m   <- (minimum . (dist:)) 'liftM' messages
  cur <- get
  when (m < cur) $ do
    set m
    sendEdges (m+)
    halt

main :: IO ()
main = do
    -- Initialization phase
    g <- <graph reading>
    modifyVertices g $
        i <- identifier
        when (i > 0) halt
    run g sssp
```

Fig. 3. The SSSP algorithm in the Palovca EDSL

The two most important types of Palovca are `Graph` for whole graphs, and `Vertex` for single vertices (see Figure 4). All type variables need to be instances of `NFData` to avoid that the evaluation of expressions is delayed due to lazy evaluation and can instead be forced inside concurrently running threads. In the following we will explain the elements of the types by going through the computation of a single superstep for a vertex-centric algorithm `f`. The computation is divided into three phases: vertex computation (which includes message passing), aggregator computation, and termination checking. Another phase, topology modification, which handles vertex and edge modifications, is not shown due to space reasons. It is similar to the aggregator phase.

All vertices are stored in a `GArray` (1) which resembles an `IOArray` but supports additional parallel map- and fold-like operations; its internal details are explained in the next section. The first phase, which is computationally most expensive, evaluates `f` on all vertices of the graph: for inactive vertices nothing is done, for active ones `f` is executed in a monadic `GraphM` context. `GraphM` is a `StateT`-based wrapper around the graph and the currently computed vertex, additionally encapsulating the `IO` monad to support channel-based concurrent communication and mutable variables:

```
type GraphM v e m = StateT (ComputeState v e m) IO

data ComputeState v e m = ComputeState {
    cVertex :: Vertex v e m
  , cGraph  :: Graph v e m
}
```

```
data (NFData v, NFData e, NFData m) ⇒ Graph v e m = Graph {
      gVertices    ::  GArray (Vertex v e m)       -- (1)
    , gSuperstep   ::  Int                         -- (2)
    , gAggregator  ::  IORef (Maybe ([v] -> v))    -- (3)
    , gAggValue    ::  Maybe v                      -- (4)
    , gAggChannel  ::  SChan v                      -- (5)
}

data (NFData v, NFData e, NFData m) ⇒ Vertex v e m = Vertex {
      vIndex       ::  Index                        -- (6)
    , vValue       ::  IORef v                       -- (7)
    , vHalt        ::  IORef Bool
    , vEdges       ::  IORef [Edge e]                -- (8)
    , vMessages    ::  (SChan m, SChan m)            -- (9)
}

type Index    = Int
type Edge a   = (Index, a)
type SChan m  = IORef [m]
```

Fig. 4. The Graph and Vertex data types contain informations for representing arbitrary graphs and BSP-based computation

Functions in the domain specific language therefore access and modify either the current vertex or the graph. For example, modifying the local vertex state (7) with set is internally defined by

```
-- User-visible functions
set  :: v -> GraphM v e m ()
set  v = modify (const v)

modify  :: (v -> v) -> GraphM v e m ()
modify f = do
     v <- vertex
     liftIO $ modifyIORef (vValue v) f

-- Internal functions
vertex :: GraphM v e m (Vertex v e m)
vertex = access cVertex

access :: (ComputeState v e m -> a) -> GraphM v e m a
access f = f `liftM` StateT.get
```

Note that the use of higher-order functions improves conciseness. Message passing is also performed in this phase and implemented as follows: each vertex has a graph-wide unique identifier (6) which serves as its index in the GArray. The directed edges to its neighbors are stored as (identifier, edge-value) tuples (8).

When a message is sent, the vertex iterates over all tuples to contact neighbors separately: it accesses a particular pair of message channels (9) over the `GArray` by

```
sendTo  ::  Index  -> m -> GraphM v e m ()
sendTo  dst  msg = do
      vs <- access (gVertices . cGraph)
      v  <- liftIO (vs 'GArray.at' dst)
      ...
```

In the BSP model messages are buffered between successive supersteps (see Section 2). We use a pair of channels for each vertex to implement this separation: in even supersteps messages are read from the first channel and written to the second one, in odd ones this is reversed; `sendTo` writes to the first channel in even supersteps to send its message:

```
      ...
      s  <- superstep
      let choose = if s 'mod' 2 == 0 then fst else snd
          chan   = choose (vMessages v)
      liftIO $ atomicModifyIORef chan (\msgs -> msg:msgs)
```

In a previous version we separated message channel pairs to prevent contention which could occur when too many threads access the channel of one vertex. Each vertex had an array of pairs of message channels, such that each thread wrote messages to its own non-shared channel. Instead of improving performance it actually slowed down the computation. We think one reason was the increased number of lookups to access the correct channel for writing. Another reason was the additional overhead of combining the input of all channels for reading. Although we use the term channel (`SChan`) to describe the different buffers, we internally implement them as a list of elements wrapped in an `IORef` and modified by `atomicModifyIORef`. In our measurements we found it to be slightly faster than traditional channels.

In the first phase, where the vertex state was updated and messages were sent, vertices might also submit values to the global aggregator by calling `aggregate`. It accesses the graph's aggregator channel (5) and writes a value to it. In the second phase a new global aggregation value is calculated if a combination function has been initially defined in (3): all values from the channel are read, combined and stored in (4), hence are available in the following superstep. In the third phase all vertices are scanned: if an inactive vertex has new messages waiting in its channel, its state is changed back to active, and it will participate again in phase one of the following superstep. It is then checked if any active vertices exist. If not, the overall computation is stopped. Otherwise, phase one is restarted.

Since all mentioned operations on vertices are performed independently, the order of execution is not important. In fact, all operations on them can be performed in parallel (using map in all phases and an additional fold in phase three). Since vertices are stored in a `GArray`, the parallel operations are implemented there and discussed in the following section.

4.2   Dynamic Arrays and Parallelizing Vertex Evaluation

The GArray data structure, which is used for storing the vertices of the graph implements a dynamic (growable) array with additional support for parallel map- and fold-like operations.

A growable array is needed for vertex addition (vertex removal is not yet supported). Our implementation uses the traditional way to implement such arrays: if the array is full, a new one with twice the original size is created and the contents copied. Initially we implemented a chunk-based growable array, but found that indexed access times to elements increase. Since vertex additions are less frequent than indexed access, we chose the copy-based approach.

The vertex operations of the last section need two parallel operations: executing a function for every element in the IO-monad, and evaluating a binary function for every successive pair of elements. They resemble the well-known mapM_-function and a fold-like foldM-function, respectively. In the following we describe parallel implementations for both.

The mapM_-implementation it similar to Prelude.mapM_ but restricted to the IO-monad and needs an additional parameter that defines a chunksize:

```
mapM_ :: ChunkSize -> (a -> IO b) -> GArray a -> IO ()
type ChunkSize = Int
```

For parallelization, (the used part of) the array is divided into chunks of the defined size (or smaller). Forked threads, whose number is defined by the -N commandline parameter, work on these chunks in parallel. For each element of the chunk the given function is called. By default the chunksize is chosen such that each thread works on one chunk. For more irregular vertex-centric algorithms with large differences in the local vertex computation time, load balancing is achieved by choosing a smaller chunk size. We intentionally did not implement a mapM-function that returns the results of the called function since it would seldom be of use for our requirements.

To collect and combine information about vertices for internal use, for example their current activation state, we need a parallelized fold-like function:

```
foldM :: ChunkSize -> (b -> a -> IO b) -> (b -> b -> b) -> b
      -> GArray a -> IO b
```

foldM calls the fold function for each chunk in parallel (using the above scheme) and returns the combined result. The combination is computed sequentially since the number of chunks is rather small and the combinator function is fast to evaluate.

5   Benchmarks

We ran our experiments on a 2.3 GHz 16-core AMD Opteron 6134 with 32 GB RAM running a Linux-kernel 2.6.38-8 with GHC 7.0.3. Similar to Pregel and to ease comparison, we measured only the pure computation time, i.e. excluded graph reading. The speedup is calculated relative to the time when using a single thread, and all stated calculation times are the average of three runs.

The number of generated messages and thus allocated short-living chunks of memory is quite high and puts a lot of stress on the parallel garbage collector. By increasing the amount of memory that is allocated at once, we decrease the calls to the garbage collector and, since the collectors runs over the allocated data in parallel, increase the overall performance. For all benchmarks we chose -A1G -H16G for sequential and -A1500M for parallel runs as additional GHC runtime parameters (found by experimentation). The option -H sets the initial heap size (with G for gigabyte and M for megabytes as potential suffixes) and -A the size of the allocation area if the garbage collector needs to allocate more memory. Although these parameters worked well for all our benchmarks, it should be stated that parameter tuning for a particular algorithm and graph might result in even better speedups.

We chose three different benchmarks with varying number of active vertices and message sizes. In the pagerank benchmark the computational time per vertex is nearly equal and all vertices work until the calculation is finished. In the single-source shortest path benchmark the number of active vertices depends on the graph structure and is more irregular. In the semi-clustering benchmark (shortly described below) computational times are also more irregular and the message size increases over the course of the computation. We used randomly generated graphs with v vertices. The probability that two vertices are connected was p. The values for v and p were as follows: For the first two benchmarks we chose $v = 10^5$ and for the third $v = 10^4$. To see the effect of additional computational load through more communication, we chose two different probabilities for edge generation, $p_1 = 0.0001$ and $p_2 = 0.0002$ such that in the second case of each benchmark the number of edges is doubled. Note that the number of vertices is much smaller than the ones used in Pregel's benchmarks since it is distributed and uses hundreds of machines and therefore can handle much larger data sets. Since Pregel is not publicy available we were not able to directly compare running times.

Pagerank Benchmark. Figure 5 shows the benchmark results for the pagerank algorithm. Since all vertices are active over the whole computation and by default each thread works on a chunk of the same size, both graphs correspond to a typical speedup curve. Linear speedup is not reached as it is typical to parallel computations. In addition, the influence of more communication is visible for p_2. For p_1, computational time becomes so small that additional threads do not increase the performance. When the number of edges is doubled, more communication and thus more computations per vertex need to be performed, which results in better scaling.

Single-Source-Shortest-Path Benchmark. Figure 6 shows the results for the SSSP algorithm. The SSSP algorithm does have a messaging model where many vertices are initially inactive and more become active with each superstep. This makes an efficient parallelization more difficult since the number of active and

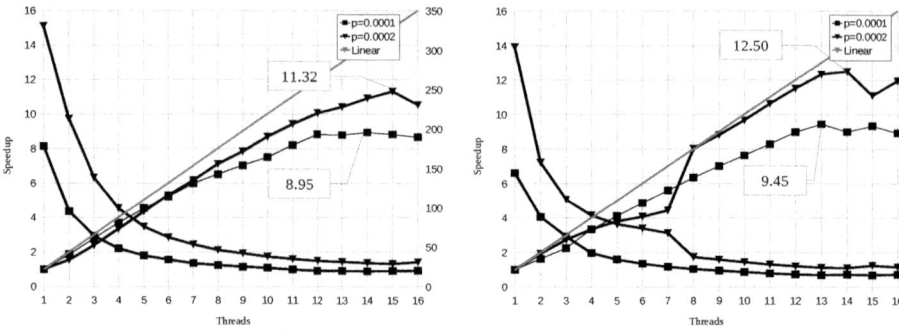

Fig. 5. Pagerank speedup and computation times for a random graph with $v = 10^5$ and $p_1 = 0.0001$ and $p_2 = 0.0002$, respectively

Fig. 6. SSSP speedup and computation times for a random graph with $v = 10^5$ and $p_1 = 0.0001$ and $p_2 = 0.0002$, respectively

thus processable vertices is initially low. Nevertheless, the first graph corresponds to a typical speedup curve since the computational load is higher than in the pagerank algorithm. The jump of the second graph at eight cores might be due to cache effects.

Semi-Clustering Benchmark. Our third benchmark implements a semi-clustering algorithm [4]. It greedily divides the graph into a set of C_{max} clusters with a maximum of V_{max} vertices in each. In contrast to traditional clustering problems, vertices can belong to more than one cluster. Semi-clusters are chosen such that their score $S_c = \frac{I_c - f_B B_c}{V_c(V_c - 1)/2}$ is maximized. Here, I_c denotes the sum of all internal edges, B_c the sum of boundary edges, V_c the number of vertices in the cluster and f_B a user-specified score factor. The local computational time is higher and more irregular than in the previous two benchmarks. Figure 7 shows the speedup graphs, which scale to about 10 for 16 threads. The difference between the graphs is low since the initial computational load in the first graph is already high.

6   Related Work

The foundation of Palovca's computational model is the Bulk Synchronous Parallel model of Valiant [2,3]. While some BSP libraries exist for classical programming languages, e.g. the Paderborn University BSP by Bonorden et al. [14] or the Green BSP library by Goudreau et al. [15], we are not aware of any Haskell-based implementations. Three Haskell approaches that could be used to implement BSP-like computations are Glasgow Distributed Haskell (GdH) [16], the CHP library [17] and data parallel Haskell [18]. GdH implements parallel and concurrent computations on distributed-memory systems. It allows to work with the same concurrent primitives that are traditionally used for concurrent

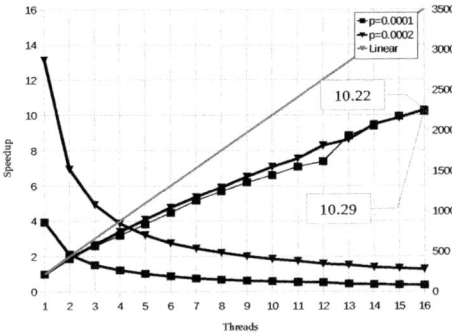

Fig. 7. Semi-clustering speedup and computation times for random graphs with $v = 10^4$, $C_{Max} = 20$, $V_{Max} = 20$. Probabilities are $p_1 = 0.0001$ and $p_2 = 0.0002$, respectively.

programming with Haskell in a distributed environment. Besides a simple BSP implementation it would be worthwhile to research if advanced BSP optimization techniques, e.g. relaxing the barrier restriction [19], could also be implemented. CHP implements combinators to allow communication of concurrent processes. Its computational model, which is based on Hoare's communicating sequential processes [20], is similar to BSP: Processes communicate over synchronous channels, interact via barriers and do not share any local data. Despite its similarity with BSP we did not choose CHP for the core of Palovca since computations in the IO-monad are rather difficult to express but were necessary for efficiency. Since vertex-centric computations are compelling data parallel, an efficient execution should be possible with automatically parallelized array operations as they are provided in data parallel Haskell. Unfortunately it is yet unclear how to handle communication between vertices in a side-effect free (pure) environment efficiently (see Section 7).

Palovca was strongly influenced by Malewicz et al.'s paper on Pregel [4]: they implement a distributed platform for large-scale vertex-centric graph algorithms with billions of vertices, programmable in C++. Albeit difficult to compare due to their different nature, their implementation achieves similar speedups as ours: when utilizing 16 times as many worker threads (absolute numbers were not stated) they reach speedups of about 10.

As we mentioned in Section 1, Haskell EDSLs are quite successful for a variety of domains. To the best of our knowledge there are no other DSLs for any problems that parallelize the execution nor libraries that allow to describe general (vertex-centric) graph algorithms. The closest approach to Palovca is the containers package, which defines the module Data.Graph. It allows to describe graphs and perform standard algorithms such as depth-first search [21].

7   Conclusion and Future Work

In this paper we defined and implemented Palovca (PArallel Local Vertex Calculations in hAskell) which consists of a Haskell-based EDSL for vertex-centric graph algorithms and an execution platform for shared-memory multicore machines. We have shown different examples of the conciseness and simplicity of the EDSL and provided benchmarks that show its scalability on modern hardware. We achieved speedups between 9 and 11 with 16 threads, depending on the particular problem and source graph. Unlike other data-parallel applications we did not yet achieve nearly linear speedups, since the irregularity of the vertex computations can be high. We found that the general approach of implementing a BSP-based computation in Haskell and applying it to vertex-centric calculations is feasible and enables good performance. Outside the scope of this paper, we developed a prototype of a pure execution platform that uses deterministic parallelism. Future work is need to improve it regarding performance and memory-consumption. Currently message passing and state update are quite memory-intensive and only a speedup of about 6 for 16 threads is achieved.

Future work may address different related topics: First, we have not used the advantages of having a restricted problem domain or the knowledge of the particular graph structures to optimize computations, e.g. by switching the execution platforms depending on the irregularity of the vertex computations. Second, experiments with Palovca's scalability regarding larger graphs could explore the efficient usage of the garbage collector with high amounts of short-living data. Third, it would be interesting to use the EDSL to generate source code in a low-level language and link it to an already existing BSP library as for example done in [22].

References

1. Grama, A., Karypis, G., Kumar, V., Gupta, A.: Introduction to Parallel Computing, 2nd edn. Addison Wesley (January 2003)
2. Valiant, L.G.: A bridging model for parallel computation. Commun. ACM 33(8), 103–111 (1990)
3. Valiant, L.G.: A bridging model for multi-core computing. Journal of Computer and System Sciences 77(1), 154–166 (2008)
4. Malewicz, G., Austern, M.H., Bik, A.J.C., Dehnert, J.C., Horn, I., Leiser, N., Czajkowski, G.: Pregel: a system for large-scale graph processing. In: Proceedings of the 2010 International Conference on Management of Data, SIGMOD 2010, pp. 135–146. ACM, New York (2010)
5. Thomas, D.E., Moorby, P.R.: The Verilog hardware description language, 4th edn. Kluwer Academic Publishers, Norwell (1998)
6. Codd, E.F.: The relational model for database management: version 2. Addison-Wesley Longman Publishing Co., Inc., Boston (1990)
7. Hudak, P.: Modular domain specific languages and tools. In: Proceedings of Fifth International Conference on Software Reuse, pp. 134–142. IEEE Computer Society Press (1998)
8. Alves, N.M.M., de Mello Schneider, S.: Implementation of an embedded hardware description language using haskell. Journal of Universal Computer Science 9(8), 795–812 (2003)
9. Elliott, C.: Programming graphics processors functionally. In: Proceedings of the 2004 Haskell Workshop. ACM Press (2004)

10. Elliott, C.: Tangible functional programming. In: International Conference on Functional Programming (2007)
11. Jones, S.P., Eber, J.M., Seward, J.: Composing contracts: an adventure in financial engineering (functional pearl). In: Proceedings of the Fifth ACM SIGPLAN International Conference on Functional Programming, ICFP 2000, pp. 280–292. ACM, New York (2000)
12. GitHub: Repository with source code, http://github.com/mlesniak/palovca
13. Brin, S., Page, L.: The anatomy of a large-scale hypertextual web search engine. In: Seventh International World-Wide Web Conference, WWW 1998 (1998)
14. Bonorden, O., Juurlink, B.H., von Otte, I., Rieping, I.: The paderborn university bsp (pub) library. Parallel Computing 29(2), 187–207 (2003)
15. Goudreau, M.W., Lang, K., Rao, S.B., Suel, T., Tsantilas, T.: Portable and efficient parallel computing using the bsp model. IEEE Trans. Comput. 48 (July 1999)
16. Pointon, R.F., Trinder, P.W., Loidl, H.-W.: The Design and Implementation of Glasgow Distributed Haskell. In: Mohnen, M., Koopman, P. (eds.) IFL 2000. LNCS, vol. 2011, pp. 53–70. Springer, Heidelberg (2001)
17. Brown, N.C.C.: Communicating haskell processes: Composable explicit concurrency using monads. In: Welch, P.H., Stepney, S., Polack, F., Barnes, F.R.M., McEwan, A.A., Stiles, G.S., Broenink, J.F., Sampson, A.T. (eds.) CPA. Concurrent Systems Engineering Series, vol. 66, pp. 67–83. IOS Press (2008)
18. Jones, S.L.P., Leshchinskiy, R., Keller, G., Chakravarty, M.M.T.: Harnessing the multicores: Nested data parallelism in haskell. In: Hariharan, R., Mukund, M., Vinay, V. (eds.) FSTTCS. LIPIcs, vol. 2, pp. 383–414. Schloss Dagstuhl - Leibniz-Zentrum fuer Informatik (2008)
19. Stewart, A., Clint, M., Gabarró, J.: Barrier synchronisation: Axiomatisation and relaxation. Formal Aspects of Computing 16, 36–50 (2004)
20. Hoare, C.A.R.: Communicating sequential processes (1985)
21. King, D.J., Launchbury, J.: Lazy depth-first search and linear graph algorithms in haskell. GLA, 145–155 (1994)
22. Anand, C.K., Kahl, W.: A domain-specific language for the generation of optimized SIMD-parallel assembly code. SQRL Report 43, Software Quality Research Laboratory, McMaster University (May 2007)

LEARNPADS++:
Incremental Inference of Ad Hoc Data Formats

Kenny Q. Zhu[1], Kathleen Fisher[2], and David Walker[3]

[1] Shanghai Jiao Tong University
[2] Tufts University
[3] Princeton University

Abstract. An ad hoc data source is any semi-structured, non-standard data source. The format of such data sources is often evolving and frequently lacking documentation. Consequently, off-the-shelf tools for processing such data often do not exist, forcing analysts to develop their own tools, a costly and time-consuming process. In this paper, we present an incremental algorithm that automatically infers the format of large-scale data sources. From the resulting format descriptions, we can generate a suite of data processing tools automatically. The system can handle large-scale or streaming data sources whose formats evolve over time. Furthermore, it allows analysts to modify inferred descriptions as desired and incorporates those changes in future revisions.[1]

1 Introduction

Ad hoc data is any *non-standard, semi-structured* data source for which processing tools and libraries are not readily available. HTML, XML, and data in relational databases are not ad hoc because many tools exist to manage such data. Despite efforts to standardize data formats, ad hoc data persists in many domains ranging from computer system administration to financial transactions to health care to computational biology. Figure 1 shows an example of a piece of ad hoc data source.

People continue to produce and use ad hoc data because such formats are expedient and compact. Typical uses of these data sources include system fault monitoring by tracking vital system health parameters in the system logs, intrusion detection by matching access patterns to intrusion models and data mining of scientific and financial data.

---

[1] This work was partially supported by NSFC Grants No. 61033002 and 61100050 and by NSF grant CCF-1016937. Any opinions, findings, and recommendations expressed in this material are those of the authors and do not necessarily reflect the views of the NSFC or NSF. The views expressed are those of the authors and do not reflect the official policy or position of the Department of Defense or the U.S. Government. The views, opinions, and/or findings contained in this article/presentation are those of the author/presenter and should not be interpreted as representing the official views or policies, either expressed or implied, of the Defense Advanced Research Projects Agency or the Department of Defense. Distribution Statement "A" (Approved for Public Release, Distribution Unlimited).

C. Russo and N.-F. Zhou (Eds.): PADL 2012, LNCS 7149, pp. 168–182, 2012.
© Springer-Verlag Berlin Heidelberg 2012

```
207.136.97.49  - - [05/May/2009:16:37:20 -0400] "GET /README.txt HTTP/1.1" 404 216
ks38.kms.com - kim [10/May/2009:18:38:35 -0400] "GET /doc/prev.gif HTTP/1.1" 304 576
```

Fig. 1. A Fragment of a Simple Web Server Log **wl**

Despite the expediency of producing ad hoc data, these data formats become very difficult to deal with because of missing documentation, the lack of tools, and corruptions caused by repeated redesign and re-engineering over time. In the past, ad hoc data analysis usually involved writing a shell script or one-off wrapper program to parse each data format, a practice which is expensive, error-prone and brittle.

The PADS project [11] aims to solve the above problems. The central technology is a declarative, type-based, data description language that allows the user to specify the physical layout of data sources as well as semantic properties of the data. PADS specifications can be compiled into a suite of processing tools such as a statistical reporting tool, an XML converter and a query engine, and programming libraries including parser, printer and traversal functions. Figure 2 shows the PADS description for the **wl** data source, and Figure 3 demonstrates the XML translator output automatically generated from the PADS description.

```
Punion client_t {                              Precord Pstruct entry_t {
    Pip        ip;      // 207.136.97.49              client_t     client;
    Phostname host;     // ks38.kms.com        ' ';   auth_id_t    remoteID;
};                                             ' ';   auth_id_t    auth;
                                               " [";  Pdate        date;
Punion auth_id_t {                             ':';   Ptime        time;
    Pchar unauthorized : unauthorized == '-';  "] ";  request_t    request;
    Pstring(:' ':) id;                         ' ';   Pint         response;
};                                             ' ';   Pint         length;
                                           };
Pstruct request_t {
    "GET ";    Ppath    path;
    " HTTP/";  Pfloat   http_ver;
    '"';
};
```

Fig. 2. PADS/C description for the **wl** format

```
<entry_t>                                    <remoteID>
  <client>                                     <unauthorized><val>-</val></unauthorized>
    <ip>                                     </remoteID>
      <elt><val>207</val></elt>              <auth>
      <elt><val>136</val></elt>                <unauthorized><val>-</val></unauthorized>
      <elt><val>97</val></elt>               </auth>
      <elt><val>49</val></elt>               <date><val>2009-05-05</val></date>
      <length>4</length>                     <time><val>16:37:20</val></time>
    </ip>                                    <timezone><val>-0400</val></timezone>
  </client>                                    ...
                                           </entry_t>
```

Fig. 3. Fragment of XML translator output from a **wl** record

The large scale as well as the streaming and evolving nature of many ad hoc sources led us to believe that a system which automatically *learns* a PADS description of a given data source and incrementally updates that description as the source evolves could significantly improve the productivity of ad hoc data users. As a first step, we developed an unsupervised algorithm LEARNPADS [7,8] that automatically infers a PADS description of a data source by computing frequency statistics for the *tokens* in the data and using an information theoretic score to guide description optimization.

This algorithm, however, has three important limitations: first, it requires that all data fit into main memory and contains procedures that are quadratic to the size of data, and therefore cannot *scale* to very large sources; second, when the data format evolves over time, the description has to be learned from scratch; and finally, machine learned description, while optimized for both precision and conciseness at the same time, may not be very user-friendly in terms of readability.

In this paper, we propose a new algorithm that *incrementally* infers descriptions of large scale or evolving ad hoc data sources. [2] The system takes as input an initial description and a new batch of data. It returns a modified description that extends the initial description and covers the new data. The initial description may be supplied by the user or automatically generated using the original LEARNPADS system. This iterative architecture enables the learning of a very large data source by partitioning it into smaller batches and updating the description from one batch to the next. It also allows the user to modify the description output at the end of an iteration (*e.g.*, renaming the automatically generated variable names), and insert the revised description back into the loop.

The main contributions of this paper are:

1. The design of a new system for generation of data descriptions and end-to-end ad hoc data processing tools from example data. The system is incremental and interactive, allowing it to process streaming data a chunk at a time, and allowing users to intercede to correct, adapt or modify intermediate results.
2. The engineering and optimization of algorithms that allow the system to handle large, industrial data sources of 30GB or more in a matter of a few hours.
3. The evaluation and analysis of the system on 16 different examples drawn from various industrial data sources.

In the rest of the paper, we describe the new incremental inference algorithm (Section 2) and give a comprehensive experimental evaluation of the system (Section 3). We then compare this system with some related work (Section 4) and finally conclude the paper (Section 5).

---

[2] A preliminary version of this paper appeared in an informal workshop [14].

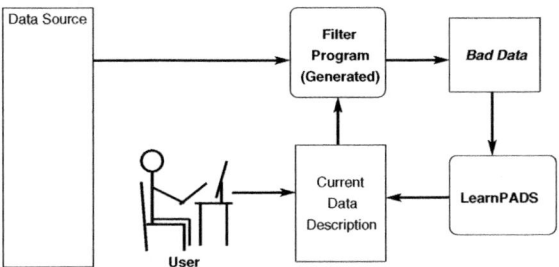

Fig. 4. An Overview of the Incremental Learning Framework

2   Main Algorithm

Our main algorithm can be characterized as a user-assisted bootstrapping processing, depicted in Figure 4. Given a candidate description D, the algorithm
uses D to parse the records in the data source. It discards records that parse
successfully, since these records are already covered by D, but it collects records
that fail to parse. Specifically, if a portion of a record fails to parse, that failure
will be detected at a particular node in D. These failed portions are collected in
an aggregation data structure A that mirrors the structure of D. When the algorithm accumulates M such records, where M is a parameter of the algorithm, it
transforms D to accommodate the places where differences were found (*i.e.*, by
introducing options where a piece of data was missing or unions where a new
type of data was discovered). It then uses the original LEARNPADS algorithm
to infer descriptions for the aggregated portions of bad data, and merge these
new sub-descriptions into the transformed description to produce a new, refined
description D'. This refined description subsumes D and describes the M new
records. In addition, the algorithm attempts to preserve as much of the structure
of D as possible, so users supplying initial descriptions can recognize the resulting
descriptions. This is so because the updates are localized to only parts of D that
incur parsing errors. At this point, the user can *optionally* get into the loop and
makes modification to the description to create D''. The algorithm then makes
D'' the new candidate description and repeats the process until it has consumed
all the input data. We call the main loop in Figure 4 the *incremental learning
step*. The initial description D can either be supplied by a user or be inferred
automatically by applying the original algorithm to N records selected from the
data source, where N is another parameter.

   In the following, we present the algorithm in more detail.

2.1   Preliminaries

Figure 5 defines the data structures for descriptions D, data representations R,
and aggregate structures A. Some data types, such as the switched union, are
omitted for the succinctness of the presentation. In these definitions, variable re

```
Basic notation:                                 Data representation:
c              (a string character)             BaseR ::= Str s | Int i | Error
s1.s2          (concatenation of strings)        SyncR ::= Good | Fail | Recovered s
first(s)       (first character of s)           R ::=
prefix(s)      (set of prefixes of s)              BaseR
sprefix(s)     (set of strict prefixes of s)     | SyncR
len(s)         (length of s)                      | PairR (R1, R2)
                                                  | Union1R R | Union2R R
Descriptions:                                     | ArrayR (R list, SyncR list, SyncR)
Base ::= Pint | PstringME(re) | PstringFW(e)      | OptionR (R option)
D ::=
   Base                (Base token)             Aggregation structure:
 | Sync s              (Synchronizing token)    A :: =
 | Pair (x:D1, D2)     (Pair with dependency)      BaseA Base
 | Union (D1, D2)      (Union)                   | SyncA s
 | Array(D, s, t)      (Array)                   | PairA(A1, A2)
 | Option D            (Option)                  | UnionA(Al, Ar)
                                                  | ArrayA (A_elem, A_sep, A_term)
                                                  | OptionA A
                                                  | Opt A
                                                  | Learn [s]
```

Fig. 5. Preliminary data structures used in incremental inference

ranges over regular expressions, e over host language expressions, s and t over strings, and i over integers. For simplicity of presentation, we assume just three base types: integers, strings that match a regular expression and strings with a fixed width specified by an expression. Synchronizing tokens, or *sync tokens* for short, correspond to string literals in PADS descriptions. Such tokens, which are often white spaces or punctuation, serve as delimiters in the data and are useful for detecting errors. The binary dependent pairs Pair (x:D1, D2) are a simplification of PADS more general Pstructs. The variable x refers to the data parsed by D1 and may be used in D2. The union Union (D1, D2) provides a choice between descriptions D1 and D2. An array description Array(D, s, t) has an element type described by D, a separator string s that appears between array elements, and a terminator string t. Finally, Option D indicates D is optional. To resolve ambiguities, unions are biased towards their first element, arrays are biased towards a longest match semantics and options are biased towards matching as opposed to not matching.

A term R is a parse tree obtained from parsing data using a description D. Parsing a base type can result in a string, an integer or an error. Parsing a sync token Sync s can give three different results: Good, meaning the parser found s at the beginning of the input; Fail, meaning s is not a substring of the current input; or Recovered s', meaning s is not found at the beginning of the input, but can be *recovered* after "skipping" string s'. The parse of a pair is a pair of representations, and the parse of a union is either the parse of the first branch or the parse of the second branch. The parse of an option is either the parse of its body or empty. The parse of an array includes a list of parses for the element type, a list of parses for the separator and a parse for the terminator which appears at the end of the array.

An aggregation structure accumulates the set of currently unparseable data fragments whose form must be learned for inclusion in the grammar. The aggregation structure mirrors the structure of the description D with two additional nodes: an Opt node and a Learn node. The Learn nodes accumulate extra data whose structure must be learned. The Opt nodes do the opposite: they mark where data were missing. An invariant of the aggregation structure is that newly inserted Opt nodes always wrap either a BaseA or a SyncA node.

2.2   Incremental Learning Step

Figure 6 gives pseudo-code for the *incremental learning step*. The input is the current description D and a batch of data records xs. The init_aggregate function initializes an empty aggregate according to description D. During parsing, the algorithm iteratively updates a list of possible aggregates As, seeded with the initial aggregate of D. For each data record x, the algorithm uses the parse function to produce a list Rs of possible parses. It then calls the aggregate function to merge each parse R in the current list of parses with each aggregate A in the current list of aggregates. (We use ' : : ' to denote prepending an element onto the front of a list.) Note that the potentially large number of parses and the growing list of aggregates in the inner loop are the performance bottleneck. We will show in Section 2.6 some strategies to alleviate this complexity.

```
incremental_step(D, xs) =
  As = [init_aggregate(D)];
  foreach x in xs {
    Rs = parse(D, x);
    As' = [];
    foreach R in Rs {
      foreach A in As {
        A' = aggregate(A, R);
        As' = A' :: As'
      }
    }
    As = As'
  }
  best_a = select_best(As);
  D' = update_desc(D, best_A);
  return D'
```

Fig. 6. Pseudo-code for the incremental learning step

When the system finishes parsing all the input data, the algorithm uses the select_best function to select the best aggregate from the list of candidate aggregates As. The select_best function counts the total number of Opt and Learn nodes in each of the aggregates, and returns the one with the smallest number. The idea is that the aggregate with the smallest number of added nodes is more likely to represent a description that is closest to the original description.

Finally, the update_desc function uses the structure of the best aggregate to update the previous description D to produce the new current description D'. The update_desc function works by doing two things. First, it converts the aggregate structure back to a PADS description with Opt nodes translated to Poption types. In addition, it invokes the LEARNPADS format inference algorithm to learn a sub-description for the data collected at each of the Learn nodes and replaces these

Learn nodes with these new sub-descriptions. Second, it uses rewriting rules to improve the overall description.

2.3 Parsing

Our parser is a top-down recursive descent parser that performs error detection and recovery using synchronizing tokens. Figure 7 describes the most important elements of the parsing algorithm. For simplicity and brevity, we describe the algorithm abstractly using a relation of the form $(R,m) \in L(D,E,s,s')$. This relation may be read "using description D and operating within the environment E, parsing the input $I = s.s'$ will consume input prefix s and leave s' as the residual input, returning the parse tree R and correctness metric m." The environment E is a mapping from variable names x to parse trees R. This environment stores the binding of variables to parse trees that the PADS dependent pair construct introduces. We use the symbol 'ϵ' to denote the empty environment.

```
Base:
(Int (atoi s), m) ∈ L(Pint,E,s,s')
    if re = (+|-)?[0-9]+
    and s ∈ L(re)
    and s'' ∈ prefix(s') and s.s'' ∉ L(re)
    and m = (0,1,0,len(s))
(Error, (1,0,0,0)) ∈ L(Pint,E,"",s'),
    if x ∈ prefix(s') then x ∉ L((+|-)?[0-9]+)
(Str s, m) ∈ L(PstringME(re),E,s,s'),
    if s ∈ L(re)
    and s'' ∈ prefix(s') and s.s'' ∉ L(re)
    and m = (0,1,0,len(s))
(Error, (1,0,0,0)) ∈ L(PstringME(re),E,"",s'),
    if x ∈ prefix(s') then x ∉ L(re)
(Str s, m) ∈ L(PstringFW(e),E,s,s')
    if E(e) = Int k and k >= 0
    and s = c1...ck and m = (0,1,0,k)
(Error, (1,0,0,0)) ∈ L(PstringFW(e),E,"",s')
    if E(e) ≠ Int k for any k > 0
(Error, (1,0,0,0)) ∈ L(PstringFW(e),E,"",s')
    if E(e) = Int k and k > 0 and len(s') < k
```

```
Sync:
(Good, (0,1,0,len(s))) ∈ L(Sync(s),E,s,s')
(Recovered s1, m) ∈ L(Sync(s2),E,s,s')
    if s = s1.s2
    and s3.s2 ∉ sprefix(s1.s2) for any s3
    and m = (1,0,len(s1),len(s2))
(Fail, (1,0,0,0)) ∈ L(Sync(s),E,"",s')
    if s ∉ prefix(s')

Pair:
(PairR (R1,R2), (m1 + m2))
        ∈ L(Pair(x:D1, D2),E,s1.s2,s')
    if  (R1, m1) ∈ L(D1,E,s1.s2.s')
    and (R2, m2) ∈ L(D2,E[x → R1],s2,s')

Union:
(Union1R R, m) ∈ L(Union(D1, D2),E,s,s')
    if (R, m) ∈ L(D1, E, s, s')
(Union2R R, m) ∈ L(Union(D1, D2),E,s,s')
    if (R, m) ∈ L(D2, E, s, s')

Main parse function:
parse(D, s) = {R | (R, m) ∈ L(D,ε,s,"")}
```

Fig. 7. Definition of parse function (excerpts)

The *parse metric* m measures the quality of a parse. It is a 4-tuple: (e, g, s, c), where the e is the number of tokens with parse errors, g is the number of tokens parsed correctly, s is the number of characters skipped during Sync token recovery, and c is the number of characters correctly parsed. To sum two parse metrics, we sum their components: $(e_1, g_1, s_1, c_1) + (e_2, g_2, s_2, c_2) = (e_1 + e_2, g_1 + g_2, s_1 + s_2, c_1 + c_2)$. We compare parse metrics by comparing the ratios of correctly parsed characters against erroneous tokens and the estimated number of skipped tokens. We estimate the number of skipped tokens by computing the fraction of the number of skipped characters over the estimated token length. Hence, $(e_1, g_1, s_1, c_1) \geq (e_2, g_2, s_2, c_2)$ iff

$$\frac{c_1}{e_1 + \frac{s_1}{\max((s_1+c_1)/(e_1+g_1),1)}} \geq \frac{c_2}{e_2 + \frac{s_2}{\max((s_2+c_2)/(e_2+g_2),1)}}$$

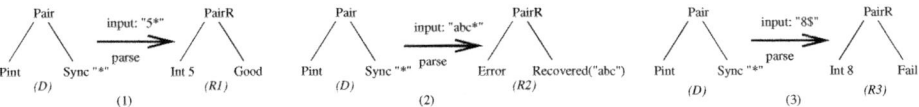

Fig. 8. Result of parsing three input lines

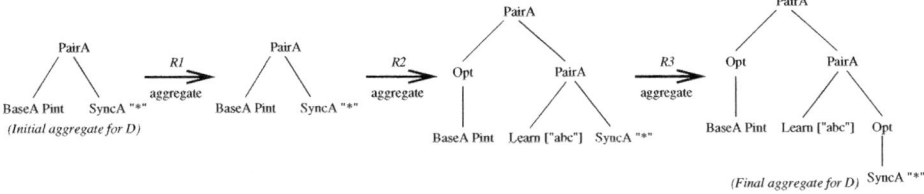

Fig. 9. Aggregation of three parses

2.4   An Example of Parsing and Aggregation

To illustrate the parsing and aggregation phases of the algorithm, we introduce a simple example. Suppose we have a description d, comprised of a pair of an integer and a sync token "*", and we are given the following three lines of new input: "5*" and "abc*" and "8$". Figure 8 shows the three data representations that result from parsing the lines, which we call $R1$, $R2$ and $R3$, respectively. Notice the first line parsed without errors, the second line contains an error for Pint and some unparseable data "abc", and the third contains a Fail node because the sync token * was missing. Figure 9 shows the aggregation of $R1$ to $R3$ starting from an empty aggregate. In general, Error and Fail nodes in the data representation trigger the creation of Opt nodes in the aggregate, while unparseable data is collected in Learn nodes.

2.5   Description Rewriting

Once we have successfully parsed, aggregated and relearned a new chunk of data, we optimize the new description using rewriting rules. Our original non-incremental algorithm already had such an optimization phase; we have modified and tuned the algorithm for use in the incremental system.

Description rewriting optimizes an information-theoretic Minimum Description Length (MDL) score [9], which is defined over descriptions D as:

$$\mathrm{MDL}(\mathrm{D}) = \mathrm{TC}(\mathrm{D}) + w \times \mathrm{ADC}(x_1, \dots, x_k \mid \mathrm{D}),$$

where $\mathrm{TC}(\mathrm{D})$ is called the *type complexity* of D and $\mathrm{ADC}(x_1, \dots, x_k \mid \mathrm{D})$ is called the *atomic data complexity*. The type complexity is a measure of the size of the abstract syntax of D. The atomic data complexity of data records $x_1, \dots, x_k$ relative to D is the number of bits required to transmit an *average* data record given the description D. The MDL score of D is the weighted sum of these two components. Our experiments indicate a weight w of approximately 10 is effective in our domain. Given a rewriting rule that rewrites D to D', the rule fires if and only if MDL(D) $\leq$ MDL(D'). Rewriting continues until no further rule can fire. Hence, our rewriting strategy is a greedy local search.

The original learning system contains many MDL-based rewriting rules, for example, to flatten nested structs and unions and to refine ranged types. *BlobFinding* is an important new rewriting rule which takes a given sub-description D and uses a heuristic to determine if the type complexity of D is too high w.r.t. the amount of data it covers. If this is true, and there is an identifiable constant string or pattern re that immediately follows D, then we rewrite D to Pstring_SE(:re:). This rule is tremendously helpful in controlling the size and complexity of learned descriptions. Without it, descriptions can grow in complexity to the point where parsing is slow and the algorithm fails to scale.

We also introduced a new *data dependent* rewriting rule called *MergeOpts* to optimize a pattern that occurs frequently in descriptions during incremental learning. Recall that the aggregate function introduces Opt nodes above a BaseA or SyncA node whenever the corresponding Base or Sync token in the description failed to parse. When faced with an entirely new form of data, the algorithm is likely to introduce a series of Opt nodes as each type in the original description fails in succession. The *MergeOpts* rule collapses these consecutive Opt nodes if they are correlated, *i.e.*, either they are all always present or all always absent.

2.6   Optimizations

The pseudo-code in Figure 6 suggests the number of aggregates is of the order $O(p^n)$, where p is the maximum number of parses for a line of input and n is the number of lines to aggregate. Clearly, this algorithm will not scale unless p and n are bounded. To deal with this problem, we have implemented several optimizations to limit the number of parses and aggregates.

The first key optimization culls parses based on the parse metric m. To be more precise, we instrument the implementation of the parse function to return a list of *parse triples* (r,m,j), where r is the data representation of the parse, m is the metric associated with r, and j is the position in the input after the parse rather than just representations. We define a clean function that retains all perfect parses or, if no perfect parse exists, the best k non-perfect parses within the same *span*. This idea is similar to the dynamic programming techniques used in Earley Parsers [6].

A second optimization, the *parse cut-off* optimization, terminates a candidate parse when parsing a struct with multiple fields f_1, f_2, ..., f_n if the algorithm encounters a threshold number of errors in succession. This may result in no possible parses for the top-level description, in which case we restart the process with this optimization turned off.

A third optimization is memoization. The program keeps a global memo table indexed by the pair of a description D and the beginning position for parsing D. This table stores the result for parsing according to D at the specific position.

Table 1. The data sources

Name (Large)	Size	Lines	Description
redstorm	34.18 GB	219096168	Supercomputer log from Sandia National Lab
liberty	30.833 GB	265569231	Supercomputer log from Sandia National Lab
dalpiv.dat	15.41 GB	25867260	Yellow pages web server log
vshkap2.log	10.33 GB	89662433	Syslog format
cosmosLog_csm.exe.log	6.09 GB	22143288	Microsoft Cosmos service manager log
free_impression.dat	2.60 GB	27644006	Impression data of yellow pages for Free users
Name (Small)	**Size**	**Lines**	**Description**
free_clickthroughs.dat	24 MB	285332	Yellow pages click through stream data
thirdpartycontent.log	40 MB	281519	Third party content stream data
eventstream.current	500 MB	1579920	Event streams on Cosmos
strace_jaccn.dat	80 MB	896490	NERSC application traces
LA-UR-EVENTS.csv	30 MB	433490	Comma separated LANL disk replacement data
messages.sdb	520 MB	5047341	/var/log/messages from CRAY
HALO_have2impression.log	360 MB	210034	Server side impression records of iPhone apps
LA-UR-NODE-NOZ.TXT	32 MB	1630479	Space separated LANL disk replacement data
searchevents.dat	90 MB	2035348	Yellow pages search event log
4046.xls	7 MB	24193	DNA Microarray data

3   Experimental Results

To evaluate the performance of our prototype system and to understand the trade-offs in setting the various parameters in the algorithm, we ran a number of experiments using 16 data sources. These sources are divided into two groups: six *large files*, each more than 1GB, and ten *smaller files*, each under 1GB. Table 1 lists the names of these data sources, the file sizes, the number of lines, and brief descriptions. We conducted our experiments on a 2.4GHz machine with 24 GBs of memory and two 64-bit quad-core Intel Xeon Processors running Linux version 2.6.18. Our system is single-threaded, so we effectively used only one of the eight available cores.

Benchmark data sources. We are interested in two kinds of performance measures: *time to learn a description* and *quality of the learned description*. The time to learn can be further broken down into two components: time to learn the initial description and time to learn with an initial description in hand.

The quality of the description can be measured in three ways: the *MDL score* [9] of the description, the *edit distance* [4] between the learned description and a "gold description" written by human expert, and the *accuracy* of the learned description. The MDL score provides a fully automated way to quantify both the precision and the compactness of a description, with smaller MDL scores corresponding to better descriptions. However, while MDL is useful, it is best seen as a proxy measure, since humans may prefer a description with a higher MDL score if that description better captures the human being's intuitions.

To address this concern, we use edit distance to measure how close the learned description is to something a human being might write. This metric counts the number of edits necessary to convert the learned description into a "gold description" written by a human being, where an edit can be either an insertion or deletion of a node in the description. More precisely, the distance measure is a *relative edit distance* score: $rel\_dist(D) = edit\_dist(D, D_{gold})/|D_{gold}|$, where

Table 2. Large data sources

Data	MDL	Dist	Accuracy	Learn (secs)	parse (secs)	PADS (secs)	wc (secs)	Blob (secs)
cosmosLog_csm.exe.log	21301.34	0.805	100%	1040	1225	430	34	89
dalpiv.dat	45785.72	0.865	100%	4012	2196	767	82	278
free_impressions.dat	6062.39	0.89	100%	2701	4032	493	15	46
liberty	8790.85	0.722	100%	21144	20851	8036	175	677
redstorm	13837.73	0.707	100%	35548	24736	9791	191	719
vshkap2.log	10063.71	1.750	100%	23337	14651	2163	57	174

$|D|$ denotes the total number of nodes in D. We have empirically determined that a relative edit distance of less than 1 indicates a relatively good description. Of course, the edit distance measure may also be imperfect as there can be a number of different but equally "good" ways to craft a gold description. Nevertheless, we have found it a useful measure.

Finally, our system would not be very useful if the learned description was not correct. Therefore, we also use an accuracy measure, which reports the percentage of original data source that the learned description parses without errors.

Large data sources. Our first experiment learns a description for each of the six large data sources in the benchmark. We set the initial batch size N to be 2000 and the incremental batch size M to be 100. Table 2 reports the MDL and distance scores, the accuracy, and the total learning time. In addition, it report various times to parse the data. The `parse` time is the time it takes the algorithm's `parse` function to parse the source data using the learned description. The PADS time is the time it takes the generated PADS parser to parse the same data. To put these parsing times in perspective, we list the time to count the total number of lines using the Unix `wc -1` command and the time to parse the data using the simple PADS type `Pstring(:Peor:)`, a.k.a *blob*, which parses each line as a newline-terminated string. The result shows that the incremental learning algorithm can learn the format of a 30GB file in a few hours. Importantly, the learned descriptions are all correct with respect to their original raw data.

Scaling performance. In the next experiment, we evaluate how the algorithm scales with increasing data size by running the system on increasingly large fractions of each of the small data files, starting with 20% and ending with 100%. For a given data source, we empirically determined which values of the batch-size parameters N and M give the best result when learning the entire source, and then used those values for this experiment. Figure 10 plots the resulting total learning time versus the percentage of the data file used in learning. The graph shows the algorithm enjoys near linear scale-up for all sources except `4046.xls`, which flattens after 40% of data. The *BlobFinding* rule is the cause of this anomaly: learning the initial description takes a relatively long time, but after the algorithm sees the first 40% of the data, the *BlobFinding* rule simplifies the description to one that parses much more quickly.

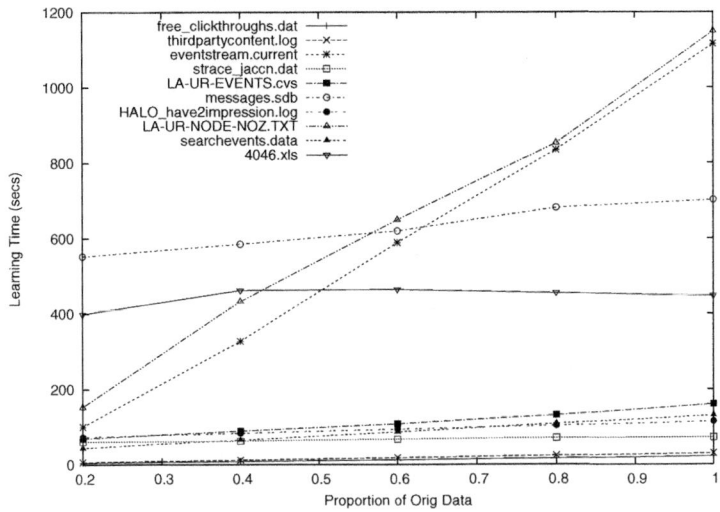

Fig. 10. Learning time vs. percentage of data sources

Initial and incremental batch size. We study the interplay of parameters N and M next. For each of the 10 small files, we repeatedly doubled N from 500 to 32000. For each N, we repeatedly quadrupled M from 25 to 6400. For each resulting pair of N and M, we ran the learning system on each data file and recorded the learning time, the MDL score and the relative distance score. All the learned descriptions parse the original data without error and therefore achieve 100% accuracy. We show only the results for `messages.sdb` in Table 3, while the remaining results are available on the web [1]. Table 3 represents a two-dimensional array, in which the N increases downward and the M increases to the right. Each table cell contains three numbers: the distance score, the MDL score and the total learning time in seconds. The number in parenthesis in the first column is the time to learn the initial batch in seconds, which is the same across all M's. As a baseline, we add a "Manual" row in which the time for the expert to produce an initial description is estimated to be 1 hour and the subsequent learning starts from that description. We highlight the best result in the table. The best description for `message.sdb` is learned with $N = 16000$ and $M = 400$ which are the parameters used for the scaling test of this source.

In general, as M goes up, the total learning time increases. With smaller batch sizes, the system updates descriptions more frequently, often simplifying them. These simplified descriptions parse more efficiently and hence require less time. When N is large, this phenomenon is not as prominent because the initial description learned from large initial batches is often good enough to cover most of the remaining data, and thus no incremental updates are needed.

Our main conclusion is that the end results of our algorithm are sensitive to the quality of the initial description, and that the quality of the initial descrip-

Table 3. N vs. M - messages.sdb

$N\backslash M$	25	100	400	1600	6400
Manual (3600)	0.62 8316.77 337.44	0.62 8355.71 438.29	0.62 8313.52 292.88	0.52 8297.47 295.68	0.52 8297.04 292.05
500 (2.13)	0.67 8098.46 123.88	0.67 8098.46 127.76	0.67 8098.46 130.17	0.67 8098.46 125.52	0.67 8098.46 124.45
1000 (5.75)	1.10 9346.35 432.61	1.10 8443.28 418.64	1.24 8549.67 425.35	1.24 8544.63 442.23	1.24 8541.95 444.56
2000 (6.55)	2.48 10881.17 3935.54	2.48 10881.17 3640.04	2.48 10881.17 3983.46	2.48 10881.17 3695.27	2.48 10881.17 3643.84
4000 (16.26)	0.57 7936.66 868.20	0.57 7936.66 881.52	0.57 7936.66 885.64	0.57 7936.66 910.99	0.57 7936.66 925.19
8000 (74.20)	0.48 7932.71 245.05	0.48 7932.71 242.79	0.48 7932.71 249.90	0.48 7932.71 244.78	0.48 7932.71 248.62
16000 (585.03)	0.57 7995.88 717.57	0.48 7932.65 758.57	**0.48 7932.65 696.82**	0.48 7932.65 760.00	0.48 7932.65 698.15

tion is dependent upon the initial batch of data. This is to be expected since our rewriting system is an incomplete, greedy local search, and therefore is sensitive to the initial candidate grammar it starts with. But given that the user can examine the intermediate descriptions during any iteration, necessary adjustments can be made to influence the final description.

To illustrate the quality of learned description and the difference between it and the gold description, we show the gold description and the best learned description of messages.sdb in Figure 11 and Figure 12. The learned description maintains a top-level structure almost identical to the gold description, except the gold description has slightly more refined details about the message_t type, which was represented by Popt Struct_6113 and the blob at the end. The gold and learned descriptions for the other files are available on the web [1].

4   Related Work

There is a long history of research in *grammar induction*, the process of discovering grammars from example data. Vidal [13] and De La Higuera [10] both give surveys of research in the area. Readers are also referred to the extensive survey in this area from our previous paper [7].

The adaptations of our algorithm to incremental processing are partly inspired by traditional compiler error detection and correction techniques. In particular, the idea of using synchronizing tokens as a means for accumulating chunks of unknown/unparseable data has long been used in parsers from programming languages (see Appel's text [2] for an introduction to such techniques). This heuristic appears to work well in our domain of systems logs as these logs are usually structured around punctuation symbols (commas, semi-colons, vertical

```
Pstruct proc_id_t {
        '[';
        Puint32 id;
        ']';
};

Pstruct daemon_t {
        Pstring_SE (:"/[:\[]/":) name;
        Popt proc_id_t v_proc_id;
        ':';
};

Pstruct msg_body_t {
        daemon_t v_daemon_pri;
        Pwhite v_space;
        Pstring_SE(:Peor:) v_msg;
};
```

```
Punion message_t  {
        msg_body_t v_normal_msg;
        Pstring_SE(:Peor:) v_other_msg;
};

Precord Pstruct entry_t {
        Pdate  v_date;
        ' ';
        Ptime v_time;
        ' ';
        Pstring(:' ':) v_id;
        ' ';
        message_t v_message;
};
Psource Parray entries_t {
        entry_t[];
};
```

Fig. 11. Gold description of messages.sdb

```
Pstruct Struct_6113 {
        Pstring(:':':)  v_blob_5869;
        ':';
};

Precord Pstruct Struct_5671 {
        Pdate  v_date_1;
        ' ';
        Ptime  v_time_6;
        ' ';
        Pstring (:' ':) v_string_33;
        ' ';
        Popt Struct_6113 v_opt_6096;
        Pstring_SE(:Peor:)  v_blob_6095;
};
```

```
Psource Parray entries_t {
        Struct_5671[];
};
```

Fig. 12. Best learned description of messages.sdb

bars, parens, newlines, *etc.*) that act as field-terminators and hence work well as synchronizing tokens.

Other incremental algorithms for learning grammars from example data have been developed in the past. For example, Parekh and Honavar [12] have developed and proven correct an incremental interactive algorithm for inferring regular grammars from positive examples and membership queries. This algorithm works quite differently than ours: it operates over automata and it uses membership queries, which ours does not. More broadly speaking, Parekh and Honavar and many other related algorithms provide beautiful theoretical guarantees. In contrast, we have focused on implementation, empirical evaluation and scaling to support massive data sets.

Another place in which grammar induction is used is in information extraction from web pages. One example (amongst many others) is work by Chidlovskii *et al.* [5], which seeks to learn wrappers (*i.e.*, data extraction functions) by using a modified edit distance algorithm. Our algorithm also uses edit distance in its guts to measure similarity between chunks of data. However, the edit distance metric we use is just one element of a larger induction algorithm related to

Arasu and Garcia-Molina's recursive descent algorithm [3]. Chidlovskii *et al.*'s algorithm is also incremental – it integrates one new record of data at a time into a grammar. Our algorithm integrates batches of new data at a time. One reason we chose a batch-oriented approach is that processing data in batches helps disambiguate between various possibilities for both token definitions and tree structure. The tagged tree-structure of XML or HTML documents eliminates many of the ambiguities that appear in log files where the separators or tags are not known *a priori*. Our ad hoc data sets also appear different from the web-based data studied by Chidlovskii et al. in terms of their scale: our data is about a million times larger.

5   Conclusion

Ad hoc data sources are extremely difficult to manage because of their large size, evolving format, and lack of documentation. In this paper, we have presented the design, implementation and evaluation of a system for incrementally learning the structure of large or stream ad hoc data files. The output of the system is a data description in PADS language which can further generate end-to-end data processing tools. The system allows the users to get into the iterative learning process and make the description more accurate and readable.

References

1. LearnPADS^{++}, http://www.padsproj.org/incremental-learning.html
2. Appel, A.W.: Modern Compiler Implementation in ML. Cambridge University Press (1998)
3. Arasu, A., Garcia-Molina, H.: Extracting structured data from web pages. In: SIGMOD, pp. 337–348 (2003)
4. Bille, P.: A survey on tree edit distance and related problems. Theor. Comput. Sci. 337(1-3), 217–239 (2005)
5. Chidlovskii, B., Ragetli, J., de Rijke, M.: Wrapper Generation via Grammar Induction. In: Lopez de Mantaras, R., Plaza, E. (eds.) ECML 2000. LNCS (LNAI), vol. 1810, pp. 96–108. Springer, Heidelberg (2000)
6. Earley, J.: An efficient context-free parsing algorithm. Communications of the ACM 13(2), 94–102 (1970)
7. Fisher, K., Walker, D., Zhu, K., White, P.: From dirt to shovels: Fully automatic tool generation from ad hoc data. In: POPL (January 2008)
8. Fisher, K., Walker, D., Zhu, K.Q.: LearnPADS: Automatic tool generation from ad hoc data. In: SIGMOD (2008)
9. Grünwald, P.D.: The Minimum Description Length Principle. MIT Press (May 2007)
10. De La Higuera, C.: Current Trends in Grammatical Inference. In: Amin, A., Pudil, P., Ferri, F., Iñesta, J.M. (eds.) SPR 2000 and SSPR 2000. LNCS, vol. 1876, pp. 28–31. Springer, Heidelberg (2000)
11. PADS project (2009), http://www.padsproj.org/
12. Parekh, R., Honavar, V.: An Incremental Interactive Algorithm for Regular Grammar Inference. In: Miclet, L., de la Higuera, C. (eds.) ICGI 1996. LNCS, vol. 1147, pp. 238–249. Springer, Heidelberg (1996)
13. Vidal, E.: Grammatical Inference: An Introduction Survey. In: Carrasco, R.C., Oncina, J. (eds.) ICGI 1994. LNCS, vol. 862, pp. 1–4. Springer, Heidelberg (1994)
14. Zhu, K.Q., Fisher, K., Walker, D.: Incremental learning of system log formats. In: ACM SOSP Workshop on the Analysis of System Logs (2009)

The Kennedy-Warren Algorithm Revisited: Ordering Attribute Grammars

Jeroen Bransen[1], Arie Middelkoop[2], Atze Dijkstra[1], and S. Doaitse Swierstra[1]

[1] Utrecht University
{J.Bransen,atze,doaitse}@uu.nl
[2] LIP6-Regal
amiddelk@gmail.com

Abstract. Attribute Grammars (AGs) are a powerful tool for defining an executable semantics of a programming language, and thus for implementing a compiler. An execution plan for an AG determines a static evaluation order for the attributes which are defined as part of an AG specification. In building the Utrecht Haskell Compiler (UHC), a large scale AG project, we discovered that the *Ordered AG* approach (Kastens, 1980) for building such plans becomes impractical: the additional dependencies between attributes introduced by this algorithm too often result in grammars for which no execution plan can be generated.

To avoid such problems we have implemented a refined version of the algorithm of Kennedy and Warren (1976) as part of our purely functional AG system and show how this algorithm solves the problems that surface with the Ordered AG approach. Furthermore, we present the results of applying this algorithm to the UHC code and show that this approach in some cases also has a positive effect on the runtime of the resulting program.

Keywords: Attribute Grammars, Haskell, Dependency graph, Ordered.

1   Introduction

Attribute Grammars (AGs) (Knuth, 1968) are well-suited for the implementation of the semantics of programming languages. An AG consists of a context-free grammar specifying the *Abstract Syntax Tree* (AST) together with a set of attribute definitions describing how the nodes in an AST are to be decorated with attributes describing the properties of that node. Semantic rules, possibly directly written in a host language, describe how attribute values can be computed out of other attributes. Attributes are either *inherited*, indicating that their value is defined in terms of the context of a node, or *synthesized*, meaning that their value is defined in terms of the tree rooted at that node.

AG based language definitions are compiled into a host language. For this we use the Utrecht University Attribute Grammar Compiler (UUAGC) (Swierstra and Baars, 2005) which uses Haskell as its host language. AG based definitions are of a purely declarative nature, since they leave the order in which

C. Russo and N.-F. Zhou (Eds.): PADL 2012, LNCS 7149, pp. 183–197, 2012.

the attributes are to be evaluated completely unspecified. A straightforward implementation, as supported by the UUAGC, uses the lazy evaluation mechanism of Haskell to determine an order at evaluation time.

One of the problems of this approach is that *circular AGs*, in which attributes can directly or indirectly depend on their own value, are not detected at compile-time, but rather may result in nontermination of the generated code. To overcome this problem the UUAGC has an option to apply the *Ordered AG* algorithm (Kastens, 1980), which tries to find such an order between the attributes of each nonterminal so that for all instances of such a nonterminal the attributes can be evaluated in that order. A side effect of this algorithm is that circular AGs are detected, since for them such an order cannot exist. Furthermore, the resulting code can be much more efficient and far less space consuming because it no longer relies on lazy evaluation. The generated compilers can thus all be evaluated in a strict manner.

Although this approach works well for simple AG examples, our experience has shown that for more complex AGs this is no longer the case: for more complex AGs the algorithm often fails to find an evaluation order, even when the AG itself is non-circular. This is caused by the additional attribute dependencies introduced by the algorithm, which quite unpredictably can lead to artificial cycles. The additional attribute dependencies are introduced by scheduling two or more unrelated attributes in the same visit, which is not always possible.

In most cases it is possible to assist the algorithm by manually adding *fake dependencies* to the source code, such that the algorithm does not run into the described problem. However, this is not a desirable situation as it is not only a tedious task to add such fake dependencies, but it also requires the programmer to have a deep understanding of the used global analysis and scheduling algorithms.

To overcome the need for manually tweaking the AGs we have implemented the *K&W* algorithm (Kennedy and Warren, 1976). In this paper we make the following new contributions:

- We describe what the problem is with Ordered AGs.
- We describe a purely functional implementation of the K&W algorithm.
- We show its effect on the Utrecht Haskell Compiler (UHC) (Dijkstra et al., 2009): not only works the algorithm as expected, but also the runtime of the resulting program decreases.

1.1 Overview

In section 2 we introduce our running example and explain the problem that shows up when using OAGs, we show how fake dependencies can be used to resolve this issue and explain why this approach eventually fails. We assume basic Haskell knowledge and will not explain the AG syntax in detail[1], understanding the AG concept should be enough to understand the example.

In the subsequent sections we continue with the implementation K&W algorithm. The implementation consists of 3 phases: the construction of *production*

---

[1] See http://www.cs.uu.nl/wiki/HUT/AttributeGrammarSystem

dependency graphs (PDG) (section 3), the construction of the visit graph (section 4) and finally the code generation (section 5). Where relevant we give code fragments.

In section 6 we dicuss related work and in section 7 we wrap up with some results of the experiments on the UHC and points of discussion.

2   A Motivating Example

The running example in this paper uses a tree with integers in its leaves, defined by:

DATA *Tree* | *Leaf val* : *Int*
          | *Bin l, r* : *Tree*

Given a type *Label* and a function *nextLabel* :: *Label* → *Label*, we associate a unique label to each leaf by threading a *Label* value through the tree from left to right. The **lhs** refers to the left hand side of the production at hand, and **loc** refers to an attribute that is local to a production:

ATTR *Tree* [*nextLabI* : *Label* | | *nextLabS* : *Label*]
SEM *Tree* | *Leaf* **loc**.*label*   = @**lhs**.*nextLabI*
              lhs.*nextLabS* = *nextLabel* @**loc**.*label*
      | *Bin l* .*nextLabI* = @**lhs**.*nextLabI*
           r .*nextLabI* = @*l*.*nextLabS*
           lhs.*nextLabS* = @*r*.*nextLabS*

The attribute *nextLab* is a *threaded* attribute, which is the combination of an inherited (*nextLabI*) and a synthesized (*nextLabS*) attribute. In the text we write *nextLab* for the combination of *nextLabI* and *nextLabS*.

Suppose now we are also interested in the sequence of all *Leaf*.*val* values that appear in the leaves as they appear from left to right. When using a cons-list as result type, the most efficient way to gather the values in a list is to introduce another threaded attribute and add the variables to the list from right to left, thereby preserving the order in the resulting list:

ATTR *Tree* [*valsI* : [*Int*] | | *valsS* : [*Int*]]
SEM *Tree* | *Leaf* **lhs**.*valsS* = @*val* : @**lhs**.*valsI*
      | *Bin r* .*valsI* = @**lhs**.*valsI*
          l .*valsI* = @*r*.*valsS*
        lhs.*valsS* = @*l*.*valsS*

At first glance there seems to be no problem with this definition, since both attribute computations are completely independent of each other, and one would expect an AG compiler to be able to generate code for such a simple AG. The OAG algorithm however fails due to induced cycles as explained below.

2.1   Induced Cycles

The problem with the OAG algorithm is that it tries to find a global ordering on the attributes and divides these into as few visits as possible. In our case there are two threaded attributes, *nextLab* and *vals*, that do not depend on each other. Therefore, they are scheduled in a single visit. However, for the *Bin* branch there now is a problem with scheduling the child visits. For the *nextLab* attribute the left child has to be visited before the right child, but for the *vals* attribute this is the other way around. It is therefore not possible to schedule both computations in a single visit, and the algorithm fails to find a solution, since it has already decided to compute them in the same visit.

To be more precise, by putting two attributes in the same visit, the dependencies of these two attributes are merged into a single set of dependencies. In this case for the *nextLab* attribute we have, amongst others, the dependencies $r.nextLabI \rightarrow l.nextLabS$ and $r.nextLabS \rightarrow r.nextLabI$. A dependency $a \rightarrow b$ means that the value of a depends on the computation of b, so b must be scheduled before a. For the *vals* attribute we have $l.valsI \rightarrow r.valsS$ and $l.valsS \rightarrow l.valsI$. It is clear that in the the AG attributes do not depend on themselves, but when we schedule the *nextLab* and *vals* attributes in the same visit we end up with the induced cycle $r.(nextLabI, valsI) \rightarrow l.(nextLabS, valsS) \rightarrow l.(nextLabI, valsI) \rightarrow r.(nextLabS, valsS) \rightarrow r.(nextLabI, valsI)$.

2.2   Fake Dependencies

There are several solutions to this problem. The most straightforward solution is to introduce a so-called *fake dependency*. We could change the **lhs**.*vals* definition of the *Leaf* production to:

SEM *Tree* | *Leaf* **lhs**.*valsS* = *const* (@*val* : @**lhs**.*valsI*) @**lhs**.*nextLabI*

The *const* :: $a \rightarrow b \rightarrow a$ function ignores its second argument, so semantically the AG has not changed. However, with this definition the scheduling does succeed because of the extra dependency from *vals* on *nextLab* that was introduced. Now *vals* does depend on *nextLab*, so there will be two visits, the first for *nextLab* and the second one for *vals*: the grammar can be evaluated by making two passes over the tree.

In our experience with the UHC, we found that patterns like this occur more often than not: that is having two or more attributes that do not depend on each other but introduce a cycle when being combined into a single visit. To keep the code compilable we had to introduce quite a few fake dependencies, and worse, it usually is unclear for a complex AG where to put such fake dependencies. In a project like the UHC this becomes a rather tedious task, as it is almost impossible to manually keep track of all dependencies between the attributes. When a new attribute is added to the code this usually introduces lots of new induced cycles, some going away as more code is written, but some requiring time consuming trial-and-error interaction with UUAGC to determine the most helpful fake dependencies.

3   Dependency Graphs

An AG is noncircular if no attributes can be defined, directly or indirectly, in terms of themselves. The algorithm from Knuth (1968), which we call Knuth-1, is an algorithm that statically determines whether an AG is *absolutely noncircular*, where absolute noncircularity is a slightly pessimistic variant of noncircularity, thus an AG that passes this stronger test is always noncircular. However, experience shows that for practical AGs the Knuth-1 algorithm is sufficient, as the programmer usually has an evaluation order in mind.

We now present our Haskell implementation of the Knuth-1 algorithm for constructing the dependency graphs for an AG. A *dependency graph* is a graph where the vertices are attributes and directed edges represent dependencies between attributes, so in order to be able to evaluate the attribute where the edge starts, the attribute where the edge points to needs to be evaluated first. We distinguish between *production dependency graphs*, the dependency graph for a single production, and *nonterminal dependency graphs*, the combined dependencies of all trees possibly derived from a nonterminal.

3.1   Production Dependency Graphs

For every production p of nonterminal N a production dependency graph PDG_p^N is constructed. We construct the initial PDG_p^N as follows. For every synthesized, inherited and local attribute that is used in any of the rules in p, so both for the production itself as for its children, we add a vertex to PDG_p^N. For every semantic rule in p we add a direct edge from the attribute in the lefthand side to each attribute in the righthand side of this rule.

Figure 1 shows PDG_{Bin}^{Tree} of our example. All solid edges are the initial edges, and the dashed edges are the edges that are added during the execution of the algorithm. The three nonterminal nodes are drawn for clarity only and are not part of the actual dependency graph.

3.2   Nonterminal Dependency Graphs

The nonterminal dependency graph NDG_N of nonterminal N represents the union over all possible dependencies induced by a tree rooted by N. To construct the initial NDG_N we add a vertex for every inherited and every synthesized attribute of this nonterminal. There are no initial edges in NDG_N.

3.3   Representation

We represent the dependency graphs in Haskell efficiently using the implementation as shown in Figure 2. An important property of the dependency graphs is that no vertices are added to the graph during the execution of the algorithm, so upon construction of the initial graph the list of all vertices is known. We use this property to assign a unique number to each vertex at construction time and we use these numbers as *Array* indices thus giving constant lookup time.

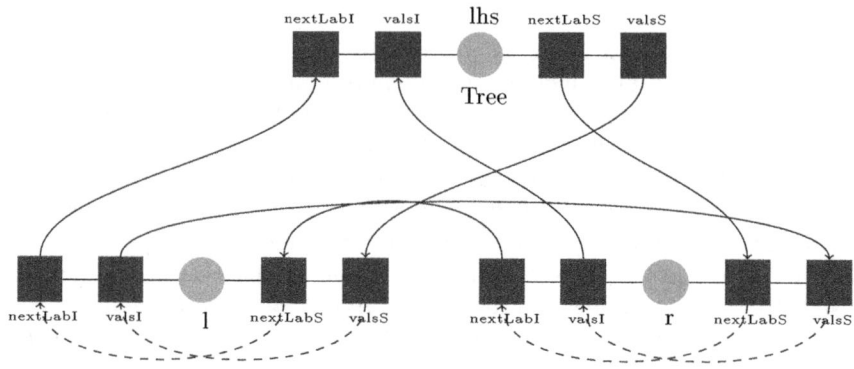

Fig. 1. Production dependency graph of production *Bin*

In the Knuth-1 algorithm there are several operations on the dependency graph for which an efficient implementation is important: *graphEdges*, the enumeration of all edges in the graph, *graphInsert*, the insertion of a new edge into the graph, and *graphContainsEdge*, a check whether two vertices are connected. Also, it is important to know which vertices become connected as a result of the insertion of a new edge.

To accomplish this we maintain the invariant that the graph is always transitively closed. We store the graph as a set of successors and a set of predecessors for each vertex. Upon insertion of a new edge we transitively close the graph in the obvious way. The return value of *graphInsert* is the list of newly added edges, excluding the one in the argument.

We use the ST Monad for performing efficient in-memory updates in a functional setting. Using the *STRef* in the successors and predecessors *Array*, the sets are updated in place without the need to update the *Array* structure itself.

3.4   Derived Edges

The idea of the Knuth-1 algorithm is that the nonterminal dependency graphs capture all dependencies of synthesized attributes on inherited attributes that are present in any of the trees rooted by that nonterminal. These nonterminal dependency graphs are then used for dependencies on the children of a production, as to obtain an approximation of the dependencies.

To add the derived edges to the production dependency graphs and the nonterminal dependency graphs, the following process is repeated until no more edges can be added. Add an edge for every pair of synthesized and inherited attributes in a nonterminal graph NDG_N, if there is a production p of N such that there is a path from this synthesized to that inherited attribute in PDG_p^N. For every edge in any NDG_N, add an edge to every PDG_p^M for every N child of p.

```
type Vertex  = ...                    -- External vertex type
type Edge    = (Vertex, Vertex)       -- External edge type
type IVertex = Int                    -- Internal representation of a vertex
type IEdge   = (IVertex, IVertex)     -- Internal representation of an edge
data DepGraph s =                     -- Representation of the graph
   DepGraph { vertexIMap :: Map   Vertex  IVertex
            , vertexOMap :: Array IVertex Vertex
            , successors  :: Array IVertex (STRef s (Set IVertex))
            , predecessors :: Array IVertex (STRef s (Set IVertex)) }
graphConstruct     :: [ Vertex ]     → [ Edge ] → ST s (DepGraph s)
graphInsert        :: DepGraph s → Edge   → ST s [ Edge ]
graphContainsEdge  :: DepGraph s → Edge   → ST s Bool
graphSuccessors    :: DepGraph s → Vertex → ST s [ Vertex ]
graphPredecessors  :: DepGraph s → Vertex → ST s [ Vertex ]
graphVertices      :: DepGraph s →          ST s [ Vertex ]
graphEdges         :: DepGraph s →          ST s [ Edge ]
```

Fig. 2. Dependency graph representation

Because there are only a finite number of possible edges this process terminates. We say that the AG is absolutely noncircular if and only if none of the production dependency graphs contains a cycle.

3.5   Worklist Algorithm

We have implemented this process as a work-list algorithm. The work-list contains the *pending* edges, edges that have been added to one of the graphs and must be potentially also added to other graphs. Initially the list of pending edges consists of all initial edges of the production dependency graphs. The main function is implemented as:

```
knuth₁ :: [NontM s] → ST s ()
knuth₁ nonts = do
   nes ← forM nonts $ λnont → do
      pend ← mapM graphEdges (productions nont)
      return (pend, nont)
   knuth'₁ nes   -- run worklist algorithm on initial graph
```

All pending edges that must be represesented in the nonterminal dependency graph and are not yet present are added to the corresponding nonterminal dependency graph by the following helper function:

```
addProdNont :: ([[Edge]], NontM s) → ST s [Edge]
```

The return value of this function is the list of all edges that are newly added due to taking transitivity into account. These edges are then taken as the new list of pending edges which are added to the production dependency graphs:

$$addNontProd :: ([\mathit{Edge}], \mathit{NontM}\ s) \to ST\ s\ [[\mathit{Edge}]]$$

This function returns per nonterminal a list of edges that were added to its PDG's due to transitivity, and which must be taken as new pending list.

The helper function $knuth'_1$ recursively alternates adding edges to the NDG's and adding edges to the PDG's, and terminates when the list of pending edges is exhausted.

$$knuth'_1 :: [([[\mathit{Edge}]], \mathit{NontM}\ s)] \to ST\ s\ ()$$

```
knuth'₁ nonts = do
    edges ← mapM addProdNont nonts
    let nontedges = concat edges
    if null nontedges
      then return ()
      else do
          perprod ← mapM (λ(_, x) → addNontProd (nontedges, x)) nonts
          newlist ← zipWithM (λ(_, nt) me → return (me, nt)) nonts perprod
          if any (not ∘ null) perprod
            then knuth'₁ newlist
            else return ()
```

4   Visit Graph

The dependency graphs induce a partial order on the evaluation of the attributes, but they do not specify an evaluator yet. For this we use the K&W algorithm.

We construct a *visit graph*, which is a directed acyclic graph. Every possible path from a starting vertex (one per nonterminal) to a leaf vertex represents a visit sequence. The vertices in the graph represent the possible states of a nonterminal, where a state is the set of attributes that have already been evaluated.

Every edge in the graph corresponds to a so-called visit to a node. A visit can start when the parent node has made some new inherited attributes available and it yields a set of newly evaluated synthesized attributes. Hence each set is labelled with an ($\{inh\}, \{syn\}$) pair.

With every edge we associate an *execution plan* for each production of the corresponding nonterminal. This execution plan describes for every synthesized attribute how it can be computed. The execution plan also includes child visits that are needed for the computation of the set of synthesized attributes.

Figure 3 shows the visit graph for our running example. The execution plans for the productions are not made explicit in this figure. There are three different visit sequences in this example. Visit v_0 is the main visit with both inherited attributes available at the start of the visit, that will be used at the top-level. For

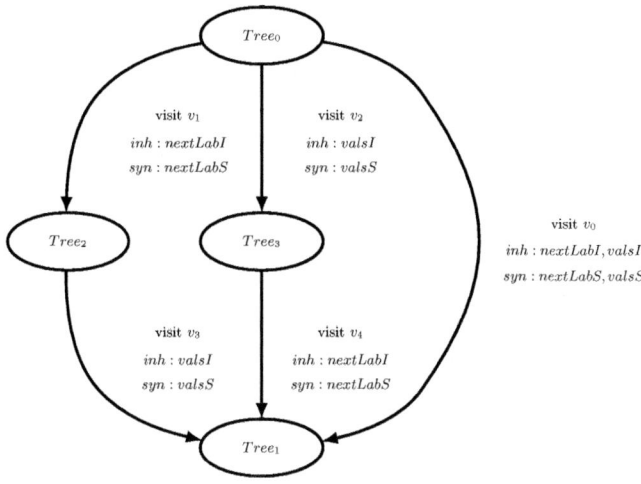

Fig. 3. The visit graph of the example

the *Leaf* it is directly possible to compute both synthesized attributes directly, but for the *Bin* production we need to perform child visits. As we have already seen it is impossible to do this in a single visit, so for the left child first visit v_1 is done and then visit v_3, and for the right child first visit v_2 and then visit v_4. It is clear that we can create execution plans for each of these visits using only these visit sequences.

The key algorithm of this paper is an adapted version of the K&W algorithm for the construction of the visit graph including the execution plans. This algorithm performs stable and predictable inference of the evaluation order which determines visits in a demand driven fashion with per visit the smallest set of inherited attributes that are needed to produce the demand set of synthesized attributes, and per visit the largest set of synthesized attributes that can be derived from the inherited attributes. If the AG is absolutely noncircular, thus none of the production dependency graphs contains a cycle, this algorithm will return a complete visit graph.

4.1   Representation

In order to implement the K&W algorithm and maintain the visit graph we use a monad, *VG*, built on top of the ST monad. In this way the representation of the visit graph is separated from the actual algorithm. This greatly improves the readability of the code.

The *VG* monad is defined as follows:

type *VG s a = ErrorT String (StateT (VGState s) (ST s)) a*

The inner monad is the *ST* monad with threaded state s. On top of this there is a *State* monad with state *VGState s*, which contains the visit graph representation.

```
runVG                  :: VG s a   → ST s a
insertInitialNode      :: NontM s → VG s VGNode
createPending          :: VGNode → [Identifier] → [Identifier] → VG s VGEdge
selectPending          :: VG s VGEdge
getInherited           :: VGEdge  → VG s [Identifier]
getSynthesized         :: VGEdge  → VG s [Identifier]
markFinal              :: VGEdge  → VG s ()
getProductions         :: VGEdge  → VG s [VGProd]
onMarkedDG             :: (ProdDepGraphM s → ST s a) → VGProd → VG s a
isDGVertexFinal        :: VGProd  → Vertex → VG s Bool
setDGVerticesFinal     :: VGProd  → [Vertex] → VG s ()
getChildState          :: VGProd  → Identifier → VG s VGNode
addChildVisit          :: VGProd  → Identifier → VGEdge → VG s VisitStep
addVisitStep           :: VGProd  → VisitStep → VG s ()
repeatM                :: VG s ()  → VG s ()
```

Fig. 4. Functions available in *VG* monad

The topmost monad is the *Error* monad which is used for capturing failure and error messages. This is also used in the implementation of the function *repeatM* :: VG s () → VG s () that repeats the execution of the argument until *mzero* (failure) is encountered. The *VGState* s is used for storing the visit graph and all necessary related data.

Type signatures of the functions that are available in the *VG* monad are shown in Figure 4.

4.2   Initial Configuration

The algorithm works by gradually building up the visit graph. We distinguish between *pending edges* and *final edges*, and we refer to a vertex as a *pending vertex* if and only if all its incoming edges are pending. Vertices with no incoming edges are called *initial vertices*.

At the start of the algorithm we create an initial vertex for each nonterminal. Additionally, we insert one pending edge (plus pending target vertex) for every starting nonterminal, containing all inherited and synthesized attributes defined on this nonterminal. In our example $Tree_0$ is the initial vertex and v_0 the initial pending edge. In the following code *wr* is the set of *wrapper* nonterminals for which a wrapper function should be generated, and *initvs* is the list of initial *VGEdge*'s, used in the code generation.

```
kennedyWarren :: Set Identifier → [NontM s] → VG s [Maybe VGEdge]
kennedyWarren wr nonts = do
    initvs ← forM nonts $ λnont → do
        nd ← insertInitialNode nont
```

```
  if (nonterminal nont) 'Set.member' wr
     then do
        initv ← createPending nd (inh nont) (syn nont)
        return $ Just initv
     else return Nothing
  ...
```

4.3 Handling Pending Edges

The main loop handles pending edges one by one, thereby potentially adding new pending edges. The pending edges are marked final and the algorithm terminates when there are no more pending edges. Again, the set of possible edges is finite so the algorithm will always terminate. It is implemented using *repeatM* as follows:

```
repeatM $ do
   pend ← selectPending
   prods ← getProductions pend
   inhs  ← getInherited pend
   syns  ← getSynthesized pend
   forM prods $ λprod → do
      ...
   markFinal pend
return initvs
```

When there are no more pending edges the *selectPending* function will result in *mzero*, thereby breaking the *repeatM* loop and the algorithm will then terminate. The final visit graph and all execution plans will be stored in the internal representation.

4.4 Dependency Graph Marks

In addition to the visit graph we keep for every vertex a list with a state for each of the the children of the productions. A state is the set of attributes that have already been computed for the child and is thus represented by a reference to a vertex in the graph. Initially every child is in the state of the initial vertex of the nonterminal of this child.

For the construction of an execution plan we use marks on the production dependency graph. Marked vertices represent the attributes that have already been evaluated and thus are available. To handle a pending edge we perform the following steps for each production of the nonterminal that this edge belongs to. We start by copying the marks on the production dependency graph from the source to the target vertex. In addition to the already existing marks we mark the vertices corresponding to the inherited attributes represented by the pending edge.

The goal of scheduling a pending edge is to mark all synthesized attributes represented by this pending edge. A vertex can be marked only if all its successors are already marked, so all its dependencies are satisfied. For synthesized attributes of children we need to do a child visit, and we maximize the number of synthesized attributes that we compute in the child visit. The vertices are recursively marked until all synthesized attributes are marked. If the production dependency graphs do not contain cycles this is always possible.

The recursive marking is implemented as recursive function that assigns a number to every vertex in a depth-first way. For every attribute the number is the maximum of all its successors, and for a synthesized child attribute it is the maximum plus one, because one extra child visit needs to be performed. The *foldChildVisits* helper function implements this behaviour.

We mark the inherited attributes as final and then call the *foldChildVisits*:

> *setDepGraphVerticesFinal prod* (*map createLhsInh inhs*)
> (*vis, i*) ← *foldM* (*foldChildVisits prod*) ([ ], 0) (*map createLhsSyn syns*)
> *setDepGraphVerticesFinal prod* (*map fst vis*)
> ...

The return value *vis* has type [(*Vertex, Int*)] and indicates the vertices that correspond to rules or attributes that need to be evaluated at this stage, together with the corresponding child visit number.

4.5   Extra Synthesized Attributes

Apart from the synthesized attributes of the children that are strictly needed for computing the desired synthesized attributes of the current nonterminal, we also add synthesized child attributes that depend only on the inherited child attributes that we already evaluate. In other words, we add synthesized child attributes that can already be computed without introducing extra child visits.

By eagerly adding such synthesized attributes we avoid constructing many almost similar visits, and thus limit the growth of the visit graph resulting from the K&W approach.

4.6   Difference to Original Algorithm

We have formulated our version of the K&W algorithm in a rather different way than the original formulation of Kennedy and Warren (1976). One important difference involves the marking of the dependency graph vertices.

In the original formulation, the child visits are done based on availability of inherited attributes. So, all child visits that can be done are done. Our approach works demand-driven, in the sense that we only do child visits that are strictly needed for the computation of the requested synthesized attributes. This optimisation thus removes unneccesary child visits.

4.7   Execution Plans

To generate the final execution plans (implemented in terms of *addVisitStep*) we group the *vis2* (*vis* combined with the extra synthesized child attributes) by visit number. For every visit we first evaluate all corresponding rules, and then add the desired child visits.

```
forM (groupSortBy (comparing snd) vis2) $ λvisit → do
   let (chattrs, rules) = partition isChildAttr $ map fst visit
      -- Rules have been added to the list in reverse order
   forM (reverse rules) $ λrule → do
      addVisitStep prod (Sem rule)
      -- Group by child
   forM (groupSortBy (comparing getChildName) chattrs) $ λchildvs → do
      let cinhs = map getName $ filter isChildInh childvs
      let csyns = map getName $ filter isChildSyn childvs
      let cname = getChildName $ head childvs
      curstate ← getChildState prod cname
      target ← createPending curstate (fromList cinhs) (fromList csyns)
      step   ← addChildVisit prod cname target
      addVisitStep prod step
```

5   Code Generation

In the code generation the generated execution plans are translated to Haskell in a relatively straightforward way. We use a monadic structure for defining the evaluation order of semantic rules. For a child visit a parameter is passed to specify which visit needs to be done. The result type of this function depends on the argument, so we use GADTs for type indices to accomplish this in a type safe way.

The generated code is purely functional and strongly typed. The type checker proves that the code has the define-before-use property and that no attribute depends indirectly on itself. The generated code can be seen as the evidence of the proof that the AG is absolutely noncircular.

It is out of the scope of the current paper to discuss the exact implementation of the code generation. We refer the interested reader to (Middelkoop, 2011).

6   Related Work

AGs were first introduced by Knuth (1968), and in the same paper the Knuth-1 algorithm that we used for the dependency graphs was introduced. The original paper claims that that this algorithm will statically determine whether an attribute grammar is noncircular. In the Knuth (1971) paper this claim was corrected to the claim that it determines *absolute* noncircularity. The latter also describes a new version of the algorithm, Knuth-2, that performs the correct noncircularity check. However, for efficiency reasons we have chosen to use the former.

The Synthesizer Generator (Reps and Teitelbaum, 1984) is a tool for creating syntax-directed editors from language descriptions. It is completely build with AGs and is a good example of applications of AGs.

Saraiva (1999) describes how AGs can be implemented in a purely functional way, amongst others based on Ordered AGs (Kastens, 1980).

7 Results and Discussion

We have experimented with the implementation of the described algorithm on the code of the UHC (Dijkstra et al., 2009), which makes extensive use of AGs. For the main AG in the UHC, the visit graph contains 895 vertices (visit states) and 1699 edges (visits).

7.1 Compile Time

Compared to the use of the OAG algorithm the time spent by the AG compiler has not changed. The compile time of the resulting code has roughly doubled, and is thus still acceptable.

One of the most important reasons for this is probably the increase of source code length. Because the K&W approach uses multiple, partially overlapping, visit sequences there is a certain level of code duplication. Although the semantic rules are not duplicated, their uses and all tupling and untupling of attributes might be duplicated.

7.2 Runtime

Our experiments with the UHC code show that the runtime of the resulting UHC executable has decreased when using the K&W approach. In table 1 we show the runtimes for a simple benchmark, with 10 runs per algorithm, in which the UHC was used to compile a set 74 of base libraries.

Table 1. Benchmark for UHC

UHC build with	Avg. runtime
OAG	2m38.538s
K&W	2m36.155s

The runtime decrease is 2.383s, which is about 1.5% of the total runtime. It is important to note that most time-consuming parts of the UHC code are the typechecking algorithms which are not AG based and are thus unchanged. Therefore, although 1.5% might seem like a minor decrease, it could be a much bigger decrease in runtime spent on the AG part of the code. We believe that this decrease is due to the fact that smaller closures are build, but further research is needed before we can draw conclusions from this.

7.3   AG Extensions

Our implementation integrates seamlessly with many AG extensions, including higher-order children and collection attributes. The possibility of splitting the generated code into multiple files is also supported, to overcome potential problems when the generated files become too large.

For obvious reasons, our implementation does not work with extensions that require demand-driven AG evaluation.

8   Conclusion

We have presented our purely function implementation of the K&W algorithm for ordering Attribute Grammars. Using an example we have shown what the problem of induced cycles with the OAG approach is, and how this problem is solved. We believe it is worth the price of a higher compilation time. For the UHC this can even lead to better runtime behaviour, but we want to make clear that this is not the core result of the paper.

References

Dijkstra, A., Fokker, J., Swierstra, S.D.: The architecture of the Utrecht Haskell compiler. In: Proceedings of the 2nd ACM SIGPLAN Symposium on Haskell, Haskell 2009, pp. 93–104. ACM, New York (2009)

Kastens, U.: Ordered attributed grammars. Acta Informatica 13, 229–256 (1980), doi:10.1007/BF00288644

Kennedy, K., Warren, S.K.: Automatic generation of efficient evaluators for attribute grammars. In: Proceedings of the 3rd ACM SIGACT-SIGPLAN Symposium on Principles on Programming Languages, POPL 1976, pp. 32–49. ACM, New York (1976)

Knuth, D.E.: Semantics of context-free languages. Theory of Computing Systems 2(2), 127–145 (1968)

Knuth, D.E.: Semantics of context-free languages: Correction. Theory of Computing Systems 5, 95–96 (1971), doi:10.1007/BF01702865

Middelkoop, A.: Inference with Attribute Grammars. PhD thesis, Utrecht University (2011)

Reps, T., Teitelbaum, T.: The synthesizer generator. SIGPLAN Not. 19, 42–48 (1984)

Saraiva, J.: Purely Functional Implementation of Attribute Grammars. PhD thesis, Utrecht University (1999)

Swierstra, S.D., Baars, A.: Attribute Grammar System (2005), http://www.cs.uu.nl/wiki/HUT/AttributeGrammarSystem

Distributed Policy Specification and Interpretation with Classified Advertisements

Nicholas Coleman

West Virginia University Institute of Technology
405 Fayette Pike, Montgomery, WV 25136
Nicholas.Coleman@mail.wvu.edu

Abstract. In a distributed system, the principle of separation of policy and mechanism provides the flexibility to revise policies without altering mechanisms and vice versa. This separation can be achieved by devising a language for specifying policy and an engine for interpreting policy. In the Condor [14] high throughput distributed system the ClassAd language [16] is used to specify resource selection policies and matchmaking algorithms are used to interpret that policy by matching jobs with available machines. We extend this framework to specify and interpret authorization policies using the SPKI/SDSI [6] public key infrastructure. SPKI/SDSI certificates are represented using the ClassAd language and certificate chain discovery is implemented using a modified matchmaking algorithm. This extension complements the resource selection policy capabilities of Condor with the authorization policy capabilities of SPKI/SDSI. Techniques for policy analysis in the context of resource selection and authorization are also presented.

1 Introduction

One of the challenges of distributed computing environments is the specification and interpretation of policy. The separation of policy and mechanism has long been one of the key principles in systems design. This principle simplifies the specification of policies and keeps them independent of implementation changes. One way of achieving separation is to provide a policy framework consisting of a language for specifying policies and an engine for interpreting these policies in the context of a given set of system conditions. The flexibility of such a framework is particularly suitable for resource allocation policy in a distributed system.

Distributed systems are dynamic in that principals and resources may join or leave the federation at any time. Allocation of resources in a decentralized environment requires policy for resource selection and access control. Resource selection is the process of finding resources that satisfy a principal's requests. Access control policies determine whether the principal is permitted to access the resources. Currently there is no single language or framework that deals with authorization and resource selection policies.

C. Russo and N.-F. Zhou (Eds.): PADL 2012, LNCS 7149, pp. 198–211, 2012.
© Springer-Verlag Berlin Heidelberg 2012

The ClassAd language is based on the concept of classified advertisements. Entities in Condor are represented by classified advertisements or ClassAds. Each job submitted by a condor user has a corresponding ClassAd as does each compute machine. The matchmaking process pairs jobs with machines based on the policies expressed in their ClassAds. Since the bilateral matchmaking framework is not sufficient for assembling three or more parties a multilateral matchmaking framework, *gangmatching*, is required in such cases. A collection of three or more ClassAds that satisfy each others `Requirements` expressions is called a *gang*.

SPKI/SDSI is an infrastructure for expressing authorization policy using public key encryption. Two kinds of certificates can be issued by a principal. An *authorization certificate* grants another principal a set of access rights for a resource as well as the permission to delegate these rights to other principals. A *name certificate* creates a name for another principal or set of principals. A combination of several certificates that authorize a principal to access a resource is called a *certificate chain*. The problem of assembling a suitable *certificate chain* for a given authorization is called the *certificate chain discovery problem* [2].

SPKI/SDSI certificates may be represented using the ClassAd language in a gangmatching context. A ClassAd representing a certificate is composed of several nested ClassAds called *ports*. One of these ports offers the certificate for use in a chain. If needed, additional ports request other certificates to resolve a SPKI/SDSI name or delegate an authorization. A gang of such ClassAds corresponds to a chain of certificates. In order to support the capability to reuse a certificate indefinitely in a chain while avoiding infinite loops, a modified algorithm for gangmatching is presented.

In the case of multilateral matching, two matchmaking analysis problems are presented along with their solutions: *Break the Chain* and *Missing Link*. The *Break the chain* problem occurs when an authorization policy grants an access that needs to be revoked. To revoke an authorization, a set of certificates must be invalidated such that no chain can be constructed granting the authorization. A new algorithm using the results of the gangmatching algorithm identifies a set of ClassAds representing such certificates. The *Missing Link* problem occurs when a desired authorization is not granted by any certificate chain. A modified version of the gangmatching algorithm identifies the additional certificate ClassAds needed to complete a gang representing a chain of certificates granting the desired authorization.

Section 2 describes the ClassAd language and the gangmatching paradigm. Section 3 provides an introduction to the SPKI/SDSI trust management system and describes a ClassAd language representation of SPKI/SDSI certificates. Section 4 discusses the structures and concepts necessary for extending the gangmatching algorithm. The algorithm itself is presented in Sect. 5. Techniques for gangmatching analysis are explored in Sect. 6. Section 7 surveys related work and Sect. 8 concludes the paper.

2   The ClassAd Language and Gangmatching

The ClassAd language is used by Condor primarily to advertise resources and requests for those resources in a distributed environment. An advertisement, called a *ClassAd*, represents an offer of or request for a resource and consists of named descriptive attributes, constraints and preferences. The constraints are expressed by an attribute named `Requirements`, and the expression of the preferences is named `Rank`. [1] A matchmaking process is used to discover offers and requests that satisfy one another's constraints and best suit one another's preferences. If more than two parties are involved – such as a job, a machine, and a license – a bilateral matchmaking scheme is insufficient and a multilateral framework, called *gangmatching* [15], must be used.

In the gangmatching framework a multilateral match is broken down into several bilateral matches. A set of ClassAds that satisfy one another's constraints is called a *gang*. Each ClassAd contains a list of nested ClassAds called *ports*, each of which represents a single bilateral match. A gang is *complete* if all ports of all ClassAds in the gang have been successfully matched to ports of other ClassAds in the gang. A port that has not been matched is an *open* port. Given a port P of a ClassAd and a potentially matching port P' of another ClassAd, a reference in P to an attribute `attr` defined in P' is represented as `other.attr` to distinguish it from a reference to an attribute in P. In addition, P has a label that is used by subsequent ports in the same ClassAd to reference attributes defined in P'. If P's label is `label`, a reference in a subsequent port to an attribute `attr` defined in P' is represented as `label.attr`. The attribute `attr` is *imported* from P' and is called an *imported attribute*.

Figure 1 shows a gangmatching ClassAd representing a job. The ClassAd has two ports: the first requests a machine to run the job, and the second requests a license to run a particular application on that machine. In the `Requirements` expression of the first port of the job ClassAd, a reference to the attribute `Memory`, imported from a matching ClassAd representing a machine, is expressed as `other.Memory`. The port is labeled `cpu`, and the subsequent port contains a reference to the `Name` attribute imported from the ClassAd matching the first port expressed as `cpu.Name`. In contrast, a locally defined attribute like `ImageSize` is referenced locally without using a prefix.

A gang is tree-structured, which means that some ClassAds may not express constraints on other ClassAds directly. For example, in Fig. 1 the job ClassAd contains a port requesting a machine and another port requesting a license. The license and machine ClassAds that match may each contain a port expressing constraints on the job, but may not have ports expressing constraints on one another. This restriction can be circumvented if the job exports attributes imported from the machine ClassAd in the license port. In Fig. 1 the `Name` attribute of the `cpu` ad is exposed in the license port by the definition `CPUName = cpu.Name`. The matching license ClassAd can indirectly reference the `Name` attribute of

---

[1] To simplify matters this paper deals only with `Requirements` expressions and omits `Rank` expressions from example ClassAds.

```
[Ports = {
  [ // request a workstation
    other = cpu; Type = "cpu_request"; ImageSize = 28M;
    Requirements = other.Type == "Machine" && other.Arch == "INTEL" &&
      other.OpSys == "LINUX" && other.Memory >= ImageSize
  ],
  [ // request a license
    other = license; Type = "license_request"; CPUName = cpu.Name;
    Cmd = "run_sim";
    Requirements = other.Type == "License" && other.App == Cmd
  ]}
]
```

Fig. 1. A gangmatching ClassAd for a job

the machine ClassAd as other.CPUName. Circular dependencies are avoided by the restriction that a port may only use imported attributes from previous ports.

3   SPKI/SDSI

SPKI/SDSI is a trust management system that specifies access control policies using certificates. A SPKI/SDSI certificate is a declaration by a principal, the *issuer* of the certificate, about the naming of another principal, the *subject* of the certificate, or the authorization for the subject to access a resource.

Principals are represented by a unique public key. They may also be referred to indirectly by a *SPKI/SDSI name*. A SPKI/SDSI name consists of a public key followed by zero or more identifiers. The identifiers navigate a hierarchical name space, similar to a hierarchical directory structure. For example, if K_A represents the principal named Alice, then the SPKI/SDSI name "K_A Bob Carol" can be resolved by looking up the identifier "Bob" in Alice's namespace. Assuming that K_A Bob resolves to K_B, Bob's public key, the identifier "Carol" must now be looked up in Bob's namespace. If Bob has defined the identifier "Carol" to resolve to K_C, Carol's public key, then "K_A Bob Carol" is equivalent to the SPKI/SDSI names "K_B Carol" and "K_C."

A name certificate (*name cert*) defines a name in the issuer's local name space by assigning an identifier to a SPKI/SDSI name that represents the subject of the certificate. An authorization certificate (*auth cert*) indicates that the issuer (represented by a public key) authorizes the subject (represented by a SPKI/SDSI name) to access a resource. Both the resource and the permission being granted are specified in an auth cert. For the purposes of this paper we are only concerned with a single anonymous resource and a generic operation on that resource. An auth cert also indicates whether or not the authorization may be delegated. In the discussion that follows, we shall adopt the representation of certificates as rewrite rules with the issuer on the left and the subject on the right as introduced in [2]. Four examples of this rewrite rule representation are shown in Fig. 2.

There are four principals involved in the example certificates in Fig. 2: the administrator of resource R (identified by the public key K_R), Alice, Bob, and Carol (identified by their public keys K_A, K_B, and K_C). Certs (2) and (4) are name certs that indicate that the identifier "Bob" in Alice's name space represents Bob's key, and the identifier "Carol" in Bob's name space represents Carol's key. Certs (1) and (3) are auth certs, denoted by the $\square$ after the subject. In cert (1), the subject "K_A Bob" is granted access to the resource R. The $\square$ at the end indicates that the subject may delegate this access right. Similarly, cert (3) grants the subject "K_B Carol" access to whatever K_B has access to. The $\blacksquare$ at the end of this cert indicates that the subject may not delegate this access right.

$$
\begin{aligned}
&(1) \; K_R \; \square \rightarrow K_A \; \text{Bob} \; \square \\
&(2) \; K_A \; \text{Bob} \rightarrow K_B \\
&(3) \; K_B \; \square \rightarrow K_B \; \text{Carol} \; \blacksquare \\
&(4) \; K_B \; \text{Carol} \rightarrow K_C
\end{aligned}
$$

Fig. 2. SPKI/SDSI certificates as rewrite rules

The use of delegation and an indirect naming scheme means that more than one certificate may be necessary for a principal to access a resource. Such a set of one or more certificates is called a *certificate chain*. A certificate chain may also be represented by a rewrite rule, derived from the composition of compatible certificates. As defined in [2], certs $C_1 = K_1 \; A_1 \rightarrow S_1$ and $C_2 = K_2 \; A_2 \rightarrow S_2$ are *compatible* if $S_1 = K_2 \; A_2 \; X$ for some sequence of zero or more identifiers X (that is $K_2 \; A_2$ is a prefix of S_1). The *composition* of C_1 and C_2, written as $C_1 \circ C_2$ is defined by replacing the prefix of S_1 with S_2. Using the term rewriting notation:

$$
\begin{aligned}
C_1 &= K_1 \; A_1 \rightarrow K_2 \; A_2 \; X \\
C_2 &= K_2 \; A_2 \rightarrow S_2 \\
C_1 \circ C_2 &= K_1 \; A_1 \rightarrow S_2 \; X
\end{aligned}
$$

Certificate chains are built by repeated use of composition.

Returning to the examples in Fig. 2, we can form cert chains by composing compatible certificates. (1) $\circ$ (2) $= K_R \; \square \rightarrow K_B \; \square$ authorizes K_B to access resource R and to delegate that access right; (3) $\circ$ (4) $= K_B \; \square \rightarrow K_C \; \blacksquare$ grants K_C access to whatever K_B has access to. Putting these two chains together we get the chain $((1) \circ (2)) \circ ((3) \circ (4)) = K_R \; \square \rightarrow K_C \; \blacksquare$ that authorizes K_C to access resource R, but not to delegate that access right. The problem of assembling such a chain is called the certificate chain discovery problem. Solutions based on formal language techniques can be found in [2, 11].

The ClassAd representation of SPKI/SDSI certificates is fairly simple. Each certificate ClassAd consists zero or more *cert request ports* and a *cert offer port*.

A cert offer port contains attributes corresponding to the type (name or auth), issuer, identifier (name certs only), and subject of the cert. The Subject attribute is a literal value if the subject of the cert is directly specified using a public key, or an attribute reference if the subject is indirectly specified using a SPKI/SDSI name with one or more identifiers. In the indirect case the ClassAd also contains one or more cert request ports, each of which requests a name cert (or chain of certs) to resolve the SPKI/SDSI name. If the ClassAd represents an auth cert with the delegation bit turned on, there is an additional cert request port requesting an additional auth cert (or chain of certs) issued by the subject of the cert.

For example, the authorization certificate designated as (1) in Fig. 2 would be represented by the ClassAd shown in Fig. 3. The name certificate designated as (2) in Fig. 2 would be represented by the ClassAd shown in Fig. 4.

```
[Ports = {
  [other = chain1; Type = "cert_request";
   Requirements = other.Type == "cert_offer" && other.CertType == "Name" &&
     other.Issuer == "K_A" && other.Identifier == "Bob";
  ],
  [other = chain2; Type = "cert_request";
   Requirements = other.Type == "cert_offer" &&
     other.CertType == "Auth" && other.Issuer == chain1.Subject
  ],
  [other = request; Type = "cert_offer"; CertType = "Auth";
   Issuer = "X"; Subject = chain2.Subject;
   Requirements = other.Type == "cert_request"
  ]}
]
```

Fig. 3. The ClassAd for cert(1)

```
[Ports = {
  [other = request; Type = "cert_offer"; CertType = "Name";
   Issuer = "K_A"; Identifier = "Bob"; Subject = "K_B";
   Requirements = other.Type == "cert_request"
  ]}
]
```

Fig. 4. ClassAd for certificate (2)

4   Gangmatching Structures and Concepts

As we have seen in the examples above, a gangmatching ClassAd is made up of a set of ports, each of which represents a request for another ClassAd. We formally define a port P as a 5-tuple $(E_P, I_P, J_P, \delta_P, \phi_P)$ where E_P is the set of all attributes defined or *exported* by P, I_P is the set of all attributes imported from the ClassAd that is matched with P, J_P is the set of all attributes referenced in P that are imported via other ports in the same ClassAd, δ_P is a function representing the attribute definitions in P, ϕ_P is a Boolean expression in disjunctive normal form (DNF) over I_P, J_P representing the Requirements expression of P. A ClassAd C is defined as an ordered list of ports.

The gangmatching process assembles a gang of ClassAds that is *complete* when all ports of all ClassAds in the gang have been matched with ports of other ClassAds in the gang. A *gangster* is an intermediate structure formed during gangmatching that represents an *open* or unmatched port in an incomplete gang. We define a gangster G as a triple (P, β, L) where $P =(E_P, I_P, J_P, \delta_P, \phi_P)$ is a port, β is a function that binds the attributes in J_P to literal values, and L associates attributes imported from elsewhere in the gang with attributes imported from the ClassAd that will ultimately be matched with P. A port connecting a ClassAd C to one of its children is called a *child port*, and the port connecting C to its parent is the *parent port*. A gang can be thought of as a tree of ClassAds where each ClassAd is connected to its parent or child through one of its ports. The ClassAd at the root of the tree is referred to as the *root ClassAd*.

The gangmatching algorithm relies heavily upon the concepts of *equivalence*, *partial evaluation* and *validity*. Two gangsters are *equivalent* if they are structurally the same, but contain attributes from different ClassAds. An individual match is *conditionally valid* if one or both of the Requirements expressions involved unresolved attribute references. Partial evaluation is used to condense these expressions, which must then be satisfied by bindings generated by subsequent matches. A gang in which all of these expressions have been satisfied is considered a *valid* gang.

The input to the algorithm is the *root* ClassAd C_0 and a set of additional ClassAds $\mathcal{C}$ that will be used to build the rest of the gang. Beginning with the gangster consisting of the single port of C_0, the algorithm creates new gangsters by matching existing gangsters to parent ports of other ClassAds. Whenever a new gangster is created, a new rule in a regular grammar is generated. When the algorithm terminates, this grammar generates all complete valid gangs built from C_0 and the ClassAds in $\mathcal{C}$. In order to avoid repeated work and infinite loops caused by the reuse of ClassAds, the algorithm must test each new gangster for equivalence to previously encountered gangsters. If an equivalent gangster is found, the algorithm adds a new rule to the grammar, but does not attempt to match the new gangster. Otherwise, the new gangster is tested against the parent port of each ClassAd in $\mathcal{C}$ for a potential match. If the match is conditionally valid, the Requirements expressions of the respective ports are partially evaluated, and the resulting expression is passed to the first new gangster created by the match. Further matches must satisfy this expression in addition to the Requirements expressions of other ports encountered later.

The structures and concepts described here are examined in more detail in [4].

5   Gangmatching Algorithm

The gangmatching algorithm builds individual gangs in a top-down (root to leaves) fashion. The premise of the algorithm is that if an infinite number of gangs can be composed from a finite set of ClassAds, then there must be a repeating pattern – in the same way that a finite automaton can define an infinite but regular language. These repetitions can be prevented by detecting new gangsters that are equivalent to previously encountered gangsters. Thus, we can assemble a finite grammar that may produce an infinite number of gangs. In addition, this algorithm makes use of the partial evaluation facility described in Sect. 4 to build gangs that satisfy conditionally valid matches.

The algorithm takes as input a set $\mathcal{C}$ of ClassAds, and a root ClassAd C_0. Without loss of generality we will assume C_0 has only one port. We also assume that each ClassAd $C \in \mathcal{C} \cup \{C_0\}$ satisfies the following properties:

1. The Requirements expression ϕ_P of each port P of C consists of a conjunction of binary or unary predicates over attributes imported via P (I_P), attributes imported via previous ports in C (J_P) and literal values (represented by the set $\mathcal{V}$) in which no predicate contains attributes imported from more than one previous port in C and every predicate contains at least one attribute imported via P.
2. The last port in C is the parent port of C, and all other ports are child ports.
3. C has no more than 2 child ports.

In order to facilitate the handling of conditionally valid matches we will add an additional component ψ_G to each gang G. The purpose of ψ_G will become clear as we discuss the algorithm.

The following methods are not explicitly defined here:

1. ADDGANGSTER - adds a new gangster to a queue to be processed later
2. ADDRULE - adds a new rule to the grammar
3. MOREGANGSTERS - returns **true** if more unprocessed gangsters are available, **false** otherwise
4. REMOVEGANGSTER - removes a gangster from the queue
5. CHECKSEEN - checks if a gangster is equivalent to a previously encountered gangster, and adds it to the previously seen gangsters if it hasn't
6. ADDEXTRARULES - finds any rules containing a gangster equivalent to given gangster, and creates duplicates of those rules for the given gangster
7. MATCHRESULTS - tests a match between a gangster and a ClassAd, and returns an expression generated by partially evaluating and conjoining the Requirements expressions of the gangster and ClassAd
8. VALIDMATCH - determines if the result of a match indicates that it is valid (both Requirements expressions evaluate to true, or can be partially evaluated to satisfiable expressions)
9. SETNEXT - adds a link to a list of gangsters in an incomplete gang
10. GETNEXT - gets then next gangster in the list of gangsters.

The GANGMATCH method shown in Fig. 5 adds a gangster created from the single port of C_0. The algorithm then enters a loop in which gangsters are removed and added to a list of gangs using the ADDGANGSTER and REMOVEGANGSTER methods. At the beginning of each loop, a gangster G is selected and tested to see if an equivalent gangster has been previously encountered using the CHECKSEEN method. If CHECKSEEN returns **true**, the ADDEXTRARULES method is called, adding new rules containing G to the grammar based on existing rules containing equivalent gangsters. If CHECKSEEN returns **false**, the PROCESSMATCH method is called on each $C \in \mathcal{C}$ to see if it matches G. When the GANGMATCH method has completed, the generated grammar will produce a set of matches representing all complete valid gangs rooted at C_0. Each gang is a list of ClassAds in order of appearance in the gang, with the parent port of each ClassAd matching the first open port of the gang made up of the previous ClassAds.

GANGMATCH(C_0, $\mathcal{C}$)
 1 $P \leftarrow C_0$'s port
 2 $G \leftarrow (P, \varnothing, \varnothing, \mathbf{T})$
 3 ADDGANGSTER(G)
 4 ADDRULE($G \rightarrow C_0$)
 5 **while** MOREGANGSTERS()
 6     $G \leftarrow$ REMOVEGANGSTER()
 7   **if** CHECKSEEN(G)
 8   ADDEXTRARULES(G)
 9   **else**
10   **for** each $C \in \mathcal{C}$
11   PROCESSMATCH(G, C)

Fig. 5. The GANGMATCH algorithm

The PROCESSMATCH method shown in Fig. 6 tests the match between G and C using the MATCHRESULTS method. The VALIDMATCH method is then used on the resulting expression to determine whether or not the match was valid or conditionally valid (i.e. further matches will be needed). If VALIDMATCH returns **true**, the MATCHBINDINGS, PROCESSPORTS, and PROCESSNEXTGANGSTER methods are called to process any new gangsters generated by the match.

The MATCHBINDINGS method shown in Fig. 7 creates a set of bindings to be used by PROCESSPORTS and PROCESSNEXTGANGSTER. The bindings are produced using the set of attribute definitions δ_P contained in C's parent port P. If any attribute defined in δ_P ($attr$, Y) corresponds to an attribute referenced in the set L_G of existing bindings in G (X, $attr$), a new binding (X, Y) is created and added to the set L_M. Additionally, a binding is created from the attribute definition itself ($attr$, Y). Once all attribute definitions in δ_P are checked, the set of bindings L_M is returned.

PROCESSMATCH(G, C)
1 $\psi_M \leftarrow$ MATCHRESULTS(G, C)
2 **if** VALIDMATCH(ψ_M)
3    $L_M \leftarrow$ MATCHBINDINGS(G, C)
4    $G_{last} \leftarrow$ PROCESSPORTS(G, C, ψ_M, L_M)
5   PROCESSNEXTGANGSTER(G, C, L_M, G_{last})

Fig. 6. The PROCESSMATCH method

MATCHBINDINGS(G, C)
1 $P \leftarrow C$'s parent port
2 $L_M \leftarrow \varnothing$
3 **for** each $(attr, Y) \in \delta_P$
3   **if** $(X, attr) \in L_G$
4       $L_M \leftarrow L_M \cup \{(X, Y)\}$
5    $L_M \leftarrow L_M \cup \{(attr, Y)\}$
6 **return** L_M

Fig. 7. The MATCHBINDINGS method

The PROCESSPORTS method shown in Fig. 8 goes through each port in C and creates a new gangster corresponding to that port based on the results of the match. The method takes as arguments G, C, the resulting expression ψ_M from the match between them, and the set of bindings L_M generated by MATCHBINDINGS. First, L_M is searched for any binding (X, Y) where Y is a member of the set I_P of imported attributes in P, and the resulting bindings are added to the set L. Second, psi_M is searched for any predicates containing an attribute in I_P, and the results are conjoined to form the expression psi. A new gangster G_{new} is then created from P, L, and psi, and is added to the queue of new gangsters. If there are no prior gangsters in the gang, a new rule $G_{new} \rightarrow G$ C is added to the grammar to indicate that G_{new} is a result of matching G and C. Finally, G_{new} is added to the linked list of gangsters comprising the current gang. The last gangster generated is returned by the method.

The PROCESSNEXTGANGSTER method shown in Fig. 9 updates the next gangster in the gang after G to reflect the results of the match between G and C. Like PROCESSPORTS the PROCESSNEXTGANGSTER method takes G, C, and L_M as arguments, along with the last gangster G_{last} created by PROCESSPORTS. The method begins by checking if there are any more gangsters in the gang after G. If there are no more gangsters, G_{last} is set as the last gangster in the gang. If there was no G_{last} the gang must be complete and the rule $S \rightarrow G$ C is added to complete the grammar. If there is a next gangster G' it must be updated.

The update of G' proceeds in a manner similar to the generation of new gangsters in PROCESSPORTS. First, L_M is searched for any binding (X, Y) where Y is a literal value, and X is a member of the set of attributes $J_{P_{G'}}$ imported in $P_{G'}$ from previous ports in the ClassAd containing $P_{G'}$. The resulting bindings

PROCESSPORTS(G, C, ψ_M, L_M)
1 $G_{last} \leftarrow$ **null**
2 **for** each child port P of C
3      $L \leftarrow \{(X, Y) \in L_M \mid Y \in I_P\}$
4      $\psi \leftarrow \wedge \{$preds in ψ_M over $i \in I_P\}$
5      $G_{new} \leftarrow (P, \varnothing, L, \psi)$
6   ADDGANGSTER(G_{new})
7   **if** $G_{last} =$ **null**
8   ADDRULE($G_{new} \rightarrow G\ C$)
9   **else**
10   SETNEXT(G_{last}, G_{new})
11      $G_{last} \leftarrow G_{new}$
12 **return** G_{last}

Fig. 8. The PROCESSPORTS method

PROCESSNEXTGANGSTER(G, C, L_M, G_{last})
1 $G' \leftarrow$ GETNEXT(G)
2 **if** $G' \neq$ **null**
3      $\beta \leftarrow \{(X, Y) \in L_M \mid X \in J_{P_{G'}}, Y \in \mathcal{V}\}$
4      $G_{new} \leftarrow (P_{G'}, \beta, L_{G'}, \psi_{G'})$
5   ADDGANGSTER(G_{new})
6   **if** $G_{last} =$ **null**
7   ADDRULE($G_{new} \rightarrow G\ C$)
8   **else** SETNEXT(G_{last}, G_{new})
9   SETNEXT(G_{new}, GETNEXT(G'))
10 **elsif** $G_{last} \neq$ **null**
11   SETNEXT(G_{last}, **null**)
12 **else**
13   ADDRULE($S \rightarrow G\ C$)

Fig. 9. The PROCESSNEXTGANGSTER method

are stored in the set of bindings β, which is added to G' to create the new gangster G_{new}. The remainder of the method is similar to lines 7-10 in PROCESSPORTS in which the rule $G_{new} \rightarrow G\ C$ is added to the grammar if it is the first gangster in the gang, and the linked list of gangs is adjusted to include G_{new}.

6   Gangmatching Analysis

Gangmatching analysis is essentially an extension of bilateral matching analysis [3]. Between any two given ports, the same techniques can be used to determine why the first port does not match the second and vice versa. However, the presence of prior ports in a ClassAd introduces the possibility that one match may be dependent on the results of other matches. In addition, new problems arise from the more complex structure of a gang as opposed to two matching ClassAds.

A common problem in authorization systems is how to revoke a principal's access to a resource. For example, in SPKI/SDSI a principal may have access to a resource via several different certificate chains containing certificates issued by several different principals. In order to revoke the principal's access to the resource, at least one certificate in each such chain must be revoked. To avoid unnecessary disruption caused by certificate revocation, the set of certificates revoked should be minimal.

The *Break the Chain* problem may be abstracted to the problem of finding a minimal element in a subset lattice that passes a given test. In this case the top set in the lattice is the set of all certificates in C. The test on a given C' $\subseteq C$ is whether the certificates in C' grant the principal access to the resource. The problem of finding all such minimal elements has been shown to be NP-hard [10], but the problem of finding one such element is linear. Furthermore, finding k such elements for a constant k is polynomial: for $k > 1$ the complexity is $O(n^{k-1})$. The algorithm itself [4] applies this abstraction, then improves the performance by optimizing to reduce repeated work.

The *Missing Link* problem is the opposite of the Break the Chain problem. In this case a principal has no access to a resource, but may have elements of a certificate chain that would grant access. The problem is to find which certificates are needed to complete a chain that will authorize the principal to access the resource. The gangmatching equivalent of this problem is finding which Class-Ads are needed to complete a gang. The solution to this problem is to run the gangmatching algorithm with a slight modification: When a port does not match any other ports, the gang is not abandoned; instead, the algorithm continues to match the rest of the ports in the gang and any dependencies on the unmatched port are ignored. When a partial gang has been completed, the "missing links" in the gang can be determined by using the Requirements expressions of the un-matched ports, and the references to imported attributes in these ports. Satisfied Requirements expressions elsewhere in the gang that contain such references can be partially evaluated to produce additional constraints for missing links. The gangmatching algorithm can be modified [4] to accept prototype ClassAds that will capture these additional constraints.

7   Related Work

There are some similarities between ClassAds and agent communication languages [9, 7, 17], though ClassAds employ a representation more akin to a database record than the rule-based representation used by these languages. There are also similarities between ClassAds matchmaking and the unification-based matching used by Linda [8] and Datalog. Linda uses tuples containing variables or literals to search a tuple space for a matching tuple. Datalog operates similarly on relational databases.

The term rewriting approach to SPKI/SDSI was introduced in [2] along with an algorithm for certificate chain discovery. It is also possible to use pushdown systems (PDS) to represent SPKI/SDSI rewrite rules [11, 12]. The enhanced gangmatching algorithm in Sect. 5 began as a generalization of the *post** algorithm for PDS reachability.

The resource selection and authorization policies discussed in this paper both fall under the category of *provisions*. Provisions are conditions that must be satisfied or actions that must occur before a decision takes place. In contrast *obligations* are conditions or actions that must be fulfilled after a decision has been made [1]. An SLA is an agreement between a service provider and a customer that specifies certain attributes of the service such as availability, serviceability, performance and operation [19]. PDL [13] expresses obligation policies as event-condition-action rules. The Ponder policy language [5] can also be used to express both obligation and authorization policies.

Several other policy languages – such as Rei and Kaos have been developed specifically for the semantic web and grid computing applications. These languages are typically based on description logics such as DAML and OWL. A comparison of Rei, Kaos and Ponder is presented here [18].

8   Conclusions

Distributed computing environments provide users with a wide range of services that a single isolated system can not provide. Policies must be designed and enforced to protect the interests of users and providers of these services. Resource selection policies address the question: What kind of resource does a principal want, and is such a resource available? Access control policies address the question: Can a principal be trusted to have access to a given resource?

The framework for policy specification and interpretation presented in this paper provides a clearing house for both types of policies. It is built on the simple yet powerful concept of matchmaking. The ClassAd language and matchmaking algorithms were initially developed to solve resource selection problems in a distributed system. As we have shown, the same framework with some minor modifications is applicable to managing access control policies.

We have demonstrated that the ClassAd language can be used to specify SPKI/SDSI authorization policies, and an enhanced gangmatching algorithm can be used to assemble SPKI/SDSI certificate chains correctly and efficiently. We have also presented the necessary theoretical underpinnings of the enhanced gangmatching algorithm which generalize beyond the specific instance of SPKI/SDSI certificate chain discovery. Finally, we have demonstrated analysis techniques for bilateral and multilateral matchmaking that serve as essential tools for comprehending matchmaking results. Taken together these contributions provide a robust framework for specifying and interpreting resource allocation policies.

References

[1] Bettini, C., Jajodia, S., Wang, S., Wijesekera, D.: Provisions and obligations in policy rule management and security applications. In: Proceedings of 28th International Conference on Very Large Data Bases (VLDB), Hong Kong, China, pp. 502–513 (August 2002)

[2] Clarke, D., Elien, J.-E., Ellison, C., Fredette, M., Morcos, A., Rivest, R.: Certificate chain discovery in SPKI/SDSI. Journal of Computer Security 9(4), 285–322 (2001)

[3] Coleman, N., Raman, R., Livny, M., Solomon, M.: Distributed policy management and comprehension with classified advertisements. Technical Report UW-CS-TR-1481, University of Wisconsin (April 2003)

[4] Coleman, N.: A Matchmaking Approach to Distributed Policy Specification and Interpretation. PhD thesis, University of Wisconsin-Madison (August 2007)

[5] Damianou, N., Dulay, N., Lupu, E., Sloman, M.: The Ponder Policy Specification Language. In: Sloman, M., Lobo, J., Lupu, E.C. (eds.) POLICY 2001. LNCS, vol. 1995, pp. 18–38. Springer, Heidelberg (2001)

[6] Ellison, C., Frantz, B., Lampson, B., Rivest, R.L., Thomas, B., Ylonen, T.: SPKI certificate theory. RFC 2693 (September 1999)

[7] Finin, T., Fritzson, R., McKay, D., McEntire, R.: KQML as an agent communication language. In: Proc. of the Third Int'l Conf. on Information and Knowledge Management, CIKM 1994. ACM Press (November1994)

[8] Gelernter, D.: Generative communication in linda. ACM Trans. Program. Lang. Syst. 7(1), 80–112 (1985)

[9] Genesereth, M., Singh, N., Syed, M.: A distributed anonymous knowledge sharing approach to software interoperation. In: Proc. of the Int'l Symposium on Fifth Generation Computing Systems, pp. 125–139 (1994)

[10] Godfrey, P.: Minimization in cooperative response to failing database queries. International Journal of Cooperative Information Systems (IJCIS) 6(2), 95–149 (1997)

[11] Jha, S., Reps, T.: Analysis of SPKI/SDSI certificates using model checking. In: Proceedings of IEEE Computer Security Foundations Workshop (CSFW). IEEE Computer Society Press (2002)

[12] Jha, S., Reps, T.W.: Model checking spki/sdsi. Journal of Computer Security 12(3-4), 317–353 (2004)

[13] Lobo, J., Bhatia, R., Naqvi, S.: A policy description language. In: AAAI/IAAI, pp. 291–298 (1999)

[14] Raman, R., Livny, M., Solomon, M.: Matchmaking: Distributed resource management for high-throughput computing. In: Proceedings of the Seventh IEEE International Symposium on High Performance Distributed Computing, HPDC7 (July 1998)

[15] Raman, R., Livny, M., Solomon, M.: Policy driven heterogeneous resource co-allocation with gangmatching. In: Proceedings of the Twelfth IEEE International Symposium on High Performance Distributed Computing (HPDC12), Seattle, WA (June 2003)

[16] Solomon, M.: The ClassAd language reference manual version 2.4 (May 2004), http://www.cs.wisc.edu/condor/classad/refman/

[17] Sycara, K., Decker, K., Pannu, A., Williamson, M., Zeng, D.: Distributed intelligent agents. IEEE Expert, 36–46 (December 1996)

[18] Tonti, G., Bradshaw, J.M., Jeffers, R., Montanari, R., Suri, N., Uszok, A.: Semantic Web Languages for Policy Representation and Reasoning: A Comparison of KAoS, Rei, and Ponder. In: Fensel, D., Sycara, K., Mylopoulos, J. (eds.) ISWC 2003. LNCS, vol. 2870, pp. 419–437. Springer, Heidelberg (2003)

[19] Westerinen, A., Schnizlein, J., Strassner, J., Scherling, M., Quinn, B., Herzog, S., Huynh, A., Carlson, M., Perry, J., Waldbusser, S.: Policy terminology. RFC 3198 (November 2001)

Handshaking in Kansas Lava Using Patch Logic

Andy Gill and Bowe Neuenschwander

Information Technology and Telecommunication Center
Department of Electrical Engineering and Computer Science
The University of Kansas
{andygill,bneuen}@ku.edu

Abstract. Designing hardware is like writing music for an orchestra - lots of pieces have to come together at the correct time for everything to work. In systems design, there is a confusing array of standards for allowing cooperating components, and little type-level support in traditional design methodologies for helping connect components with pre-arranged protocols. In this paper, we explore bringing protocol-level types to communicating processes. Inside our hardware description language Kansas Lava we introduce the notation of a patch, which is a communicating component with well-understood protocols. We build a theory round the notion of patches, which we call patch logic, and then use the patch abstraction to build a small driver for an FPGA board.

1   Introduction

When writing cooperative components for hardware fabrics like FPGAs, some form of handshaking or inter-component cooperation is required. One common solution is using central control logic. This allows for maximizing global throughput, but at the cost of composability of the sub-components. Another solution is to allow components to act independently, and throttle the communication between components using bus protocols. In this paper, we take the second approach to hardware design, and build a set of types and combinators to facilitate the construction of hardware using composition.

We program in the language Haskell [12], and design hardware using Kansas Lava [8,7], our version of a Haskell library for describing hardware. Kansas Lava, like other the versions of Lava before it [4,14], makes extensive use of types to describe signals. Kansas Lava has distinct types for combinatorially and sequentially generated values, a family of lifting functions to coerce between these two styles of hardware logic, and various structured types for complex signals. This paper takes this type-based approach one step further, where we express the *protocol* between components using types, and build abstractions around these types.

The contribution of this paper is explaining in detail how Lava may be successfully used in the large by utilizing both the traditional idioms and a new Lava idiom which we call patches. Of course, all circuits could be described using simple logic and structural composition. Types, higher-order functions and

C. Russo and N.-F. Zhou (Eds.): PADL 2012, LNCS 7149, pp. 212–226, 2012.

mathematical structures like monads give functional language-based hardware description languages the advantage of powerful and composable abstractions. Specifically, we make the following contributions.

- We introduce a new Haskell structure for constructing large circuits, a `Patch`, which facilitates the construction of cooperating components.
- We give the laws for our patches, and show how complex dataflow can be managed and connected to the interfaces of our circuits.
- To support our thesis that this new abstraction support the modular construction of circuits we give an extended example of building an LCD driver.

2   Kansas Lava

Kansas Lava is a Haskell library for simulating and generating hardware components, in the spirit of Chalmers Lava and Xilinx Lava. Like Chalmers Lava, Kansas Lava uses observable sharing [5,6] to represent and capture cycles in hardware, but uniquely uses an explicit monad to represent external connectivity. The major novel feature of Kansas Lava is the aggressive use of types and type extensions to capture hardware restrictions and concerns. This paper represents an extension of this initiative, by giving a typed interface to protocols.

All variants of Lava are based around the idea that you can write a structural description of hardware, and then observe or extract the description of the described hardware. The classical example is the half-adder.

```
halfAdder :: Seq Bool -> Seq Bool -> (Seq Bool,Seq Bool)
halfAdder a b = (carry,sum) where
   carry = and2 a b
   sum   = xor2 a b
```

In this example, two arguments are combined to make two results, the carry and the result of the sum. The `Seq` :: * -> * type constructor lifts its argument to make it observable; a well-understood Domain Specific Language trick [11,8,2]. Seq here is a sequence of values of time, interpreted by an implicit clock, in much the same way as `signal` is typically used in VHDL.

There are several structures like Seq in Kansas Lava; here is a short taxonomy of the major structures.

- There are fixed width values, signed (Sn), unsigned (Un), and fixed range values (Xn).
- These values, and other built-in Haskell types, like tuples and `Bool`, can be lifted into an observable signal using `Comb`, `CSeq c`, a signal interpreted by a given clock type, or `Seq`, a signal interpreted by a global clock. For the remainder of this paper we will use Seq with its global clock for conciseness, the ideas presented here generalize to multi-clock designs.
- We have what we call the protocol gap, where types are used to represent protocol. Filling this gap is the subject of this paper. As an example of a protocol, `Enabled` represents an optional value implemented using an extra ENABLE status flag.

- Finally, we have the Fabrics. Fabric is the monad used to connect a Kansas Lava program to an external device, like a LCD screen or RJ-45 port. We have two implementations of Fabric: one for use on real hardware, and one for use in simulation.

These different type classifications are connected using combinators. There is a lift function that lifts pure Haskell functions into a function that operates on signals, and a fixed set of lift functions that lifts Comb-based functions into Seq-based functions. As well as these functions, many primitives are provided, and overloaded to work over Signal, a class that abstracts over Comb and Seq.

Fabric is the monad for connecting to the outside world, via specific pins on the FPGA. As an example, consider listening to physical switches and pushbuttons on a specific FPGA board, and lighting up a row of LEDs. In Kansas Lava, this would read:

```
test_leds :: Fabric ()
test_leds = do sw <- switches
               bu <- buttons
               leds (sw 'M.append' bu)

-- switches, buttons and leds are provided by a board-specific prelude
switches :: Fabric (Matrix X4 (Seq Bool))
switches = do
        inp <- inStdLogicVector "SW" :: Fabric (Seq (Matrix X4 Bool))
        return (unpack inp)

buttons :: Fabric (Matrix X4 (Seq Bool))
buttons = do i0 <- inStdLogic "BTN_WEST"
             i1 <- inStdLogic "BTN_NORTH"
             i2 <- inStdLogic "BTN_EAST"
             i3 <- inStdLogic "BTN_SOUTH"
             return (matrix [i0,i1,i2,i3])

leds :: Matrix X8 (Seq Bool) -> Fabric ()
leds inp = outStdLogicVector "LED" (pack inp :: Seq (Matrix X8 Bool))
```

There is a Haskell class for each FPGA board supported, with peripherals being provided as overloaded Fabric-based functions. Furthermore, each board is given two instances, one for programming the physical device using an associated UCF specification, and one for programming a board simulator. In this way, programs can be developed for specific boards, and tested offline before being actually deployed.

3   Protocols

When building larger Lava circuits, we want some typed idioms to help us with our hardware development. The need for an idiom appears when allowing two components to communicate when a new datum does not appear every cycle. We

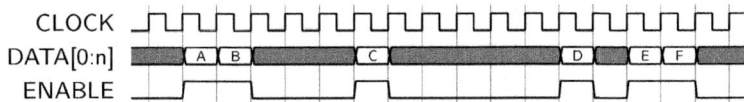

Fig. 1. The Enabled Protocol

now introduce two such well-understood idioms, built on top of `Seq`: sequences of optionally defined values, and sequences of handshaken values.

3.1 The `Enabled` Protocol

The basic way of arranging one-direction optional communication is marking data as valid or invalid at each clock cycle. In Kansas Lava, we call this protocol the `Enable` protocol. Figure 1 gives the timing table for `Enabled`. On every clock cycle, DATA is either transmitted with the ENABLE bit high, or the DATA is unknown/ignored and ENABLE is low. In this example, the sequence A,B,C,D,E,F is transmitted, taking just over a dozen cycles to do so.

In order to help describe our use of protocols, we use a simple notation to give a type to this agreement between producer and consumer. We notate the `Enabled` protocol using a pair of **E** α, indicated an `Enabled` value of type α is sent; and •, to indicate that nothing is sent from consumer to producer. We place the outgoing type above the back-edge type, and group with Oxford-style brackets, to notate the use of `Seq` to do the actual transmission.

$$\left[\negthinspace\left[\begin{array}{c} \text{E } \alpha \\ \bullet \end{array} \right]\negthinspace\right] \tag{1}$$

3.2 Handshaking

The basic shortcoming of `Enabled` is the inability of the consumer to slow down the dataflow. This is overcome by handshaking. There are two general types of handshaking: sending an acknowledgment to an `Enabled` datum ("Yes, I got that, please send the next one."), or indicating readiness to receive an `Enabled` datum ("If you send me something, I promise to be ready for it."). In Kansas Lava, we support both, but standardize around the acknowledge, simply because this use of acknowledge complies with the `opencores.org` Wishbone bus protocol, and one standard protocol with necessary coercions is more manageable than supporting both handshake styles everywhere. Figure 2 gives the timing diagram for standardized handshaking, which we called AckBox (acknowledge/mailbox). Again using our invented notation, we can describe this protocol mnemonically.

$$\left[\negthinspace\left[\begin{array}{c} \text{E } \alpha \\ \text{A} \end{array} \right]\negthinspace\right] \tag{2}$$

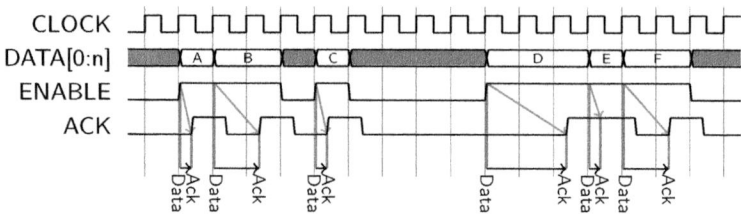

Fig. 2. The Handshake Protocol

Like before, we transmit datums using the `Enable` protocol. This time, however, we have an acknowledgment, A, which asynchronously responds to the EN-ABLE line, and provides actionable evidence of receipt of data. In Kansas Lava, the acknowledgment is typed `Ack`, and `Ack` is always used to indicate successful receipt of data.

The issue with sending acknowledgment to a producer of data is purely logistical. If Lava was based on relations, like Ruby [10], this would be easy. However, we need to instead take an extra output from the consumer, and feed it backwards, as an extra input into the transmitter. This wiring is error-prone and cumbersome to do manually.

4   Patches

A patch is what we call a circuit, or stream processor, between two protocols. There can be communication patches, that act as bridges between protocols, and there can be computational patches, that perform some computation on the input to generate the output. A patch becomes a mid-level unit of expressing computation on an FPGA fabric.

In Kansas Lava, we can represent a patch with a function that takes input from the left hand protocol and the acknowledge from the right hand protocol, and returns the acknowledge to the left hand protocol, and the output for the right hand protocol. A patch is a function from two-tuple to two-tuple. For example, a fifo (a bounded channel in hardware, a pipe in UNIX), could have the type:

```
--                  lhs input * rhs ack      lhs ack * rhs output
fifo :: ... -> (Seq (Enabled a), Seq Ack) -> (Seq Ack, Seq (Enabled a))
```

The connection and direction of each input and output in not as clear as could be here. We found using this tuple convention confusing, and wiring between patches tedious, because wiring is needed in both directions.

We want to find a good type abstraction to clarify the relationship between data-flow direction and protocol used. Further, with this abstraction we hope to build combinators that make the wiring of patches straightforward in practice. Towards this, we choose to represent our patches using the following notation, based on the idea that both input and output is performed on a specific protocol.

$$\texttt{fifo} \; :: \; \left[\!\!\left[\begin{matrix} \text{E } \alpha \\ \text{A} \end{matrix}\right]\!\!\right] \triangleright \left[\!\!\left[\begin{matrix} \text{E } \alpha \\ \text{A} \end{matrix}\right]\!\!\right]$$

This notates, using a left-to-right dataflow assumption, that a component called
fifo takes an enabled, handshaken value using the AckBox protocol from a (un-
represented) component, and passes on results, also using the AckBox protocol.
The diagram presents the types of values being passed, and how the protocol is
used, but says nothing about what fifo actually does.

We can capture the cleaner notational style of the protocol based patch description in Haskell, by using a type synonym. Specifically, a Patch is defined
as

```
type Patch lhs_dat rhs_dat
          lhs_ack rhs_ack = (lhs_dat,rhs_ack) -> (lhs_ack,rhs_dat)
```

Now Patch can mirror the []▷[] notation for patches, by making use of whitespace.

```
fifoP :: (...) => Patch (Seq (Enabled a)) (Seq (Enabled a))
                        (Seq Ack)          (Seq Ack)
```

The first and the third argument line up as a column, to specify the protocol
used as input. Likewise for the output, with the second and forth arguments
respectively. We use the suffix P to denote the use of a patch, as M is sometimes
used to denote the use of a monad.

Patches can, of course, be used as coercions between different sequence-based
protocols. For example, the Enabled protocol can be translated into AckBox
protocol, assuming frequent enough handshakes, using latch:

$$\texttt{latch} \; :: \; \left[\!\!\left[\begin{matrix} \text{E } \alpha \\ \bullet \end{matrix}\right]\!\!\right] \triangleright \left[\!\!\left[\begin{matrix} \text{E } \alpha \\ \text{A} \end{matrix}\right]\!\!\right] \tag{3}$$

Therefore, latch would have the following Haskell type:

```
latchP :: (...) => Patch (Seq (Enabled a)) (Seq (Enabled a))
                         ()                 (Seq Ack)
```

4.1   Multi-protocol Patches

Some patches have multiple input or output protocols. We notate a multi-
protocol interface using multiple columns inside our protocol box. A multi-
protocol interface consisting of two AckBox protocols that send an α and β
respectively, can be notated using:

$$\left[\!\!\left[\begin{matrix} \text{E } \alpha & \text{E } \beta \\ \text{A} & \text{A} \end{matrix}\right]\!\!\right] \tag{4}$$

Having multi-protocol patches allows various standard list processing idioms to
be captured at the protocol level. For example, zip and unzip are possible:

$$\text{zip} :: \begin{bmatrix} \text{E } \alpha & \text{E } \beta \\ \text{A} & \text{A} \end{bmatrix} \triangleright \begin{bmatrix} \text{E } (\alpha, \beta) \\ \text{A} \end{bmatrix} \tag{5}$$

$$\text{unzip} :: \begin{bmatrix} \text{E } (\alpha, \beta) \\ \text{A} \end{bmatrix} \triangleright \begin{bmatrix} \text{E } \alpha & \text{E } \beta \\ \text{A} & \text{A} \end{bmatrix} \tag{6}$$

When writing multi-protocol interfaces, we use an infix tupling constructor :>, and line up the columns to mirror the patch description. We give the type of zip here; the unzip follows from the patch description in the same way.

```
data a :> b = a :> b

zipP :: (...)
    => Patch (Seq (Enabled a) :> Seq (Enabled b)) (Seq (Enabled (a,b)))
           (Seq Ack           :> Seq Ack)          (Seq Ack)
```

This ability to write multi-protocol patches allows the implementation of data-flow style hardware descriptions, furthering abstractions provided to the Kansas Lava user.

4.2   Patches for Kansas Lava Sequences

So far, patches and protocols are a hand-shake of sequences, mapping to signals in VHDL. However, there is a powerful generalization that can be introduced. We want to generalize patches and protocols to other transport mechanisms other than just Kansas Lava sequences. The protocols rendered with Oxford brackets can be written explicitly, using single-line brackets. We therefore define our Oxford brackets in terms of the more primitive notation.

$$\begin{bmatrix} \alpha_1 \ldots \alpha_n \\ \beta_1 \ldots \beta_n \end{bmatrix} \equiv \begin{bmatrix} (\text{Seq } \alpha_1) & \ldots & (\text{Seq } \alpha_n) \\ (\text{Seq } \beta_1) & \ldots & (\text{Seq } \beta_n) \end{bmatrix} \tag{7}$$

We take a small liberty with the rewriting using rule (7), where $\bullet$ inside Oxford brackets represents (), not Seq (). We appeal to the isomorphism between () and Seq (), where our use of () is unlifted, to justify this syntactical shortcut. We retain, however, the Oxford-style brackets for conciseness.

This generalization allows us to insert and extract Haskell values straight into our patches. We can have a patch that has conventional Haskell values on one side, and uses Kansas Lava Seq on the other. For example, we can have patches that coerce to and from Haskell lists, here called toAckBox and fromAckBox.

$$\text{toAckBox} :: \begin{bmatrix} [\text{E } \alpha] \\ \bullet \end{bmatrix} \triangleright \begin{bmatrix} \text{E } \alpha \\ \text{A} \end{bmatrix} \tag{8}$$

$$\text{fromAckBox} :: \begin{bmatrix} \text{E } \alpha \\ \text{A} \end{bmatrix} \triangleright \begin{bmatrix} [\text{E } \alpha] \\ \bullet \end{bmatrix} \tag{9}$$

We call these patches "shallow" because they have a shallow embedding; that is, they can never be rendered into hardware because of the direct use of the Haskell lists; they exist for simulation and test-bench use only. The protocol

$$\begin{bmatrix} [\text{E } \alpha] \\ \bullet \end{bmatrix} \tag{10}$$

is implemented directly as a Haskell list of `Maybe` (and the returned ().)

There is no requirement for the left-hand side of a patch to share the same timings as the right-hand side. In the case of `toAckBox` the left-hand side is a Haskell list, the right hand side is a Lava sequence. The use of [E α] inside (10), rather than simply a [α] allows `toAckBox` to generate a punctured use of the AckBox protocol; `toAckBox` can literally be told to send `Nothing`.

4.3 Chaining Together Patches

The principal thing we can do with patches is combine them into bigger patches. We do this using a type-safe bus builder, $\$\$$.

$$\$\$ \ :: \ \begin{bmatrix} \alpha \\ \beta \end{bmatrix} \triangleright \begin{bmatrix} \gamma \\ \delta \end{bmatrix} \ \longrightarrow \ \begin{bmatrix} \gamma \\ \delta \end{bmatrix} \triangleright \begin{bmatrix} \pi \\ \phi \end{bmatrix} \ \longrightarrow \ \begin{bmatrix} \alpha \\ \beta \end{bmatrix} \triangleright \begin{bmatrix} \pi \\ \phi \end{bmatrix} \tag{11}$$

Unsurprisingly, $\$\$$ is also associative:

$$([]\triangleright_1[] \ \$\$ \ []\triangleright_2[]) \ \$\$ \ []\triangleright_3[] \ = \ []\triangleright_1[] \ \$\$ \ ([]\triangleright_2[] \ \$\$ \ []\triangleright_3[]) \tag{12}$$

When chaining components together, we sometimes use an infix variant of our signatures, where the $\triangleright$ is replaced by the name of the component, and $\$\$$ to notate a bus.

$$\cdots \ \left(\begin{bmatrix} \text{E } \alpha \\ \bullet \end{bmatrix} \text{latch} \begin{bmatrix} \text{E } \alpha \\ \text{A} \end{bmatrix}\right) \$\$ \left(\begin{bmatrix} \text{E } \alpha \\ \text{A} \end{bmatrix} \text{fifo} \begin{bmatrix} \text{E } \alpha \\ \text{A} \end{bmatrix}\right) \ \cdots \tag{13}$$

The bus can also be collapsed, by replacing the $\$\$$ and the duplicate protocol description with a single instance of the protocol, thus:

$$\cdots \ \begin{bmatrix} \text{E } \alpha \\ \bullet \end{bmatrix} \text{latch} \begin{bmatrix} \text{E } \alpha \\ \text{A} \end{bmatrix} \text{fifo} \begin{bmatrix} \text{E } \alpha \\ \text{A} \end{bmatrix} \ \cdots \tag{14}$$

This gives us a concise notation to describe a pipeline of cooperating components.

5 Patch Logic

At this point of the discourse of protocols and patches, traditional functional programming kicks in. Do we have a unit for our patch, for example? What are the laws for patches? This section introduces patch logic.

First, we have the combinators for lifting into the patch world and for executing a patch, called `output` and `run` respectively, and the law that they form an identity.

$$\text{output} :: \alpha \longrightarrow \begin{bmatrix} \bullet \\ \bullet \end{bmatrix} \triangleright \begin{bmatrix} \alpha \\ \bullet \end{bmatrix} \tag{15}$$

$$\text{run} :: \begin{bmatrix} \bullet \\ \bullet \end{bmatrix} \triangleright \begin{bmatrix} \alpha \\ \bullet \end{bmatrix} \longrightarrow \alpha \tag{16}$$

$$\text{run} \circ \text{output} = \text{id}_\alpha \tag{17}$$

The next primitive is empty, which is the identity for patches.

$$\text{empty} :: \begin{bmatrix} \alpha \\ \beta \end{bmatrix} \triangleright \begin{bmatrix} \alpha \\ \beta \end{bmatrix} \tag{18}$$

$$\text{empty} \$\$ \, []\triangleright[] = []\triangleright[] = []\triangleright[] \, \$\$ \, \text{empty} \tag{19}$$

We have a way of changing the incoming or outgoing component of a protocol. using forward and backward.

$$\text{forward} :: (\alpha \to \beta) \longrightarrow \begin{bmatrix} \alpha \\ \gamma \end{bmatrix} \triangleright \begin{bmatrix} \beta \\ \gamma \end{bmatrix} \tag{20}$$

$$\text{forward } f \$\$ \text{ forward } g = \text{forward } (g \circ f) \tag{21}$$

$$\text{forward id} = \text{empty} \tag{22}$$

$$\text{backward} :: (\beta \to \alpha) \longrightarrow \begin{bmatrix} \gamma \\ \alpha \end{bmatrix} \triangleright \begin{bmatrix} \gamma \\ \beta \end{bmatrix} \tag{23}$$

$$\text{backward } f \$\$ \text{ backward } g = \text{backward } (f \circ g) \tag{24}$$

$$\text{backward id} = \text{empty} \tag{25}$$

$$\text{forward } f \$\$ \text{ backward } g = \text{backward } g \$\$ \text{ forward } f \tag{26}$$

Finally, we have a way of stacking patches.

$$\text{stack} :: \begin{array}{c} \begin{bmatrix} \alpha_1 \\ \beta_1 \end{bmatrix} \triangleright \begin{bmatrix} \gamma_1 \\ \delta_1 \end{bmatrix} \\ \times \\ \begin{bmatrix} \alpha_2 \\ \beta_2 \end{bmatrix} \triangleright \begin{bmatrix} \gamma_2 \\ \delta_2 \end{bmatrix} \end{array} \longrightarrow \begin{bmatrix} \alpha_1 \ \alpha_2 \\ \beta_1 \ \beta_2 \end{bmatrix} \triangleright \begin{bmatrix} \gamma_1 \ \gamma_2 \\ \delta_1 \ \delta_2 \end{bmatrix} \tag{27}$$

As a note, stack has the property of a form of distributivity between stacks.

$$\text{stack}([]\triangleright_1[] \times []\triangleright_2[]) \$\$ \text{stack}([]\triangleright_3[] \times []\triangleright_4[])$$
$$=$$
$$\text{stack}(([]\triangleright_1[] \$\$ []\triangleright_3[]) \times ([]\triangleright_2[] \$\$ []\triangleright_4[])) \tag{28}$$

From these primitives, a number of useful combinators can be constructed. Often, forward and backward are used together to jointly built the edge of a stack. For example, open, which opens a new channel, has the protocols

$$\text{open} \;::\; \begin{bmatrix} \alpha \\ \beta \end{bmatrix} \triangleright \begin{bmatrix} \bullet\; \alpha \\ \bullet\; \beta \end{bmatrix} \tag{29}$$

and can be defined thus:

$$\begin{bmatrix} \alpha \\ \beta \end{bmatrix} \text{forward } (\lambda x \to () \; :> \; x) \begin{bmatrix} \bullet\; \alpha \\ \beta \end{bmatrix} \text{backward } (\lambda(() \; :> \; x) \to x) \begin{bmatrix} \bullet\; \alpha \\ \bullet\; \beta \end{bmatrix} \tag{30}$$

From experience, forward and backward are often used as a pair in this way.

6   Case Study: LCD Driver

As an extended example of a real hardware driver, consider the problem of controlling the LCD panel on the Xilinx Spartan3e FPGA, which is driven by the Sitronix ST7066U Dot Matrix LCD controller. The LCD panel has 16x2 character elements, each of which can display a single ASCII character. Laying aside the more advanced features like user-definable character sets and auto-scroll modes, we want to write a simple memory-mapped driver for this LCD in Kansas Lava.

6.1   Description of the Sitronix ST7066U

Control commands for the LCD are sent to the ST7066U in 9-bit datums. We can represent possible control commands using a Haskell data-structure, with representative constructors shown here, and a table (not given) which maps between these Haskell values, and the relevant 9-bit pattern.

```
data LCD
  = ClearDisplay
  | ReturnHome
  | EntryMode    {moveRight::Bool, displayShift::Bool}
  | SetDisplay   {displayOn::Bool, cursorOn::Bool, blinkingCursor::Bool}
  | FunctionSet  {eightBit::Bool, twoLines::Bool, fiveByEleven::Bool}
  | SetDDAddr    {dd_addr::U7}
  | WriteChar    {char::U8}
  | ...
```

The ST7066U itself is programmed on the Spartan3e board via a slow 4-bit data-bus, with a number of control wires, as explained in Figure 3.

Each command is physically transmitted by using two 4-bit nibbles, with a small $1\mu s$ delay between them. The 9th bit (a status-bit) of the command is is sent with *both* nibbles, on the LD_RS line. The gap between 9-bit commands is longer, at least $40\mu s$. Figure 4 explains how complete commands are transmitted. There is also a boot sequence for setting up the ST7066U.

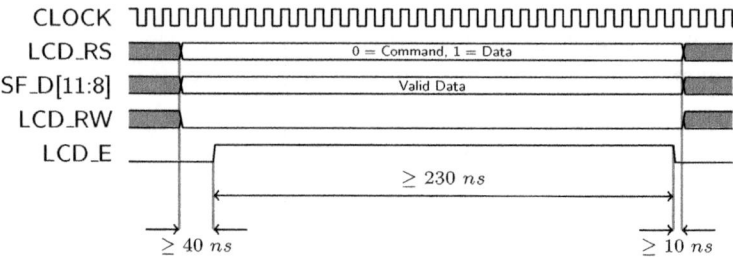

Fig. 3. Timing for the ST7066U 4-bit asynchronous bus (with 50MHz clock)

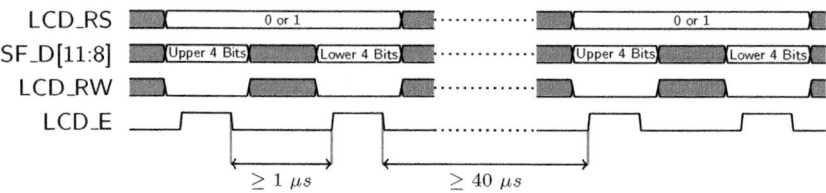

Fig. 4. Sending 9-bit commands to ST7066U over the 4-bit asynchronous bus

- There is a nibble-based boot sequence, with 4 separate nibbles sent, with non-standard delays between them.
- After the nibble boot sequence has been sent, a small sequence of 9-bit LCD commands are required to be sent to reset the device.
- After *most* 9-bit commands, a $40\mu s$ delay is required; with 2 exceptions requiring a $1.40ms$ delay – the joy of hardware interfaces.

6.2   LCD Driver Design

From these specifications, a design based on four separate patches emerges.

- A patch that takes memory writes, and outputs a sequence of LCD commands.
- A patch that prepends the fixed LCD command boot sequence to a stream.
- A patch that takes LCD commands, and outputs nibbles and intra-nibble pause durations. This patch can be responsible for issuing the correct nibble boot sequence.
- Finally, a patch that takes nibbles and intra-nibble pause durations, and drives the bus according to Figure 3, then waits for the given duration before accepting the next nibble, based on Figure 4.

The pipeline of patches we therefore need is:

$$
\left[\!\!\left[\begin{array}{c} \text{E }((\text{X2},\text{X16}),\text{U8}) \\ \text{A} \end{array}\right]\!\!\right] \triangleright \left[\!\!\left[\begin{array}{c} \text{E LCD} \\ \text{A} \end{array}\right]\!\!\right] \triangleright \left[\!\!\left[\begin{array}{c} \text{E LCD} \\ \text{A} \end{array}\right]\!\!\right] \triangleright \left[\!\!\left[\begin{array}{c} \text{E }(\text{U5},\text{U18}) \\ \text{A} \end{array}\right]\!\!\right] \triangleright \left[\!\!\left[\begin{array}{c} (\text{U1},\text{U4},\text{Bool}) \\ \bullet \end{array}\right]\!\!\right]
$$

The use of patches has informed our design decisions here, and modularized our implementation into reusable components. We now discuss the implementation of these components, in right-to-left order.

6.3   LCD Bus Driver

The lowest-level patch takes 5-bit nibble-and-status values, a delay before accepting the next nibble, and physically drives the bus, including pausing after each nibble for the prescribed delay.

```
phy_4bit_LCD :: Patch (Seq (Enabled (U5,U18))) (Seq (U1,U4,Bool))
                      (Seq Ack)                ()
```

phy_4bit_LCD is implemented in Kansas Lava using an internal 6-state state-machine and a 20-bit counter, taking approximately 40 lines of code. We use a flip-flop on the output signal to clean up any glitches; perhaps an extension could require this using types in the future.

6.4   LCD Instruction Compiler

The LCD instruction compiler is the heart of the LCD driver, so we give the complete code here (some whitespace has been removed for space reasons).

```
phy_Inst_4bit_LCD :: Patch (sig (Enabled LCD))  (sig (U1,U4,Bool))
                           (sig Ack)            ()
phy_Inst_4bit_LCD = mapP splitCmd
                 $$ matrixExpandP
                 $$ prependP bootCmds
                 $$ phy_4bit_LCD       -- invokes patch from section 6.3

bootCmds :: Matrix X4 (U5,U18)
bootCmds = matrix [ (3, 205000), (3, 5000), (3, 2000), (2, 2000) ]

splitCmd :: Comb LCD -> Comb (Matrix X2 (U5,U18))
splitCmd cmd = pack $ matrix
    [ pack ( high_op 'KL.append' mode, smallGap )
    , pack ( low_op 'KL.append' mode, otherGap ) ]
  where
    otherGap = mux ((bitwise) cmd .<=. (0x03 :: Comb U9)) (bigGap,hugeGap)

    (op :: Comb U8, mode :: Comb U1) = unappend ((bitwise) cmd :: Comb U9)
    (low_op :: Comb U4, high_op :: Comb U4) = unappend op

    smallGap = 50     -- between nibbles
    bigGap   = 2000   -- between commands
    hugeGap  = 100000 -- after clear display or return cursor home
```

The compiler is itself built from three patches, and because the only possible client of the nibble instructions is the LCD bus driver, phy_4bit_LCD it is directly

Fig. 5. Example of using the LCD driver

invoked by `phy_Inst_4bit_LCD`. The three patches split the commands into nibbles, intersperse the nibbles in one channel, then prepend the nibble-based boot sequence, as given by `bootCmds`.

6.5 LCD Instruction Boot Sequence

The `init_LCD` patch prepends the instruction-level boot sequence, which is not magic instructions, but rather the setting of the LCD into a sensible state (no cursor, correct LCD hardware setup, no display shift). Though this is the recommended sequence, it may certainly be possible for a user to use a different setup sequence, so we have `init_LCD` as its own patch. We include the code for `initCmds`, because it demonstrates that we are programming using Haskell structures not bit-level representations at this point.

```
init_LCD :: Patch (sig (Enabled LCD)) (sig (Enabled LCD))
                  (sig Ack)           (sig Ack)
init_LCD = prependP initCmds

initCmds :: Matrix X4 LCDInstruction
initCmds = matrix
    [ FunctionSet { eightBit=False, twoLines=True, fiveByEleven=False }
    , EntryMode { moveRight=True, displayShift=False }
    , SetDisplay { displayOn=True, cursorOn=False, blinkingCursor=False }
    , ClearDisplay ]
```

6.6 Memory-Mapped LCD Interface

Finally, we have a simple memory mapped interface, that is (2-dimensional) index-value pairs, and an enable. The user literally writes, using this interface, to the LCD. This implementation is almost trivial; for each write command sent to the memory mapped LCD interface, we can simply issue two LCD instructions, one to place the cursor, and the second to place the specified character. There is no reason to optimize the commands sent; the entire display can be rewritten in a fraction of a second. The memory mapped LCD interface has the type:

```
mm_LCD_Inst :: Patch (sig (Enabled ((X2,X16),U8))) (sig (Enabled LCD))
                     (sig Ack)                      (sig Ack)
```

Chaining our sub-components together gives us our working LCD driver, taking character write operations, and returning the bus interactions for our LCD controller. Figure 5 gives an example of using the LCD driver.

7   Discussion

Kansas Lava builds on a long history of hardware description languages, which can be traced back to μFP [13]. There have also been many code generators for VHDL, including JHDL [3], and the combinations of Xilinx Lava to JBits [15].

The use of `Patch` resembles an early feature of Lava: to suggest layout; for example Chapter 16 of [9]. In early versions of Lava, implementations could be configured to work like systolic arrays, with data flowing left to right on every clock cycle, and extra information like carry being passed in the vertical direction. Kansas Lava explicitly chooses to rely on the Xilinx tools for physical layout, based on the improvements made by Xilinx over the last decade. Use of `Patch` is about channels between components, not proximity, though there is no reason why patches could not be extended to give layout hints.

A `Patch` could be represented in Wired [1], a DSL that uses Chalmers Lava. Wired uses a monad called `Let`, and a writable `Var` constructor that allows the acknowledge back-edge to be wired. For example, a fifo could be given the following type:

```
fifo :: (...)
      => (Seq (Enabled a), Var (Seq Ack)) -- left hand side
      -> Let (Seq (Enabled a), Var (Seq Ack)) -- right hand side
```

The differences are that in Wired traditional monadic constructions can be used, though `Var` needs to be dynamically checked for single usage at code generation time. In Kansas Lava the back-edge connection can only be connected using juxtapositioning, avoiding the need for this check. In Wired however, the bidirections of a protocol can be expressed inside a single tuple, perhaps allowing for new protocol abstractions.

The `Patch` idiom emerged from frustration when developing a FPGA-centric protocol stack we call λ-bridge. We experimented with different variations of `Patch`, for example originally there were additional control and status signals for each `Patch`. This was later subsumed when needed by simply using extra columns of protocol interactions.

It turns out that `Patch` is a useful place to hide an environment, and we plan to make `Patch` abstract in the future, then experiment with passing in resource hints. It would be useful to know, for example, if a 1-element FIFO will suffice with the necessary bubbles, or if a larger fifo is required.

Overall, we are pleased with how the `Patch` idiom has helped us structure our Kansas Lava programs. Extensions to the simple `Patch` logic, however, would be useful to show specific properties, like compliance to protocol. Patches such as `forward` and `backward` can be used to break the protocol abstraction, in the same way that mapping over an even-only list can destroy the even-only property. Higher level combinators, on top of `forward` and `backward`, will help here.

Acknowledgments. We would like to thank the anonymous referees for their useful comments, Garrin Kimmell who wrote the Haskell datatype in section 6.1, as well as Andrew Farmer, Ed Komp, and the other members of the CSDL lab at KU for their feedback. This work was partially supported by NSF grant CCF-1117569.

References

1. Axelsson, E.: Functional Programming Enabling Flexible Hardware Design at Low Levels of Abstraction. Ph.D. thesis, Department of Computer Science and Engineering Chalmers University of Technology and University of Gothenburg (2008)
2. Axelsson, E., Claessen, K., Dvai, G., Horvth, Z., Keijzer, K., Lyckegrd, B., Persson, A., Sheeran, M., Svenningsson, J., Vajdax, A.: Feldspar: A domain specific language for digital signal processing algorithms. In: MEMOCODE 2010, pp. 169–178 (2010)
3. Bellows, P., Hutchings, B.: JHDL - an HDL for reconfigurable systems. In: Annual IEEE Symposium on Field-Programmable Custom Computing Machines, p. 175 (1998)
4. Bjesse, P., Claessen, K., Sheeran, M., Singh, S.: Lava: Hardware design in Haskell. In: International Conference on Functional Programming, pp. 174–184 (1998)
5. Claessen, K., Sands, D.: Observable Sharing for Functional Circuit Description. In: Thiagarajan, P.S., Yap, R.H.C. (eds.) ASIAN 1999. LNCS, vol. 1742, pp. 62–73. Springer, Heidelberg (1999)
6. Gill, A.: Type-safe observable sharing in Haskell. In: Proceedings of the 2009 ACM SIGPLAN Haskell Symposium (September 2009)
7. Gill, A.: Declarative FPGA circuit synthesis using Kansas Lava. In: The International Conference on Engineering of Reconfigurable Systems and Algorithms (ERSA 2011), Las Vegas, Nevada, USA (July 2011)
8. Gill, A., Bull, T., Farmer, A., Kimmell, G., Komp, E.: Types and Type Families for Hardware Simulation and Synthesis. In: Page, R., Horváth, Z., Zsók, V. (eds.) TFP 2010. LNCS, vol. 6546, pp. 118–133. Springer, Heidelberg (2011)
9. Hauck, S., DeHon, A.: Reconfigurable Computing: The Theory and Practice of FPGA-Based Computation. Morgan Kaufmann Publishers Inc., San Francisco (2007)
10. Jones, G., Sheeran, M.: Circuit design in ruby. In: Staunstrup (ed.) Formal Methods for VLSI Design. Elsevier Science Publications (1990)
11. Matlage, K., Gill, A.: ChalkBoard: Mapping Functions to Polygons. In: Morazán, M.T., Scholz, S.-B. (eds.) IFL 2009. LNCS, vol. 6041, pp. 55–71. Springer, Heidelberg (2010)
12. Peyton Jones, S. (ed.): Haskell 98 Language and Libraries – The Revised Report. Cambridge University Press, Cambridge (2003)
13. Sheeran, M.: mufp, a language for vlsi design. In: LFP 1984: Proceedings of the 1984 ACM Symposium on LISP and Functional Programming, pp. 104–112. ACM, New York (1984)
14. Singh, S.: Designing reconfigurable systems in lava. In: International Conference on VLSI Design, p. 299 (2004)
15. Singh, S., James-Roxby, P.: Lava and JBits: From hdl to bitstream in seconds. In: FCCM 2001: Proceedings of the the 9th Annual IEEE Symposium on Field-Programmable Custom Computing Machines, pp. 91–100. IEEE Computer Society, Washington, DC (2001)

Virtualizing Real-World Objects in FRP

Daniel Winograd-Cort[1], Hai Liu[2], and Paul Hudak[3]

[1] Yale University
daniel.winograd-cort@yale.edu
[2] Intel, Inc.
hai.liu@intel.com
[3] Yale University
paul.hudak@yale.edu

Abstract. We begin with a *functional reactive programming* (FRP) model in which every program is viewed as a *signal function* that converts a stream of input values into a stream of output values. We observe that objects in the real world – such as a keyboard or sound card – can be thought of as signal functions as well. This leads us to a radically different approach to I/O: instead of treating real-world objects as being external to the program, we expand the sphere of influence of program execution to include them within. We call this *virtualizing real-world objects*. We explore how *virtual objects* (such as GUI widgets) and even *non-local effects* (such as debugging and random number generation) can be handled in the same way.

The key to our approach is the notion of a *resource type* that assures that a virtualized object cannot be duplicated, and is safe. Resource types also provide a deeper level of transparency: by inspecting the type, one can see exactly what resources are being used. We use arrows, type classes, and type families to implement our ideas in Haskell, and the result is a safe, effective, and transparent approach to stream-based I/O.

Keywords: Functional Programming, Arrows, Functional Reactive Programming, Stream Processing, Haskell, Unique Types, I/O.

1 Introduction

Every programming language has some way of communicating with the outside world. Usually we refer to such mechanisms as *input/output*, or I/O. In most imperative languages the mechanisms have effects almost entirely outside the program, serving a purpose typically unrelated to the internal computation of an answer to the program. In Haskell, programs engage in I/O by using the *IO monad* [20,19]. An advantage of Haskell is that we can determine from the type of a function whether or not it is engaged in I/O – if any one part of a program is, then the type of the whole program reflects this. The monadic framework assures us that the overall program is well defined, and in particular, that the I/O operations are executed in a deterministic, sequential manner. However, even in Haskell, the *IO* monad is "special" compared to other monads. I/O

C. Russo and N.-F. Zhou (Eds.): PADL 2012, LNCS 7149, pp. 227–241, 2012.

commands often represent an awkward disconnect between the internal execution of a program and the objects, devices, and protocols of the real world.

In this paper, we take a different approach. Instead of using an imperative or even monadic basis for overall program execution, we use *arrows* [13]. Specifically, we assume that a program is a *signal function* having the (over-simplified for now) type *SF inp out*, where both the input and output are time-varying signals: *inp* is the type of the instantaneous values of the input, and *out* is the type of the instantaneous values of the output. Just as *IO* is a monad, *SF* is an arrow, and like a monad, the arrow framework composes program components in a way that assures us that the streams are well-defined and that I/O is done in a deterministic, sequential manner.

This approach is the basis for arrow-based versions of *functional reactive programming* (FRP), such as *Yampa* [12,3] (which has been used for animation, robotics, GUI design, and more), *Nettle* [23] (for networking), and *Euterpea* [11] (for audio processing and sound synthesis). In fact, our work was motivated by Euterpea, and in this paper we use examples from that domain: synthesizers, speakers, keyboards, and MIDI devices.[1]

Our research is based on three insights. First, we observe that *objects and devices in the real world can also be viewed as signal functions.* For example, a MIDI keyboard takes note events as input and generates note events as output. Similarly, a speaker takes a signal representing sound as input and produces no output, and a microphone produces a sound signal as output while ignoring its input. So it would seem natural to simply include these signal functions as part of the program – i.e. to program with them directly and independently rather than merge everything together as one input and one output for the whole program. In this sense, the real-world objects are being *virtualized* for use in the program.

A major problem with this approach is that one could easily duplicate one of these virtualized objects – after all, they are just values – which would cause the semantics of the program to become unclear. For example, how does a single concrete device handle the multiple event streams that would result from its virtualized duplicates? This leads to our second insight, namely that *the uniqueness of signal function can be realized at the type level.* In particular, we introduce the notion of a *resource type* to ensure that there is exactly one signal function that represents each real-world device.

Our final insight is that *many unsafe functions can be treated as unique signal functions* as well. Examples include GUI widgets, random number generators, and "wormholes" (mutable variables that are written to at one point in a program and safely read from at another).

The advantages of our approach include:

1. *Virtualization.* I/O devices can be treated conveniently and independently as signal functions that are just like any other signal function in a program. I/O is no longer a special case in the language design.

---

[1] MIDI = Musical Instrument Digital Interface, a standard protocol for communication between electronic instruments and computers.

2. *Transparency.* From the type of a signal function, we can determine immediately *all* of the resources that it consumes. In particular, this means that we know all the resources that a complete program uses (with monads, all we know is that some kind of I/O is being performed).

3. *Safety.* As long as each resource is uniquely assigned, a signal function engaged in I/O or non-local effects is *safe* – despite the side effects, equational reasoning is preserved.

4. *Modularity.* Certain non-local effects – the lack of which is often cited as a lack of moduarity in functional languages – can be handled safely.

5. *Extensibility.* A user can define his or her own resource type and signal function that capture a new I/O device or some kind of non-local effect.

In the remainder of this paper we first introduce arrow syntax and the basis of our language design. In Section 3, we present our main ideas and the purpose of resource types and then show the type inference rules for them in Section 4. We next work through a number of examples in Section 5 before delving into the implementation details in Section 6. Finally, we discuss limitations and future work in Section 7 and related work in Section 8.

2   A Signal-Processing Language

The simplest way to understand our language is to think of it as a language for expressing *signal processing diagrams*. We refer to the lines in such a diagram as *signals*, and the boxes (that convert one signal into another) as *signal functions*. Conceptually, signals are continuous, time-varying quantities, but, they can also be streams of events.

For example, this very simple diagram has two signals, an input x and an output y, and one signal function, *sigfun*:

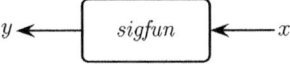

This is written as a code fragment in our framework as:

$$y \leftarrow sigfun \prec x$$

using Haskell's *arrow syntax* [18]. The above program fragment cannot appear alone, but rather must be part of a **proc** construct, much like a **do** construct for monads. The expression on the left must be a variable, whereas the expression on the right can be any well-typed expression that matches the signal function's input type. Signal functions such as *sigfun* have a type of the form $SF\ T_1\ T_2$, for some types T_1 and T_2; subsequently, x must have type T_1 and y must have type T_2. Although signal functions act on signals, the arrow notation allows one to manipulate the instantaneous values of the signals. For example, here is a definition for *sigfun* that integrates a signal that is one greater than its input:

$sigfun :: SF\ Double\ Double$
$sigfun = \mathbf{proc}\ x \rightarrow \mathbf{do}$
    $y \leftarrow integral \prec x + 1$
    $returnA \prec y$

The first line declares *sigfun* to be a signal function that converts a time-varying value of type *Double* into a time-varying value of type *Double*. The notation "**proc** $x \rightarrow$ **do**..." introduces a signal function, binding the name x to the instantaneous values of the input. The third line adds one to each instantaneous value and sends the resulting signal to an integrator, whose output is named y. Finally, we specify the output by feeding y into *returnA*, a special signal function that returns the result.

Streams of Events. With respect to I/O, continuous signals can be useful in many contexts, such as the position of a mouse (as input to a program) or the voltage to a robot motor (as output from a program). However, there are many applications where instead we are interested in *streams of events*. We represent event streams in our language as continuous signals that only contain data at discrete points in time. A signal that periodically carries information of some type T has type *Event T*, whose values are either *NoEvent* or *Event x*, where $x :: T$.[2] For example, a signal function that converts an event stream carrying values of type M_1 into an event stream carrying values of type M_2 has type $SF\ (Event\ M_1)\ (Event\ M_2)$.

3   Resource Types

The Problem. As mentioned earlier, we wish to treat I/O devices as signal functions. Consider, for example, a MIDI sound synthesizer with type:

$midiSynth :: SF\ (Event\ Notes)\ ()$

midiSynth takes a stream of *Notes*[3] events as input, synthesizes the appropriate sound of those simultaneous notes, and returns unit values. Now consider this code fragment:

    $\_ \leftarrow midiSynth \prec notes_1$
    $\_ \leftarrow midiSynth \prec notes_2$

We intend for *midiSynth* to represent a single real-world device, but here we have two occurrences – so what is the effect? Are the event streams $notes_1$ and $notes_2$ somehow interleaved or non-deterministically joined together?

Likewise, suppose *randomSF* is intended to be a random number generator initialized with a random seed from the OS:

$randomSF :: SF\ ()\ Double$

---

[2] The name *Event* is overloaded as both the type and data constructor.

[3] The *Notes* type represents a set of simultaneously sounding notes such as a chord or just a single note.

Now consider this code fragment:

$$rands_1 \leftarrow randomSF \prec ()$$
$$rands_2 \leftarrow randomSF \prec ()$$

What is the relationship between $rands_1$ and $rands_2$? Do they share the same result, or are they different? If they are the same, what if we want them to be different?

A Solution. Our solution to these problems consists of four parts. First, to prevent duplication of signal functions, we introduce the notion of a *resource type*. There may be many resource types in a program, and, as we shall see, the user can easily define new ones. For example, in the cases above, we introduce the resource types *MidiSynthRT* and *RandomRT* (by convention, we always use *RT* as the suffix for resource type names).

Second, to keep track of resource types, we introduce three type-level constructors: *Empty*, *S* and ∪. *Empty* is the empty set of resource types; the type *S MidiSynthRT* is the singleton set containing only *MidiSynthRT*; and the binary operator ∪ constructs the union of two sets of resource types.

Third, we add a "phantom" type parameter to each signal function that captures the set of resource types that it uses. A signal function of type *SF r a b* accesses the resources represented by r, while converting a signal of type a into a signal of type b. Following the examples above, this leads to:

$$midiSynth :: SF \ (S \ MidiSynthRT) \ (Event \ Notes) \ ()$$
$$randomSF :: SF \ (S \ RandomRT) \quad () \qquad\qquad Double$$

Finally, to facilitate working with resource types, we provide three functions to convert monadic I/O actions into signal functions tagged with the appropriate resource type:

$$source :: IO \ c \qquad\quad \rightarrow SF \ (S \ r) \ () \ c$$
$$sink \ \ :: (b \rightarrow IO \ ()) \rightarrow SF \ (S \ r) \ b \ ()$$
$$pipe \ \ :: (b \rightarrow IO \ c) \rightarrow SF \ (S \ r) \ b \ c$$

In each case, the resultant signal function has a singleton resource type because it is expected to be applied to a monadic I/O action of a single I/O device, thus consuming a single resource.

For event-based signal functions (as described in Section 2) we provide three analagous functions: *sourceE*, *sinkE*, and *pipeE* with the expected types.

Running Examples. Continuing with our running examples, suppose that: $midiSynthM :: Notes \rightarrow IO \ ()$ is the monadic action that sends a set of notes to the synthesizer. We can then define *midiSynth* as follows:

data *MidiSynthRT*

$$midiSynth :: SF \ (S \ MidiSynthRT) \ (Event \ Notes) \ ()$$
$$midiSynth = sinkE \ midiSynthM$$

Note that *MidiSynthRT* is an empty data type – all we need is the type name –
and that *midiSynth* is an event-based signal function.

Similarly, although *randomSF* does not access an I/O device, it is a source of
non-local effects from the OS. We can define it from scratch using the *randomIO*::
IO Double function from Haskell's *Random* library:

> **data** *RandomRT*
>
> *randomSF* :: *SF* (*S RandomRT*) () *Double*
> *randomSF* = *source randomIO*

We treat *randomSF* as a continuous signal function, and its range, inherited
from *randomIO*, is the semi-closed interval $[0, 1)$.

Redefining the Arrow Class. Our key technical result is that, because we
are using arrows, we can now re-type each of the combinators in the *Arrow* class
in such a way that the problematical code fragments given earlier *will not type
check*. The details of how this is done are described in the next Section, but for
now the key intuition is that whenever two signal functions, say $sf_1 :: SF \ r_1 \ a \ b$
and $sf_2 :: SF \ r_2 \ b \ c$ are composed, we require that r_1 and r_2 be *disjoint* –
otherwise, they may compete for the same resource. Both of the problematical
code fragments given earlier fall into this category. For example:

> _ ← *midiSynth* —≺ *notes*$_1$
> _ ← *midiSynth* —≺ *notes*$_2$

is essentially the composition of two instances of *midiSynth* – but each of them
has the same set of resource types, namely *S MidiSynthRT*; thus they are not
disjoint, and not well typed. One way to fix this is to explicitly merge *notes*$_1$
and *notes*$_2$:

> _ ← *midiSynth* —≺ *noteMerge notes*$_1$ *notes*$_2$

Now there is one occurence of *midiSynth*, and all is well.

The problematical example involving random numbers leads to a more interesting result if we wish to have *two independent* random number generators. We
achieve this by defining two different resource types, and two different versions
of *randomSF*:

> **data** *RandomRT*$_1$
> **data** *RandomRT*$_2$
>
> *randomSF*$_1$ :: *SF* (*S RandomRT*$_1$) () *Double*
> *randomSF*$_1$ = *source randomIO*
>
> *randomSF*$_2$ :: *SF* (*S RandomRT*$_2$) () *Double*
> *randomSF*$_2$ = *source randomIO*

A slight variation of the problematical code yields the desired well-typed result:

> *rands*$_1$ ← *randomSF*$_1$ —≺ ()
> *rands*$_2$ ← *randomSF*$_2$ —≺ ()

(Because each element produced by *randomIO* is independently random, multiple calls will not interfere with each other. Therefore, we can use alternating
calls to *randomIO* to produce two independent random streams.)

$$(arr)\frac{\vdash E : \alpha \to \beta}{\vdash arr\ E : SF\ \emptyset\ \alpha\ \beta} \qquad (loop)\frac{\vdash E : SF\ \tau\ (\alpha,\gamma)\ (\beta,\gamma)}{\vdash loop\ E : SF\ \tau\ \alpha\ \beta}$$

$$(first)\frac{\vdash E : SF\ \tau\ \alpha\ \beta}{\vdash first\ E : SF\ \tau\ (\alpha,\gamma)\ (\beta,\gamma)} \qquad (init)\frac{\vdash E : \alpha}{\vdash init\ E : SF\ \emptyset\ \alpha\ \alpha}$$

$$(\ggg)\frac{\begin{array}{c}\vdash E_1 : SF\ \tau'\ \alpha\ \beta \\ \vdash E_2 : SF\ \tau''\ \beta\ \gamma \\ \emptyset = \tau' \cap \tau'' \\ \tau = \tau' \cup \tau''\end{array}}{\vdash E_1 \ggg E_2 : SF\ \tau\ \alpha\ \gamma} \qquad (|||)\frac{\begin{array}{c}\vdash E_1 : SF\ \tau'\ \alpha\ \gamma \\ \vdash E_2 : SF\ \tau''\ \beta\ \gamma \\ \tau = \tau' \cup \tau''\end{array}}{\vdash E_1 ||| E_2 : SF\ \tau\ (\alpha + \beta)\ \gamma}$$

Fig. 1. Resource Type Inference Rules

4   Type Inference Rules

In Haskell, the arrow syntax is translated into a set of combinators that are captured by the type classes *Arrow*, *ArrowLoop*, *ArrowChoice*, and *ArrowInit*. Space limitations preclude a detailed discussion of this translation process (see [18]). Once translated, the type inference rules that form the basis of our implementation are shown in Figure 1. There is one rule for each of the operators in the above type classes. The + symbol denotes the disjoint (i.e. discriminated) sum type. Set intersection is denoted by ∩ and set union by ∪. Let's examine each of the rules in turn:

1. The (*arr*) rule states that the set of resource types for a pure function lifted to the arrow level is empty.
2. The (*first*) rule states that transforming a signal function using *first* does not alter the resource type.
3. The ($\ggg$) rule is perhaps the most important; it states that when two signal functions are composed, their resource types must be disjoint, and the resulting resource type is the union of the two.
4. The (*loop*) rule states that the loop combinator must pass the resource type unchanged (i.e. as a loop invariant), reflecting the fact that in a recursively defined signal function, the resource type must be the same at every level of recursion.
5. The (*init*) rule states that the set of resource types for the *init* operator (from the *ArrowInit* class) is empty.
6. The final rule is for the choice operator (|||) in the *ArrowChoice* class. The resulting resource type is the union of those of its inputs, which are not required to be disjoint (as discussed in Section 5).

Note that the new signal functions created by *init* and *arr* have empty resource types. But when defining a new signal function, we need a way to specify its resource type. Thus, we define a function *tag*, whose type inference rule is:

$$\frac{\vdash E : SF\ \tau\ \alpha\ \beta}{\vdash tag\ E : SF\ \tau'\ \alpha\ \beta}$$
$$(tag)\ \frac{\tau \subseteq \tau'}{}$$

The *tag* function has no run-time effect; it merely adds resource types to the signal function it acts upon.

5   More Examples

Recursion. A MIDI keyboard is a stream transformer that adds the notes played on the keyboard in real time to the stream it operates on. It has the type:

$midiKB :: SF\ (S\ MidiKBRT)\ (Event\ Notes)\ (Event\ Notes)$

We can define a signal function that creates an "echo" effect for notes played on the keyboard by delaying and looping them through the keyboard itself, attenuating each note by some percentage on each loop:

$echo :: SF\ (S\ MidiKBRT)\ (Double, Double)\ (Event\ Notes)$
$echo = \mathbf{proc}\ (rate, freq) \to \mathbf{do}$
   rec $notesOut \leftarrow midiKB \prec notes$
      $notes\ \ \ \leftarrow delayt\ \ \ \prec (1.0/freq, decay\ rate\ notesOut)$
  $returnA \prec notesOut$

Note the use of the **rec** keyword – this will induce the loop rule from Section 4, and everything is well typed.

   echo is a signal function that takes a decay rate and frequency as time varying arguments and uses them to add an echo to the notes played on the MIDI keyboard. It uses two helper functions: *decay rate ns* attenuates each note in *ns* by *rate*, and *delayt* $\prec (t, ns)$ delays each event in *ns* by the time t.

Conditionals. As discussed earlier, signal function composition requires that the resource types of the arguments be *disjoint*. However, for conditionals (i.e. case statements), the proper semantics is to take the *natural union* of the resource types. Consider the following functions for sending sound data to speakers:

$playLeft\ \ :: SF\ (S\ LeftRT)\ \ \ Sound\ ()$
$playRight :: SF\ (S\ RightRT)\ Sound\ ()$
$playStereo :: SF\ (S\ LeftRT \cup S\ RightRT)\ Sound\ ()$

We can use these to define a signal function for routing sound to the proper speaker (often called a demultiplexer):

data $SpeakerChoice = Left \mid Right \mid Stereo$

$routeSound :: SF\ (S\ LeftRT \cup S\ RightRT)\ (SpeakerChoice, Sound)\ ()$
$routeSound = \mathbf{proc}\ (sc, sound) \to \mathbf{do}$

case *sc* **of**
>   *Left*   → *playLeft*   —≺ *sound*
>   *Right* → *playRight*   —≺ *sound*
>   *Stereo* → *playStereo* —≺ *sound*

This is well typed, since the case statement in arrow syntax invokes the inference rule for the choice operator (|||) in the *ArrowChoice* class given in Section 4.

Virtual Objects. Virtual (GUI) components can be treated the same as concrete devices in our framework. In this section we extend the echo example given earlier to allow the user to pick the decay rate and frequency using GUI "sliders" and for the echo result to be graphed in real time.

To write this program, we use a different type of signal function than used previously. The type *UISF r a b* is designed especially for GUIs, and we can lift ordinary *SF*s to *UISF*s by using the function *toUISF*. In addition, we use two built-in GUI functions: (1) Given a range and initial value, *hslider* creates a horizontal slider; (2) Given some step parameters, a size, and a color, *realTimeGraph* creates a graph that varies in real-time as its input changes. We begin by defining three signal functions for the three widgets we use:

>   *decSlider* :: *UISF* (*S DSlider*) ()   *Double*
>   *freqSlider* :: *UISF* (*S FSlider*) ()   *Double*
>   *graph*   :: *UISF* (*S Graph*)   *Double* ()
>
>   *decSlider* = *title* "Decay Rate" $ *hSlider* (0, 0.9) 0.5
>   *freqSlider* = *title* "Frequency" $ *hSlider* (1, 10) 10
>   *graph*   = *realtimeGraph* (400, 300) 400 20 *Black*

We also require *renderNotes*::*SF Empty* (*Event Notes*) *Double*, a signal function that transforms our *Notes* events into sound data. With these functions we can define our main application:

>   *echoGUI* :: *UISF* (*S MidiKBRT* ∪ *S DSlider* ∪ *S FSlider* ∪ *S Graph*) () ()
>   *echoGUI* = **proc** _ → **do**
>   *rate* ← *decSlider*   —≺ ()
>   *freq* ← *freqSlider*   —≺ ()
>   *notes* ← *toUISF echo*   —≺ (*rate*, *freq*)
>   *sound* ← *toUISF renderNotes* —≺ *notes*
>   _   ← *graph*   —≺ *sound*
>   *returnA* —≺ ()

Note that the type of *echoGUI* lists all of the resources that it uses: both the physical MIDI keyboard as well as the virtual sliders and graph. If one were to use this module in another GUI, it would be clear from the type what the major components would be. Figure 2a at the end of this section shows a screenshot of the program in action.

Wormholes. Resource types allow us to safely perform I/O actions within signal functions, and although they were designed with physical resources in mind, the idea extends to other kinds of effectful computation as well. For example,

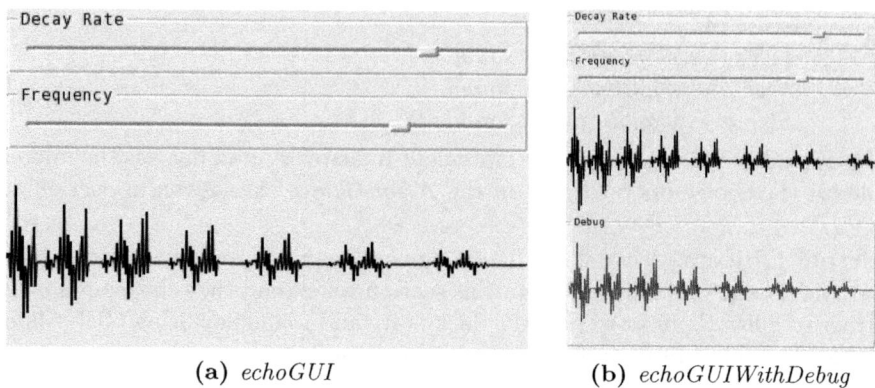

(a) *echoGUI*   (b) *echoGUIWithDebug*

Fig. 2. Screenshots of the GUI signal functions from Section 5 just after a note has been played on the MIDI keyboard

mutation and direct memory access, techniques that are typically plagued by difficult-to-find bugs, can be made safe. We begin by defining:

data *Wormhole* r_1 r_2 a = *Wormhole* {*whitehole* :: *SF* (*S* r_1) () a,
    blackhole :: *SF* (*S* r_2) a ()}
makeWormhole :: $a \rightarrow$ *Wormhole* r_1 r_2 a

makeWormhole takes an initial value for the hidden mutable variable and returns a pair of signal functions, the first for reading and the second for writing, with each independently typed.

Continuing with our *echo* example from previous sections, suppose we want to add debugging information. There were two values we created in *echo* – *notesOut* and *notes* – but we only return the former. However, if we try to change *echo* to return both note streams, then we need to adjust *echoGUI* and any other functions that rely on *echo* to match. So instead, we use a wormhole:

wormhole :: *Wormhole* *DebugW* *DebugB* (*Event Notes*)
wormhole = *makeWormhole* *Nothing*

echo :: *SF* (*S* *MidiKBRT* $\cup$ *S* *DebugB*) (*Double*, *Double*) (*Event Notes*)
echo = **proc** (*rate*, *freq*) $\rightarrow$ **do**
  rec *notesOut* $\leftarrow$ *midiKB* $\prec$ *notes*
    notes $\leftarrow$ *delayt* $\prec$ (1.0/*freq*, *decay rate notesOut*)
  _ $\leftarrow$ *blackhole wormhole* $\prec$ *notes*
  returnA $\prec$ *notesOut*

The set of resource types for *echo* changes to include *S* *DebugB*; the set of resource types for *echoGUI* changes similarly, but its implementation remains the same.

Now, we can define a new *echoGUI* that uses the debug info. Because of the nature of signal functions, this is quite easy:

debugGraph :: *UISF* (*S* *DebugGraph*) *Double* ()
debugGraph = *title* "Debug" $ *realtimeGraph* (400, 300) 400 20 *Red*
echoGUIWithDebug = **proc** _ $\rightarrow$ **do**

$$
\begin{aligned}
\_ &\leftarrow echoGUI & &\prec () \\
debugVal &\leftarrow toUISF \ (whitehole \ wormhole) & &\prec () \\
rendered &\leftarrow toUISF \ renderNotes & &\prec debugVal \\
\_ &\leftarrow debugGraph & &\prec rendered \\
returnA &\prec ()
\end{aligned}
$$

Figure 2b shows a screenshot of the program in action.

6   Implementation

Implementing Resource Types. To implement resource types in Haskell we need a way to represent sets of resource types, integrate them appropriately with our signal functions, and make them consistent with the type inference rules given earlier. Our implementation is inspired by Haskell's *HList* library [14] for heterogeneous lists.

We lack the space to show the complete code, but here we show the most relevant type class, *Disjoint*:

```
class Disjoint xs ys
instance Disjoint Empty ys
instance (NotElemOf x ys HTrue) ⇒ Disjoint (S x) ys
instance (Disjoint xs₁ ys, Disjoint xs₂ ys) ⇒ Disjoint (xs₁ ∪ xs₂) ys
```

Disjoint s_1 s_2 declares that s_1 and s_2 are disjoint sets (of resource types). The first instance of the *Disjoint* class declares that the empty set is disjoint from all other sets. The second instance says that if x is not an element of ys, then the singleton set containing x is disjoint from ys. And the final instance says that if both xs_1 and xs_2 are disjoint from ys, then their union is also disjoint from ys.

Re-Typing the Arrow Operators. We now have a method to represent sets of types as well as type classes for combining them. What remains is to use these types in the typing of the arrow operators, as we did in Section 4.

```
class Arrow a where
    arr   :: (b → c) → a Empty b c
    first :: a r b c  → a r (b, d) (c, d)
    (⋙) :: (Disjoint r₁ r₂, Union r₁ r₂ r₃) ⇒ a r₁ b c → a r₂ c d → a r₃ b d
    tag   :: Subset r₁ r₂ ⇒ a r₁ b c → a r₂ b c
```

arr and *first* are easily adapted, as the resource types do not actually affect their behavior. The (⋙) operator is more complex as it needs to perform a disjoint union on the resource types of its arguments. The *Disjoint* type class from the previous section assures the arguments are well-typed, and the *Union* type class behaves like the ∪ operator except that it simplifies degenerate cases like $r \cup Empty$ to just r. Lastly, we add the *tag* operator to the class as well.

Monadic Signal Functions. With the types prepared, we can instantiate the *Arrow* class. We begin with a standard implementation of a signal function, such as from Yampa [15], but with an additional resource type parameter:

data $SigF\ r\ a\ b = SigF\ \{\ sfFunction :: a \rightarrow (b, SigF\ r\ a\ b)\}$

Here, a signal function consumes a value of its input type and produces a value of its output type along with a new function for the next input value.

However, this definition does not allow us to perform monadic IO actions within the signal function. Although our newly adopted model of program execution is based on signal functions, we still have to implement everything in Haskell, which is based on monadic I/O. To address this, we add a monad parameter to the signal function data type. This leads to the following design:

data $SFM\ m\ r\ a\ b = SFM\ \{\ sfmFun :: a \rightarrow m\ (b, SFM\ m\ r\ a\ b)\}$

Note that this is the automaton arrow transformer specialized to the Kleisli arrow, with an added resource type parameter. The instances for *Arrow*, etc. follow directly. For example, for the *Arrow* class:

```
instance Arrow (SFM m) where
  arr f = SFM h where h x = return (f x, SFM h)
  first (SFM f) = SFM (h f)
    where h f (x, z) = do (y, SFM f') ← f x
                          return ((y, z), SFM (h f'))
  SFM f ⋙ SFM g = SFM (h f g)
    where h f g x = do (y, SFM f') ← f x
                       (z, SFM g') ← g y
                       return (z, SFM (h f' g'))
  tag (SFM f) = SFM h where h x = do (y, sf') ← f x
                                     return (y, tag sf')
```

At this point, the astute reader may guess the definition of SF that we introduced in Section 3:

newtype $SF = SFM\ IO$

Auxiliary Functions. Now that we have a complete description of SF, we can easily show the definitions of *source*, *sink*, and *pipe* from Section 3:

```
source f = SF h where h _ = f   ≫= return ∘ (λ x → (x, SF h))
sink f   = SF h where h x = f x ≫ return ((), SF h)
pipe f   = SF h where h x = f x ≫= return ∘ (λ x → (x, SF h))
```

7 Limitations and Future Work

Reusing Resource Types. The benefits of resource types rely on their proper assignment to actual resources, which is not something we can enforce. Even assuming that the user marks every appropriate signal function with a resource type, he or she may still accidentally use the same resource type for different signal functions that don't share a resource. This will not cause a program to be unsafe, but it might prevent perfectly safe programs from type-checking. Alternatively (and more dangerously), the user could use *different* resource types for signal functions that access the *same* resource. This would allow one to use the same resource multiple times without the type-checker complaining. We have no easy way to detect or dissuade this behavior; we simply demand that the programmer take care when assigning resource types.

We should point out that this "flaw" is also a "feature," in that it is what allows us to instantiate the two independent random number generators described in Section 3. In general, if two signal functions will not interfere with each other, even if they access the same resource, then they can have different resource types.

Dynamically Created Types. It is very likely, especially when dealing with virtual objects like widgets, that one would want to create a dynamic number of signal functions each with its own resource. For example, a program could present some variable number of sliders to a user depending on user input. However, despite the fact that any number of signal functions can be created, only the limited number of types declared at compile time are available as resource types.

Of course, one could create a compound signal function that displays an arbitrary number of sliders yet only has one resource type. Although this is a practical way to deal with the problem, it reduces the effectiveness of resource typing, so we are exploring alternative solutions.

Type Explosion. Although resource types provide an elegant means to managing resources, lengthy programs making use of many resources can become unwieldy. Ideally, we would have some way to hide particular "sets" of types from being displayed, so that, for example, a fully-used wormhole's types would not appear in the signal function's type. Currently, the best way to do this is to group the set of unwanted resource types into a type synonym like so:

type $ExtraRTs = S\ Blackhole_1 \cup S\ Whitehole_1 \cup S\ Blackhole_2 \cup ...$
$mySF :: SF\ (S\ Resource_1 \cup S\ DebugB \cup ExtraRTs)\ a\ b$

Here, $mySF$ uses $Resource_1$ and a debugging black hole and hides the rest of its internal resource types in $ExtraRTs$. However, a more desirable method to achieve this would be to have locally-scoped types that could only be used with similarly scoped signal functions.

Parallelism and Asynchrony. Because resource types clearly show where particular resources are being used and assure that resources will not be accidentally touched in other places, they provide a great setting for safely parallelizing programs. Furthermore, constructs like wormholes (but made thread-safe) could provide an easy way for parallel threads to communicate. In addition to parallelism, resource types allow for elegant asynchronous computation. Rather than the typical parallel synchronous model, where each input correspdons to one output, we can allow slow performing signal functions to run as event-based ones in separate threads that only supply data when their computations complete.

8   Related Work

The idea of using continuous modeling for dynamic, reactive behavior (now often referred to as "functional reactive programming") is due to Elliott, beginning with early work on TBAG, a C++ based model for animation [6]. Subsequent work on Fran ("functional reactive animation") embedded the ideas in Haskell [5,9]. The design of Yampa [3,12] adopted arrows as the basis for FRP, an approach that is used in most of our research today, including Euterpea. The use of Yampa to program GUI components was explored in [2,1], which relates to our work in the use of signal functions to represent GUI widgets. So, for example, in Fruit, a model very similar to our *UISF* was proposed, but it does not require resource types. They avoid the problem of reource duplicaton by making their "widgets" essentially pure functions with well defined but restricted output (e.g. *Picture*). Our work allows us to lift this restriction as we address the duplication problem through resource types. Also related is Elliott's recent work on Eros [4].

There is a long history of programming languages designed specifically for audio processing and computer music applications – indeed, the Wikipedia entry for "Audio Programming Language" currently lists 34 languages, including our original work on *Haskore* [10]. Obviously we cannot mention every language. It is worth noting that, except for our recent work on Euterpea, none of these efforts attempt to address the safe virtualization of devices.

With regard to types, the idea of linear typing is somewhat similar to our work. For example, the language *Clean* [21] has a notion of *uniqueness types*. In Clean, when an I/O operation is performed on a device, a value is returned that represents a new instantiation of that device; this value, in turn, must be threaded as an argument to the next I/O operation, and so on. This single-threadedness can also be tackled using *linear logic* [7]. In fact, various authors have proposed language extensions to incorporate linear types, such as [24,8]. In contrast, we do not concern ourselves with single-threadedness since we only have one signal function to represent any particular I/O device. Our focus is on ensuring that resource types do not conflict.

It seems clear that a language with dependent types, such as Agda [16], could easily encode the resource type constraints that we showed in this paper. However, Agda and related proof assistants (Coq, Epigram, etc.) are aimed primarily at verification, and not general programming as Haskell is.

Separation logic [17,22] is also relevant, in which specifications and proofs of a program component refer only to the portion of memory used by that component, and not the entire global state. An extension of this idea might provide a theoretical basis for our work, although we have yet to explore it.

Acknowledgements. This research was supported in part by a gift from Microsoft Research and a grant from the National Science Foundation (CCF-0811665).

References

1. Courtney, A.: Modelling User Interfaces in a Functional Language. Ph.D. thesis, Department of Computer Science, Yale University (May 2004)
2. Courtney, A., Elliott, C.: Genuinely functional user interfaces. In: 2001 Haskell Workshop (September 2001)

3. Courtney, A., Nilsson, H., Peterson, J.: The Yampa arcade. In: Proceedings of the 2003 ACM SIGPLAN Haskell Workshop (Haskell 2003), pp. 7–18. ACM Press, Uppsala (2003)

4. Elliott, C.: Tangible functional programming. In: International Conference on Functional Programming (2007), http://conal.net/papers/Eros/

5. Elliott, C., Hudak, P.: Functional reactive animation. In: International Conference on Functional Programming, pp. 263–273 (June 1997)

6. Elliott, C., Schechter, G., Yeung, R., Abi-Ezzi, S.: Tbag: A high level framework for interactive, animated 3d graphics applications. In: Proceedings of SIGGRAPH 1994, pp. 421–434. ACM SIGGRAPH (July 1994)

7. Girard, J.Y.: Linear logic. Theoretical Computer Science 50, 1–102 (1987)

8. Hawblitzel, C.: Linear types for aliased resources (extended version). Tech. Rep. MSR-TR-2005-141, Microsoft Research, Redmond, WA (October 2005)

9. Hudak, P.: The Haskell School of Expression – Learning Functional Programming through Multimedia. Cambridge University Press, New York (2000)

10. Hudak, P.: Describing and interpreting music in Haskell. In: The Fun of Programming, ch. 4. Palgrave (2003)

11. Hudak, P.: The Haskell School of Music – from Signals to Symphonies (Version 2.0) (January 2011), http://haskell.cs.yale.edu/?post_type=publication&p=112

12. Hudak, P., Courtney, A., Nilsson, H., Peterson, J.: Arrows, Robots, and Functional Reactive Programming. In: Jeuring, J., Jones, S.L.P. (eds.) AFP 2002. LNCS, vol. 2638, pp. 159–187. Springer, Heidelberg (2003)

13. Hughes, J.: Generalising monads to arrows. Science of Computer Programming 37, 67–111 (2000)

14. Kiselyov, O., Lämmel, R., Schupke, K.: Strongly typed heterogeneous collections. In: Haskell 2004: Proceedings of the ACM SIGPLAN Workshop on Haskell, pp. 96–107. ACM Press (2004)

15. Nilsson, H., Courtney, A., Peterson, J.: Functional Reactive Programming, continued. In: ACM SIGPLAN 2002 Haskell Workshop (October 2002)

16. Norell, U.: Dependently Typed Programming in Agda. In: Koopman, P., Plasmeijer, R., Swierstra, D. (eds.) AFP 2008. LNCS, vol. 5832, pp. 230–266. Springer, Heidelberg (2009)

17. OHearn, P., Reynolds, J., Yang, H.: Local reasoning about programs that alter data structures. Computer Science Logic, p. 1

18. Paterson, R.: A new notation for arrows. In: ICFP 2001: International Conference on Functional Programming, Firenze, Italy, pp. 229–240 (2001)

19. Peyton Jones, S., Wadler, P.: Imperative functional programming. In: Proceedings 20th Symposium on Principles of Programming Languages, pp. 71–84. ACM (January 1993)

20. Peyton Jones, S., et al.: The Haskell 98 language and libraries: The revised report. Journal of Functional Programming 13(1), 0–255 (January 2003)

21. Plasmeijer, R., van Eekelen, M.: Clean – version 2.1 language report. Tech. rep., Department of Software Technology, University of Nijmegen (November 2002)

22. Reynolds, J.: Separation logic: A logic for shared mutable data structures. In: Proc. Logic in Computer Science (LICS 2002), pp. 55–74 (July 2002)

23. Voellmy, A., Hudak, P.: Nettle: Taking the Sting Out of Programming Network Routers. In: Rocha, R., Launchbury, J. (eds.) PADL 2011. LNCS, vol. 6539, pp. 235–249. Springer, Heidelberg (2011)

24. Wadler, P.: Is there a use for linear logic? In: Symposium on Partial Evaluation and Semantics Based Program Manipulation, pp. 255–273. ACM/IFIP (1991)

Resource-Safe Systems Programming with Embedded Domain Specific Languages

Edwin Brady and Kevin Hammond

University of St Andrews, KY16 9SX, Scotland/UK
{eb,kh}@cs.st-andrews.ac.uk

Abstract. We introduce a new overloading notation that facilitates programming, modularity and reuse in Embedded Domain Specific Languages (EDSLs), and use it to reason about safe resource usage and state management. We separate the structural language constructs from our primitive operations, and show how precisely-typed functions can be lifted into the EDSL. In this way, we implement a generic framework for constructing state-aware EDSLs for systems programming.

Keywords: Dependent Types, Resource Usage, (Embedded) Domain-Specific Languages, Program Verification.

1   Introduction

Domain Specific Languages (DSLs) are designed to solve problems in specific domains (e.g. Matlab/Simulink for real-time systems or SQL for database queries). One popular implementation technique is to embed a DSL in a *host* language, so creating an Embedded Domain Specific Language (EDSL) [12]. This allows rapid development of a DSL by exploiting host language features, such as parsing/code generation. However, host-language specific information, such as details of host language constructs, often "leaks" into the DSL, inhibiting usability and reducing abstraction. In order to be truly *practical*, we must address such issues so that our EDSL is modular, composable and reusable. This paper introduces a new overloading notation that allows EDSLs to be more easily used in practice, and shows how it can be used to develop an EDSL for reasoning about safe resource usage and state management. We make the following specific contributions:

1. We present the dsl construct, a modest extension to the dependently-typed language IDRIS that allows host language syntax, in particular variable binding, to be overloaded by an Embedded DSL (Section 3).
2. Using the dsl construct, we show how to embed languages with alternative forms of binding: we embed an *imperative* language, which manages mutable local variables in a type-safe way, and extend this to a *state-aware* language which manages linear resources (Section 4).
3. We show how to convert a protocol described by state transitions into a verified implementation (Sections 5 and 6).

C. Russo and N.-F. Zhou (Eds.): PADL 2012, LNCS 7149, pp. 242–257, 2012.

By embedding the DSL within a dependently-typed language, we obtain the key advantage of *correctness by construction*: the host language type system *automatically* verifies the required DSL properties without needing to first translate into an equivalent set of state transitions and subsequently checking these. As Landin said, "Most programming languages are partly a way of expressing things in terms of other things, and partly a basic set of given things" [14]. In our state-aware DSL, the basic set of given things explains how resources are created and how states interact. Like Landin's ISWIM, this DSL can be problem-oriented by providing functions for creating, updating and using primitive values. The embedding then *composes* these constructs into a complete and verifiable EDSL. Example code for the resource language presented in this paper is available from http://idris-lang.org/code/padl12-resources.tgz.

2   The Well-Typed Interpreter

Dependent types, in which *types* may be predicated on *values*, allow us to express a program's specification and constraints precisely. In the context of EDSLs, this allows us to express a precise type system, describing the exact properties that EDSL programs must satisfy, and have the host language check those properties. The well-typed interpreter [1,6,20] for a simple functional language is commonly used to illustrate the key concepts of dependently-typed programming. Here, the type system ensures that only well-typed source programs can be represented and interpreted. In this section, we use the well-typed interpreter example to introduce Domain Specific Language implementation in IDRIS. IDRIS [5] is an experimental functional programming language with dependent types, similar to Agda [19] or Epigram [9,16]. It is eagerly evaluated and compiles to C via the Epic compiler library [4]. It is implemented on top of the IVOR theorem proving library [3], giving direct access to an interactive tactic-based theorem prover. A full tutorial is available online at http://idris-lang.org/tutorial/.

2.1   Language Definition

Figure 1 defines a simple functional expression language, **Expr**, with integer values and operators. The `using` notation means that wherever G is used it can be treated as an implicit argument with type Vect Ty n. Terms of type Expr are indexed by i) a context (of type Vect Ty n), which records types for the variables that are in scope; and ii) the type of the term (of type Ty). The valid types (Ty) are integers (TyInt) or functions (TyFun). We define terms to represent variables (Var), integer values (Val), lambda-abstractions (Lam), function calls (App), and binary operators (Op). Types may either be integers (TyInt) or functions (TyFun), and are translated to IDRIS types using `interpTy`. Our definition of Expr also states its typing rules, in some context, by showing how the type of each term is constructed. For example:

```
Val : (x:Int)    -> Expr G TyInt
Var : (i:Fin n) -> Expr G (vlookup i G)
```

```
data Ty = TyInt | TyFun Ty Ty;

interpTy : Ty -> Set;
interpTy TyInt = Int;
interpTy (TyFun A T) = interpTy A -> interpTy T;

data Fin : Nat -> Set where
      f0 : Fin (S k)
   | fS : Fin k -> Fin (S k);

using (G:Vect Ty n) {
  data Expr : Vect Ty n -> Ty -> Set where
      Var : (i:Fin n) -> Expr G (vlookup i G)
   | Val : (x:Int) -> Expr G TyInt
   | Lam : Expr (A::G) T -> Expr G (TyFun A T)
   | App : Expr G (TyFun A T) -> Expr G A -> Expr G T
   | Op  : (interpTy A -> interpTy B -> interpTy C) ->
            Expr G A -> Expr G B -> Expr G C;
}
```

Fig. 1. The Simple Functional Expression Language, **Expr**

The type of Val indicates that values have integer types (TyInt), and the type of Var indicates that the type of a variable is obtained by looking up i in context G. For any term, x, we can read x : Expr G T as meaning "x has type T in the context G". Expressions in this representation are *well-scoped*, as well as *well-typed*. Variables are represented by *de Bruijn* indices, which are guaranteed to be bounded by the size of the context, using i:Fin n in the definition of Var. A value of type Fin n is an element of a finite set of n elements, which we use as a reference to one of n variables. Evaluation is via an interpretation function, which takes an expression and and environment corresponding to the context in which that expression is defined. The definition can be found in [8].

```
    interp : Env G -> Expr G T -> interpTy T;
```

We can now define some simple example functions. We define each function to work in an arbitrary context G, which allows it to be applied in any subexpression in any context. Our first example function adds its integer inputs:

```
    add : Expr G (TyFun TyInt (TyFun TyInt TyInt));
    add = Lam (Lam (Op (+) (Var (fS f0)) (Var f0)));
```

We can use add to define the double function:

```
    double : Expr G (TyFun TyInt TyInt);
    double = Lam (App (App add (Var f0)) (Var f0));
```

2.2   Control Structures and Recursion

To make **Expr** more realistic, we add boolean values and an If construct. These extensions are shown in Figure 2. Using these extensions, we can define a (recursive) factorial function:

```
data Ty = TyInt | TyBool | TyFun Ty Ty;
interpTy TyBool = Bool;

data Expr : (Vect Ty n) -> Ty -> Set where
   ...
  | If : Expr G TyBool -> Expr G A -> Expr G A -> Expr G A;
```

Fig. 2. Booleans and If construct

```
fact : Expr G (TyFun TyInt TyInt);
fact = Lam (If (Op (==) (Val 0) (Var f0)) (Val 1)
           (Op (*) (Var f0)
             (App fact (Op (-) (Var f0) (Val 1)))));
```

We have all the fundamental features of a full programming language here: a type system, variables, functions and control structures. While **Expr** itself is clearly too limited to be of practical use, we could use similar methods to represent more complex systems, e.g. capturing sizes, resource usage or linearity constraints. In the rest of this paper, we will explore how to achieve this.

3   Syntax Overloading

We would like to use the well-typed interpreter approach to implement *domain specific* type systems capturing important properties of a particular problem domain, such as *resource correctness*. Unfortunately, this at first appears to be impractical because of the need to write programs as syntax trees, and in particular the need to represent variables as *de Bruijn* indices. In this section, we present a new host language construct that allows host language syntax to be used when constructing programs in the EDSL, and use it to implement a practical embedded DSL for resource- and state-aware programs.

3.1   do-Notation

In Haskell, we can overload do-notation to give alternative interpretations of variable binding in monadic code. We have implemented a similar notation in IDRIS using syntactic overloading. For example, we can use do-notation for Maybe by declaring which bind and return operators to use:

```
data Maybe a = Nothing | Just a;

maybeBind : Maybe a -> (a -> Maybe b) -> Maybe b;

do using (maybeBind, Just) {
   m_add : Maybe Int -> Maybe Int -> Maybe Int;
   m_add x y = do { x' <- x;
                    y' <- y;
                    return (x' + y'); };
}
```

```
dsl expr {
    lambda      = Lam, variable = Var,
    index_first = f0,  index_next = fS,
    apply       = App, pure = id
}
```

Fig. 3. Overloading syntax for **Expr**

```
add    = expr (\x, y => Op (+) x y );
double = expr (\x => [| add x x |]);

fact : Expr G (TyFun TyInt TyInt);
fact = expr (\x => If (Op (==) x (Val 0)) (Val 1)
                      (Op (*) x [| fact (Op (-) x (Val 1)) |] ));
```

Fig. 4. Expr programs after overloading

Overloading do-notation is useful for EDSL implementation, in that it allows us to use a different binding construct provided by the EDSL. However, do-notation provides only one kind of binding. What if we need e.g. λ and let binding? What if we need a different notion of application, for example with effects [17]?

3.2   The dsl Construct

In order to allow multiple kinds of binding and application, we introduce a new construct to IDRIS. A dsl declaration gives a name for a language and explains how each *host* language construct is translated into the required EDSL construct. Figure 3 shows, for example, how IDRIS's binding syntax is overloaded for **Expr**. We give a language name, expr, and say that IDRIS lambdas correspond to Lam, and that variables correspond to Var applied to a *de Bruijn* index, which is constructed from f0 and fS. Applications are built using App, with the pure, functional part of the application built using id. The programs that we presented in the previous section can now be written using IDRIS's binding construct, as in Figure 4. Since we called the DSL expr, an expression expr e applies the syntactic overloading to the sub-expression e. Application overloading applies only under explicit "idiom brackets" [17]. Intuitively, expr e translates e according to the following rules:

- Any expression \x => a is translated to Lam a', where a' is a with instances of the variable x is translated to a de Bruijn indexed Var i. The index i is built from f0 and fS counting the number of names bound since x.
- Any application under idiom brackets [| f a1 a2 ... an |] is translated to App (App (App (id f) a1) a2) ... an

Within a dsl declaration, we can provide several overloadings:

- bind and return, for overloading do-notation.
- pure and apply, for overloading application under idiom brackets.

$$
\begin{array}{llll}
e ::= & x & \text{(Variable)} & \mid\quad e\ e & \text{(Application)} \\
& \mid\ \backslash\ x \Rightarrow e & \text{(lambda binding)} & \mid\quad \text{let } x = e_1 \text{ in } e_2 & \text{(let binding)} \\
& \mid\ \text{[|}\ e\ \text{|]} & \text{(Idiomatic application)} & \mid\quad \text{do } \{\ ds\ \} & \text{(do block)} \\
& \mid\ return & \text{(return keyword)} & \mid\quad dsl\ e & \text{(Overloaded expression)} \\[6pt]
d ::= & x \mathrel{\text{<-}} e & \text{(Binding)} & ds ::= d;\ ds \mid e \\
& \mid\ e & \text{(Expression)}
\end{array}
$$

Fig. 5. Core IDRIS expressions

- lambda, let, variable, index_first and index_next, for overloading lambda and let bindings.

It is not necessary to define all of these overloadings. However, if either lambda or let is defined, all of variable, index_first and index_next must be defined, otherwise there is no valid translation for the bound variable.

3.3   Formal Definition

To give a precise definition of the dsl construct, we define four translation schemes on core IDRIS expressions as defined in Figure 5.

- $\mathcal{D}[\![\cdot]\!]$ dsl, defined in Figure 6, transforms an IDRIS expression by a given set of overloadings dsl.
- $\mathcal{V}[\![\cdot]\!]$ $x\ i$, defined in Figure 7, converts a variable name x to de Bruijn index i in an expression.
- $\mathcal{I}[\![\cdot]\!]$, defined in Figure 8, converts an application under idiom brackets
- $\mathcal{M}[\![\cdot]\!]$, also defined in Figure 8, converts a do-block.

Mostly, these schemes are a straightforward traversal of the structure of IDRIS expressions. In $\mathcal{D}[\![\cdot]\!]$, we can nest dsl declarations, updating the set of overloadings. We leave the overloading parameter o implicit in $\mathcal{V}[\![\cdot]\!]$, $\mathcal{I}[\![\cdot]\!]$ and $\mathcal{M}[\![\cdot]\!]$. The definition of each of the overloadable names is extracted from this parameter. Note that $\mathcal{D}[\![\cdot]\!]$ combines the other translation schemes, which each do a specific job. This means in particular that lambda bindings generated by $\mathcal{M}[\![\cdot]\!]$ can further be translated to an overloaded lambda.

4   Resource Management

In a typical file management API, such as that in Haskell, we might find the following typed operations:

```
open  : String -> Purpose -> IO File;
read  : File              -> IO String;
close : File              -> IO ();
```

$$
\begin{aligned}
\mathcal{D}[\![x]\!]\, o &\;\longmapsto\; x \\
\mathcal{D}[\![e_1\, e_2]\!]\, o &\;\longmapsto\; (\mathcal{D}[\![e_1]\!]\, o)\, (\mathcal{D}[\![e_2]\!]\, o) \\
\mathcal{D}[\![\backslash\, x => e]\!]\, o &\;\longmapsto\; \mathcal{D}[\![\texttt{lambda}\, (\mathcal{V}[\![e]\!]\, x\, 0)]\!]\, o \quad\;\; (\text{if } \texttt{lambda} \text{ defined}) \\
&\;\longmapsto\; \backslash\, x => \mathcal{D}[\![e]\!]\, o \qquad\qquad (\text{otherwise}) \\
\mathcal{D}[\![\texttt{let } x = e_1 \texttt{ in } e_2]\!]\, o &\;\longmapsto\; \mathcal{D}[\![\texttt{let } e_1\, (\mathcal{V}[\![e_2]\!]\, x\, 0)]\!]\, o \quad (\text{if } \texttt{let} \text{ defined}) \\
&\;\longmapsto\; \texttt{let } x = \mathcal{D}[\![e_1]\!]\, o \texttt{ in } \mathcal{D}[\![e_2]\!]\, o \; (\text{otherwise}) \\
\mathcal{D}[\![[l\ e\ l]]\!]\, o &\;\longmapsto\; \mathcal{D}[\![\mathcal{I}[\![e]\!]]\!]\, o \\
\mathcal{D}[\![\texttt{do } \{\, ds\, \}]\!]\, o &\;\longmapsto\; \mathcal{D}[\![\mathcal{M}[\![ds]\!]]\!]\, o \\
\mathcal{D}[\![return]\!]\, o &\;\longmapsto\; \texttt{return} \\
\mathcal{D}[\![dsl\ e]\!]\, o &\;\longmapsto\; \mathcal{D}[\![e]\!]\, dsl
\end{aligned}
$$

Fig. 6. The $\mathcal{D}[\![\cdot]\!]$ translation schemes

$$
\begin{aligned}
\mathcal{V}[\![x_1]\!]\, x_2\, i &\;\longmapsto\; \texttt{variable}\, (\textsc{MkVar}\, i) \qquad\qquad (\text{if } x_1 = x_2) \\
&\;\longmapsto\; x_1 \qquad\qquad\qquad\qquad\qquad\quad (\text{otherwise}) \\
\mathcal{V}[\![e_1\, e_2]\!]\, x\, i &\;\longmapsto\; (\mathcal{V}[\![e_1]\!]\, x\, i)\, (\mathcal{V}[\![e_2]\!]\, x\, i) \\
\mathcal{V}[\![\backslash\, x_1 => e]\!]\, x_2\, i &\;\longmapsto\; \backslash\, x_1 => \mathcal{V}[\![e]\!]\, x_2\, (i+1) \qquad (\text{if } \texttt{lambda} \text{ defined}) \\
&\;\longmapsto\; \backslash\, x_1 => \mathcal{V}[\![e]\!]\, x_2\, i \qquad\quad\;\; (\text{otherwise}) \\
\mathcal{V}[\![\texttt{let } x_1 = e_1 \texttt{ in } e_2]\!]\, x_2\, i &\;\longmapsto\; \texttt{let } x_1 = \mathcal{V}[\![e_1]\!]\, x_2\, i \texttt{ in } \mathcal{V}[\![e_2]\!]\, x_2\, (i+1) \;(\text{if } \texttt{let} \text{ defined}) \\
&\;\longmapsto\; \texttt{let } x_1 = \mathcal{V}[\![e_1]\!]\, x_2\, i \texttt{ in } \mathcal{V}[\![e_2]\!]\, x_2\, i \qquad (\text{otherwise}) \\
\mathcal{V}[\![[l\ e\ l]]\!]\, x\, i &\;\longmapsto\; [l\ \mathcal{V}[\![e]\!]\, x\, i\ l] \\
\mathcal{V}[\![\texttt{do } \{\, ds\, \}]\!]\, x\, i &\;\longmapsto\; \texttt{do } \{\, \mathcal{V}[\![ds]\!]\, x\, i\, \} \\
\mathcal{V}[\![return]\!]\, x\, i &\;\longmapsto\; return \\
\mathcal{V}[\![dsl\ e]\!]\, x\, i &\;\longmapsto\; dsl\, (\mathcal{V}[\![e]\!]\, x\, i)
\end{aligned}
$$

$$
\begin{aligned}
\textsc{MkVar}\, 0 &\;\longmapsto\; \texttt{index\_first} \\
\textsc{MkVar}\, (n+1) &\;\longmapsto\; \texttt{index\_next}\, (\textsc{MkVar}\, n)
\end{aligned}
$$

Fig. 7. The $\mathcal{V}[\![\cdot]\!]$ translation scheme

Unfortunately, it is easy to construct programs which are well-typed, but nevertheless fail at run-time, for example, if we read from a file opened for writing:

```
fprog filename = do { h <- open filename Writing;
                      content <- read h;
                      close h; };
```

If we make the types more precise, parameterising open files by purpose, `fprog` is no longer well-typed, and will therefore be rejected at compile-time.

```
data Purpose = Reading | Writing;

open  : String -> (p:Purpose) -> IO (File p);
read  : File Reading          -> IO String;
close : File p                -> IO ();
```

However, there is still a problem. The following program is well-typed, but fails at run-time — although the file has been closed, the handle h is still in scope:

$$\mathcal{I}[\![e_1\ e_2]\!] \quad \mapsto \textbf{apply}\ (\mathcal{I}[\![e_1]\!])\ e_2 \qquad \text{(top level application)}$$
$$\mathcal{I}[\![e]\!] \qquad \mapsto \textbf{pure}\ e \qquad\qquad \text{(all other expressions)}$$

$$\mathcal{M}[\![x <- e; ds]\!] \quad \mapsto \textbf{bind}\ e\ (\backslash\ x => \mathcal{M}[\![ds]\!])$$
$$\mathcal{M}[\![e; ds]\!] \qquad \mapsto \textbf{bind}\ e\ (\backslash\ \_ => \mathcal{M}[\![ds]\!])$$
$$\mathcal{M}[\![e]\!] \qquad\quad \mapsto e$$

Fig. 8. The $\mathcal{I}[\![\cdot]\!]$ and $\mathcal{M}[\![\cdot]\!]$ translation schemes

```
fprog filename = do { h <- open filename Reading;
                      content <- read h;
                      close h; read h; };
```

Furthermore, we did not check whether the handle h was created successfully. Resource management problems such as this are common in systems programming — we need to deal with files, memory, network handles, etc, ensuring that operations are executed only when valid and errors are handled appropriately.

4.1   An EDSL for Generic Resource Correctness

To tackle this problem, we present an EDSL which tracks the *state* of resources at any point during program execution, and ensures that any resource protocol is correctly executed. We begin by categorising resource operations into creation, update and usage operations, by lifting them from IO. We illustrate this using Creator; Updater and Reader can be defined similarly.

```
data Creator a = MkCreator (IO a);
ioc : IO a -> Creator a;
ioc = MkCreator;
```

The MkCreator constructor is left abstract, so that a programmer can lift an operation into Creator using ioc, but cannot run it directly. IO operations can be converted into resource operations, tagging them appropriately:

```
open  : String -> (p:Purpose) -> Creator (Either () (File p));
close : File p                 -> Updater ();
read  : File Reading           -> Reader String;
```

Here: open creates a resource, which may be either an error (represented by ()) or a file handle that has been opened for the appropriate purpose; close updates a resource from a File p to a () (i.e., it makes the resource unavailable); and read accesses a resource (i.e., it reads from it, and the resource remains available). They are implemented using the relevant (unsafe) IO functions from the IDRIS library. Resource operations are executed via a resource management EDSL, **Res**, with resource constructs (Figure 9), and control constructs (Figure 10).

As we did with **Expr** in Section 2, we index **Res** over the variables in scope (which represent resources), and the type of the expression. This means that firstly we can refer to resources by *de Bruijn* indices, and secondly we can express precisely how operations may be combined. Unlike **Expr**, however, we allow

```
data Res : Vect Ty n -> Vect Ty n -> Ty -> Set where
   Let    : Creator (interpTy a) ->
            Res (a :: gam) (Val () :: gam') (R t) -> Res gam gam' (R t)
 | Update : (a -> Updater b) -> (p:HasType gam i (Val a)) ->
            Res gam (update gam p (Val b)) (R ())
 | Use    : (a -> Reader b) -> HasType gam i (Val a) ->
            Res gam gam (R b)
   . . .
```

Fig. 9. Resource constructs

```
data Res : Vect Ty n -> Vect Ty n -> Ty -> Set where
   . . .
 | Check  : (p:HasType gam i (Choice (interpTy a) (interpTy b))) ->
            (failure:Res (update gam p a) (update gam p c) T) ->
            (success:Res (update gam p b) (update gam p c) T) ->
            Res gam (update gam p c) T
 | While  : Res gam gam (R Bool) ->
            Res gam gam (R ()) -> Res gam gam (R ())
 | Lift   : IO a -> Res gam gam (R a)
 | Return : a -> Res gam gam (R a)
 | Bind   : Res gam gam'  (R a) -> (a -> Res gam' gam'' (R t)) ->
            Res gam gam'' (R t);
```

Fig. 10. Control constructs

types of variables to be updated. Therefore, we index over the input set of resource states, and the output set:

```
data Res : Vect Ty n -> Vect Ty n -> Ty -> Set
```

We can read Res gam gam' T as, "an expression of type T, with input resource states gam and output resource states gam'". Expression types can be resources, values, or a choice type:

```
data Ty = R Set | Val Set | Choice Set Set;
```

The distinction between *resource* types, R a, and *value* types, Val a, is that resource types arise from IO operations. A choice type corresponds to Either — we use Either rather than Maybe as this leaves open the possibility of returning informative error codes:

```
interpTy : Ty -> Set;
interpTy (R t) = IO t;
interpTy (Val t) = t;
interpTy (Choice x y) = Either x y;
```

We represent variables by proofs of context membership, rather than directly by *de Bruijn* indices. As we will see shortly, this allows a neater representation of some language constructs:

```
data HasType : Vect Ty n -> Fin n -> Ty -> Set where
     stop : HasType (a :: gam) fO a
   | pop  : HasType gam i b -> HasType (a :: gam) (fS i) b;

envLookup : HasType gam i a -> Env gam -> interpTy a;
envUpdate : (p:HasType gam i a) -> (val:interpTy b) ->
            Env gam -> Env (update gam p b);
```

The type of the Let construct explicitly shows that, in the scope of the Let expression a new resource of type a is added to the set, having been made by a Creator operation. Furthermore, by the end of the scope, this resource must have been consumed (i.e. its type must have been updated to Val ()):

```
Let : Creator (interpTy a) ->
      Res (a :: gam) (Val () :: gam') (R t) -> Res gam gam' (R t)
```

The Update construct applies an Updater operation, changing the type of a resource in the context. Here, using HasType to represent resource variables allows us to write the required type of the update operation simply as a -> Updater b, and put the operation first, rather than the variable.

```
Update : (a -> Updater b) -> (p:HasType gam i (Val a)) ->
         Res gam (update gam p (Val b)) (R ())
```

The Use construct simply executes an operation without updating the context, provided that the operation is well-typed:

```
Use : (a -> Reader b) -> HasType gam i (Val a) ->
      Res gam gam (R b)
```

Finally, we provide a small set of control structures: Check, a branching construct that guarantees that resources are correctly defined in each branch; While, a loop construct that guarantees that there are no state changes during the loop; Lift, a lifting operator for IO functions[1]; and Bind and Return to support do-notation. The type of Bind captures updates in the resource set. We use dsl-notation to overload the IDRIS syntax, in particular providing a let-binding to bind a resource and give it a human-readable name:

```
dsl res {
    let          = Let,   variable  = id,
    bind         = Bind,  return    = Return,
    index_first = stop, index_next = pop
}
```

The interpreter for **Res** is written in continuation-passing style, where each operation passes on a result and an updated environment (containing resources):

```
interp : Env gam -> Res gam gam' t ->
         (Env gam' -> interpTy t -> IO u) -> IO u;

run : Res VNil VNil (R t) -> IO t;
run prog = interp Empty prog (\env, res => res);
```

---

[1] This requires us to hide the resource operations, e.g. in a module.

5   First Example: File Management

We can use **Res** to implement a safe file-management protocol, where each file must be opened before use, opening a file must be checked, and files must be closed on exit. We define the following operations for opening, closing, reading a line[2], and testing for the end of file.

```
open   : String -> (p:Purpose) -> Creator (Either () (File p));
close  : File p                -> Updater ();
read   : File Reading          -> Reader String;
eof    : File Reading          -> Reader Bool;
```

Simple example. Returning to our simple example from Section 4, we now write the file-reading program as follows:

```
fprog : {gam:Vect Ty n} -> String -> Res gam gam (R String);
fprog filename =
    res do { let h = open filename Reading;
             Check h
             (Lift (putStrLn "File error"))
             (do { content <- Use read h;
                   Update close h; }); };
```

This is well-typed because the file is opened for reading, and by the end of the scope, the file has been closed. Syntax overloading allows us to name the resource h rather than using a *de Bruijn* index or context membership proof. Although this is a big improvement, the syntax is still somewhat unsatisfactory:

- The type of fprog is hard to read and write (and for practical use, we need programmers to write these signatures!)
- The need to apply Use, Read and Lift explicitly is a little ugly.

Fortunately, both problems can be addressed using IDRIS's syntax macros:

```
syntax RES x = {gam:Vect Ty n} -> Res gam gam (R x);

syntax rclose      h = Update close h;
syntax rread       h = Use read h;
syntax reof        h = Use eof h;
syntax rputStrLn x = Lift putStrLn x;
```

We use macros rather than functions, as the types of Update and Use are context dependent. We now use RES x as the type of *any* resource safe program which returns an x, and rclose and rread as the file operations:

---

[2] Reading a line may fail, but we consider this harmless and return an empty string.

```
fprog : String -> RES String;
fprog filename =
   res do { let h = open filename Reading;
            Check h
              (rputStrLn "File error")
              (do { content <- rread h;
                    rclose h; }) };
```

Using loops. In the following program, we open a file, read each line of the file and output it using a While loop, then close it:

```
dump : String -> RES String;
dump filename =
   res do { let h = open filename Reading;
            Check h
              (rputStrLn "File error")
              (do { While (do { end <- reof h;
                                return (not end); })
                          (do { str <- rread h;
                                rputStrLn str; });
                    rclose h; }) };
```

This program has a similar structure to the equivalent Haskell program written using the IO monad However, here the IDRIS type system guarantees that each operation is executed only when it is valid. We *cannot*, for instance, close the file during the loop, or try to read from the file in the branch where opening has failed. We have achieved this by writing ordinary monadic IO functions and lifting them intro a general framework which guarantees linear use of resources.

Embedding functions. We can improve the program by lifting out the While loop into a function. Since this is an EDSL, we can use a host language function, but its type must refer to the EDSL's context. A **Res** function which uses a resource a but does not update it, and returns a value b is denoted by a :-> b:

```
syntax (:->) a b = {gam:Vect Ty n} ->
    HasType gam i (Val a) -> Res gam gam b;

readFile : File Reading :-> R ();
readFile h = res (While (do { end <- reof h;
                              return (not end); })
                        (do { str <- rreadLine h;
                              rputStrLn str; }));
```

We can use this function directly in a **Res** program:

```
dump filename = res do { let h = open filename Reading;
                         Check h
                           (rputStrLn "File error")
                           (do { readFile h; rclose h; }) };
```

Correspondingly, updating a resource variable is denoted by a |-> b:

```
syntax (|->) a b = {gam:Vect Ty n} ->
    (p:HasType gam i (Val a)) -> Res gam (update gam p b) (R ()) ;
```

6   Second Example: Network Transport

As well as defining high-level APIs, we can also use **Res** to implement low-level operating systems components such as reliable network transport. Let us briefly consider a simple automatic repeat request (ARQ) protocol, in which a machine S attempts to send packets reliably to a machine R.

1. S opens a connection to R and waits for R to acknowledge the connection.
2. For each packet, with a sequence number n:
   (a) S sends a packet with sequence number n, and waits for an acknowledgement from R.
   (b) If an acknowledgement is not received within a timeout period, retry.
3. S requests that the connection be closed.

Each operation may have pre-/post-conditions on the state of the connection.

```
connect    : Receiver        -> Creator (Either () (Net (Ready 0)));
send       : Net (Ready n)   -> Updater (Net (Waiting n));
recvAck    : Net (Waiting n) -> Updater (Either (Net (Ready n))
                                                (Net (Ready (S n))));
disconnect : Net (Ready n)   -> Updater ();
```

We implement the protocol by lifting these functions into **Res**, defining a function sendList which iterates across a list of packets, either sending them successfully or timing out:

```
sendList : List Packet -> (Net (Ready n) |-> R ());

arq : Receiver -> List Packet -> RES ();
arq r pkts = res do { let h = connect r;
                      Check h (rputStrLn "Couldn't open connection")
                              (do { sendList pkts h; }); };
```

Note that sendList's type requires that it also closes the connection. It is written as a combination of send and recvAck, retrying if an acknowledgement is not received. As before, the primitives are composed using the constructs in **Res** to guarantee that resources are managed according to the protocol.

7   Related Work

We have previously explored the use of IDRIS for implementing EDSLs in domains such as networking [2,5] and concurrency [7]. The work described here is similar to that of [7]. However, by using *de Bruijn* indices we obtain the key advantage of compositionality, a neat way to build contexts, etc. Unlike other approaches to resource usage verification based on e.g. model-checking [13,15,21], which translate the program into a (hopefully) equivalent set of state transitions that can subsequently be checked, the EDSL approach we have used here relates the *actual* program to the abstract state machine model, so guaranteeing correctness *by construction*. **Res** is inspired by work on linear types for resource management [10,11], and an alternative approach would have been to add linear types to IDRIS's type system. We have avoided this for two reasons: firstly, we prefer to keep the core type theory of IDRIS as small and as easy to reason about as possible; secondly, as **Res** demonstrates, dependent types alone are strong enough to capture the linearity property. Finally, Hoare Type Theory has also been used in the Ynot system [18] to reason about imperative programs with side effects, as we have done in **Res**. However, our approach is much lighter weight: it involves writing the state transition functions directly, as normal IDRIS functions, then "promoting" them into the resource language. This makes it much easier to plug in new functionality, for example, in our system.

8   Conclusion

We have shown a new way to write resource-safe systems programs using domain-specific languages embedded in a dependently-typed host language. The dsl-notation introduced in this paper raises the abstraction level when programming EDSLs, adding the important properties of compositionality and modularity over previous approaches. The notation captures common patterns in EDSL implementation, in particular variable binding and function application, and can easily be extended to overload other language features, for example literal values. Using this notation over a dependently-typed host language, we are able to produce automatically verified EDSL programs, provided the primitive state transitions are correctly written. We have also demonstrated the applicability and generality of the notation by developing a generic resource usage framework and applying it to two realistic systems programming scenarios. Like Landin's ISWIM, the EDSL can be problem-oriented, providing functions for creating, updating and using primitive values. These primitives are then embedded into a generic composition framework, here exemplified by **Res**. Although not shown here, the approach can easily handle other constructs such as (higher-order) functions, further extending its applicability. We have not considered how to e.g. embed resources within data structures, although we expect this to be achievable by indexing larger data structures over a resource context. This may be important for some examples, particularly where we have long-lived resources, or a collection of live resources such as a list of open file handles.

There are a number of obvious future applications of this work in systems programming. In particular, we intend to study larger applications in network protocols, and consider how to capture and reason about security issues. The use of dependent types simplifies the task of producing verifiable systems programs as EDSLs, providing a lightweight, extensible and composable framework that is tightly integrated with the actual systems program. The dsl-notation itself also deserves further study. At present it provides straightforward syntactic overloadings, but there is no checking of whether the overloadings interact safely and reliably other than by type checking the resulting term. It would be interesting to investigate whether they can be give a more theoretically sound presentation, for example using type classes.

Acknowledgments. This work was partly funded by the Scottish Informatics and Computer Science Alliance (SICSA), by EPSRC grant EP/F030592/1 (Islay), and by EU Framework 7 Project No. 248828 (ADVANCE).

References

1. Augustsson, L., Carlsson, M.: An exercise in dependent types: A well-typed interpreter (1999)
2. Bhatti, S., Brady, E., Hammond, K., McKinna, J.: Domain specific languages (DSLs) for network protocols. In: International Workshop on Next Generation Network Architecture, NGNA 2009 (2009)
3. Brady, E.: IVOR, a Proof Engine. In: Horváth, Z., Zsók, V., Butterfield, A. (eds.) IFL 2006. LNCS, vol. 4449, pp. 145–162. Springer, Heidelberg (2007)
4. Brady, E.: Epic — a library for generating compilers. In: Trends in Functional Programming, TFP 2011 (to appear, 2011)
5. Brady, E.: Idris — systems programming meets full dependent types. In: Programming Languages meets Program Verification (PLPV 2011), pp. 43–54 (2011)
6. Brady, E., Hammond, K.: A Verified Staged Interpreter is a Verified Compiler. In: Proc. GPCE 2006: Conf. on Generative Prog. and Component Eng. (2006)
7. Brady, E., Hammond, K.: Correct-by-construction concurrency: Using dependent types to verify implementations of effectful resource usage protocols. Fundamenta Informaticae 102(2), 145–176 (2010)
8. Brady, E., Hammond, K.: Scrapping your Inefficient Engine: using Partial Evaluation to Improve Domain-Specific Language Implementation. In: Proc. ICFP 2010: ACM Intl. Conf. on Functional Programming, pp. 297–308 (2010)
9. Chapman, J., Dagand, P.-E., McBride, C., Morris, P.: The Gentle Art of Levitation. In: Proc. ICFP 2010: ACM Intl. Conf. on Funct. Prog., pp. 3–14 (2010)
10. Hawblitzel, C.: Linear types for aliased resources. Technical Report MSR-TR-2005-141, Microsoft Research (2005)
11. Hofmann, M., Jost, S.: Static prediction of heap space usage for first-order functional programs. In: Proc. POPL 2003 — 2003 ACM Symp. on Principles of Programming La nguages, pp. 185–197. ACM (2003)
12. Hudak, P.: Building domain-specific embedded languages. ACM Computing Surveys 28A(4) (December 1996)
13. Igarashi, A., Kobayashi, N.: Resource usage analysis. ACM Trans. Program. Lang. Syst. 27, 264–313 (2005)
14. Landin, P.: The next 700 programming languages. Communications of the ACM 9(3) (March 1966)
15. Marriott, K., Stuckey, P., Sulzmann, M.: Resource Usage Verification. In: Ohori, A. (ed.) APLAS 2003. LNCS, vol. 2895, pp. 212–229. Springer, Heidelberg (2003)
16. McBride, C., McKinna, J.: The view from the left. Journal of Functional Programming 14(1), 69–111 (2004)
17. McBride, C., Paterson, R.: Applicative programming with effects. J. Funct. Program. 18, 1–13 (2008)
18. Nanevski, A., Morrisett, G., Shinnar, A., Govereau, P., Birkedal, L.: Ynot: Reasoning with the Awkward Squad. In: Proc. ICFP 2008: 2008 ACM Intl. Conf. on Functional Programming, pp. 229–240. ACM (2008)

19. Norell, U.: Towards a practical programming language based on dependent type theory. PhD thesis, Chalmers University of Technology (September 2007)
20. Pašalíc, E., Taha, W., Sheard, T.: Tagless Staged Interpreters for Typed Languages. In: Proc. ICFP 2002: Intl. Conf. on Functional Programming. ACM (2002)
21. Walker, D.: A Type System for Expressive Security Policies. In: Proc. POPL 2000: ACM Intl. Symp. on Principles of Programming Languages, pp. 254–267 (2000)

Node-Based Connection Semantics for Equation-Based Object-Oriented Modeling Languages

David Broman[1] and Henrik Nilsson[2]

[1] Department of Computer and Information Science, Linköping University, Sweden
david.broman@liu.se
[2] School of Computer Science, University of Nottingham, United Kingdom
nhn@cs.nott.ac.uk

Abstract. Declarative, Equation-Based Object-Oriented (EOO) modeling languages, like Modelica, support modeling of physical systems by composition of reusable component models. An important application area is modeling of cyber-physical systems. EOO languages typically feature a connection construct allowing component models to be assembled into systems much like physical components are. Different designs are possible. This paper introduces, formalizes, and validates an approach based on *explicit nodes* that expressly is designed to work for *functional* EOO languages supporting *higher-order modeling*. The paper also considers Modelica-style connections and explains why that design does not work for functional EOO languages, thus mapping out the design space.

Keywords: Declarative Languages, Modeling, and Simulation.

1 Introduction

Equation-based Object-Oriented (EOO) languages is an emerging class of declarative Domain-Specific Languages (DSLs) for modeling the dynamic aspects of systems using (primarily) differential equations [6]. These languages are characterized by *acausal* modeling of individual objects in the domain(s) of interest and composition of such object models into a complete system model[1]. Acausal modeling means there is no a priori assumption about the directionality of equations (known vs. unknown variables). This greatly facilitates reuse and composition [10], a crucial advantage for large models that can consist of thousands of equations. Moreover, EOO languages are typically capable of expressing models from arbitrary physical domains (e.g., mechanical, electrical, hydraulic) and of supporting *hybrid modeling*: modeling of both continuous-time and discrete-time aspects. State-of-the-art EOO languages include *Modelica* [11,19], VHDL-AMS [15]

---

[1] Some of these languages share typical traits of object-oriented programming languages, such as a class system, but this is not essential: object-oriented here refers to the focus on composition of reusable *models* that have a direct correspondence to *objects* in the *physical world*. Also, note that, unlike (imperative) object-oriented programming languages, EOO languages have no notion of mutable state.

C. Russo and N.-F. Zhou (Eds.): PADL 2012, LNCS 7149, pp. 258–272, 2012.

and Verilog-AMS [1]. Taken together, the characteristics of EOO languages make them particularly suitable for modeling Cyber-Physical Systems: complex systems that combine embedded computers and networks (the cyber) with physical processes [17]. Examples include cars, aircraft, and power plants.

Most EOO languages provide a mechanism to *connect* component models together in a way that mimics how physical components may be interconnected. To obtain a purely mathematical model, these connections have to be translated into equations. This translation is the *connection semantics*. Unsurprisingly, the connection semantics is grounded in physical reality, such as the conservation principles of various physical domains. Because these principles share a common mathematical structure, it is possible to formulate the connection semantics in a *domain-neutral* way. To that end, two kinds of physical quantities are distinguished: *flow* quantities and *potential* quantities. Connected flow quantities are translated into sum-to-zero equations, as a connection point itself does not provide any capability of storing the flowing quantity, while connected potential quantities are translated into equality constraints, as there can only be one potential at a connection point. Modelica is one language taking this approach.

While state-of-the-art EOO languages like Modelica are highly successful, they do have acknowledged weaknesses, including limited support for structurally dynamic systems and limited meta-modeling capabilities per se [20,26]. These and other considerations have led researchers to investigate a different approach to EOO language design that supports *higher-order* modeling. The common idea is to make models *first class* entities in the setting of a *functional language* and using pure functions as the central abstraction mechanism [6,14,20].

Unfortunately, the connection semantics of Modelica-like languages is predicated on specific design aspects of such languages and does not readily carry over to a functional setting with first-class models. Moreover, at least the Modelica connection semantics is complex and has not been fully formalized, making it difficult to understand it precisely (for end users as well as for implementors).

In this paper we propose an alternative approach to specifying the connection semantics based on *explicit* connection points, from now on *nodes*. The idea of explicit nodes is not new; for example, it is used in VHDL-AMS, Verilog-AMS, and other hardware description languages. The novel insight demonstrated in this paper is how a node-based approach solves the problem of defining the connection semantics in *functional* EOO languages. The resulting semantics is also pleasingly clear. In more detail, our specific contributions are:

- We relate Modelica-style connection semantics (Section 2) and the node-based approach (Section 3), thus mapping out part of the design space, and we explain why the former approach does not work in a functional setting.
- We formalize the semantics of the node-based approach (Section 4).
- We describe and validate a prototype implementation of the node-based approach in the *Modeling Kernel Language (MKL)* [6] (Section 5). (Note that MKL is just a vehicle: the approach as such is language-independent.)

2   Modelica-Style Approach

This section gives an informal overview of Modelica-style connection semantics and explains why this approach does not work in a functional setting. Our examples are from the analog electrical domain. However, we re-iterate that connection semantics in this paper is domain-neutral unless stated otherwise [8].

2.1   Models and Equation Generation

Fig. 1(a) depicts a graphical *model* of a simple electrical circuit. The model consists of five *component models*, in this case a voltage source VS, a resistor R, a capacitor C, an inductor L, and a ground G. At the lowest level of abstraction, a model consists of a set of *Differential-Algebraic Equations (DAEs)* [16]. For example, the behavior of resistor R is expressed declaratively by the algebraic equation R*i = v (Ohm's law) and the inductor's behavior is stated using the differential equation L*der(i) = v, where der(i) is the time derivative of i.

Each component model has one or more *ports* (or *connectors*) specifying its connection points. For example, the negative ports (white boxes) of the capacitor C and the inductor L are connected to the positive port (black box) of resistor R. In the analog electrical domain, each port has two variable instances, a *potential* variable v and a *flow* variable i, representing voltage and current respectively.

The connection semantics specifies how a *set of connected ports* is translated into equations over their instance variables. Two kinds of equations are generated: pairwise equalities among the potential variables, and a sum-to-zero equation for the flow variables. We use Modelica's dot-notation to refer to variables; e.g, C.n.v refers to v of the negative port n of the capacitor C. As an example, the port set {G.p, R.n, VS.n} (node a_3) is translated into the two equations R.n.v = G.p.v and VS.n.v = G.p.v for the potential variables and the sum-to-zero equation G.p.i + R.n.i + VS.n.i = 0 for the flow variables.

2.2   Abstraction and Composition

In an EOO language, such as Modelica, a model is fundamentally a DAE system. However, to promote reuse and facilitate construction, models are usually

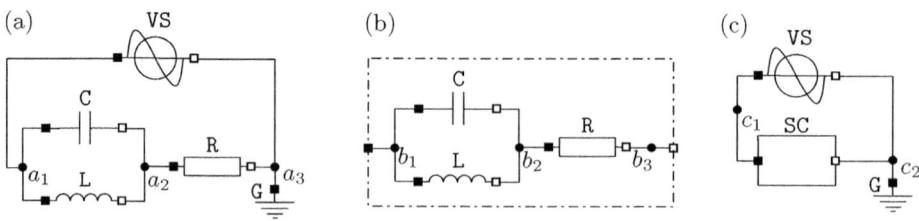

Fig. 1. Example of how parts of a circuit can be composed into a new model abstraction. Figure (a) shows the full circuit and (b) shows how three of the components are composed into a new model. Figure (c) shows how the model in (b) is used.

constructed hierarchically: related equations are grouped into models of physical components; such models can then be instantiated any number of times and further grouped into models of systems at progressively higher levels of abstraction.

For example, the model in Fig. 1(b) represents an abstraction of the components R, C, and L from Fig. 1(a). The dashed box represents the outside border of the abstracted model. Fig. 1(c) shows another way to model the circuit in (a), this time as a *composed* model using the sub-circuit in (b) (named SC) as one of the components. Hence, (a) and (c) model the exact same system, the only difference being that (c) introduces one more hierarchical level of abstraction.

The question is how to define connection semantics for composed models with several hierarchical levels of abstraction. In the Modelica-style, each port is considered either an *outside* or an *inside* port, depending on whether the current viewpoint is inside or outside a model. For example, in Fig. 1(b), when generating the sum-to-zero equation for the connection b_3, SC.n is considered an outside port and SC.R.n an inside port. The Modelica specification [19] states that outside connectors shall have a negative sign in sum-to-zero equations. The sum-to-zero equation at node b_3 is thus -SC.n.i + SC.R.n.i = 0. On the other hand, in model (c), port SC.n is considered an inside port, hence the resulting sum-to-zero equation for c_2 is VS.n.i + SC.n.i + G.p.i = 0. Information about the hierarchical structure is thus exploited when generating the equations.

2.3   Problems in a Functional Setting

In the Modelica-style approach, models have ports that define instance variables. A port is a *part* of the model it belongs to, and as such, its position in a compositional hierarchy becomes unambiguously determined; in particular, each port can be classified as inside or outside with respect to a specific model context and then treated accordingly for connection purposes.

In contrast, a functional EOO language uses *function abstraction* (or some variant thereof) for expressing model abstractions, with "ports" becoming *formal parameters*. As a result, a port is no longer *per se* a part with an implied position that can inform the generation of sum-to-zero equations. We can attempt to overcome this by introducing connection nodes as an independent notion. A model abstraction is then seen as a function mapping nodes to equations. But a node is just a node, a value like any other, without any special relation to specific abstractions, meaning that the notions inside and outside become meaningless. For example, assume that the model SC is defined as a function with two formal parameters. A function call SC(c1,c2) results in the nodes c1 and c2 being substituted into the function body of SC, yielding a collapsed hierarchy without any possibility to say whether a port is inside or outside.

Thus, the Modelica-style connection semantics does not carry over to a functional setting essentially because it is predicated on exploiting contextual information alien to this setting. To address this, we develop in the following an alternative approach that *is* suitable, based on nodes *and branches* (Electrical Engineering terminology; here essentially a directed edge annotated with variables) forming an explicit graph. Other possibilities are discussed in Sec. 6.3.

3   Node-Based Approach

This section informally describes the node-based approach to connection semantics. It has two phases: (1) Collapsing the hierarchical model structure into a
directed graph of nodes, branches, and equations; (2) Translation of nodes and
branches into additional equations, yielding a pure system of equations; i.e.,
the *connection semantics* proper. The approach is demonstrated using a small
research language called the *Modeling Kernel Language (MKL)* [6]: a typed functional language specifically designed for embedding equation-based DSLs. However, note that the approach as such is language-independent.

3.1   Phase 1: Collapsing the Model Hierarchy

In an functional EOO-language, functions are used as the abstraction mechanism for describing composed models. For example, consider the following MKL
model, which is the textual representation of Fig. 1(a):

```
def CircuitA() = {
    def a1,a2,a3:Electrical;
    SineVoltage(220,50,a1,a3);
    Capacitor(0.02,a1,a2);
    Inductor(0.1,a1,a2);
    Resistor(200,a2,a3);
    Ground(a3);
}
```

The model CircuitA is defined as a function without parameters. Three nodes
a1, a2, and a3 of type Electrical are defined. The five component models of the circuit are instantiated using function application; e.g., the application Capacitor(0.02,a1,a2) instantiates a capacitor of 0.02 F. The connection
topology is defined by supplying the electrical nodes to the components; e.g.,
Capacitor is applied to nodes a1 and a2. Note how both parallel and serial
connections are expressed in this way (cf. Fig. 1(a)). The Capacitor model

```
def Capacitor(C:Real,p:Electrical,n:Electrical) = {
    def i:Current;
    def v:Voltage;
    Branch(i,v,p,n);
    C * der(v) = i;
}
```

has parameters C (capacitance) p (positive port), and n (negative port). Two
unknown continuous-time signals i (current) and v (voltage) are defined inside
the body. The third line in the body instantiates a Branch with four elements.
Conceptually, a *branch* is a path between two nodes through a component model.
Branches are essential for the translational connection semantics because they
capture information necessary to generate correct signs in sum-to-zero equations.

Fig. 2 shows the resulting graph from evaluating the expression CircuitA().
Filled black arrows represent the branches (labeled edges). The nodes a1, a2,

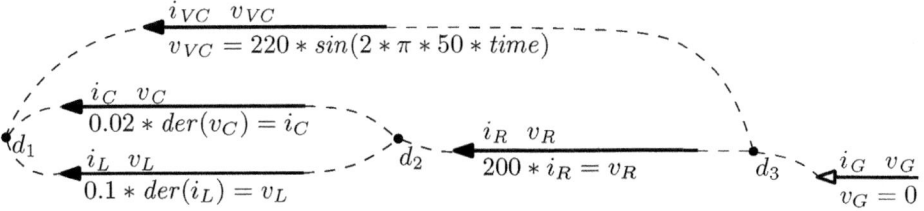

Fig. 2. The connection graph after collapsing the model hierarchy of `CircuitA` or `CircuitC`

and a3 maps to d_1, d_2, and d_3 respectively. The graph is *directed* where the arrow head represents the positive position (the third element of a branch-instantiation) and the tail the negative position (forth element). The unknowns for a specific component are listed above each arrow. For example, i_R is the current flowing *through* the resistor branch and v_R is the voltage drop *across* the branch. The behavior equation for a specific component model is given below the arrow; e.g., Ohm's law in the resistor case. The unfilled arrow represents a *reference branch* (`RefBranch`) as used in the `Ground` model, for example:

```
def Ground(p:Electrical) = {
    def i:Current;
    def v:Voltage;
    RefBranch(i,v,p);
    v = 0;
}
```

Note that the `RefBranch` is only connected to one node. The intuition is that a reference branch makes the *absolute values* for a *specific node* accessible; i.e., the absolute potential value in relation to a global implicit reference value. The ground model states that the potential in the ground node is zero (v = 0).

So far we have only used basic components, such as `Resistor` and `Capacitor`. We now consider a model where one of the components itself is a composite model. The following is an MKL model of the sub-circuit from Fig. 1(b):

```
def SubCircuit(p:Electrical,n:Electrical) = {
    def b2:Electrical;
    Capacitor(0.02,p,b2);
    Inductor(0.1,p,b2);
    Resistor(200,b2,n);
}
```

The `SubCircuit` model is a function with two parameters p and n, both of type `Electrical`. A minor difference compared with Fig. 1(b) is that only node b2 is defined inside the model: because a user of `SubCircuit` will supply the nodes between which it is going to be connected via parameters p and n (nodes being first-class), those nodes should *not* be defined inside `SubCircuit`. The model

```
def CircuitC (SC:TwoPin) = {
    def c1,c2:Electrical;
    SineVoltage (220,50,c1,c2);
    SC (c1,c2);
    Ground (c2);
}
```

is the MKL version of Fig. 1(c). It has one parameter SC of type TwoPin. This is an example where *Higher-Order Acausal Models (HOAMs)* [7] is used, i.e., where a model is parametrized with another model. The type TwoPin,

```
type TwoPin = Electrical -> Electrical -> Equations
```

is defined as a curried function[2] from nodes (type Electrical) to a system of equations (type Equations). Because SubCircuit is of type TwoPin, the expression CircuitC(SubCircuit) is well-typed and evaluating it results in a connection graph. During evaluation, SC is replaced with SubCircuit, meaning SubCircuit gets applied to the nodes c1 and c2. Hence c1 and c2 are substituted for the formal parameters p and n respectively. The resulting connection graph for CircuitC(SubCircuit) is the same as that for Fig. 1(a), up to renaming of nodes. Thus, for CircuitA() the following holds: $d_1 = a_1$, $d_2 = a_2$, and $d_3 = a_3$, while for CircuitC(SubCircuit): $d_1 = c_1$, $d_2 = b_2$, and $d_3 = c_2$.

3.2   Phase 2: The Connection Semantics

In the second phase, we translate the connection graph into a set of equations. We describe this translation process by defining three translation rules.

In contrast to the Modelica semantics, ports do not define instance variables. Nodes are instead defined explicitly in the model (e.g., d_1, d_2, and d_3 in Fig. 2), with each node corresponding to a *set* of connected ports in the Modelica approach. Instead of enforcing the equality of all potential variables of a port set by generating equality constraints, we apply the following rule:

> **Rule 1 - Potential variables:** Associate a distinct variable with each node in the system representing the potential in that node.

Three new distinct continuous-time variables v_{p1}, v_{p2}, and v_{p3} are thus associated with nodes d_1, d_2, and d_3 respectively.

A sum-to-zero equation must be created for each node and the signs in the equation must be chosen appropriately. This is where the information captured by *branches* comes into play. Consider the definition of Capacitor again. The first argument to Branch is the *flow variable* representing the current i through the branch, the second argument the *relative potential variable* representing the voltage v across the branch, the third argument the positive node p, and the fourth argument the negative node n. We can now define the second rule:

---

[2] All functions are curried in MKL even though the syntax of function definitions and applications uses parentheses. This design choice was made to make the functional style of programming more familiar to engineers used to the syntax of main-stream programming and modeling languages.

Rule 2 - Sum-to-zero equations: For each node n in the circuit, create a sum-to-zero equation, such that the flow variables for the branches connected to node n get a positive sign if the branch is pointing towards the node, and a negative sign if it is pointing away from the node. For reference branches, the positive sign is always used.

Rule 2 results in the sum-to-zero equations $i_{VC} + i_C + i_L = 0$, $i_R - i_C - i_L = 0$, and $i_G - i_R - i_{VC} = 0$ for nodes d_1, d_2, and d_3 respectively.

The last translation rule defines the voltage across components:

Rule 3 - Branch equations: For each branch in the model, create an equation stating that the *relative potential* across a branch is equal to the difference between the potential variable of the positive node and the one of the negative node. For a reference branch the relative potential is equal to the potential variable of the associated node.

Rule 3 results in one equation for each component; i.e., $v_{VC} = v_{p1} - v_{p3}$, $v_C = v_{p1} - v_{p2}$, $v_L = v_{p1} - v_{p2}$, $v_R = v_{p2} - v_{p3}$, and $v_G = v_{p3}$.

In the example, there are 13 variables in total: 10 variables originate from the potential and flow variables of each component, while 3 are generated from the nodes by rule 1. 5 behavior equations are explicitly stated for the model, 3 further equations are generated by rule 2 (sum-to-zero), and 5 more by rule 3. There are thus 13 equations and 13 variables: a necessary but not sufficient condition for solving a set of independent equations.

We note the following invariants. First, for each node, rule 1 adds one variable and rule 2 adds one equation. Second, two variables are always defined for each component: one flow variable and one relative potential variable. There are also always two equations for each component: one behavior equation defined in the original component model, and one branch equation generated by rule 3.

These invariants make it clear that the balance between the number of variables and equations is preserved under interconnection of correctly defined components. The approach is thus correct in that sense. However, the number of generated equations is not minimal; for example, a sum-to-zero equation can always be eliminated by using it to solve for one variable and substitute the result into other equations. However, we are not concerned with such issues here as that has to do with solving the equations, not with the semantics of connections.

4   Formalization of the Connection Semantics

In this section we formalize the node-based connection semantics. Note that the formalization is independent of MKL.

4.1   Notation and Syntax

Let N be a finite set of nodes and $n \in N$ denote a node element. Let V be a finite set of variables and $v \in V$ a variable. Let B_{bin} be the set of binary branches and B_{ref} be the set of unary reference branches. A binary branch is a quadruple $(v_f, v_{rp}, n_1, n_2) \in B_{bin}$, where v_f is a flow variable, v_{rp} a relative potential variable, n_1 a first and n_2 a second node connected to the branch. A reference branch is a triple $(v_f, v_{rp}, n_1) \in B_{ref}$, where v_f is the flow variable, v_{rp} a relative potential variable, n_1 a connected node. Let $B = B_{bin} \cup B_{ref}$ be the set of all branches. The syntax of expressions e is given by the grammar rules

$$e ::= e + e \mid e - e \mid 0 \mid v$$

where + and - are the plus and minus operators, 0 the value zero, and v a variable. The syntax for an equation is $e_1 = e_2$, where e_1 and e_2 are expressions. Let E be a multiset of equations. A multiset is needed as equations could be repeated in a model[3].

We use braces to denote sets and square brackets to denote multisets. When pattern matching on sets, the pattern $A \cup \{a\}$ matches a non-empty set with a being bound to an arbitrary element of the set and A being bound to the rest of the set, *not* including a.

We postulate an overloaded function *vars* that returns the set of variables occurring in a branch, an expression, or a (multi)set of branches or expressions. Similarly, we postulate an overloaded function *nodes* that returns the set of nodes occurring in a branch or set of branches.

4.2 Semantics of Rules

Fig. 3 defines the connection semantics using (recursive) function definitions. The functions are categorized according to the informal rules in previous section.

Rule 1 associates a new potential variable with each node. The function *potvar* returns a bijective function pv mapping each node to a corresponding potential variable, distinct from any of the existing variables V_{BE}.

Rule 2 describes the generation of the multiset of sum-to-zero equations. The rule defines one main function *sumzeroeqns* and one auxiliary function *sumexpr*. The function *sumezeroeqns* takes two arguments, where the first argument N is the set of nodes and the second argument B the set of branches. For each $n \in N$, the function creates the corresponding sum-to-zero expression using set-builder notation for multisets together with calling *sumexpr*. The first three cases of *sumexpr* concern binary branches by matching on the quadruple (v_f, v_{rp}, n_1, n_2). Only branches directly connected to the node under consideration contribute to the expression. The last two cases handle reference branches in the same manner. Note that a literal 0 is inserted at the end of the recursion. This zero could easily be eliminated by introducing unary minus in the expression syntax. However, this would make the formalization less readable.

Rule 3 describes the generation of the multiset of relative potential equations. The rule defines a function *brancheqns* that takes two arguments. The first argument pv is the mapping between nodes and potential variables (see Rule 1).

---

[3]   We do not wish to eliminate redundant equations here, and we note that syntactic equality on equations would not suffice for this purpose anyway.

The second argument B is the set of branches. Different equations are generated depending on whether a branch is a binary branch or a reference branch.

The last function definition *consem* takes the set B of branches and multiset E of equations that already exists in the model (i.e, the behavior equations) as arguments. The function returns the final multiset of model equations; i.e., the initial equations along with all generated equations.

A branch starting and ending at the same node is a bit of a special case. The relative potential across such a branch is, of course, 0, and no special consideration is needed in rule 3 for the associated potential variable. However, such a branch *in itself* imposes *no* constraints on the flow through it. Rule 2 thus

Rule 1 - Potential variables $\boxed{potvar(N, V_{BE})}$

$potvar(N, V_{BE}) = pv$ where $pv : N \rightarrow V_P$ is bijective, $V_P \subseteq V$, and $V_P \cap V_{BE} = \emptyset$

Rule 2 - Sum-to-zero equations $\boxed{sumzeroeqns(N, B)}$

$sumzeroeqns(N, B) = [\ sumexpr(n, B) = 0 \mid n \in N\ ]$

$\boxed{sumexpr(n, B)}$

$sumexpr(n, \emptyset) = 0$

$$sumexpr(n, B \cup \{b\}) = \begin{cases} sumexpr(n, B) + v_f & \text{if } (v_f, v_{rp}, n_1, n_2) = b \text{ and} \\ & \quad n = n_1 \text{ and } n \neq n_2 \\ sumexpr(n, B) - v_f & \text{if } (v_f, v_{rp}, n_1, n_2) = b \text{ and} \\ & \quad n \neq n_1 \text{ and } n = n_2 \\ sumexpr(n, B) & \text{if } (v_f, v_{rp}, n_1, n_2) = b \text{ and} \\ & \quad ((n \neq n_1 \text{ and } n \neq n_2) \text{ or} \\ & \quad (n = n_1 \text{ and } n = n_2)) \\ sumexpr(n, B) + v_f & \text{if } (v_f, v_{rp}, n_1) = b \text{ and } n = n_1 \\ sumexpr(n, B) & \text{if } (v_f, v_{rp}, n_1) = b \text{ and } n \neq n_1 \end{cases}$$

Rule 3 - Branch equations $\boxed{brancheqns(pv, B)}$

$brancheqns(pv, B) = [\ eqn(b) \mid b \in B\ ]$ where

$$eqn(b) = \begin{cases} v_{rp} = pv(n_1) - pv(n_2) & \text{if } b = (v_f, v_{rp}, n_1, n_2) \\ v_{rp} = pv(n_1) & \text{if } b = (v_f, v_{rp}, n_1) \end{cases}$$

Translational connection semantics $\boxed{consem(B, E)}$

$consem(B, E) = E \cup sumzeroeqns(N, B) \cup brancheqns(pv, B)$ where

$$N = nodes(B)$$
$$V_{BE} = vars(B) \cup vars(E)$$
$$pv = potvar(N, V_{BE})$$

Fig. 3. Formalization of the node-based connection semantics

carefully ignores any such branch, meaning that the associated flow variable will not appear in any sum-to-zero equation. (Of course, it would usually appear in other equations, like component equations relating the relative potential and flow.)

5   Implementation and Evaluation

We have developed a prototype implementation of the node-base connection semantics as a functional EOO DSL in MKL. The prototype has three parts:

- Libraries for defining the elaboration semantics of a functional EOO DSL supporting acausal modeling in the continuous-time domain. The connection semantics that is part of the elaboration semantics was implemented according to the formalization presented in this paper, with certain optimizations together with more efficient data structures.
- Libraries for defining reusable components (models of physical objects) within the analog electrical domain, the rotational mechanical domain, and automatic control domain.
- Test models that use the modeling libraries.

The evaluation of the prototype so far was concerned with testing the correctness of the node-based approach compared to Modelica's approach. The selected test models were chosen according to the following criteria:

- Size of the model, where the largest model contained more than 1000 equations after translation.
- Combination of and interaction between different physical domains, like electrical, mechanical, and control, to ensure domain-neutrality.
- Modeling abstraction and generation mechanisms, such as higher-order models and recursively defined models.

The test procedure was as follows:

1. The model was created in Modelica using standard components in Modelica standard library.
2. The same model was created by using components from MKL's standard library. This library has been modeled according to the Modelica library.
3. The Modelica model was simulated using Dymola 6 [9], a Modelica environment. Data from the sensors was plotted and visualized.
4. The MKL model was translated into flat equations by the prototype implementation following the connection semantics defined in this paper. Dymola 6 was then used as a simulation backend to simulate and plot these flat equations. Using the same simulation backend for both the model expressed in Modelica and for the model expressed in MKL eliminates the risk of differences in the results due to differences in employed simulation methods.
5. The plotted results from the Modelica model and the MKL model were visually compared.

In all cases the simulation result from the Modelica models were found to coincide with the results from the corresponding MKL version of the model; i.e., the results were the same. This confirms the described approach works as intended, in a functional setting, and is applicable for multi-physical modeling. Moreover, preliminary performance measurements of the translational semantics show that the approach can scale up to hundreds of thousands equations. Our approach has not yet been evaluated for structurally dynamic systems, which we see as the next step of future work.

6   Related Work

6.1   Modelica

The work most closely related to the node-based approach is the connection semantics for Modelica [11,19]. As we saw (Sec. 2), Modelica lets the modeler specify sets of interconnected component ports. Each such set corresponds to a node and is translated into connection equations by taking the context-dependent classification of individual ports as being outside or inside into account. However, nodes are *not* an explicit notion. In contrast, to provide connection functionality without relying on specific language design aspects (beyond the standard notion of functions), nodes along with branches are made *explicit* notions in the node-based approach and used to construct an *explicit* interconnection graph containing all necessary information for subsequent translation into connection equations. This approach is thus a good fit for e.g. functional EOO languages as the kind of contextual information used in Modelica is not available (Sec. 2.3).

Furic [12] proposes an alternative connection semantics for Modelica. The main objective is to make models compose better and to support structural dynamism. For example, in Modelica, missing or "duplicated" ground references in electrical models typically lead to under- and over-constrained systems of equations respectively, and ideal switches might mean there is no one way of "grounding" the model that works for all structural configurations. Furic's approach is based on nodes, like our approach, but, following VHDL-AMS, it employs *relative* potentials across branches between nodes, referred to as *effort*, while *absolute* potentials at nodes are of no concern, unlike in our approach and the standard Modelica approach. The end result is an explicit representation of the model topology in the form of a graph, like in our case, which suggests that it may be possible to adapt Furic's approach to a functional setting. However, like for VHDL-AMS, special source and sensor constructs are necessary to mediate between the "effort/flow world" and the "signal world", e.g. to feed in external stimuli or make observations. This is more direct in our setting. Furic's work has not yet been formalized or thoroughly evaluated outside the electrical domain, but constitute another interesting node-based approach.

6.2   Hardware Description Languages

Hardware Description Languages, such as VHDL and Verilog, are primarily used for describing digital electrical circuits. However, there exist *analog and mixed signal (AMS)* extensions to both these languages: VHDL-AMS [2] and Verilog-AMS [1] respectively. These variants allow modeling of continuous systems from various physical domains. Both VHDL-AMS and Verilog-AMS have a node-based connection semantics, where nodes connect components together via ports. However, in contrast to the work presented in this paper, neither language has a *formally* specified semantics for connections. The VHDL-AMS specification [15] describes the connection semantics informally as part of the elaboration phase of the language. Similarly, Verilog-AMS definition states that DAE equations are generated according to Kirchhoff's laws, but does not specify how.

Lava [4] is a tool for specifying and verifying hardware circuits. It is embedded in Haskell and makes use of higher-order functions and combinators for composing circuits. Wired [3] is a relational language that is based on Lava, but also models the layout of a circuit, including the wires. Both Lava and Wired are used for describing *digital* circuits; the kind of connections discussed here grounded in abstraction over phenomena from continuous physics is thus not relevant. However, both employ a notion of explicit nodes for describing circuits.

SPICE [23] is a circuit simulation program originally developed at UC Berkeley in the 1970s. Circuits are defined using *netlists*, a textual description where electrical components are connected together using nodes. SPICE uses a modified nodal analysis method with special treatment for voltage sources to enable numerical approximation. In contrast, our approach generates DAEs as output and relies on symbolic/numerical methods developed in the 1980s-1990s for solving DAEs [18,21,22]. Also, SPICE is designed for analog circuit simulation, whereas our approach is based on ideas from Modelica and is domain-neutral.

6.3   Functional Acausal Languages

The Flow λ-calculus [5] is a minimal EOO language developed by the first author. It is an extension of the λ-calculus with primitives for generating flow equations. The approach to connections taken by the Flow λ-calculus inspired the node-based approach presented here, but its semantics was more complex.

Functional Hybrid Modeling (FHM) [20] combines functional programming and acausal modeling. It can be seen as a generalization of causal Functional Reactive Programming (FRP) [25]. Hydra is a DSL within the FHM paradigm developed by Giorgidze and Nilsson [14]. At present, the language is realized as an embedding in Haskell [24], with just-in-time compilation of simulation code for speed. FHM supports highly structurally dynamic systems and it makes a strict distinction between time-invariant and time-varying entities, relegating the latter to secondary status. The central FHM modeling-specific abstraction is the *signal relation*. It is similar to model abstraction in MKL, but formally parametrized on *signals*, time-varying values, not nodes.

Modelica-style connections are not applicable to FHM for the reasons outlined in Sec. 2.3. Instead, a scheme is adopted with one `connect`-specification per node enumerating *all* variables related by that node [13]. By assuming that flow is always directed into a signal relation, the signs of the flow variables in the generated sum-to-zero equations are always positive, independent of context.

Signal relation *application* then takes care of the necessary sign-reversal for flow quantities (what flows into one signal relation, flows out of another).

While this scheme is simple and quite effective, it does require connections to be expressed in a particular way. For example, and perhaps unexpectedly, connection by transitivity does not work. While static checks can be employed to catch mistakes, the node-based approach would be an interesting alternative.

7   Conclusions

We presented and formalized a new, node-based approach to specifying model composition through connections in the context of equation-based, acausal languages for modeling of physical systems. The main benefit compared to the connect-based approach used in Modelica is that it does not assume much about the language design. Thus it works well for, for example, functional EOO languages, which, indeed, was the goal of the design. Additional advantages include its simplicity and clarity, as evidenced by the formalization.

Acknowledgements. The authors would like to thank Peter Fritzson and John Capper for useful comments. The first author was funded by the ELLIIT project.

References

1. Accellera Organization. Verilog-AMS Language Reference Manual - Analog & Mixed-Signal Extensions to Verilog HDL Version 2.3.1 (2009)
2. Ashenden, P.J., Peterson, G.D., Teegarden, D.A.: The System Designer's Guide to VHDL-AMS: Analog, Mixed-Signal, and Mixed-Technology Modeling. Morgan Kaufmann Publishers, USA (2002)
3. Axelsson, E., Claessen, K., Sheeran, M.: Wired: Wire-Aware Circuit Design. In: Borrione, D., Paul, W. (eds.) CHARME 2005. LNCS, vol. 3725, pp. 5–19. Springer, Heidelberg (2005)
4. Bjesse, P., Claessen, K., Sheeran, M., Singh, S.: Lava: hardware design in Haskell. In: Proceedings of the Third ACM SIGPLAN International Conference on Functional Programming, pp. 174–184. ACM Press, New York (1998)
5. Broman, D.: Flow Lambda Calculus for Declarative Physical Connection Semantics. Technical Reports in Computer and Information Science No. 1. LiU Electronic Press (2007)
6. Broman, D.: Meta-Languages and Semantics for Equation-Based Modeling and Simulation. PhD thesis, Department of Computer and Information Science, Linköping University, Sweden (2010)
7. Broman, D., Fritzson, P.: Higher-Order Acausal Models. Simulation News Europe 19(1), 5–16 (2009)
8. Cellier, F.E.: Continuous System Modeling. Springer, New York (1991)
9. Dassault Systems. Multi-Engineering Modeling and Simulation - Dymola - CATIA - Dassault Systemes, http://www.dymola.com (last accessed: September 16, 2011)
10. Elmqvist, H., Mattsson, S.E., Otter, M.: Modelica - A Language for Physical System Modeling, Visualization and Interaction. In: Proceedings of the IEEE International Symposium on Computer Aided Control System Design (1999)

11. Fritzson, P.: Principles of Object-Oriented Modeling and Simulation with Modelica 2.1. Wiley-IEEE Press, New York (2004)
12. Furic, S.: Enforcing model composability in Modelica. In: Proceedings of the 7th International Modelica Conference, Como, Italy, pp. 868–879 (2009)
13. Giorgidze, G., Nilsson, H.: Embedding a Functional Hybrid Modelling Language in Haskell. In: Scholz, S.-B., Chitil, O. (eds.) IFL 2008. LNCS, vol. 5836, pp. 138–155. Springer, Heidelberg (2011)
14. Giorgidze, G., Nilsson, H.: Higher-Order Non-Causal Modelling and Simulation of Structurally Dynamic Systems. In: Proceedings of the 7th International Modelica Conference, Como, Italy, pp. 208–218. LiU Electronic Press (September 2009)
15. IEEE Std 1076.1-2007. IEEE Standard VHDL Analog and Mixed-Signal Extensions. IEEE Press (2007)
16. Kunkel, P., Mehrmann, V.: Differential-Algebraic Equations Analysis and Numerical Solution. European Mathematical Society (2006)
17. Lee, E.A.: CPS foundations. In: Proceedings of the 47th Design Automation Conference, DAC 2010, pp. 737–742. ACM Press, New York (2010)
18. Mattsson, S.E., Söderlind, G.: Index reduction in differential-algebraic equations using dummy derivatives. SIAM Journal on Scientific Computing 14(3), 677–692 (1993)
19. Modelica Association. Modelica - A Unified Object-Oriented Language for Physical Systems Modeling - Language Specification Version 3.2 (2010), http://www.modelica.org
20. Nilsson, H., Peterson, J., Hudak, P.: Functional Hybrid Modeling. In: Dahl, V. (ed.) PADL 2003. LNCS, vol. 2562, pp. 376–390. Springer, Heidelberg (2002)
21. Pantelides, C.C.: The Consistent Initialization of Differential-Algebraic Systems. SIAM Journal on Scientific and Statistical Computing 9(2), 213–231 (1988)
22. Petzold, L.R.: A Description of DASSL: A Differential/Algebraic System Solver. In: IMACS Trans. on Scientific Comp., 10th IMACS World Congress on Systems Simulation and Scientific Comp., Montreal, Canada (1982)
23. Quarles, T.L., Newton, A.R., Pedersen, D.O., Sangiovanni-Vincentelli, A.: SPICE3 Version 3f3 User's Manual. Technical report, Department of Electrical Engineering and Computer Sciences, University of California, Berkeley (1993)
24. Jones, S.P.: Haskell 98 Language and Libraries – The Revised Report. Cambridge University Press (2003)
25. Wan, Z., Hudak, P.: Functional reactive programming from first principles. In: PLDI 2000: Proceedings of the ACM SIGPLAN 2000 Conference on Programming Language Design and Implementation, pp. 242–252. ACM Press, New York (2000)
26. Zimmer, D.: Enhancing Modelica towards variable structure systems. In: Proceedings of the 1st International Workshop on Equation-Based Object-Oriented Languages and Tools, Berlin, Germany, pp. 61–70. LiU Electronic Press (2007)

A Declarative Specification of Tree-Based Symbolic Arithmetic Computations

Paul Tarau

Department of Computer Science and Engineering
University of North Texas
tarau@cs.unt.edu

Abstract. We use Prolog as a flexible meta-language to provide executable specifications of some interesting mathematical objects and their operations. In the process, isomorphisms are unraveled between natural numbers and rooted ordered trees representing hereditarily finite sequences and rooted ordered binary trees representing Gödel's System **T** types. Our isomorphisms result in an interesting "paradigm shift": we provide recursive definitions that perform the equivalent of arbitrary-length integer computations directly on rooted ordered trees. Besides the theoretically interesting fact of "breaking the arithmetic/symbolic barrier", our arithmetic operations performed with symbolic objects like trees or types turn out to be genuinely efficient – we derive implementations with asymptotic performance comparable to ordinary bitstring implementations of arbitrary-length integer arithmetic. The Prolog code of the paper, organized as a literate program, is available at http://logic.cse.unt.edu/tarau/research/2012/padl12.pl

Keywords: modeling finite mathematics in logic programming, symbolic arbitrary precision arithmetic, ranking/unranking of hereditarily finite sequences, balanced parenthesis languages.

1 Introduction

This paper exhibits a creative use of logic programming as a modeling tool for several interesting concepts at the intersection of combinatorics, formal languages, foundation of mathematics and coding theory. It builds on the declarative data transformation framework introduced in [1,2], where we introduce a methodology to derive bijective mappings between fundamental data types used in programming languages (sets, multisets, sequences to graphs, digraphs, DAGs, hypergraphs etc.)

At the same time, with practical uses for arbitrary size integer arithmetic in mind, we focus on keeping the asymptotic complexity of various operations similar to that of operations on conventional bitstrings.

Like [1], this paper is organized as a literate Prolog program. This means that our "lingua franca" is logic programming rather than the usual mathematical notation.

C. Russo and N.-F. Zhou (Eds.): PADL 2012, LNCS 7149, pp. 273–288, 2012.

It has been a long tradition in logic programming to model program properties and behaviors in terms of mathematical reasoning. We pay it back this time, and model mathematical concepts as logic programs. The paper is organized as follows. Section 2 overviews, following [1], a bijection between natural numbers and sequences that is extended in section 3, by recursive application, to hereditarily finite sequences. Section 4 describes a novel way to perform arbitrary length arithmetic computations using ordered rooted tree representations of hereditarily finite sequences and discusses some potential applications for implementation of arithmetic operations with numbers that do not fit in computer memory with conventional binary encodings. It is followed by a sketch of a similar mechanism in section 5 for the type language of Gödel's system **T**. Section 6 introduces a bijection between hereditarily finite sequences and balanced parenthesis languages providing a succinct representation for them. Sections 7 and 8 discuss related work and conclude the paper.

2   A Bijection between Finite Sequences and Natural Numbers

Let $\mathbb{N}$ be the set of natural numbers and $[\mathbb{N}]$ the set of finite sequences of natural numbers (that can also be seen as the set of functions from an initial segment of $\mathbb{N}$ to $\mathbb{N}$ - or even more generally, as *finite functions*). We first derive, following [1] a bijection $\mathbb{N} \to [\mathbb{N}]$.

We define the following predicates working on natural numbers:

```
cons(X,Y,XY):-X>=0,Y>=0,XY is (1+(Y<<1))<<X.

hd(XY,X):-XY>0,P is XY /\ 1,hd1(P,XY,X).

  hd1(1,_,0).
  hd1(0,XY,X):-Z is XY>>1,hd(Z,H),X is H+1.

tl(XY,Y):-hd(XY,X),Y is XY>>(X+1).

null(0).
```

After observing that the relations cons(X,Y,Z), hd(Z,X), tl(Z,Y) hold if and only if $Z = 2^X(2Y + 1)$, it can be proven by structural induction that:

Proposition 1. *The predicates* cons/3, hd/2, tl/2, null/1 *emulate the list functions CONS,CAR,CDR,NIL as defined in [3] (see proof in [1]).*

Note also that hd/2 implements the *2-adic valuation* function $\nu_2(z)$ i.e. it computes the largest exponent x of 2 such that 2^x divides z.

Using these predicates we define a bijection between finite sequences represented as lists of their values and natural numbers, described by the predicates list2nat/2 and nat2list/2.

```
list2nat([],0).
list2nat([X|Xs],N):-list2nat(Xs,N1),cons(X,N1,N).
```

```
nat2list(0,[]).
nat2list(N,[X|Xs]):-N>0,hd(N,X),tl(N,T),nat2list(T,Xs).
```

The following example shows this bijection at work:

```
?- nat2list(2012,Ns),list2nat(Ns,N).
Ns = [2, 0, 0, 1, 0, 0, 0, 0],
N = 2012
```

3 Ranking Hereditarily Finite Sequences

Definition 1. *The* ranking problem *for a family of combinatorial objects is finding a unique natural number associated to each object, called its* rank. *The inverse* unranking problem *consists of generating a unique combinatorial object associated to each natural number.*

Definition 2. *A hereditarily finite sequence is* [] *or a finite sequence of hereditarily finite sequences.*

We describe, by instantiating the data type transformation described in [1], how to extend a bijection $\mathbb{N} \to [\mathbb{N}]$ to trees representing *hereditarily finite sequences*. The two sides of the bijection are expressed as two higher order predicates rank and unrank parameterized by two transformations F and G:

```
unrank(F,N,Rs):-call(F,N,Ns),maplist(unrank(F),Ns,Rs).

rank(G,Ts,Rs):-maplist(rank(G),Ts,Xs),call(G,Xs,Rs).
```

These predicates can be seen as a form of "structured recursion" that propagate a simpler operation (F and G) guided by the structure of the underlying data type. We can instantiate this mechanism to derive a bijection between natural numbers and trees representing hereditarily finite sequences using rank and unrank as:

```
nat2hfseq(N,T):-unrank(nat2list,N,T).

hfseq2nat(T,N):-rank(list2nat,T,N).
```

They work as follows:

```
?- nat2hfseq(2012,HFSEQ),hfseq2nat(HFSEQ,N).
HFSEQ = [[[[]]], [], [], [[]], [], [], [], []],
N = 2012
```

One can represent the recursive *unfolding* of a natural number into a hereditarily finite sequence as a directed ordered multigraph (Fig. 1). Note that as the mapping nat2list generates a sequence where the order of the edges matters, this order is indicated with integers starting from 0 labeling the edges.

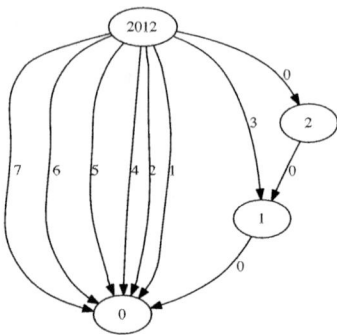

Fig. 1. 2012 as a HFSEQ

4   Computing with Hereditarily Finite Sequences

This section describes a surprising possibility derived from the existence of bijections between various data types and natural numbers. It answers positively the following question: can we turn such bijections into actual isomorphisms such that operations like additions or multiplications defined on symbolic objects (e.g. trees or parenthesis languages) mimic their natural number equivalents? Moreover, we want a genuinely constructive proof that this can be done, which means that we need to build inductive definitions, starting with successor and predecessor and then extend them to implement everything else.

We build these operations incrementally. We start with successor/predecessor operations and simple (but slow) mappings to natural numbers. We then provide efficient implementations, working, like in the case of bitstring representations, in time proportional to the size of the operands.

4.1   Successor and Predecessor

To derive efficient successor and predecessor operations we recall that the equation Z=[X|Y] on hereditarily finite sequences corresponds bijectively to the equation

$$Z = 2^X(2Y + 1) \tag{1}$$

on natural numbers. Successor and predecessor predicates s/2 and p/2 are defined as:

```
s([],[[]]).
s([[K|Ks]|Xs],[[],K1|Xs]):-p([K|Ks],K1).
s([[]|Xs],[[K1|Ks]|Ys]):-s(Xs,[K|Ys]),s(K,[K1|Ks]).

p([[]],[]).
p([[],K|Xs],[[K1|Ks]|Xs]):-s(K,[K1|Ks]).
p([[K|Ks]|Xs],[[]|Zs]):-p([K|Ks],K1),p([K1|Xs],Zs).
```

The two predicates are deterministic and implement functions when their first arguments are ground, given that the patterns used in the heads of the rules share no instances. If executed under a breadth-first evaluation rule (or if impure Prolog operations are used) the two predicates can be merged into a single reversible predicate. We have preferred pure Horn clause definitions, however, and reordered the goals in the clause bodies as needed. However, the fact that s and p are defined by the same Prolog predicate except for a reordering in their 3-rd clause has the following immediate consequence.

Proposition 2. *If f_s and f_p are the functions defined as the result computed by the second argument of* s *and respectively* p, *given their first argument, then* $\forall x, f_p(f_s(x)) = x$ *and* $\forall x <> [], f_s(f_p(x)) = x$.

It follows from this that HFSEQ is a model of (second order) Peano's axioms. Given that all such models are isomorphic to $\mathbb{N}$, one could "non-constructively" conclude that f_s provides an implementation of the successor function on $\mathbb{N}$.

However, we will prefer to derive a constructive proof of this equivalence based on our direct transformations between HFSEQ and $\mathbb{N}$. The following propositions hold:

Proposition 3. *If T is such that* hfseq2nat(T,N), s(T,T1) *and* hfseq2nat (T1,N1) *hold, then N1=N+1.*

Proposition 4. *If* T *(assumed different from []) is such that* hfseq2nat(T,N), p(T,T1) *and* hfseq2nat(T1,N1) *hold, then N1=N-1.*

This means that the pair hfseq2nat and nat2hfseq acts as an *isofunctor* that transports successor and predecessor operations between natural numbers and hereditarily finite sequences. A proof is obtained by structural induction on the first argument of the two predicates, after defining a mapping between an ordered rooted tree type and a natural number type supporting an axiomatization of Peano arithmetic. After

1. replacing [] by 0
2. replacing each relation of the form [X|Y]=Z in the inductive definition of s and t with equations of the form $2^X * (2 * Y + 1) = Z$,

one can obtain arithmetic formulas equivalent to the usual arithmetic relations defining s and p. This means that we can prove correctness of s and p with respect to the corresponding successor and predecessor operations on $\mathbb{N}$, by verifying that, when interpreting each constructor in terms of equation (1) on $\mathbb{N}$, the resulting formulas become identities.

For instance, s([],[[]]) becomes $s(0, 2^0 * (2*0+1))$ and then $s(0, 1)$ which states that the successor of 0 is 1.

On the other hand the second and third recursive equations in the definitions of s and p become logical implications between arithmetic identities, relatively easy to prove through a sequence of simplifications.

For instance, the second equation in the definition of s/2 becomes, after putting $[K|Ks] \to x, Xs \to y, K1 \to z$ with $x, y, z \in \mathbb{N}$.

$$s([x|y], [0, z|y]) : -p(x, z). \tag{2}$$

After interpreting :- as inverse logical implication $\Leftarrow$ we obtain

$$s(2^x * (2 * y + 1), 2^0 * 2 * (2^z * (2 * y + 1)) + 1) \Leftarrow p(x, z). \tag{3}$$

After interpreting s and p as successor and predecessor on $\mathbb{N}$ we obtain:

$$1 + (2^x * (2 * y + 1) = 2 * 2^z * (2 * y + 1) + 1 \Leftarrow (x = z + 1). \tag{4}$$

After replacing x by $z + 1$ on the left side we obtain:

$$2^{z+1} * (2 * y + 1) = 2^{z+1} * (2 * y + 1) \tag{5}$$

which is clearly an identity in $\mathbb{N}$.

Note that the ability to reason about the correctness of our programs is clearly facilitated by the declarative semantics of Prolog, for instance when interpreting :- as reverse logical implication.

After defining a generator for the infinite stream of hereditarily finite sequences mapped to successive natural numbers

```
n([]).
n(S):-n(P),s(P,S).
```

one can confirm empirically that our two symbolic s/2 and p/2 operations provide indeed emulations of their standard counterparts:

```
?- n(X),hfseq2nat(X,N).
X = [], N = 0 ;
X = [[]], N = 1 ;
X = [[[]]], N = 2 ;
X = [[], []], N = 3 ;
.......
```

4.2   Simple Arithmetic Operations in Terms of Successor and Predecessor

The s/2 and p/2 predicate pair can be used to implement the usual arithmetic operations in time O(N) where N is the natural number corresponding to the first operand. For instance, addition can be defined as follows:

```
slow_add([],X,X).
slow_add([X|Xs],Y,Z):-p([X|Xs],P),s(Y,Y1),slow_add(P,Y1,Z).
```

It works indeed as expected:

```
?- nat2hfseq(42,T),slow_add(T,T,R),hfseq2nat(R,N).
T = [[[]], [[]], [[]]], R = [[[[]]], [[]], [[]]], N = 84
```

We next define efficient operations, with asymptotic complexity comparable to typical bignum packages provided by various languages.

4.3   Basic Recognizers and Constructors

We start with recognizers for odd numbers o_/2, strictly positive even numbers i_/2 and zero e_/1.

```
o_([[]|_]).
i_([[_|_]|_]).
e_([]).
```

Next, we define our constructors. The first one, o/2 builds odd numbers, as if provided by the leftshift+increment operation 2*X+1. The second one, i/2, applies the successor predicate to the result of the first, as if provided by the 2*X+2 operation.

```
o(X,[[]|X]).
i(X,Y):-s([[]|X],Y).
```

The predicate e_/1 can also be seen as a constructor for the empty list representing 0.

Note that by interpreting o and i as the two successors in WS2S arithmetic one can obtain a decision procedure on HFSEQ similar to that of [4].

4.4   Arithmetic Operations with Hereditarily Finite Sequences –
Efficiently

To provide efficient, possibly practical implementations of arithmetic operations, we need a few more steps towards emulating binary representations including variants of left and right shifting operations.

Deconstructing. Let us first build a deconstructor r/2, working as a decrement + rightshift operation on bitstrings such that it maps both 2*X+1 and 2*X+2 to X, i.e. such that it reverses the action of the constructors o/2 and i/2.

```
r([[]|Xs],Xs).
r([[X|Xs]|Ys],Rs):-p([[X|Xs]|Ys],[[]|Rs]).
```

Note that the first clause maps to n a term corresponding to an odd number of the form 2*n+1, while the second applies the predecessor to an even number while trimming the result (an odd number) in a similar way to the first clause.

Converting back and forth. Given the deconstructor r/2 and the constructors o/2 and i/2, we can empirically validate the intuitions behind our symbolic representations, by mapping them one-to-one to conventional natural numbers.

We first define a converter s2n/2, mapping tree representations of hereditarily finite sequences to conventional natural numbers:

```
s2n([],0).
s2n(X,R):-o_(X),r(X,S),s2n(S,N),R is 1+2*N.
s2n(X,R):-i_(X),r(X,S),s2n(S,N),R is 2+2*N.
```

then a converter n2s/2 from natural numbers to our symbolic representations:

```
n2s(0,[]).
n2s(N,R):-N>0,P is N mod 2,N1 is (N-1) // 2,
  n2s(N1,X),
  ( P=:=0→i(X,R)
  ; o(X,R)
  ).
```

They work as expected, and s2n can be seen as enumerating the stream of natural numbers correctly.

```
?-n(X),s2n(X,N).
X = [], N = 0 ;
X = [[]], N = 1 ;
X = [[[]]], N = 2 ;
X = [[], []], N = 3 ;
.......
```

Note also that they work in time proportional to the size of the representations.

Efficient Addition. Guided by this mapping, that sees our symbolic representations as if they were bitstrings in *bijective base-2*, we can implement an addition operation working in time proportional to the size of the operands:

```
a([],Y,Y).
a([X|Xs],[],[X|Xs]).
a(X,Y,Z):-o_(X),o_(Y),a1(X,Y,R),   i(R,Z).
a(X,Y,Z):-o_(X),i_(Y),a1(X,Y,R), a2(R,Z).
a(X,Y,Z):-i_(X),o_(Y),a1(X,Y,R), a2(R,Z).
a(X,Y,Z):-i_(X),i_(Y),a1(X,Y,R), s(R,S),i(S,Z).

  a1(X,Y,R):-r(X,RX),r(Y,RY),a(RX,RY,R).
  a2(R,Z):-s(R,S),o(S,Z).
```

To validate the intuitions behind the algorithm one can interpret o_ and i_ as tests for odd and even natural numbers, o(A,B) as B=2*A+1, i(A,B) as B=2*A+2 and r(A,B) as B = (A-1) // 2. After simplifications, one can observe that the relation Z=X+Y holds for each of the clauses. A test on large natural numbers illustrates the fact that its asymptotic efficiency is comparable to its conventional bitstring counterpart.

```
?-n2s(12345678901234567890,A),n2s(10000000000000000000,B),a(A,B,S),s2n(S,N).
A = [[[]], [[[]]], [[]], [], [[]], [[]], [[[...]]], [], []|...],
B = [[[], [], [[[]]]], [[]], [], [], [], [[[]]], [[], []], [[...]]...|...],
S = [[[]], [[[]]], [[]], [], [[]], [[]], [[[...]]], [], []|...],
N = 22345678901234567890 .
```

One can observe that this property holds because each recursive rule reduces its operands to less then "half" (a seen through their mapping to N) and that s and p are asymptotically equivalent to their bitstring counterparts.

Efficient Multiplication. We can implement efficient multiplication guided by intuitions about binary multiplication in base 2 and bijective-base 2 as follows:

```
m([],_,[]).
m(_,[],[]).
m(X,Y,Z):-p(X,X1),p(Y,Y1),m0(X1,Y1,Z1),s(Z1,Z).

m0([],Y,Y).
m0([[]|X],Y,[[]|Z]):- m0(X,Y,Z).
m0(X,Y, Z):-i_(X),r(X,X1),m0(X1,Y,Z1),a(Y,[[]|Z1],Y1),s(Y1,Z).
```

One can see that it handles easily large numbers (the *googol*= 10^{100} included!):

```
?-n2s(12345678901234567890,A),n2s(10000000000000000000,B),m(A,B,S),s2n(S,N).
A = [[[]], [[[]]], [[]], [], [[]], [[]], [[[...]]]], [], []|...],
B = [[[], [], [[[]]]], [[]], [], [], [], [[[]]], [[], [[]], [[...]]]|...],
S = [[[[[]]]], [[]]], [[]], [[]], [[]]], [], [[[[]]]], [[]], []|...],
N = 123456789012345678900000000000000000000000 .

?- n2s((10^100),Googol),m(Googol,Googol,S),s2n(S,N).
Googol = [[[[[]]]], [[[]]], []], [[], [[]], [], [], [], [[], [[]], [[]] |...],
S = [[[[], []], [[[]]], []], [[[[]]]], [], [], [[]], [[[]]], [] |...],
N = 100000000...............0000000000000000000000000000000000000
```

Let $< \mathbb{T}, a, m >$ denote the algebraic structure induced by the operations a and m on the set of ordered rooted trees representing hereditarily finite sequences and $< \mathbb{N}, +, * >$ the corresponding algebraic structure on natural numbers with addition and multiplication. The following holds:

Proposition 5. *The addition and multiplication operations* a/3 *and* m/3 *induce an isomorphism between the semirings with commutative multiplication* $< \mathbb{N}, +, * >$ *and* $< \mathbb{T}, a, m >$.

We conclude this first part of the paper by confessing that inventing (the asymptotically efficient) Horn clause definitions of various arithmetic operations would not have been possible without the "reverse engineering" capabilities provided by the data transformation framework in [1], which has enabled us to move at will between representations like bijective base-2 binary numbers, bit-stacks, hereditarily finite sets, hereditarily finite sequences and watch the internal workings of ordinary operations through functors defined between these domains.

While page limits do not allow us to describe this process in full detail, we have extended these operations to cover, with asymptotic complexity comparable to standard bignum packages, to comparaisons, subtraction, division, powers etc.

5 Computing with Binary Trees Representing Gödel's System T Types

Definition 3. *In Gödel's System* **T** *[5] a type is either N or* $t \to s$ *where t and s are types.*

The basic type N usually stands for the type of natural numbers. We briefly show here that natural numbers can be emulated directly with types, by using a single constant e as basic type, representing 0.

First, we observe that, guided by the known isomorphism between ordered rooted trees and ordered rooted binary trees[1], we can bring with a *functor* defined from hereditarily finite sequences to rooted binary trees the definitions of s/2 and p/2 into corresponding definitions in the language of system **T** types, s_/2 and p_/2.

```
s_(e, (e→e)).
s_(((K→Ks)→Xs), (e→(K1→Xs))) :- p_((K→Ks), K1).
s_((e→Xs), ((K1→Ks)→Ys)) :- s_(Xs, (K→Ys)), s_(K, (K1→Ks)).
```

```
p_((e→e), e).
p_((e→(K→Xs)), ((K1→Ks)→Xs)) :- s_(K, (K1→Ks)).
p_(((K→Ks)→Xs), (e→Zs)) :- p_((K→Ks), K1), p_((K1→Xs), Zs).
```

The following example illustrates that s_ and p_ work as expected:

```
?- s_(e,One),s_(One,Two),s_(Two,Three),s_(Three,Four),p_(Four,Three).
One = (e->e),
Two = ((e->e)->e),
Three = (e->e->e),
Four = (((e->e)->e)->e)
```

We only give here the code of a generator n_/1 for the infinite stream of natural numbers represented as types in system **T**, and a simple converter to usual natural numbers t2n, modeled after tree2nat/2.

```
n_(e).
n_(S):-n_(P),s_(P,S).

t2n(e,0).
t2n((T→S),N):-p_((T→S),U),t2n(U,M),N is M+1.
```

confirming empirically that our computations mimic the usual ones:

```
?-  n_(T),t2n(T,N).
T = e, N = 0 ;
T = (e->e), N = 1 ;
T = ((e->e)->e), N = 2 ;
T = (e->e->e), N = 3 ;
. . .
```

Fast arithmetic computations, operating directly on types, can be derived using the corresponding code for hereditarily finite sequences as "boilerplate".

Deriving a bidirectional successor/predecessor predicate. The predicates s_ and p_ are mutually recursive and structurally similar. Moreover, each of them would

---

[1] That manifests itself in languages like Prolog or LISP as the dual view of lists as a representation of sequences or binary CONS-cell trees.

run reversibly under a breadth-first evaluation order. An interesting challenge is to derive a bidirectional variant replacing both predicates. One could achieve this by using impure operations like nonvar/1 to check which argument is instantiated or, equivalently, checking the instantiation of the arguments using negation as failure. We proceed by merging the two predicates' shared clauses and adding an extra argument taking the values up or down to indicate which way the the computation goes.

```
sp(e, (e->e), _).
sp(((K->Ks)->Xs), (e->(K1->Xs)),Dir) :- flip(Dir,Other),
  sp(K1,(K->Ks), Other).
sp((e->Xs), ((K1->Ks)->Ys), up) :-
  sp(Xs, (K->Ys) ,up),
  sp(K, (K1->Ks), up).

sp((e->Xs), ((K1->Ks)->Ys), down) :-
  sp(K, (K1->Ks), down),
  sp(Xs, (K->Ys) ,down).

flip(up,down).
flip(down,up).

up_or_down(_X,Y,down):- \+(Y=other).
up_or_down(X,_Y,up):- \+(X=other).

sp(X,Y):-up_or_down(X,Y,Dir),sp(X,Y,Dir).
```

Note also the auxiliary predicate flip/2, which indicates a change of direction, and the auxiliary predicate up_or_down, that choses among the two possible directions, based on the instantiation of at least one of the arguments of sp/2. We detect instantiation of the arguments testing them against the atom other, assumed not to be part of the Herbrand Universe of our program.

One step further, we push the call to sp/3 into flip/2 (as it is the only continuation of flip/2), and merge the last two clauses, while delegating the ordering of the recursive calls to the auxiliary predicate order_sp. Note that we also fold up_or_down as part of the definition of sp/2.

```
sp(e, (e→e), _).
sp(((K→Ks)→Xs), (e→(K1→Xs)), Dir):-flip_sp(Dir, K1, (K→Ks)).
sp((e→Xs), ((K1→Ks)→Ys), Dir):-order_sp(Dir, Xs, (K→Ys), K, (K1→Ks)).

flip_sp(up,X,Y)  :- sp(X,Y,down).
flip_sp(down,X,Y) :- sp(X,Y,up).

order_sp(up,A,B,C,D)  :- sp(A,B,up), sp(C,D,up).
order_sp(down,A,B,C,D) :- sp(C,D,down), sp(A,B,down).

sp(X,Y) :- \+(X=other), sp(X,Y,up).
sp(X,Y) :- \+(Y=other), sp(X,Y,down).
```

One can try out `sp/2` working as a bidirectional successor/predecessor predicate when at least one of its arguments is instantiated:

```
?- sp(Pred,((e->e)->e)).
Pred = (e->e) .
```

```
?- sp((e->e),Succ).
Succ = ((e->e)->e) .
```

6   Mapping Hereditarily Finite Sequences to Parenthesis languages

We next explore the bijection between hereditarily finite sequences and the language of balanced parenthesis, known to combinatorialists [6,7,8] as a member of the *Catalan family*, which also includes the ordered rooted binary trees representing `System T` types.

An encoder for the balanced parenthesis language is obtained by combining a parser and a writer, which, with some ingenuity, can be made one and the same in a language like Prolog.

As hereditarily finite sequences naturally map one-to-one to parenthesis expressions expressed as bitstrings, we choose them as target of the transformers. Our parser recurses over a bitstring (encoding balanced parentheses '[' as 0, ']' as 1) and builds a `HFSEQ` tree T:

```
pars_hfseq(Xs,T):-pars2term(0,1,T,Xs,[]).

pars2term(L,R,Xs) ⟶ [L],pars2args(L,R,Xs).

pars2args(_,R,[]) ⟶ [R].
pars2args(L,R,[X|Xs])⟶pars2term(L,R,X),pars2args(L,R,Xs).
```

Note that `pars_hfseq` is *bidirectional* i.e. it works both as an encoder and a decoder:

```
?- pars_hfseq([0,0,1,0,1,1],T),pars_hfseq(Ps,T).
T = [[], []],
Ps = [0, 0, 1, 0, 1, 1]
```

One can see the bijection defined by `pars_hfseq` as a bridge between a family of formal languages and hereditarily finite sequences, represented as ordered rooted trees.

Kraft's inequality. As the sequences computed by `pars_hfseq` are elements of the balanced parenthesis language (also called Dyck primes) [9], they implement *uniquely decodable self-delimiting* codes. Moreover, each of them is also a *prefix code*, i.e. there's no way to add a string made of any combination of balanced left or right parenthesis at the end of a code and obtain another code. For a similar reason, each of them is also a *suffix code*. Such codes are known in the literature under a variety of different names i.e. as *reversible variable-length codes, bifix codes* or *fix-free* codes[2].

In particular, given that they are *uniquely decodable* codes, it follows that the *Kraft inequality* [10] holds for them, i.e. if $l_0, l_1 \ldots l_k \ldots$ denote the length of the codes, then

$$\sum_{k \geq 0} 2^{-l_k} \leq 1 \qquad (6)$$

We define the function computing the left side of the *Kraft* inequality (called *Kraft-sum*), and the corresponding test as follows.

```
kraft_sum(M,S):- M1 is M-1, numlist(0,M1,Ns),
  maplist(kraft_term,Ns,Ls),
  sumlist(Ls,S).

kraft_term(N,X):-parsize(N,L), X is 1/2^L.
```

```
parsize(N,L):- nat2hfseq(N,HFSEQ), pars_hfseq(Xs,HFSEQ), length(Xs,L).

kraft_inequality(M):-kraft_sum(M,S),S=<1.
```

The following example illustrates that the Kraft's inequality holds and it is likely that the Kraft-sum converges to a value below 0.5:

```
?- maplist(kraft_sum,[10,100,1000,2000,3000,4000],R).
R = [0.364258, 0.382935, 0.390383, 0.391615, 0.392292, 0.392598]
```

The bijection between hereditarily finite sequences and balanced parenthesis languages provides a succinct alternative representation for purposes of efficient arithmetic operations using bitvector operations – by encoding the two parenthesis as 0 and 1. As a possible practical application, this allows building in Prolog, at source level, a library supporting arbitrary length arithmetic operations.

7   Related Work

A version of this paper has been presented at the CICLOPS'2011 workshop with only informal proceedings at the arxiv.org repository.

Ranking functions can be traced back to Gödel numberings [11,12] associated to formulae. Together with their inverse *unranking* functions they are also used in combinatorial generation algorithms [13,14]. Natural number encodings of hereditarily finite sets have triggered the interest of researchers in fields ranging from Axiomatic Set Theory and Foundations of Logic to Complexity Theory and Combinatorics [15,16,17].

---

[2] A nice property of such codes is that parallel bidirectional decoding is possible. Also, the ability to decode from either the beginning or the end makes them suitable for encoding media streams.

The encodings of hereditarily finite sets and sequences described in this paper originate in [1,18,19,20]. The key difference is that while in our previous work we use pairs of bijections encapsulated as higher order predicates/functions to define various isomorphisms directly, here we provide actual algorithms for arithmetic operations, ordering etc. while in our previous work the existence of such algorithms was only implied "non-constructively".

In [21] ordered multiway trees and binary trees are used to describe computations with countable ordinals as well as applications to termination analysis. While [21] has a very different focus from our paper, it would be interesting to study in depth the connection between the total order induced by our successor and predecessor functions and ordinal theory.

An emulation of Peano and conventional binary arithmetic operations in Prolog, is described in [22]. Their approach is similar as far as a symbolic representation is used. The key difference with this paper is that our operations work on tree structures, and as such, they are not based on previously known algorithms. Our tree-based algorithms are also likely to support parallel execution in a way similar to the powerlists of [23]. Arithmetic computations with types expressed as C++ templates are described in [24] and in online articles by Oleg Kiselyov using Haskell's type inference mechanism. However, the mechanism advocated there is basically the same as [22], focusing on Peano and binary arithmetics. The connection between hereditarily finite sequences and balanced parenthesis languages places them the context of *Catalan families* [6,7,8], the well known to combinatorialists.

8   Conclusion

We have derived a few algorithms expressing arithmetic computations symbolically, in terms of hereditarily finite sequences and types in Gödel's system **T**.

This has been made possible by extending the techniques introduced in [1] that allow observing the internal working of intricate mathematical concepts through isomorphisms transporting operations between fundamental data types.

At the same time, we have shown that logic programming provides a flexible framework for modeling mathematical concepts from fields as diverse as combinatorics, formal languages, type theory and coding theory.

Arithmetic operations with hereditarily finite sequences are likely to be interesting for hardware (FPGA) implementations of large integer operations used in cryptography. They are also subject to parallelization by adapting techniques introduced by Misra's powerlists [23] and can provide computations with giant numbers that do not fit in any computer memory with a flat bitstring representation[3].

Reversible variable length (bifix) codes like the ones we derived in section 6 have found uses in image and video coding [25] (including MPEG4!). Prefix codes

---

[3] Something as simple as [[[[[[[[]]]]]]]] expresses a very large number - as such numbers correspond to towers of exponents of the form $2^{\cdot^{\cdot^{2^{2}}}}$.

are used in defining modern versions of Kolmogorov complexity [26]. The fact that this property holds, recursively, for arbitrary parts of the code, combined with their *ability to express programming language constructs*, as shown in [1], makes them an interesting alternative to the Elias codes [27] typically used in the field.

Acknowledgment. We thank NSF (research grant 1018172) for support.

References

1. Tarau, P.: An Embedded Declarative Data Transformation Language. In: Proceedings of 11th International ACM SIGPLAN Symposium PPDP 2009, Coimbra, Portugal, pp. 171–182. ACM (September 2009)
2. Tarau, P.: Everything Is Everything Revisited: Shapeshifting Data Types with Isomorphisms and Hylomorphisms. Complex Systems (18) (2010)
3. McCarthy, J.: Recursive functions of symbolic expressions and their computation by machine, part i. Commun. ACM 3(4), 184–195 (1960)
4. Rabin, M.O.: Decidability of second-order theories and automata on infinite trees. Transactions of the American Mathematical Society 141, 1–35 (1969)
5. Gödel, K.: Über eine bisher noch nicht benützte Erweiterung des finiten Standpunktes. Dialectica 12, 280–287 (1958)
6. Berstel, J., Boasson, L.: Formal properties of XML grammars and languages. Acta Informatica 38(9), 649–671 (2002)
7. Liebehenschel, J.: Ranking and unranking of a generalized Dyck language and the application to the generation of random trees. Séminaire Lotharingien de Combinatoire 43, 19 (2000)
8. Bertoni, A., Choffrut, C., Palano, B.: Context-Free Grammars and XML Languages. In: Ibarra, O.H., Dang, Z. (eds.) DLT 2006. LNCS, vol. 4036, pp. 108–119. Springer, Heidelberg (2006)
9. Berstel, J., Boasson, L.: Balanced Grammars and Their Languages. In: Brauer, W., Ehrig, H., Karhumäki, J., Salomaa, A. (eds.) Formal and Natural Computing. LNCS, vol. 2300, pp. 3–25. Springer, Heidelberg (2002)
10. Kraft, L.: A device for quantizing, grouping, and coding amplitude-modulated pulses. Master's thesis, Massachusetts Institute of Technology. Dept. of Electrical Engineering (1949)
11. Gödel, K.: Über formal unentscheidbare Sätze der Principia Mathematica und verwandter Systeme I. Monatshefte für Mathematik und Physik 38, 173–198 (1931)
12. Hartmanis, J., Baker, T.P.: On Simple Goedel Numberings and Translations. In: Loeckx, J. (ed.) ICALP 1974. LNCS, vol. 14, pp. 301–316. Springer, Heidelberg (1974)
13. Martínez, C., Molinero, X.: Generic Algorithms for the Generation of Combinatorial Objects. In: Rovan, B., Vojtáš, P. (eds.) MFCS 2003. LNCS, vol. 2747, pp. 572–581. Springer, Heidelberg (2003)
14. Knuth, D.E.: The Art of Computer Programming. Fascicle 1: Bitwise Tricks & Techniques; Binary Decision Diagrams, vol. 4. Addison-Wesley Professional (2009)
15. Takahashi, M.O.: A Foundation of Finite Mathematics. Publ. Res. Inst. Math. Sci. 12(3), 577–708 (1976)

16. Kaye, R., Wong, T.L.: On Interpretations of Arithmetic and Set Theory. Notre Dame J. Formal Logic 48(4), 497–510 (2007)
17. Kirby, L.: Addition and multiplication of sets. Math. Log. Q. 53(1), 52–65 (2007)
18. Tarau, P.: A Groupoid of Isomorphic Data Transformations. In: Carette, J., Dixon, L., Coen, C.S., Watt, S.M. (eds.) Calculemus/MKM 2009. LNCS (LNAI), vol. 5625, pp. 170–185. Springer, Heidelberg (2009)
19. Tarau, P.: Isomorphisms, Hylomorphisms and Hereditarily Finite Data Types in Haskell. In: Proceedings of ACM SAC 2009, Honolulu, Hawaii, pp. 1898–1903. ACM (March 2009)
20. Tarau, P.: Declarative Combinatorics: Isomorphisms, Hylomorphisms and Hereditarily Finite Data Types in Haskell, pages 150 (January 2009), unpublished draft, http://arXiv.org/abs/0808.2953, updated version at http://logic.cse.unt.edu/tarau/research/2010/ISO.pdf
21. Dershowitz, N.: Trees, Ordinals and Termination. In: Gaudel, M., Jouannaud, J. (eds.) CAAP 1993, FASE 1993, and TAPSOFT 1993. LNCS, vol. 668, pp. 243–250. Springer, Heidelberg (1993)
22. Kiselyov, O., Byrd, W.E., Shan, C.-c.: Pure, Declarative, and Constructive Arithmetic Relations (Declarative Pearl). In: Garrigue, J., Hermenegildo, M. (eds.) FLOPS 2008. LNCS, vol. 4989, pp. 64–80. Springer, Heidelberg (2008)
23. Misra, J.: Powerlist: a structure for parallel recursion. ACM Transactions on Programming Languages and Systems 16, 1737–1767 (1994)
24. Kiselyov, O.: Type arithmetics: Computation based on the theory of types. CoRR cs.CL/0104010 (2001)
25. Wen, J., Villasenor, J.: Reversible variable length codes for efficient and robust image and video coding. In: Proceedings Data Compression Conference, pp. 471–480 (1998)
26. Li, M., Vitányi, P.: An introduction to Kolmogorov complexity and its applications. Springer-Verlag New York, Inc., New York (1993)
27. Elias, P.: Universal codeword sets and representations of the integers. IEEE Transactions on Information Theory 21(2), 194–203 (1975)

Typing the Numeric Tower

Vincent St-Amour[1], Sam Tobin-Hochstadt[1], Matthew Flatt[2], and Matthias Felleisen[1]

[1] Northeastern University
{stamourv,samth,matthias}@ccs.neu.edu
[2] University of Utah
mflatt@cs.utah.edu

Abstract. In the past, the creators of numerical programs had to choose between simple expression of mathematical formulas and static type checking. While the Lisp family and its dynamically typed relatives support the straightforward expression via a rich numeric tower, existing statically typed languages force programmers to pollute textbook formulas with explicit coercions or unwieldy notation. In this paper, we demonstrate how the type system of Typed Racket accommodates both a textbook programming style and expressive static checking. The type system provides a hierarchy of numeric types that can be freely mixed as well as precise specifications of sign, representation, and range information—all while supporting generic operations. In addition, the type system provides information to the compiler so that it can perform standard numeric optimizations.

1 Designing the Numeric Tower

From the classic two-line factorial program to financial applications to scientific computation to graphics software, programs rely on numbers and numeric computations. Because of this spectrum of numeric applications, programmers wish to use a wide variety of numbers: the inductively defined natural numbers, fixed-width integers, floating-point numbers, complex numbers, etc. Supporting this variety demands careful attention to the design of programming languages that manipulate numbers.

Most languages have taken one of two approaches to numbers. Many untyped languages, drawing on the tradition of Lisp and Smalltalk, provide a hierarchy of numbers whose various levels can be freely used together, known as the *numeric tower*. For example, the following Racket expression mixes arbitrary precision integers with inexact floating-point numbers and produces a complex result:

```
(sqrt (/ 3.14159 (- (expt 2 32))))
```

That is, the numeric tower supports concise expression of mathematical formulas.

Other languages provide static checking of various numeric operations, ensuring that results conform to machine representations of numbers. Static checking helps programmers reason about the requirements, behavior, and performance of their programs. Some languages also provide a limited ability to combine different forms of numbers together in arithmetic operations for a small set of numeric representations. No existing typed language provides as rich a numeric hierarchy nor as many generic operations as those found in Smalltalk, Scheme, or Racket.

C. Russo and N.-F. Zhou (Eds.): PADL 2012, LNCS 7149, pp. 289–303, 2012.

In this paper, we describe the design of the numeric tower in Typed Racket (Tobin-Hochstadt and Felleisen 2008), which combines expressiveness with static checking. Typed Racket is an explicitly and statically typed sister language to Racket, a mostly-functional language (Flatt and PLT 2010). Using Typed Racket, programmers may convert untyped Racket programs by adding explicit type declarations. In the existing type system, we can encode fine distinctions in the hierarchy of numeric types and express numerous mathematical properties of numeric operations in their types. Combining these features allows programmers to state and enforce static properties about their numeric programs while maintaining the concise mathematical expression of untyped Racket. Furthermore, we can reuse standard optimization techniques to reap the performance benefits of static typing.

Three features of Typed Racket support this design. Due to *true union types* (Buneman and Pierce 1999) the choices of numeric types do not need to reflect the underlying runtime representation of numbers nor do they affect the representation. For example, Integer is the union of positive and negative integers, yet Racket's run-time representation has no knowledge of this division. Due to *overloading with intersection types* (Coppo and Dezani-Ciancaglini 1978; Reynolds 1988) the type system supports precise specification of the behavior of numeric operations such as + without necessitating multiple implementations. Thus it can express that adding two positive integers produces a positive integer and adding a negative integer to a negative floating point number produces a negative floating point value. Due to *occurrence typing* (Tobin-Hochstadt and Felleisen 2008, 2010) the type checker can "lower" the numeric types of variables based on dynamic tests including predicates and numeric comparisons.

The remainder of the paper begins with a series of examples that illustrate Typed Racket's approach to numeric computations. We then describe the encoding of the type hierarchy in section 3, the typing of numeric operations using overloading in section 4, and the use of occurrence typing to refine types in section 5. Finally, in section 6, we describe our implementation, focusing on challenges concerning usability.

2 A Rich Numeric Tower

We introduce Typed Racket and its approach to numeric programming with a series of small examples. The mathematical absolute value function, $|-|$, takes real numbers to non-negative real numbers. As figure 1 shows, a programmer can naturally express this simple fact via types. Furthermore, the function definition itself transliterates the textbook definition of abs into the concrete syntax of a functional programming language; Typed Racket's type system accomplishes the rest.

The pythagorean function also benefits from encoding sign information in the type system. Racket's sqrt function, like its mathematical counterpart, optionally may yield complex numbers. Programmers often write programs, however, that depend on real-valued results from sqrt. To accommodate the latter, the type of sqrt in Typed Racket maps non-negative reals to non-negative reals. Because the square of any real number is provably always non-negative and the sum of two non-negative numbers is also non-negative, the type system can validate that the length of the hypotenuse of any right triangle is non-negative. See the type of the pythagorean function in figure 1.

```
(: abs : Real → Nonnegative-Real)
(define (abs x) (if (> x 0) x (- x)))
```

```
(: pythagorean : Real Real → Nonnegative-Real)
(define (pythagorean a b) (sqrt (+ (sqr a) (sqr b))))
```

```
(: nat->hex : Natural → (Listof Byte))
(define (nat->hex n)
  (cond [(= n 0) '()]
        [else (cons (modulo n 16) (nat->hex (quotient n 16)))]))
```

```
(: sum-vector : (Vectorof Integer) → Integer)
(define (sum-vector v)
  (define n (vector-length v))
  (let loop ([i 0] [sum 0])
    (if (< i n) (loop (+ i 1) (+ sum (vector-ref v i))) sum)))
```

```
(: gen-random : Float Float → Float)
(define (gen-random min max)
  (next) (+ min (/ (* (- max min) x) p)))
(define p (- (expt 2 31) 1))
(define A (expt 7 5))
(define x 42) ; state of the PRNG
(define (next) (set! x (modulo (* A x) p))) ; x_{i+1} ≡ A · x_i (mod p)
```

Fig. 1. Numeric programs in Typed Racket

Sign properties are a special case of range properties, another common set of properties that programmers want to establish. For instance, two program fragments may need to communicate via a protocol that limits the range of encoded values. A type system that supports subtyping and overloading makes it possible to mix and match fixed-width and unbounded integers, both widely used by Racket programmers. Hence, programmers can have the mathematically correct behavior of unbounded integers as the default and may still enforce range properties when desired, without explicit coercions.

In the third example of figure 1, Typed Racket's type system guarantees that the result of (modulo n 16) fits within a byte. Arguments to nat->hex can be unbounded integers, and the range properties still hold. Similarly, in the fourth example, the type system guarantees that i is of type Index, which is bounded by the maximum length of Racket vectors. This ensures that vector index computations are performed directly using machine arithmetic instead of costly arbitrary precision operations; all index computations in sum-vector use machine integers directly. Furthermore, the results of these functions can be freely mixed with unbounded integers in subsequent computations, without introducing explicit coercions.

The ability to freely mix numbers from different levels of the numeric tower in arithmetic expressions is another convenience of blackboard mathematics that is important for programmers. Again, many type systems require explicit coercions for mixed value expressions, as in Standard ML, Ocaml or Haskell, or provide a limited set of built-in implicit coercions, as in C or Java. A type system that can encode the promotion rules of arithmetic operations when used on operands of mixed types saves the programmer from having to repeatedly encode these rules in his programs in an ad-hoc manner.

The last example in figure 1 presents an implementation of Lewis et al. (1969)'s multiplicative congruential pseudo-random number generator that features mixed-type arithmetic with integer and floating-point numbers. Local type inference (Pierce and Turner 2000) determines that p, A and x are of type Integer and both arguments to gen-random (min and max) are of type Float. In the boldface section, the result of the subtraction, a floating-point number, is multiplied by an integer, which results in a floating-point number. This implementation is structurally that of a textbook; the actual mathematical operations are unobscured by coercions or other artifacts.

3   Encoding the Numeric Hierarchy

To encode arithmetic specifications, a type system must classify numbers. For example, if a type system is to encode specifications involving sign properties, it needs to distinguish between positive and negative numbers at the type level. To reason about exactness of results, a type system needs to encode exactness of numbers as part of their type. We express distinctions along these axes using true unions and subtyping.

3.1   Union Types

Typed Racket provides general union types. For example, (U Integer Float) contains all integers as well as all floating-point numbers. Subtyping follows the usual rules for union types, e.g., both the Integer type and Float type are subtypes of (U Integer Float). It thus is possible to use either an integer or a floating-point number as a value of the union without injection.

Since true unions do not add tags to the values of their constituents, they do not impose constraints on the underlying machine-level representation of data, which has several benefits. First, we can overlay a type hierarchy on top of Racket's existing representations, without requiring changes to the compiler and runtime. Second, we can make finer-grained distinctions at the type level than at the representation level. For example, while Racket uses the same IEEE 754 floating-point representation scheme for positive and negative floating-point numbers, Typed Racket distinguishes the two at the type level by providing both a Positive-Float and a Negative-Float type. Finally, because we build our numeric types as unions of non-overlapping base types, the intersection of any two numeric types is necessarily a union of some of those non-overlapping base types and thus denotes a valid type. Therefore, we reap some of the benefits of useful intersection types without the need for general intersection types.

3.2 Layers of Numbers

Figure 2 shows Typed Racket's *layers* of the numeric hierarchy. Most layers correspond to well-known sets, such as integers, rationals, and complex numbers. Others correspond to numbers with specific machine representations, such as floating-point.

These layers are similar to the numeric types offered by most programming languages. In addition to the usual integer and floating-point layers, Typed Racket offers exact rationals and both exact and floating-point complex numbers. Members of these layers are integrated with the rest of the numeric tower: operations on numbers from other layers of the tower can produce rationals or complex numbers. For example, the result of dividing 2 by 5 is the fraction $\frac{2}{5}$. Rationals and complex numbers can also be mixed freely with numbers from the other layers of the tower; e.g., the addition of the rational $\frac{2}{5}$ and the integer 3 yields the rational $\frac{17}{5}$.

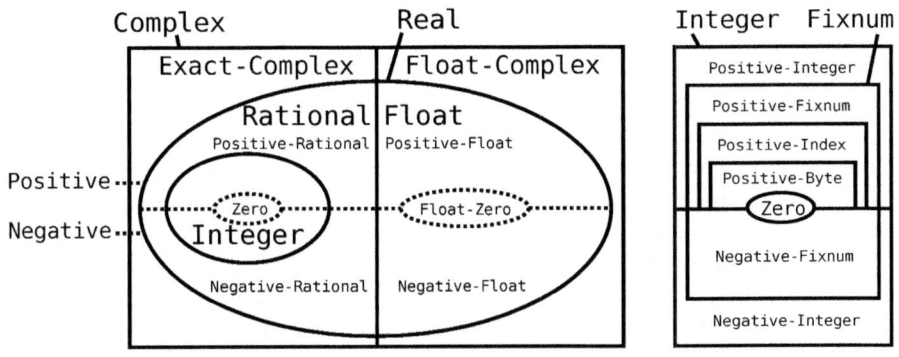

Fig. 2. Typed Racket's numeric type hierarchy, with signs

Layers are related by subtyping in the expected fashion; Integer is a subtype of Rational, which is a subtype of Real. Float is also a subtype of Real. All numeric types in Typed Racket are subtypes of Complex. For convenience, Typed Racket provides a Number type as a synonym for Complex; we use the two interchangeably.

3.3 Signed Types

As a refinement of layers, Typed Racket distinguishes numbers based on their sign. Typed Racket offers positive and negative subdivisions of all layers except Complex, as well as types for integer zero and for both of the floating-point zeroes, producing types such as Positive-Integer and Negative-Rational.

In addition, unions can express types such as Natural, which corresponds to the union of Positive-Integer and Zero, the type of the integer zero. It would be possible to subdivide the Complex layer into quadrants to achieve a similar effect.

The different zero types are singleton types that contain only the appropriate zero. Singleton types for first-order values are straightforward, and fit nicely in our subtyping hierarchy. For convenience, a Float-Zero type containing both floating-point zeroes is provided, as well as a Real-Zero type that also includes the integer zero. Since these different zero values cause distinct behavior when used as arguments, we distinguish them both at the type level as well as at the value level. As explained in section 5, zero types are most useful for comparisons. Since comparisons are not defined on complex numbers, complex zero types are of limited usefulness and are not provided.

As expected, the sign distinctions preserve the subtyping of layers: Positive-Integer is a subtype of Positive-Rational. In addition, signed subsets are subtypes of their parent layer: Positive-Integer is also a subtype of Integer. In fact, Integer is the union of Positive-Integer, Negative-Integer and Zero. Similarly, the Positive type is the union of the "positive" types. Figure 2 shows how sign distinctions refine the numeric hierarchy; see the dotted lines.

3.4   Encoding Range Information

The integer layer is further subdivided into fixed-width integer types, corresponding to different ranges. The Byte type contains the integers from 0 to 255, the Index type is bounded by zero and the length of the longest possible Racket vector. The Fixnum type contains all integers that Racket stores as tagged machine integers on every platform.[1] Those ranges capture a large number of use cases in existing Racket programs. Other ranges could be provided as needed. To prevent base types from overlapping, we fix the ranges when implementing the type system. In addition, bounds on range types are static; bounds cannot depend on values, unlike in dependently-typed systems.

Sign distinctions can also apply to these types to express types such as Positive-Byte or Negative-Fixnum. These types are also related by subtyping: Byte is a subtype of Index, which is a subtype of Nonnegative-Fixnum. Figure 2 shows a close-up view of the subdivisions of the integer layer.

4   Typing Operations

To exploit our numeric tower, we need type signatures for primitive operations that are generic and yet as tightly specified as possible. For example, if x and y are Integers, then (+ x y) is also an Integer, yet if x and y are Float-Complex numbers, then that should be the result type as well. In this section, we present both the properties of our basic type environment and the mechanisms for expressing such properties.

4.1   Overloading with Ordered Intersection Types

Untyped Racket already provides overloading for numeric operations. The function + produces exact results when given exact inputs, and otherwise produces inexact results. The challenge for Typed Racket is to represent these overloadings in the type system and to refine them using the distinctions that only exist in the type environment.

We use *ordered intersection types* to express the multiple possible behaviors of numeric operations. Intersection types (Coppo and Dezani-Ciancaglini 1978; Reynolds

---

[1] This last point is discussed further in section 6.4.

1988) are well known in the type system literature and have been extensively studied in many contexts. In their most general form, intersection types are too expressive and undecidable. Typed Racket instead offers a pragmatic flavor of intersections of function types.[2] To increase the predictability of the system for programmers, intersections of function types are considered in order, with earlier types taking precedence over later types.[3] Thus, the following types are equivalent in Typed Racket:

$$\top \rightarrow \top \qquad (\top \rightarrow \top) \wedge (\texttt{Integer} \rightarrow \texttt{Integer})$$

because $\top$ is a supertype of Integer, and thus the first conjunct applies in all possible cases. Typed Racket provides the case→ type constructor to build function intersection types. Using this type constructor, we can express this fragment of the type of +:

```
(: + (case→ (Integer Integer → Integer)
            (Float   Float   → Float)
            (Number  Number  → Number)))
```

Although intersection types are useful for functions that branch based on their input type, conditionals are not required. For example, this program type checks:

```
(: f (case→ (Number → Number) (String → Number))
(define (f x) 0))
```

A function definition with an intersection type must check properly for *each* branch in the intersection, but no other restrictions are imposed.

In the remainder of this section, we consider several varieties of numeric operations, and show how fine-grained numeric types and overloading via ordered intersections help us express a variety of semantic properties in our type system.

4.2 Simple Numeric Operations

The most basic use of overloading for numeric operations is to express the closure properties of arithmetic operations such as + and *. For example, the type of + includes conjuncts specifying that the sum of two Integers is an Integer, and that the sum of two Real numbers is also Real. These properties hold for * as well.

Signed types provide scope for expressing useful mathematical properties. For example, the type fragment

```
(Negative-Real Negative-Real → Positive-Real)
```

expresses that * produces positive real numbers when given negative inputs. Using overloading, the types of *, /, and other operations can express these properties precisely.

Range-bounded types are trickier, because they enjoy fewer closure properties. For example, the sum of two Indexes may not be an Index itself, because integer addition

---

[2] Intersections of function types are especially interesting because they reify overloading.

[3] The need for ordered intersection types is further motivated by Racket's case-lambda construct whose operational behavior calls for an ordered execution of clauses.

in Racket can exceed the length of the largest possible vector. However, the sum of two Indexes *is* a Fixnum.

Further, Racket and Typed Racket support mixed-typed arithmetic. Hence, the types of primitive operations must describe this behavior as well. For example, the sum of a Float and an Integer is a Float by the promotion rules for addition.

4.3   Other Operations

Many numeric operations in Racket have semantic properties that are expressible using the combination of overloading and our numeric type hierarchy. For example, the modulo operation, when given a bounded modulus, produces a bounded result. This property is key to typing the nat->hex function in figure 1. Other operations that are given similarly expressive types include floor, ceiling, and round.

Coercion operators can also be precisely typed using overloading. The function exact->inexact, which converts exact integers and rationals to floating point values, comes with a type that includes the clauses Real $\rightarrow$ Float and Complex $\rightarrow$ Float-Complex.

Finally, some operations have special properties on parts of their domain. The sqrt function potentially produces Complex results, but it produces Nonnegative-Reals for non-negative inputs. The pythagorean function in figure 1 relies on this overloading to prove that the third side of a right triangle always has non-negative length.

5   Refining Types with Dynamic Tests

In many cases programs use dynamic tests to determine properties of numeric values. The Typed Racket type system uses occurrence typing (Tobin-Hochstadt and Felleisen 2008, 2010) to refine the types in the program using dynamic type tests such as exact-integer? and positive?. In addition, we can also express useful properties of comparison operators using occurrence typing, thus refining types even further.

5.1   Numeric Predicates

The key idea of occurrence typing is expressed with the abs function from figure 1:

```
(: abs : Real → Nonnegative-Real)
(define (abs x) (if (positive? x) x (- x)))
```

To check this function, the type checker proceeds as follows.

- The function signature assigns Real to x.
- Based on (positive? x), the type system determines that if the condition holds, x must have the type Positive in the *then* branch.
- Since restricting Real to Positive produces a subtype of Nonnegative-Real, the *then* branch type checks correctly.
- In the *else* branch, the type of x must be both a Real and not Positive, yielding the Nonpositive-Real type, which via negation yields the Nonnegative-Real type, as desired.

To express that `positive?` determines whether its argument has type `Positive`, its type is

$$\text{positive?} \ : \ \left(x : \text{Real} \xrightarrow{\text{Positive}_x} \text{Boolean} \right)$$

The annotation above the arrow is a *proposition* about the parameter x. Specifically, it says that x is positive if the result is true and it is not positive otherwise. With types such as this one, Typed Racket understands many more numeric predicates than simply `positive?`, including `real?`, `inexact?`, `fixnum?` and others.

Because Typed Racket has a precise type hierarchy, a wide variety of predicates can refine types. For example, `Positive` is a union of positive integers represented both as machine integers and bignums, as well as positive exact rationals and positive floating point numbers. A type hierarchy with coarser-grained distinctions would sacrifice some of the precision available for describing the behavior of `positive?`.

Another advantage of occurrence typing in combination with numeric predicates is that it greatly reduces the need for explicit downward coercions within the numeric hierarchy. For example, the following function verifies that its input is an exact integer:

```
(: assert-exact-integer : Any → Integer)
(define (assert-exact-integer in)
  (if (exact-integer? input) in (error "not an integer")))
```

Without occurrence typing, this program would require an explicit injection into the exact integer type. Instead, we leverage both the untagged union representation of Racket numbers and the handling of predicates by the type system to avoid coercions.

5.2 Comparison Operators

While occurrence typing is useful for predicates, programmers are more likely to employ comparison operators than predicates in numerical programs. Returning to the `abs` function, we can rewrite its body to use a comparison and it still type checks:

```
(if (> x 0) x (- x))
```

From the programmer's perspective, the two versions of the function are identical. The `>` function is not a predicate, however. We can still use the expressiveness of the types to encode this information in the type of `>`, leading to (among other overloadings):

$$> \ : \ \left(x : \text{Real} \ y : \text{Zero} \xrightarrow{\text{Positive}_x} \text{Boolean} \right)$$

That is, when the second argument (y) of `>` is `Zero`, the result of the comparison is true only if the first argument (x) is `Positive`.

Comparison with distinguished integer literals is a special case that appears only in a few types of the base environment. More commonly, comparison operators are used as in the `sum-vector` function given in figure 1. Its definition is

```
(define (sum-vector v)
  (define n (vector-length v))
  (let loop ([i 0] [sum 0])
    (if (< i n) (loop (+ i 1) (+ sum (vector-ref v i))) sum)))
```

There are several aspects of this definition to note. First, n is the result of vector-length, which must be of type Index. Second, i is initially 0 and it is only incremented, classifying it as a Natural. Now, when we consider the comparison operation, we see that if (< i n) is true, then i must be both greater than 0 and smaller than the largest possible vector, meaning that i must be an Index itself in the *then* branch. This is exactly the needed information to prove that i is *always* a Fixnum, allowing the compiler to optimize both the addition and comparison to use simple and efficient machine instructions.

To express this information, we again use the mechanism of associating propositions about argument types with the boolean result of functions:

$$< : \left(x : \texttt{Natural} \; y : \texttt{Index} \xrightarrow{\texttt{Index}_x} \texttt{Boolean} \right)$$

Further, this technique applies to comparison operators for all range-bounded types, such as Fixnum, as well as signed types such as Negative.

Using occurrence typing in conjunction with overloadings of comparison operators, Typed Racket can automatically prove tight bounds on numeric types based solely on the dynamic checks *already present* in programs. This supports both optimization and static checking for programs such as sum-vector.

6   Implementation

Over the past year, we implemented the type environment of sections 3 through 5 in Typed Racket without changing the basic type system. More precisely, the type assignment for the primitive operations now encodes basic mathematical theorems. Building a practical type system from these encodings has posed some challenges, however. We discuss the interesting ones in this section.

6.1   Precise Types and Invariance

While it is generally desirable to assign precise types that include sign and range information, doing so can sometimes lead to unexpected behavior. Consider the program

```
(define x (box 3))
(set-box! x 2000)
```

This program defines a mutable box that contains the integer 3. The most precise type we can locally infer for 3 is Positive-Byte, and if we were willing to use this type, x could be assigned the type (Boxof Positive-Byte). This type assignment implies, however, that attempting to set the contents of x to 2000 is a type error. Similar issues arise with any invariant type constructor.

Although this behavior is perfectly correct from a theoretical perspective, it has severe usability drawbacks. In the code bases we studied, initializing a box with a small integer, often zero, and later assigning significantly larger ones is a common occurrence. We therefore make this common case the default.

This decision means that the typechecker generalizes types that are used as arguments to invariant type constructors. In the above example, Positive-Byte would be generalized to Natural, and x would be of type (Boxof Natural), which is more broadly useful. Generalization requires balancing of course. For example, we could use Complex instead of Natural, but doing so would discard all the information contained in the original type. The generalization function takes into account heuristics inspired by our corpus of numeric Racket programs as well as feedback from users of Typed Racket.

Finally, programmers can override the results of local type inference with explicit annotations to assign more permissive or restrictive types.

6.2   Precise Types and Arguments

Precise types make it possible to enforce interesting numerical properties, but it may be inconvenient to enforce them at all times. For example, we could restrict vector-ref, which indexes into a vector, to accept only indices of type Index, which are guaranteed to not exceed the length of the longest possible vector.

An experiment with this choice indicates, however, that it leads to severe usability issues in practice. Consider this variant of sum-vector from figure 1:

```
(define (sum-vector v)
  (define n (vector-length v))
  (let loop ([i (- n 1)] [sum 0])
    (if (> i -1) (loop (- i 1) (+ sum (vector-ref v i))) sum)))
```

This loop should produce identical results to the original version of sum-vector, despite iterating backwards over the input vector. In this case though, the index i cannot be assigned the Index type, since its value is -1 for the last iteration of the loop. If we enforce that vector-ref can only accept indices of type Index, this program would not type check and the programmer would have to rewrite the loop to appease the type checker. Our experience suggests that this typechecking failure is both confusing and frustrating to programmers.

To avoid such usability problems, our type system abides by Postel's law (Postel 1980) as a guiding principle for the types of the Typed Racket standard library. Library functions typically feature somewhat permissive argument types—vector-ref accepts Integer as an index, and errors if necessary—and the most precise return type possible. That way, the proof obligations do not overwhelm the programmer. And yet, programmers can benefit from precise return types when they do want to enforce stricter properties in their own code.

Thus, if a program wants to communicate that vector indices can only be of type Index, it is possible:

```
(: picky-vector-ref : (∀ (X) (Vectorof X) Index → X))
(define picky-vector-ref vector-ref)
```

Since the new restrictive type is a subtype of the original type of vector-ref, the program typechecks just fine. This technique could also be used to statically enforce that the second argument of the division operator cannot be zero.

6.3   Printing Types

Encoding properties in types means types become large. Although manipulating, and operating on, such large types intuitively impacts type-checking time, we have not noticed a significant impact in practice. The large size of these types is problematic, however, when a programmer must see them.

Error reporting is the most important point of contact between programmers and the types of primitives. If a function is given arguments of the wrong type, an error message is displayed, along with the valid argument types of this function. By displaying the domains of the function, the error informs the programmer of what constitutes a valid argument to the function. As such, this type is useful information.

Unfortunately, the large number of cases in some numeric types causes an explosion in the size of error messages. An example of such an error message is shown in the left column of figure 3. Each of these domains are associated to a different return type: adding two Bytes results in an Index, adding two Floats results in a Float, and so on. It makes sense to have all these domains as part of the type, but this information does not belong in error messages. If a programmer passes a string to the + function, the error message should merely say that + accepts only numbers.

To reduce the extraneous information in error messages, the type checker filters out domains that are subtypes of other domains. In the above example, since all domains are subtypes of Number, only this last one is displayed, as shown in the right column of figure 3. The error message is just as informative and much easier to digest than the original. This heuristic also ensures that the type checker does not discard unrelated domains. For example, if a function has just two domains, Integer and Float, both are present in the error message because they are unrelated by subtyping. This is desirable because both branches carry useful information.

In addition, before filtering subsumed domains, we remove any domains that would lead to results that are inconsistent with the expected return type. For example, if the type checker expects an Integer as the result of an application of +, it can safely discard domains involving Float and Complex. After this initial filtering, it can remove subsumed domains as before. As a result, the error message that is shown when applying + with an expected type of Integer mentions only Integer.

The same techniques are used when printing types at the REPL, which is the other important point of contact between programmers and types. Full types can be displayed on demand if programmers want to explore them.

```
> (+ 1 "A")
Type Checker: No function domains
  matched in function application:
Domains:
  Zero Zero
  Zero Positive-Byte
  Byte Positive-Byte
  Byte Byte
          ... <snip 58 lines> ...
  Real Real
  Float-Complex Number
  Number Float-Complex
  Number Number
Arguments: Positive-Byte String
 in: (+ 1 "A")
```

```
> (+ 1 "A")
Type Checker: No function domains
  matched in function application:
Domains: Number Number
Arguments: Positive-Byte String
  in: (+ 1 "A")
```

Fig. 3. Original typechecking error message versus simplified error message

6.4 Typechecking Literals

Finally, the fine-grained distinctions among types affect the type-checking of literals. When assigning a type to a literal, the typechecker needs to know where that literal falls with regards to the divisions discussed previously. Since the typechecker has access to the value of literals, this is for the most part straightforward. Portability between platforms complicates matters, however, and compiled Racket programs are portable. In particular, it is possible to typecheck and compile a program on one architecture and to run it on a different one. While the range of integers that fit within a byte is constant, the range of numbers that Racket stores as tagged machine integers is architecture-dependent. Hence, the typechecker must make conservative assumptions and assigns fixed-width integer types only if it is correct to do so on all architectures supported by Racket. For this reason, the Index type is limited to the closed interval $[0, 2^{28} - 1]$ and Fixnum is limited to $[-2^{30}, 2^{30} - 1]$.

6.5 Optimization

Numeric types guide compiler optimizations, and the Typed Racket compiler (Tobin-Hochstadt et al. 2011) is no exception. It reuses existing optimization technology with few major changes. Most of the time, the optimizer ignores the fine-grained distinctions, for example, the distinctions among the various subtypes of Float. Doing so gives the compiler a view similar to what optimizers would see in other typed languages, making the reuse of existing optimization techniques straightforward. Examples of numeric optimizations performed by the Typed Racket compiler are dispatch elimination, unboxing and arity-raising of complex number operations.[4]

---

[4] Wright and Cartwright (1997)'s typing efforts for Scheme-like languages, as well as those of others, lacked the expressive power to distinguish between different classes of numbers and to optimize numeric code in this fashion.

7   Related Work

Many dynamic languages, such as Common Lisp (Steele Jr. 1994), Scheme (Sperber et al. 2009) and Smalltalk (Goldberg and Robson 1983) provide numeric towers. They also allow for mixed-type arithmetic and dynamically moving from one level of the tower to another. As far as programmer convenience is concerned, they offer most of the benefits of Typed Racket. Due to their dynamic nature, however, these languages provide little in terms of static checking. Other dynamic languages such as Python, and Ruby provide mixed type arithmetic and a numeric tower, but with fewer types, typically omitting exact rationals, complex numbers, and sometimes arbitary size integers as well.

Languages in the SIMULA 67 (Dahl 1968) tradition such as Java (Gosling et al. 2005), C (ISO 1999) and C++ (Stroustrup 2000) provide static checking, but let programmers escape the type system. These languages provide mixed-type arithmetic for a small number of specific cases, but beyond that, programmers have to rely on labor-intensive operator overloading tricks in C++ or settle for an inconvenient notation. Typed functional languages, such as Haskell (Marlow 2010), Standard ML (Milner et al. 1997) and Ocaml (Leroy et al. 2010) provide static checking equivalent to numeric layers alone without subtyping. Haskell provides a large and extensible set of layers, but it does not support the sign and range properties of Typed Racket. Also, each of these languages have different stances on overloading. Ocaml does not provide any overloading for numeric operations. Programmers must choose between the + and +. operators depending on whether they are adding integers or floating-point numbers respectively. SML provides overloading in a small number of cases in the same way Java does. Finally, Haskell's type classes provide overloading, but disallow mixed-type arithmetic. Special handling of literals makes mixed-type arithmetic unnecessary in some cases, but in general explicit coercions between numeric types are necessary.

Finally, the Habit (Jones 2010) language is a dialect of Haskell for systems programming. Its type system enforces arithmetic properties about integers, provides a large variety of fixed-width integer types and aims to provide a large array of strong static guarantees. However, this significantly increases the proof obligation on the programmer. Although the kinds of guarantees Habit provides are valuable when writing highly reliable systems software, the costs of these guarantees are inconvenient for a general-purpose language. In addition, Habit focuses on integers and does not seem to provide support for interesting properties of other numeric layers.

8   Conclusion

To facilitate numeric programming in Typed Racket, we have supplemented an existing practical type system with a base type environment that supports rich specification, concise expression, static checking and effective optimization. The environment makes crucial use of several existing Typed Racket features: union types for defining a precise numeric hierarchy, function overloading via intersection types for expressing properties of operations, and occurrence typing for reasoning about predicates and comparisons.

Our design supports both the convenience of a numeric tower as found in untyped languages as well as the static checking available with modern typed languages. Additionally, we support strong specifications expressing sign, range, and layer information about numeric values. Our Typed Racket implementation demonstrates the effectiveness of the approach both in typechecking existing code as well as providing static information for effective optimizations of numeric programs.

References

1. Buneman, P., Pierce, B.: Union types for semistructured data. In: Proc. Works. On Database Programming Languages, pp. 184–207 (1999)
2. Coppo, M., Dezani-Ciancaglin, M.: A new type assignment for λ-terms. Archiv Math. Logik 19, 139–156 (1978)
3. Dahl, O.-J.: SIMULA 67 Common Base Language. Norwegian Computing Center (1968)
4. Flatt, M., PLT.: Reference: Racket. PLT Inc., PLT-TR-2010-1 (2010), `http://racket-lang.org/tr1/`
5. Goldberg, A., Robson, D.: Smalltalk-80: the Language and its Implementation. Addison-Wesley (1983)
6. Gosling, J., Joy, B., Steele Jr., G.L., Bracha, G.: The Java™ Language Specification, 4th edn. Addison-Wesley (2005)
7. ISO. ISO C Standard 1999 (1999)
8. Jones, M.P.: The Habit programming language: the revised preliminary report (2010)
9. Leroy, X., Doligez, D., Frisch, A., Garrigue, J., Rémy, D., Vouillon, J.: The Objective Caml system, Documentation and user's manual (2010)
10. Lewis, P.A.W., Goodman, A.S., Miller, J.M.: A pseudo-random number generator for the System/360. IBM Systems Journal 8(2), 136–146 (1969)
11. Marlow, S. (ed.): Haskell 2010 Language Report (2010)
12. Milner, R., Tofte, M., Harper, R., MacQueen, D.: The Definition of Standard ML, Revised edn. MIT Press (1997)
13. Pierce, B.C., Turner, D.N.: Local type inference. ACM Transactions on ProgrammingLanguages and Systems 22(1), 1–44 (2000)
14. Postel, J.: DoD standard Transmission control protocol. IETF RFC 761 (1980)
15. Reynolds, J.C.: Preliminary design of the programming language Forsythe. Technical report CMU-CS-88-159, Carnegie-Mellon University (1988)
16. Sperber, M., Flatt, M., Van Straaten, A., Kent Dybvig, R., Findler, R.B., Matthews, J.: Revised[6] report on the algorithmic language Scheme. J. of Functional Programming 19(S1), 1–301 (2009)
17. Steele Jr., G.L.: Common Lisp: the Language, 2nd edn. Digital Press (1994)
18. Stroustrup, B.: The C++ Programming Language, 3rd edn. Addison-Wesley (2000)
19. Tobin-Hochstadt, S., Felleisen, M.: The design and implementation of Typed Scheme. In: Proc. Symp. on Principles of Programming Languages, pp. 395–406 (2008)
20. Tobin-Hochstadt, S., Felleisen, M.: Logical types for untyped languages. In: Proc. International Conf. on Functional Programming, pp. 117–128 (2010)
21. Tobin-Hochstadt, S., St-Amour, V., Culpepper, R., Flatt, M., Felleisen, M.: Languages as libraries. In: Proc. Programming Language Design and Implementation, pp. 132–141 (2011)
22. Wright, A.K., Cartwright, R.: A practical soft type system for Scheme. ACM Transactions on Programming Languages and Systems 19(1), 87–152 (1997)

Author Index

Albert, Elvira   123
Antoy, Sergio   33
Arenas, Puri   123

Balduccini, Marcello   78
Brady, Edwin   242
Bransen, Jeroen   183
Broman, David   258

Campagna, Dario   108
Carro, Manuel   138
Casas, Amadeo   138
Chico de Guzmán, Pablo   138
Christiansen, Henning   93
Coleman, Nicholas   198

Dijkstra, Atze   183

Eisenbach, Susan   48

Felleisen, Matthias   289
Fisher, Kathleen   168
Flatt, Matthew   289

Gill, Andy   212
Gill, Harjot   1
Goldberg, Mayer   18
Gómez-Zamalloa, Miguel   123

Hammond, Kevin   242
Hanus, Michael   33
Hermenegildo, Manuel V.   138
Hudak, Paul   227

Lesniak, Michael   153
Lierler, Yuliya   63, 78
Liu, Changbin   1
Liu, Hai   227
Loo, Boon Thau   1

Mao, Yun   1
Marczak, William R.   1
Martins, Pedro M.   48
McCann, Julie A.   48
Middelkoop, Arie   183

Neuenschwander, Bowe   212
Nilsson, Henrik   258

Sarna-Starosta, Beata   108
Schrijvers, Tom   108
Sherr, Micah   1
Smith, Shaden   63
St-Amour, Vincent   289
Stewart, Don   17
Swierstra, S. Doaitse   183

Tarau, Paul   273
Theil Have, Christian   93
Tobin-Hochstadt, Sam   289
Truszczynski, Miroslaw   63

Walker, David   168
Wang, Anduo   1
Westlund, Alex   63
Wiener, Guy   18
Winograd-Cort, Daniel   227

Zhou, Wenchao   1
Zhu, Kenny Q.   168